T0181049

IFIP Advances in Information and Communication Technology 596

Editor-in-Chief

Kai Rannenberg, Goethe University Frankfurt, Germany

IFIP – The International Federation for Information Processing

IFIP was founded in 1960 under the auspices of UNESCO, following the first World Computer Congress held in Paris the previous year. A federation for societies working in information processing, IFIP's aim is two-fold: to support information processing in the countries of its members and to encourage technology transfer to developing nations. As its mission statement clearly states:

IFIP is the global non-profit federation of societies of ICT professionals that aims at achieving a worldwide professional and socially responsible development and application of information and communication technologies.

IFIP is a non-profit-making organization, run almost solely by 2500 volunteers. It operates through a number of technical committees and working groups, which organize events and publications. IFIP's events range from large international open conferences to working conferences and local seminars.

The flagship event is the IFIP World Computer Congress, at which both invited and contributed papers are presented. Contributed papers are rigorously refereed and the rejection rate is high.

As with the Congress, participation in the open conferences is open to all and papers may be invited or submitted. Again, submitted papers are stringently refereed.

The working conferences are structured differently. They are usually run by a working group and attendance is generally smaller and occasionally by invitation only. Their purpose is to create an atmosphere conducive to innovation and development. Refereeing is also rigorous and papers are subjected to extensive group discussion.

Publications arising from IFIP events vary. The papers presented at the IFIP World Computer Congress and at open conferences are published as conference proceedings, while the results of the working conferences are often published as collections of selected and edited papers.

IFIP distinguishes three types of institutional membership: Country Representative Members, Members at Large, and Associate Members. The type of organization that can apply for membership is a wide variety and includes national or international societies of individual computer scientists/ICT professionals, associations or federations of such societies, government institutions/government related organizations, national or international research institutes or consortia, universities, academies of sciences, companies, national or international associations or federations of companies.

More information about this series at http://www.springer.com/series/6102

Jason Staggs · Sujeet Shenoi (Eds.)

Critical Infrastructure Protection XIV

14th IFIP WG 11.10 International Conference, ICCIP 2020
Arlington, VA, USA, March 16–17, 2020
Revised Selected Papers

 Springer

Editors
Jason Staggs
University of Tulsa
Tulsa, OK, USA

Sujeet Shenoi
University of Tulsa
Tulsa, OK, USA

ISSN 1868-4238   ISSN 1868-422X (electronic)
IFIP Advances in Information and Communication Technology
ISBN 978-3-030-62842-0   ISBN 978-3-030-62840-6 (eBook)
https://doi.org/10.1007/978-3-030-62840-6

This Springer imprint is published by the registered company Springer Nature Switzerland AG
The registered company address is: Gewerbestrasse 11, 6330 Cham, Switzerland

Contents

Contributing Authors

David Balenson is a Senior Computer Scientist in the Infrastructure Security Group at SRI International, Arlington, Virginia. His research interests include critical infrastructure protection, experimentation and testing, and technology transition.

Elena Bernardini is an M.Sc. student in Management and Automation Engineering at the University of Roma Tre, Rome, Italy. Her research interests include modeling critical infrastructures and telecommunications networks.

Addison Betances is an Assistant Professor of Computer Engineering at the Air Force Institute of Technology, Wright-Patterson Air Force Base, Ohio. His research interests include software-defined radios, device fingerprinting, programmable hardware, embedded systems security and critical infrastructure protection.

Zachary Birnbaum is a Senior Professional Staff Member at Johns Hopkins University Applied Physics Laboratory, Laurel, Maryland. His research interests include quantitative cyber and resilience modeling and simulation, and behavior-based anomaly detection in cyber-physical systems.

Brett Borghetti is an Associate Professor of Computer Science at the Air Force Institute of Technology, Wright-Patterson Air Force Base, Ohio. His research interests include applying machine learning to problem spaces such as human-machine teaming in cyber security.

Chun-Fai Chan is a Ph.D. student in Computer Science at the University of Hong Kong, Hong Kong, China. His research interests include penetration testing, digital forensics and Internet of Things security.

Raymond Chan is a Lecturer of Information and Communications Technology at Singapore Institute of Technology, Singapore. His research interests include cyber security, digital forensics and critical infrastructure protection.

Kam-Pui Chow is an Associate Professor of Computer Science at the University of Hong Kong, Hong Kong, China. His research interests include information security, digital forensics, live system forensics and digital surveillance.

David Crow recently completed his M.S. degree in Computer Science at the Air Force Institute of Technology, Wright-Patterson Air Force Base, Ohio. His research interests include machine learning, cyber-physical systems security and critical infrastructure protection.

Matthew Dallmeyer is a Research Engineer at the Air Force Institute of Technology, Wright-Patterson Air Force Base, Ohio. His research interests include programmable hardware, cyber-physical systems security and embedded systems security.

Matthew Davis is a Senior Professional Staff Member at Johns Hopkins University Applied Physics Laboratory, Laurel, Maryland. His research interests include information security, modeling and simulation, and cyber-physical systems security.

Stephen Dunlap is a Cyber Security Research Engineer at the Air Force Institute of Technology, Wright-Patterson Air Force Base, Ohio. His research interests include embedded systems security, cyber-physical systems security and critical infrastructure protection.

Tim Ellis is a Senior Principal Research Engineer at SRI International, San Diego, California. His research interests include critical infrastructure protection and information system privacy and security.

Chiara Foglietta is an Assistant Professor of Automatic Control at the University of Roma Tre, Rome, Italy. Her research interests include industrial control systems, data fusion techniques and controls for energy management systems.

Yanan Gong is an M.Phil. student in Computer Science at the University of Hong Kong, Hong Kong, China. Her research interests include cyber security and digital forensics.

Scott Graham is an Associate Professor of Computer Engineering at the Air Force Institute of Technology, Wright-Patterson Air Force Base, Ohio. His research interests include embedded and communications systems security, vehicle cyber security and critical infrastructure protection.

Micah Hayden recently completed his M.S. degree in Computer Engineering at the Air Force Institute of Technology, Wright-Patterson Air Force Base, Ohio. His research interests include computer communications, avionics security and critical infrastructure protection.

Nicholas Kovach is a Senior Research Engineer at the Air Force Research Laboratory, Wright-Patterson Air Force Base, Ohio. His research interests include avionics security, critical infrastructure protection and embedded systems security.

Brandon Kow is a B.Sc. student in Computing Science at the University of Glasgow, Glasgow, United Kingdom. His research interests include the Internet of Things and cyber security.

Rajesh Kumar is an Assistant Professor of Computer Science at Birla Institute of Technology and Science, Pilani, India. His research interests include information security risk management, and safety and security risk analysis using formal models and model checking.

Jennifer Leopold is an Associate Professor of Computer Science at Missouri University of Science and Technology, Rolla, Missouri. Her research interests include data mining, especially graph data mining, and cyber-physical systems.

Michael Locasto is a Principal Computer Scientist at SRI International, New York. His research focuses on understanding software faults and developing fixes.

Nathan Lutes is a Ph.D. student in Mechanical Engineering at Missouri University of Science and Technology, Rolla, Missouri. His research interests include automatic control and machine learning, with an emphasis on intelligent control and decision making.

Jake Magness recently completed his M.S. degree in Computer Engineering at the Air Force Institute of Technology, Wright-Patterson Air Force Base, Ohio. His research interests include cyber-physical systems security, avionics security and critical infrastructure protection.

Yonghao Mai is a Professor of Information Technology at Hubei Police University, Wuhan, China. His research interests include digital forensics and cyber law.

Bruce McMillin is a Professor of Computer Science at Missouri University of Science and Technology, Rolla, Missouri. His research interests include cyber-physical systems security, distributed systems and formal methods.

Robert Mills is a Professor of Electrical Engineering at the Air Force Institute of Technology, Wright-Patterson Air Force Base, Ohio. His research interests include network security and management, cyber situational awareness and electronic warfare.

Lucas Mireles recently completed his M.S. degree in Computer Engineering at the Air Force Institute of Technology, Wright-Patterson Air Force Base, Ohio. His research interests include communications systems security, avionics security and critical infrastructure protection.

Stefano Panzieri is a Professor of Automatic Control and Head of the Models for Critical Infrastructure Protection Laboratory at the University of Roma Tre, Rome, Italy. His research interests include industrial control systems, robotics, sensor fusion and models for critical infrastructure protection.

Shruti Paul is a Cyber Security Engineer at PayPal, Scottsdale, Arizona. Her research interests include cyber security, network security and penetration testing.

Dillon Pettit recently completed his M.S. degree in Cyber Operations at the Air Force Institute of Technology, Wright-Patterson Air Force Base, Ohio. His research interests include cyber security risk management, unmanned aerial vehicles and cyber-physical systems security.

Stefan Rass is an Associate Professor of Computer Science at the University of Klagenfurt, Klagenfurt, Austria. His research interests include decision theory and game theory applications in security, complexity theory and applied cryptography.

Salman Salman is a Cyber Security Engineer at Aerospace Corporation, Chantilly, Virginia. His research interests include operational technology/information technology cyber defense, high latency network optimization, penetration testing and networking.

James Cervini is a D.Eng. student at Johns Hopkins University, Baltimore, Maryland. His research interests include cyber-physical systems security, virtualization, fog computing and penetration testing.

Stefan Schauer is a Senior Scientist at the Austrian Institute of Technology, Klagenfurt, Austria. His research interests include mathematical models for risk and security management, and the assessment of cascading effects in critical infrastructures.

Rachel Stiffler is a Ph.D. student in Mechanical Engineering at Missouri University of Science and Technology, Rolla, Missouri. Her research interests include combustion and cyclic dynamics in internal combustion engines.

Patrick Sweeney is an Assistant Professor of Computer Engineering at the Air Force Institute of Technology, Wright-Patterson Air Force Base, Ohio. His research interests include avionics security, critical infrastructure protection and embedded systems security.

Forest Tan is a Cluster Director and Associate Professor of Information and Communications Technology at Singapore Institute of Technology, Singapore. His research interests include the Internet of Things, and intelligent and secure systems.

Ulric Teo is a B.Sc. student in Computing Science at the University of Glasgow, Glasgow, United Kingdom. His research interests include industrial control systems and cyber security.

Simon Thougaard is a Ph.D. student in Computer Science at Missouri University of Science and Technology, Rolla, Missouri. His research interests include cyber-physical systems security, consensus systems and emergent behavior in distributed systems.

Anusha Thudimilla recently completed her Ph.D. degree in Computer Science at Missouri University of Science and Technology, Rolla, Missouri. Her research interests include cyber-physical systems security and deep learning.

Matthew Wagner recently completed his Ph.D. degree in Computer Science at Missouri University of Science and Technology, Rolla, Missouri. His research interests include cyber-physical systems security and cryptography.

Lanier Watkins is an Associate Research Scientist at the Information Security Institute, Whiting School of Engineering, Johns Hopkins University, Baltimore, Maryland; and a Senior Professional Staff Member at Johns Hopkins University Applied Physics Laboratory, Laurel, Maryland. His research interests include algorithms and frameworks for defending critical infrastructure networks and systems.

Saikiran Yamajala is a Software Engineer at Cisco Systems, Research Triangle Park, North Carolina. Her research interests include information security, cryptosystems and cloud security.

Jun Zhang is a Professor of Information Technology at Hubei Police University, Wuhan, China. His research interests include information security and digital forensics.

Preface

The information infrastructure – comprising computers, embedded devices, networks and software systems – is vital to operations in every sector: chemicals, commercial facilities, communications, critical manufacturing, dams, defense industrial base, emergency services, energy, financial services, food and agriculture, government facilities, healthcare and public health, information technology, nuclear reactors, materials and waste, transportation systems, and water and wastewater systems. Global business and industry, governments, indeed society itself, cannot function if major components of the critical information infrastructure are degraded, disabled or destroyed.

This book, *Critical Infrastructure Protection XIV*, is the fourteenth volume in the annual series produced by IFIP Working Group 11.10 on Critical Infrastructure Protection, an active international community of scientists, engineers, practitioners and policy makers dedicated to advancing research, development and implementation efforts related to critical infrastructure protection. The book presents original research results and innovative applications in the area of critical infrastructure protection. Also, it highlights the importance of weaving science, technology and policy in crafting sophisticated, yet practical, solutions that will help secure information, computer and network assets in the various critical infrastructure sectors.

This volume contains sixteen selected papers from the Fourteenth Annual IFIP Working Group 11.10 International Conference on Critical Infrastructure Protection, held at SRI International in Arlington, Virginia, USA on March 16–17, 2020. The papers were refereed by members of IFIP Working Group 11.10 and other internationally-recognized experts in critical infrastructure protection. The post-conference manuscripts submitted by the authors were rewritten to accommodate the suggestions provided by the conference attendees. The sixteen selected papers were subsequently revised by the editors to produce the final chapters published in this volume.

The chapters are organized into six sections: (i) aviation infrastructure security; (ii) vehicle infrastructure security; (iii) telecommunications systems security; (iv) industrial control systems security; (v) cyberphysical systems security; and (vi) infrastructure modeling and simulation. The coverage of topics showcases the richness and vitality of the discipline, and offers promising avenues for future research in critical infrastructure protection.

This book is the result of the combined efforts of several individuals and organizations. In particular, we thank David Balenson for his tireless work on behalf of IFIP Working Group 11.10. We also thank the National Science Foundation, U.S. Department of Homeland Security, National Security Agency and SRI International for their support of IFIP Working Group 11.10 and its activities. Finally, we wish to note that all opinions, findings, conclusions and recommendations in the chapters of this book are those of the authors and do not necessarily reflect the views of their employers or funding agencies.

JASON STAGGS AND SUJEET SHENOI

I

AVIATION INFRASTRUCTURE SECURITY

Chapter 1

CYBER-PHYSICAL SECURITY OF AIR TRAFFIC SURVEILLANCE SYSTEMS

Anusha Thudimilla and Bruce McMillin

Abstract   Cyber-physical system security is a significant concern in the critical infrastructure. Strong interdependencies between cyber and physical components render cyber-physical systems highly susceptible to integrity attacks such as injecting malicious data and projecting fake sensor measurements. Traditional security models partition cyber-physical systems into just two domains – high and low. This absolute partitioning is not well suited to cyber-physical systems because they comprise multiple overlapping partitions. Information flow properties, which model how inputs to a system affect its outputs across security partitions, are important considerations in cyber-physical systems. Information flows support traceability analysis that helps detect vulnerabilities and anomalous sources, contributing to the implementation of mitigation measures.

This chapter describes an automated model with graph-based information flow traversal for identifying information flow paths in the Automatic Dependent Surveillance-Broadcast (ADS-B) system used in civilian aviation, and subsequently partitioning the flows into security domains. The results help identify ADS-B system vulnerabilities to failures and attacks, and determine potential mitigation measures.

Keywords: Cyber-physical systems, ADS-B system, integrity, privacy

1.   Introduction

Recent years have seen significant increases in the development and deployment of cyber-physical systems – smart, mission-critical computing systems that are characterized by tightly-coupled embedded devices in physical environments [7]. Since cyber-physical systems comprise physical components, computational resources and communications in-

© IFIP International Federation for Information Processing 2020
Published by Springer Nature Switzerland AG 2020
J. Staggs and S. Shenoi (Eds.): Critical Infrastructure Protection XIV, IFIP AICT 596, pp. 3–23, 2020.
https://doi.org/10.1007/978-3-030-62840-6_1

frastructures [14], it is equally important to ensure cyber security and physical security.

Cyber-physical systems are exposed to new forms of risk due to the tight couplings between their cyber and physical components. These risks have not been considered adequately in cyber-physical systems due to the lack of tools for identifying vulnerabilities that arise from the complex interactions between their cyber and physical components. These risks can be classified as: (i) cyber elements that impact the physical environment; and (ii) physical elements that impact the cyber components. This chapter addresses these risks by identifying failures and attacks using information flow analysis, an important cyber-physical security paradigm that determines if inputs to a process or system can change its outputs.

Air traffic surveillance systems have complex cyber-physical interactions. Significant increases in civilian airline traffic in recent years have led the Federal Aviation Administration (FAA) to introduce NextGen technologies to ensure flight predictability, efficiency and safety. Automatic Dependent Surveillance-Broadcast (ADS-B), a key NextGen component, is a powerful cyber-physical system that integrates computational intelligence with physical components to provide reliable and efficient communications between air traffic control (ATC) and aircraft. ADS-B uses the Global Positioning System (GPS) and onboard sensors to determine aircraft identity, position, altitude and velocity. Because ADS-B broadcasts all information over unauthenticated and unencrypted wireless channels, it is imperative to protect against false data injection, spoofing, flooding, jamming, message modification and eavesdropping attacks [10]. Unfortunately, ADS-B does not employ adequate security mechanisms [10, 12, 18].

This chapter employs information flow analysis to identify faulty components in the ADS-B system and detect attacks. Two scenarios are discussed, one involving aircraft altimeter failure and the other involving GPS satellite failure.

2.   ADS-B System

ADS-B is an airborne surveillance system designed to enable seamless surveillance, and collision detection and avoidance, and to provide situational awareness in the air and on the ground. It replaces radar-based surveillance by having every aircraft broadcast its identity, position, altitude, velocity and other data over unencrypted data links once per second. An aircraft equipped with ADS-B collects this data from sources such as a GPS device, barometric altimeter and other nearby aircraft, and processes the data to determine its accuracy and integrity. The processed information is then encoded and broadcast as an ADS-B message to nearby aircraft and ground stations. ADS-B also enables pilots to receive other information such as flight restrictions and weather data in real time.

An aircraft equipped with ADS-B broadcasts information in an omnidirectional manner so that it can be received by ground stations and other aircraft with compatible receiving devices. These broadcasts differ from other transponder interrogations such as those performed by the Traffic Collision and Avoidance System (TCAS).

ADS-B has two functional operations: (i) ADS-B OUT; and (ii) ADS-B IN. ADS-B OUT is a surveillance technology responsible for generating ADS-B broadcasts that transmit aircraft identity, position, altitude and velocity data in real time to air traffic control and nearby aircraft. ADSB-IN is used to receive transmissions from nearby aircraft and ground stations (i.e., ADS-B OUT information). The information includes weather updates, conflict detection and de-confliction guidance, graphical displays of aircraft position and along-track guidance [11].

3. Related Work

Cyber-physical systems are widely deployed to monitor and control operations in critical infrastructure assets. Due to their importance, it is vital to protect them from failures and attacks. Several methods have been proposed to address security issues posed by denial-of-service attacks [2], false data injection attacks [9], stealthy deception attacks [19] and replay attacks [13].

Information flow security is a powerful approach for preventing sensitive data from leaking to malicious entities. Its primary variants are static and dynamic approaches. A static approach merely executes information security policies whereas a dynamic approach uses labels to describe security levels and propagates the labels to ensure data integrity with respect to invariants or predefined policies. Much work in the area has focused on proving the non-interference property that describes information flow restrictions and using a combination of language features and system models to implement information flow security [16].

Considerable research has focused on using information flow analysis in aviation security. The real challenge in the case of information flow security is to apply the vast theory and language-based designs such as Jif [3] and Flow Caml [15, 17] to real-world problems [23].

In the context of ADS-B security, Kim et al. [8] have devised a timestamp method based on signal propagation time to identify and reject spoofed ADS-B messages between senders and receivers. Yang et al. [21] have proposed a lightweight security solution that integrates crypto-primitives such as FFX and TESLA to ensure ADS-B message integrity and privacy [21]. Other researchers [22] have conducted similar work with a focus on congested data links and resource-constrained avion-Thudimilla and McMillin [20] have employed ProVerif to identify attacks attacks on ADS-B and TCAS, but their analysis is limited to proving observational equivalence (anonymity property) via process composition. Several researchers have investigated security vulnerabilities, failures and attacks in ADS-B systems [10, 12, 18]. A survey of the literature reveals that research in the area of ADS-B security either focuses on cyber attacks or physical component failures, but not both. This work stands out in that it considers cyber- and physically-enabled attacks and failures using automated graph-based information flow analysis to identify security risks and develop mitigation measures.

4.　　Threat Model

An adequate threat model is crucial to assessing security vulnerabilities in a system and determining mitigation measures. The following threat model is at the foundation of this work:

- *Source:* The threat source is an entity that initiates threats, which include system failures, adversarial attacks and environmental factors.

- *Goal:* The goal of the threat model is to capture system features that may lead to system failure and identify the features that are modified as a result of an attack.

- *Consequences:* The consequences include compromises to system integrity, safety or availability.

The threat model assumes that failures and attacks exhibit similar behavior, and they are arbitrary and unbounded. The adversary is assumed to have full control of the target – specifically, the adversary can eavesdrop, intercept and modify messages sent and received by a component.

The threat model also assumes that the adversary cannot exploit certain aspects of the system. Specifically:

- The adversary cannot corrupt or modify a proposed model.

- The adversary cannot modify more than half of the participating entities while traversing the graph with respect to a feature in the proposed model.

Table 1. Modal logic symbols and descriptions.

Symbol	Description
W	Set of worlds.
φ	Boolean statement that is true or false in world $w \in W$.
$w \vdash \varphi$	Statement φ is valid in world w.
$w \models \varphi$	Values from world w cause φ to evaluate to true.
$\Box\varphi$	Statement φ always evaluates to true or false.
$V_{S_x}^i$	Valuation function of entity i with respect to state variable S_x.

5.   MSDND

Multiple security domain nondeducibility (MSDND), introduced by Howser and McMillin [5], engages modal logic [4] to address the shortings of traditional security models that partition a security space into two domains, high and low. Traditional models work well only when the boundaries of the security domains are defined precisely. The MSDND model checks for nondeducibility – the inability to deduce the values of two states in a system at any point in time. Computing the security domains for complex cyber-physical systems is difficult. However, this work addresses the issue by automating the MSDND process to partition security domains based on information flow traversal.

Table 1 lists the modal logic symbols used in this work along with their descriptions.

The state of a system is represented by a set of variables that help determine the future system states and outputs. A state variable φ represents the state of a dynamic system, which is evaluated to either true or false. For example, a mechanical system may contain state variables such as position and velocity that describe its components. A combination of state variables S_x is represented as:

$$S_x = \varphi_0 \wedge \varphi_1 \wedge \varphi_2 \wedge \varphi_3 \wedge \ldots \tag{1}$$

The set of worlds W contains all possible combinations of m state variables $S_0, S_1, \ldots S_m$. If a state variable S_x has no valuation function, then MSDND fails to determine the value associated with the state variable or the value of any logical expression associated with the state variable [5]. A valuation function $V_{S_x}^i$ indicates the value of a state variable S_x as observed by an entity i in world w.

Each state variable is associated with a component identifier. Figure 1 shows the ADS-B system architecture with components represented as nodes and connections between components represented as edges. In the

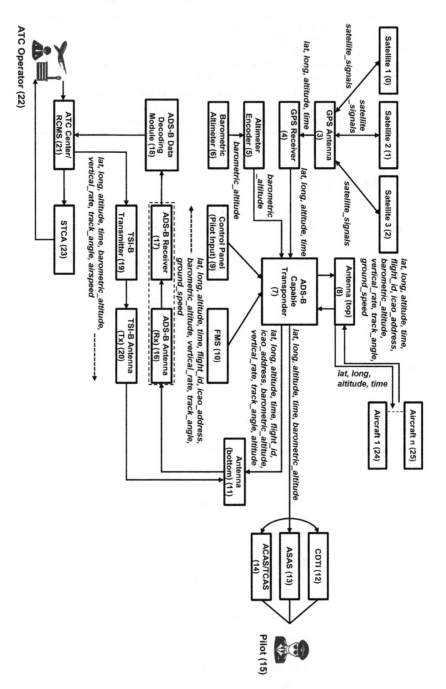

Figure 1.   ADS-B system architecture with components (nodes) and connections (edges).

figure, Satellite 1 has the component identifier 0, Barometric Altimeter has the component identifier 6 and Control Panel has the component identifier 9. Every edge is labeled with attributes that denote the data that flows from one component to another [1]. The state variables associated with Satellite 1, Barometric Altimeter and Control Panel are denoted by φ_0, φ_6 and φ_9, respectively. These state variables are used later in the chapter to perform MSDND analysis.

Definition 1 (Multiple Security Domain Exclusivity). There exists some world with multiple states $S_a, S_b, S_c, \ldots$ in which, at any instant, the system is in one true state and all the others are false:

$$f(S_a, S_b, S_c, \ldots) = \begin{cases} \text{True} & \text{when one of } S_a, S_b, S_c, \ldots \text{ is True} \\ \text{False} & \text{otherwise} \end{cases} \quad (2)$$

In the MSDND model, an entity i is any part of the system that is capable of independent observation or action. The event system ES comprises multiple security domains SD^i as viewed by each entity i in the model. These domains may or may not overlap depending on the complexity of the event system [5, 6].

Definition 2 (Multiple Security Domain Nondeducibility). A system is MSDND if:

$$MSDND(ES) = \exists w \in W : [w \vdash \Box f(S_a, S_b, S_c, \ldots)]$$
$$\wedge \, [w \models (\nexists V^i_{S_a} \wedge \nexists V^i_{S_b} \wedge \nexists V^i_{S_c} \ldots] \quad (3)$$
$$\bigcup_{i=1}^{n} SD^i = ES \quad (4)$$

An MSDND proof creates a logical argument based on conditions on the observable state of the system under consideration. These conditions are assessed for their valuation in a particular security domain. If no valuation function can be found, then the system is MSDND secure. This is a bad thing because it means attacker actions can be hidden in the security domain. Preventing MSDND is a good thing because it means the system can detect the attack.

6.   Graph-Based Detection System

The graph-based detection system presented in this chapter considers the entire aircraft system as a directed acyclic graph, where a node represents a system component and an edge represents the information flow between two nodes. Each edge has a set of labels, where each label has a value associated with it.

The graph-based detection algorithm has the following three steps:

1. Identify all the paths in the network using depth-first search with respect to a label and sort the result set in descending order of subgraph size.

2. Identify the subgraphs and eliminate them to obtain a reduced unique subgraph set.

3. In the reduced set, traverse each edge to check for discrepancies such as inconsistent values associated with a particular label. If there is a discrepancy, find the in-degree of each node.

4. A node with in-degree no less than three will break the MSDND property because it contains more than two information flow paths that help identify the faulty component or the component under attack that is sending incorrect data during design time or runtime.

Definition 3 (Directed Acyclic Graph/Subgraph). A directed acyclic graph $G = (V, E, L)$ comprises a set of nodes V, set of edges E and set of labels L associated with each edge.
A directed acyclic graph $S = (V_s, E_s, L_s)$ is a subgraph of directed acyclic graph $G = (V, E, L)$ iff $V_s \subseteq V$, $E_s \subseteq E$ and L_s contains the label l under consideration.

Figure 1 shows the ADS-B system of an aircraft, which has 26 components (nodes). Each edge has a set of labels and values associated with the labels that represent information flows.

Figure 2 shows the ADS-B system in Figure 1 represented as a graph without edge labels. Each component is identified by its node identifier and the directional edges represent information flows.

Algorithms 1 and 2 are used to find all the graphs associated with each label and eliminate the subpaths to obtain unique graphs corresponding to each label. Source code for the algorithms is available at github. com/anushaat/MSDND.

6.1   Finding Independent Paths

Algorithm 1 uses depth-first search to find all the paths with edges labeled l. The algorithm has a runtime complexity of $\mathcal{O}(|V| + |E|)$, where $|V|$ is the number of nodes and $|E|$ is the number of edges.

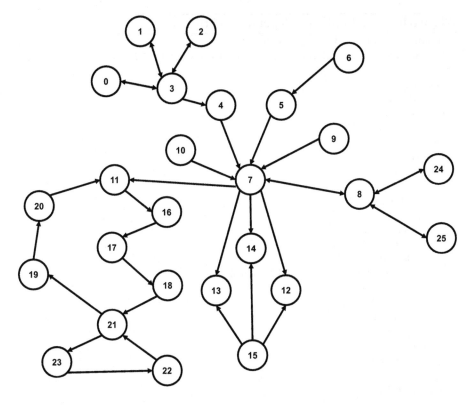

Figure 2. ADS-B system graph.

The following theorem proves the correctness of Algorithm 1:

Theorem 1. During a depth-first search of a directed acyclic graph $G = (V, E, L)$, vertex s is a descendent of vertex d iff the search discovers a path from s to d comprising entirely of edges labeled l.

Proof: Assume that a depth-first search is performed on the directed acyclic graph $G = (V, E, L)$ to determine the independent paths for each vertex $v_i \in V$. It suffices to show that for any pair of distinct vertices $s, d \in V$, the graph G contains an edge from s to d. If $s = d$, then the path from s to d contains only s, which indicates it is source or initial node. If d is an immediate descendent of u, then the path from s to d contains label l. If d is a descendent of s, then all the edges on the simple path from s to d contain label l. □

Algorithm 1 : Finding independent paths.

Inputs: graph $G = (V, E, L)$; node u
Output: alg1-res (set of graphs associated with a label $l \in L$)

    alg1-res ← null
    on_path ← null
    path ← null
    visited ← null
    label ← l
    function DFS(G, u)
       visited.add(u)
       if on_path.contains(u) **then**
         alg1-res.add(path)
       else
         on_path.add(v);
         path.push(v);
         for all v ∈ adj[u] **do**
           if v.labels.contains(label) **then**
             DFS(G, u)
           end if
         end for
         path.pop()
       end if
       on_path.remove(u)
       return alg1-res
    end function

6.2　　Eliminating Subpaths

Algorithm 2 eliminates subpaths that occur more than once. This achieves non-redundancy, which helps identify the faulty component or the component under attack.

Algorithm 2 operates on the sorted result set (alg1-res) provided by Algorithm 1. The if-statement in the outer for loop obtains the longest path of length k and saves the paths with length k in the final result without any processing. The first inner for-loop uses a variant of the sliding window technique to obtain the non-redundant paths and save them in the result. The return statement returns the non-redundant paths in the list of paths provided by Algorithm 1. The runtime complexity of the algorithm is $\mathcal{O}(nmk)$ where n is the size of the result set, m is the subpath length and k is the sliding window size.

The following theorem proves the correctness of Algorithm 2:

Theorem 2. Let $G = (V, E, L)$ be a directed acyclic graph. Let l_m be a label in L based on which the graph traversal is done. The algorithm

---

Algorithm 2 : Eliminating subpaths.

Input: alg1-res (set of graphs associated with a label $l \in L$ (Algorithm 1 result))
Output: alg2-res (set of independent paths associated with a label $l \in L$)

function ELIMINATESUBPATHS(alg1-res)
    alg2-res ← null
    maxSize ← alg1-res.get(0).size()
    for path ← 0 to alg1-res.size() **do**
        S ← alg1-res.get(path)
        k ← alg1-res.get(path).size()
        if k==maxSize **then**
            alg2-res.add(S)
        end if
        for all s in alg2-res **do**
            count ← 0
            N ← s.size()
            for i ← 0 to N-k+1 **do**
                if s(i)==alg1-res.get(i) **then**
                    for j ← 0 to k **do**
                        if s(i+j)==alg1-res.get(j) **then**
                            count++
                      else
                        break
                      end if
                    end for
                end if
            end for
            if count!=k **then**
                alg2-res.add(alg1-res.get(i))
            end if
        end for
    end for
    return alg2-res
end function

---

produces nonempty subpaths S_p with edges containing values associated with l_m in the result of Algorithm 1 (alg1-res).

Proof: Let S_p be the maximum-size subset of paths associated with label l_m in the result of Algorithm 1 (alg1-res). Let $(n_i, ..., n_j, ..., n_k)$ where $i < j < k$ be the set of nodes connected by edges E_p associated with label l_m in S_p. If the edges connecting $n_i \rightarrow n_j$ and $n_j \rightarrow n_k$ are equal (i.e., $e_{ij} = e_{jk}$), then the result contains paths with label l_m because e_{jk} is an element of edge set E_p associated with label l_m. If $e_{ij} \neq e_{jk}$, let the edge set $E'_p = E_p - \{e_{jk}\} \cup \{e_{ij}\}$. Upon substituting e_{ij} for e_{jk}, $E'_p = E_p$ is obtained, which shows that e_{ij} and e_{jk} belong to the same set (i.e., have the same label). This is true because n_i is a child of n_j and n_k is a child of n_j. Since $E'_p = E_p$, it can be concluded that E'_p contains edges with label l_m, and it includes e_{jk}.   □

7.   MSDND Analysis

This section presents an analysis of the vulnerabilities associated with the ADS-B air traffic surveillance system. This is accomplished in two steps. The first step is to identify the compromised component. The second step is to employ the graph-based model to identify information flow paths and use the MSDND model to identify the faulty paths associated with the ADS-B system.

Two scenarios are presented in this section, altimeter failure and satellite failure. They demonstrate that MSDND is an effective tool for identifying system vulnerabilities by analyzing information flow paths. The analyses could be performed at design time to enable security mechanisms to be proactively implemented to handle component failures or attacks.

7.1   Altimeter Failure

This section analyzes an altimeter failure scenario. The result is expressed by the following theorem:

Theorem 3. In the event of an altimeter compromise, automated graph-based analysis can show that the MSDND model yields deducibility. This means that, despite the altimeter failure, critical information can flow to the pilot and air traffic control.

Proof: Consider a scenario in which the barometric altimeter is faulty and sends incorrect altitude data to the pilot. Specifically, the altimeter displays incorrect altitude values, which makes them nondeducible to the pilot.

Between ten to 60 graphs are associated with each label. The graphs are generated based on three labels: (i) *barometric_altitude*; (ii) *altitude*; and (iii) *airspeed*.

Figures 3 through 5 show three graphs generated with respect to the label *altitude*. For example, Figure 3 presents the information flow with respect to *altitude* from node 3 (GPS Antenna) to node 20 (TSI-B Antenna). After the graphs are generated, a variant of the sliding window technique is used to eliminate subpaths from the set of graphs.

Graph 3 in Figure 5 is a subpath of Graph 2 in Figure 4. Algorithm 2 is used to eliminate occurrences such as Graph 3 from the result set.

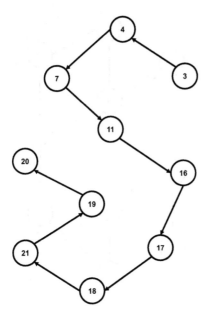

Figure 3.   Graph 1.

After eliminating the subpaths, the value associated with each label is evaluated to check for consistency. If an inconsistency exists, then the in-degree of each node in the inconsistent set is computed. If a node has an in-degree of two or more (indicating that more than one information flow path carries similar information), then it is considered to have a valuation function that eventually breaks the nondeducibility property. If a valuation function exists for a node, then the incoming edges are evaluated to identify the faulty source.

Applying the MSDND model yields two security domains (sources of data) in this scenario: (i) SD^{BA} (Barometric Altimeter domain) and (ii) SD^{GPS} (GPS Satellite domain). Combining the valuation functions in SD^{BA} with respect to the *altitude* value from the Pilot domain yields:

$$S_{ba} = \neg\varphi_6 \wedge \neg\varphi_5 \wedge \neg\varphi_7 \wedge \neg\varphi_{15} \Rightarrow \nexists V^P_{\sim a} \tag{5}$$

Since the information from the Barometric Altimeter domain is faulty, the Pilot domain cannot evaluate the correctness of the *altitude* data.

Combining the valuation functions in SD^{GPS} with respect to the *altitude* value from the Pilot domain yields:

$$S_{gps} = \varphi_3 \wedge \varphi_4 \wedge \varphi_7 \wedge \varphi_{15} \Rightarrow \nexists V^P_a \tag{6}$$

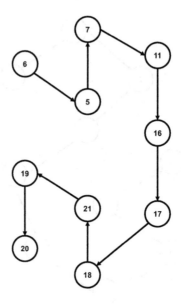

Figure 4.   Graph 2.

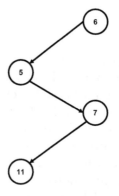

Figure 5.   Graph 3.

Although the information received from the GPS Satellite domain is not faulty, the Pilot domain cannot evaluate the correctness of the *altitude* data because there are just two information flow paths.

According to Equations (5) and (6), the Pilot domain sees two different information flow paths that result in different *altitude* values. Combining the two equations yields:

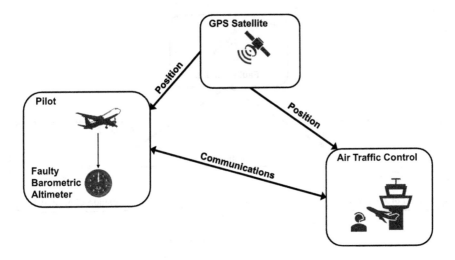

Figure 6. Pilot can deduce the correct altitude value.

$$MSDND(ES) = \exists w \in W : [w \vdash \Box f(S_{ba}, S_{gps})]$$
$$\wedge [w \models (\nexists V_{\sim a}^P \wedge \nexists V_a^P] \tag{7}$$

Therefore, the Pilot domain cannot deduce that the Barometric Altimeter domain is faulty and is sending incorrect *altitude* data. This situation can be resolved by having an additional information flow path that enables the Pilot domain to resolve the conflict (Figure 6).

The additional information flow path comes from the Air Traffic Control domain, which is responsible for sending *altitude* data:

$$S_{atc} = \varphi_{21} \wedge \varphi_{19} \wedge \varphi_{20} \wedge \varphi_{11} \wedge \varphi_7 \wedge \varphi15 \Rightarrow \exists V_a^P \tag{8}$$

Combining Equations (5), (6) and (8) yields:

$$MSDND(ES) = \exists w \in W : [w \vdash \Box f(S_{ba}, S_{gps}, S_{atc})]$$
$$\wedge [w \models (\nexists V_{\sim a}^P \wedge \exists V_a^P \wedge \exists V_a^P] \tag{9}$$

Hence, the ADS-B system is not MSDND secure and the Pilot domain can deduce the correct *altitude* value and resolve the conflict by relying on the alternate information flow path from the Air Traffic Control domain. $\quad\Box$

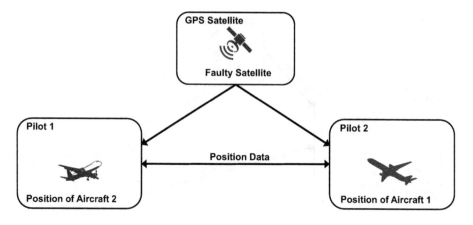

Figure 7. Satellite failure.

7.2   GPS Satellite Failure

This section analyzes a GPS satellite failure scenario. The result is expressed by the following theorem:

Theorem 4. In the event of a GPS satellite failure, automated graph-based analysis can show that the MSDND model yields nondeducibility. This means that critical information cannot flow to the pilots.

Proof: Consider a scenario where a GPS satellite responsible for sending position data is faulty and sends incorrect position data to two aircraft. Assume that the pilots of the two aircraft can communicate with each other. The potential for incorrect decisions by the pilots and a mid-air collision exist if the two pilots cannot identify the source of the incorrect data (Figure 7).

Pilots trust the position data sent by a GPS satellite. When two aircraft are near each other, both the pilots communicate based on the data received from the GPS satellite. This scenario has the Pilot 1 domain and the Pilot 2 domain. If pilots in the two domains cannot identify the problem soon enough, there could be a breakdown in safe aircraft separation. Automated MSDND analysis can enable the pilots to check the consistency of the information flow paths and identify the source of the faulty data.

Figure 8 shows the subgraph generated with respect to the labels *satellite_signals*, *lat* and *long* corresponding to the position data. After the graph is generated, a variant of the sliding window technique is used to eliminate the subgraphs from the set of graphs. Algorithm 2 is then

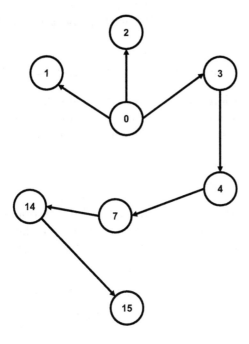

Figure 8. Graph 4.

applied to eliminate the subgraphs to avoid redundancy. In this case, no subgraphs exist and Algorithm 2 does not reduce the set of paths.

After eliminating the subgraphs, the value associated with each label is evaluated to check for consistency. If an inconsistency exists, then the in-degree of each node in the inconsistent set is computed. If a node has an in-degree of two or more (indicating that more than one information flow path carries similar information), then it is considered to have a valuation function and eventually breaks the nondeducibility property. If a valuation function exists for a node, then the incoming edges are evaluated to identify the faulty source.

In this case, none of the nodes have an in-degree greater than two. Therefore, the pilots of the two aircraft cannot deduce that the GPS satellite failure is causing the transmission of incorrect information.

The two security domains in this scenario are SD^{P1} (Pilot 1 domain) and SD^{P2} (Pilot 2 domain). After the flight position is retrieved, the Pilot 1 domain trusts the information sent by the Pilot 2 domain and vice-versa. However, the Pilot 1 domain and Pilot 2 domain cannot identify the problem until they are too close, leading to a breakdown in aircraft separation.

Combining the states in SD^{P1} with respect to the Pilot 1 domain yields:

$$S_{p1} = \neg\varphi_{a1} \wedge \neg\varphi_{a2} \wedge \neg\varphi_{a3} \wedge \neg\varphi_{a4} \wedge \neg\varphi_{a7} \wedge \neg\varphi_{a15} \Rightarrow \nexists V^{P1}_{\sim pos} \qquad (10)$$

Since the information received from the Pilot 2 domain is faulty, the Pilot 1 domain cannot evaluate the correctness of the *position* data.

Combining the states in SD^{P2} with respect to the Pilot 2 domain yields:

$$S_{p2} = \neg\varphi_{b1} \wedge \neg\varphi_{b2} \wedge \neg\varphi_{b3} \wedge \neg\varphi_{b4} \wedge \neg\varphi_{b7} \wedge \neg\varphi_{b15} \Rightarrow \nexists V^{P2}_{\sim pos} \qquad (11)$$

Since the information received from the Pilot 1 domain is faulty, the Pilot-2 domain cannot evaluate the correctness of the *position* data.

Combining Equations (10) and (11) yields:

$$MSDND(ES) = \exists w \in W : [w \vdash \Box f(S_{p1}, S_{p2})]$$
$$\wedge [w \models (\nexists V^{P1}_{\sim pos} \wedge \nexists V^{P2}_{\sim pos}] \qquad (12)$$

Therefore, the pilots of the two aircraft cannot deduce that the GPS satellite failure is causing the transmission of incorrect information. Hence, the system is MSDND secure to the pilots and they cannot deduce the true positions of their aircraft. □

8.   Conclusions

MSDND works by identifying independent information flow paths and partitioning them into security domains based on the consistency of information flows. The model effectively detects failures and attacks in cyber-physical systems with complex state transitions.

Two scenarios using MSDND in the ADS-B system were discussed, one involving an aircraft altimeter failure and the other involving a GPS satellite failure. The analyses were conducted using various interacting components in an aircraft ADS-B system. Such analyses, when applied to the entire system, enable manufacturers and pilots to identify vulnerabilities at design-time and in real time, respectively.

Future research will focus on automatically defining the optimal number of security domains for attack scenarios. This will be done by clustering system components based on validated information flow paths, where information flow paths qualified as secure would be in the secure security domain and the other information flow paths would be in the non-secure security domain. Each of these security domains would have additional security partitions based on the labels associated with the information flow paths. Research will also attempt to use MSDND to model confidentiality, integrity and availability vulnerabilities. Finally, future research will extend the MSDND model to evaluate cyber-physical risks in other critical infrastructures.

Acknowledgement

This research was supported by the National Science Foundation under Grant No. CNS-1837472 and by the Missouri S&T Intelligent Systems Center.

References

[1] B. Ali, W. Ochieng, A. Majumdar, W. Schuster and T. Chiew, ADS-B system failure modes and models, *The Journal of Navigation*, vol. 67(6), pp. 995–1017, 2014.

[2] S. Amin, A. Cardenas and S. Sastry, Safe and secure networked control systems under denial-of-service attacks, in *Hybrid Systems: Computation and Control*, R. Majumdar and P. Tabuada (Eds.), Springer, Berlin Heidelberg, Germany, pp. 31–45, 2009.

[3] S. Chong, A. Myers, K. Vikram and L. Zheng, Jif: Reference Manual, Department of Computer Science, Cornell University, Ithaca, New York (www.cs.cornell.edu/jif/doc/jif-3.3.0/manual.html), 2009.

[4] J. Garson, Modal logic, in *The Stanford Encyclopedia of Philosophy Archive*, E. Zalta (Ed.), Metaphysics Research Laboratory, Center for the Study of Language and Information, Stanford University, Stanford, California (plato.stanford.edu/archives/fall2018/entries/logic-modal), 2018.

[5] G. Howser and B. McMillin, A multiple security domain model of a drive-by-wire system, *Proceedings of the Thirty-Seventh Annual IEEE Computer Software and Applications Conference*, pp. 369–374, 2013.

[6] G. Howser and B. McMillin, Using information flow methods to analyze the security of cyber-physical systems, *IEEE Computer*, vol. 50(4), pp. 17–26, 2017.

[7] A. Humayed, J. Lin, F. Li and B. Luo, Cyber-physical systems security – A survey, *IEEE Internet of Things Journal*, vol. 4(6), pp. 1802–1831, 2017.

[8] Y. Kim, J. Jo and S. Lee, ADS-B vulnerabilities and a security solution with a timestamp, *IEEE Aerospace and Electronic Systems*, vol. 32(11), pp. 52–61, 2017.

[9] Y. Liu, P. Ning and M. Reiter, False data injection attacks against state estimation in electric power grids, *ACM Transactions on Information and System Security*, vol. 14(1), article no. 13, 2011.

[10] M. Manesh and N. Kaabouch, Analysis of vulnerabilities, attacks, countermeasures and overall risk of the Automatic Dependent Surveillance-Broadcast (ADS-B) system, *International Journal of Critical Infrastructure Protection*, vol. 19, pp. 16–31, 2017.

[11] D. McCallie, Exploring Potential ADS-B Vulnerabilities in the FAA's NextGen Air Transportation System, Graduate Research Project, Department of Electrical and Computer Engineering, Air Force Institute of Technology, Wright-Patterson Air Force Base, Ohio, 2011.

[12] D. McCallie, J. Butts and R. Mills, Security analysis of the ADS-B implementation in the next generation air transportation system, *International Journal of Critical Infrastructure Protection*, vol. 4(2), pp. 78–87, 2011.

[13] Y. Mo and B. Sinopoli, Secure control against replay attacks, *Proceedings of the Forty-Seventh Annual Allerton Conference on Communications, Control and Computing*, pp. 911–918, 2009.

[14] F. Pasqualetti, F. Dorfler and F. Bullo, Cyber-physical security via geometric control: Distributed monitoring and malicious attacks, *Proceedings of the Fifty-First IEEE Conference on Decision and Control*, pp. 3418–3425, 2012.

[15] F. Pottier and V. Simonet, Information flow inference for ML, *Proceedings of the Twenty-Ninth ACM SIGPLAN-SIGACT Symposium on Principles of Programming Languages*, pp. 319–330, 2002.

[16] A. Sabelfeld and A. Myers, Language-based information flow security, *IEEE Journal on Selected Areas in Communications*, vol. 21(1), pp. 5–19, 2003.

[17] V. Simonet, Flow Caml in a nutshell, *Proceedings of the First Applied Semantics II Workshop*, pp. 152–165, 2003.

[18] M. Strohmeier, M. Schafer, V. Lenders and I. Martinovic, Realities and challenges of NextGen air traffic management: The case of ADS-B, *IEEE Communications*, vol. 52(5), pp. 111–118, 2014.

[19] A. Teixeira, S. Amin, H. Sandberg, K. Johansson and S. Sastry, Cyber security analysis of state estimators in electric power systems, *Proceedings of the Forty-Ninth IEEE Conference on Decision and Control*, pp. 5991–5998, 2010.

[20] A. Thudimilla and B. McMillin, Multiple security domain nondeducibility air traffic surveillance systems, *Proceedings of the Eighteenth IEEE International Symposium on High Assurance Systems Engineering*, pp. 136–139, 2017.

[21] H. Yang, M. Yao, Z. Xu and B. Liu, LHCSAS: A lightweight and highly-compatible solution for ADS-B security, *Proceedings of the IEEE Global Communications Conference*, 2017.

[22] H. Yang, Q. Zhou, M. Yao, R. Lu, H. Li and X. Zhang, A practical and compatible cryptographic solution to ADS-B security, *IEEE Internet of Things Journal*, vol. 6(2), pp. 3322–3334, 2018.

[23] S. Zdancewic, Challenges for information flow security, *Proceedings of the First International Workshop on Programming Language Interference and Dependence*, 2004.

Chapter 2

SIMULATION-BASED LOGIC BOMB IDENTIFICATION AND VERIFICATION FOR UNMANNED AERIAL VEHICLES

Jake Magness, Patrick Sweeney, Scott Graham and Nicholas Kovach

Abstract   This chapter presents a novel methodology for detecting logic bombs hidden in unmanned aerial vehicle autopilot code without source code analysis by executing mission runs in a software-in-the-loop simulator and defining safe unmanned aerial vehicle operating areas. The methodology uses preplanned flight paths as a baseline, greatly reducing the input space that must be searched to have confidence that an unmanned aerial vehicle will not encounter a triggering condition during its mission. While the focus is on detecting logic bombs in ArduPilot autopilot software, the methodology is general enough to be applicable to other unmanned aerial vehicle systems.

Keywords: Unmanned aerial vehicles, logic bombs, detection, ArduPilot

1.   Introduction

Military and civilian entities are continually finding new use cases for unmanned aerial vehicles (UAVs). Important use cases are manifesting themselves in the critical infrastructure sectors. Unmanned aerial vehicles are being used to monitor forest fires, inspect power lines and oil and gas pipelines, and function as rapidly-deployable communications nodes in remote areas [7]. As applications of unmanned aerial vehicles in the critical infrastructure grow, securing them has become a priority.

A wide variety of exploits have been developed and employed against unmanned aerial vehicles. The exploits include network-based attacks that target Wi-Fi connectivity to interrupt command and control, GPS spoofing and base station compromises [10, 11, 16, 17, 20, 22]. While these exploits pose clear threats, many of them are the result of poor practices that can be mitigated using Wi-Fi passwords or secure proto-

© IFIP International Federation for Information Processing 2020
Published by Springer Nature Switzerland AG 2020
J. Staggs and S. Shenoi (Eds.): Critical Infrastructure Protection XIV, IFIP AICT 596, pp. 25–44, 2020.
https://doi.org/10.1007/978-3-030-62840-6_2

cols. However, other nefarious exploits potentially exist. As announced by the U.S. military and U.S. Department of Homeland Security, some unmanned aerial vehicle vendors implant malware in the source code of their aircraft [17, 22]. The types of malware that can be implanted are numerous. However, this work focuses on logic bombs implanted by vendors or malicious actors that are triggered when certain conditions are met.

This chapter presents a methodology for detecting logic bombs in unmanned aerial vehicle autopilot code without source code access by executing mission runs in a software-in-the-loop simulator and defining safe unmanned aerial vehicle operating areas. The methodology uses preplanned flight paths to greatly reduce the search space, providing confidence that an unmanned aerial vehicle – whether autonomous or manually-controlled – will not encounter a logic bomb triggering condition during its mission. Since the vast majority of small unmanned aerial vehicles are procured from outside entities, the ability of the methodology to provide high levels of assurance without source code access or firmware reverse engineering is especially significant.

2.   Background

This section provides background information related to the research. In particular, it discusses applications of unmanned aerial vehicles in the critical infrastructure, unmanned aerial vehicle vulnerabilities, logic bombs and black box testing.

2.1   Critical Infrastructure Applications

The U.S. Department of Homeland Security currently identifies 16 critical infrastructure sectors [24]. Unmanned aerial vehicles are becoming essential tools in all these sectors because they provide distinct advantages over other means for monitoring and managing critical infrastructure assets. The advantages include the ability to fly into high-risk areas, fly with high-fidelity navigational precision, carry different sensors depending on mission type, capture large-scale images and create overlapped images, all with low operational costs [1].

An important use case is emergency response operations in disaster scenarios such as forest fires, adverse weather events and industrial accidents [1]. These operations would be extremely dangerous or impossible to conduct on the ground, and very expensive to perform via other aerial means such as helicopters and airplanes.

Unmanned aerial vehicles have numerous applications in the energy sector as well. They are used by oil and gas companies to survey proposed drilling sites and monitor infrastructure assets such as pipelines and refineries for leaks and other potential problems, including malicious attacks [7]. Timely, accurate and low cost monitoring of these sites are vital as compromises of essential energy assets pose direct threats to national security and societal wellbeing.

As unmanned aerial vehicles take on increased roles in the critical infrastructure sectors, it is essential to ensure that they are secured from current and emergent threats, including logic bombs.

2.2 Documented Vulnerabilities

Unmanned aerial vehicles have been around since 1918, but it is only during the past decade that their capabilities and affordability have generated significant interest [23]. As the use of unmanned aerial vehicles has become more pervasive, vulnerabilities have been identified and exploitation techniques have been developed, and it is certain that many of them have not been addressed. Attacks on civilian unmanned aerial vehicles vary widely, with the vast majority of them targeting communications protocols and networks, GPS integrity, vehicle operating systems and base stations [16, 17, 20, 22].

Figure 1 shows an unmanned aerial vehicle/base station architecture and the associated attack vectors and targets [16]. At this time, a large number of vulnerabilities stem from traditional network-based attacks, protocol weaknesses and operating system flaws. For example, researchers from the University of Brandenburg were able to seize control of a Parrot AR.Drone 2.0 quadcopter using the default FTP and Telnet root accounts [19]. Other vulnerabilities associated with commercial unmanned aerial vehicles stem from the use of unsecured Wi-Fi networks for command and control [11]. In fact, the Wi-Fi networks were found to be vulnerable to nearly all standard attacks, including ARP cache poisoning, DHCP poisoning and MAC cloning. Unmanned aerial vehicles are also susceptible to other attacks, especially GPS spoofing. However, the focus of this research is logic bomb malware embedded in the autopilot code of unmanned aerial vehicles by vendors or malicious actors.

2.3 Logic Bombs

A logic bomb is "malicious application logic that is executed or triggered only under certain (often narrow) circumstances" [13]. Early logic bombs were employed to render software unusable after their free trial periods had expired, requiring license payments from users for continued access [13]. However, it was not long before logic bombs were used for

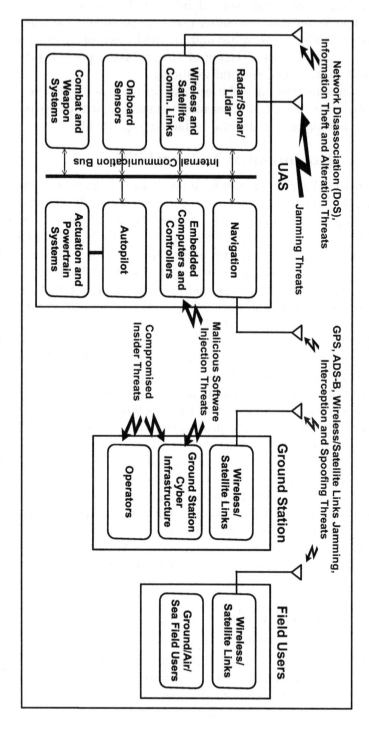

Figure 1. Attack vectors and targets [16].

nefarious purposes such as deleting files and destroying network equipment based on triggering events [13, 25].

Logic bombs can be difficult to detect because they are often planted by developers and other experts who have intimate knowledge of the systems [25]. Additionally, most malware analysis techniques focus on malicious code in running applications instead of malicious code residing quietly in "clean" code [2]. Insider threat exploitation of logic bombs means that administrators have few active options for searching for logic bombs in information technology systems and networks. Preventative measures for logic bombs are typically administrative in nature such as password management protocols and employee privilege monitoring [25]. While these administrative measures make it more difficult for malicious actors to introduce logic bombs, they do not help identify or mitigate logic bombs resident in systems and networks.

Most efforts at detecting logic bombs involve static and/or dynamic analyses of source code. The analysis techniques attempt to cover as many conditional branches in the code as possible to determine if logic bomb conditions are present. Branches that are very rarely reached and those that involve extremely specific conditions are most suspicious.

The SQA tool, which was developed to detect logic bombs hidden in critical infrastructure software, analyzes test conditions while maximizing code coverage [2]. Its high level of code coverage ensures that potential malicious code is detected and removed from critical infrastructure software before it is sent to customers. Another example is the TriggerScope tool, which was designed to find logic bombs in Android applications [9]. The tool employs "trigger analysis," a static program analysis technique that locates logic bomb triggering conditions. Interestingly, TriggerScope has detected several previously-unknown logic bombs in Google Play Store applications. Unfortunately, while SQA and TriggerScope have promising applications, they are not directly useful in this research because they rely on source code and Android APK, respectively.

2.4 Black Box Testing

Tools like SQA and TriggerScope assist in detecting latent logic bombs in code. However, most commercial unmanned aerial vehicle platforms are not open source. Analyzing firmware is a possibility, but this involves difficult and time-consuming reverse engineering; moreover, the firmware may have hardware protections that prevent its extraction. Thus, a different testing technique is required.

Traditional software testing techniques fall in three categories: (i) white box testing; (ii) gray box testing; and (iii) black box testing [15]. This research is concerned with black box testing. Black box testing is conducted without access to or an understanding of the inner workings of a system, just the ability to provide input values to the system and examine the resulting output values [18]. Black box testing has some advantages over other software validation techniques, including that it is faster on large pieces of code and does not require intimate knowledge of the system and programming languages [14, 15].

Given the assumption that autopilot source code is not available, an unmanned aerial vehicle must be treated as a black box. The proposed logic bomb detection methodology utilizes a black box testing technique called "equivalence partitioning." Equivalence partitioning divides input data into partitions and test cases are derived from the data partitions [14]. This greatly reduces the input space while maximizing the test conditions. In the case of an unmanned aerial vehicle, equivalence partitioning is achieved using the flight profiles in its mission set as a baseline for inputs instead of conducting brute-force testing of every combination of potential inputs in the area of operation.

3. Proposed Methodology

This section describes the proposed methodology for detecting logic bombs in unmanned aerial vehicle autopilot code.

3.1 Goals

The proposed detection methodology is intended to reduce the risk of an unmanned aerial vehicle encountering a logic bomb triggering event without having to test all the potential triggering conditions encountered during its operation. Because it was not possible to find a logic bomb developed for the ArduPilot autopilot software or even for unmanned aerial vehicles in general, a key task was to develop a simple logic bomb from scratch. Also, the logic bomb had to be represented and triggered within the ArduPilot Software-in-the-Loop (SITL) simulation software, which served as a key component of the suite used to validate the logic bomb detection methodology. Finally, a program had to be developed for parsing and analyzing log files gathered from flights to define a "safe corridor" through which an unmanned aerial vehicle could travel with a high degree of confidence that it would not trigger a logic bomb.

3.2   General Approach

The general approach is to use the ArduPilot SITL simulator to execute autopilot software on simulated missions prior to a real mission. The simulated missions expose the autopilot software to realistic conditions that the unmanned aerial vehicle would expect to encounter during the course of the real mission. By verifying that these conditions do not trigger a malicious logic bomb, mission planners can be confident that the unmanned aerial vehicle would perform as expected during its mission. Additionally, by partitioning the flight plan and considering likely flight variations, safe corridors can be developed in which the unmanned aerial vehicle may transit and operate.

The proposed detection methodology has the following steps:

- **Step 1:** Partition the flight according to the expected type – either point-to-point or free space.

- **Step 2:** For a point-to-point flight, develop a safe travel corridor for the unmanned aerial vehicle with a specified confidence level.

- **Step 3:** Within the safe travel corridor, exhaustively search all the flight paths based on the minimum resolution.

- **Step 4:** For a free space flight, exhaustively search all the flight paths based on the minimum resolution.

- **Step 5:** If no logic bombs are triggered after exhaustive searches in Steps 3 and 4, proceed with the mission.

3.3   Test Suite Overview

The test suite used in the experiments comprised the ArduPilot SITL simulation software, MAVProxy ground control software (GCS), Mission Planner ground control software and Python analysis code. These programs worked in conjunction to define the test flight profiles, execute the flight profiles and analyze the log files gathered from the flights. Figure 2 shows how the autopilot software interacts with the MAVProxy and Mission Planner ground control software. Also, the figure shows how the autopilot receives input from the physics and flight engines to perform accurate testing.

The ArduPilot desktop executable interacts with MAVProxy and Mission Planner via TCP over a serial connection and interacts with the physics simulator over a UDP connection. This simulation setup enables the autopilot software to interact with the physics engine.

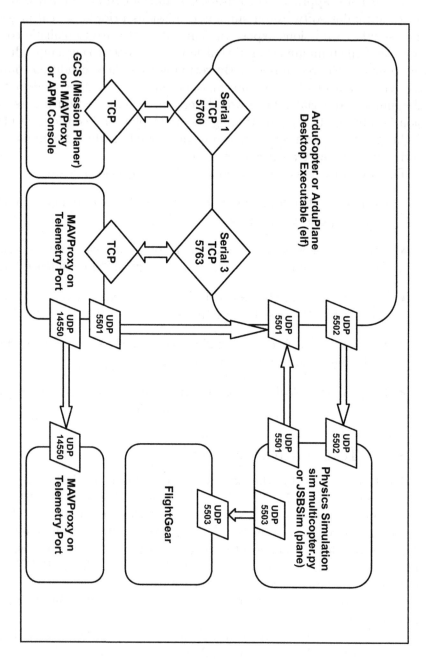

Figure 2.   ArduPilot SITL interaction [6].

The following four components comprised the test suite used in the experiments:

- **ArduPilot SITL:** ArduPilot is an open-source autopilot system used in many types of unmanned aerial vehicles [3]. It provides advanced logging capabilities along with simulation and analysis tools. The principal benefit of the ArduPilot software is that it is open source, which enables the code to be augmented with logic bomb malware to validate the detection methodology. Note that, although ArduPilot is open source by nature, the detection methodology considers it to be closed source.

- **MAVProxy Ground Control Software:** MAVProxy is designed for unmanned aerial vehicles [4]. At its core, the software is responsible for sending commands to and receiving information from an unmanned aerial vehicle. MAVProxy provides features such as command-line control with basic graphical user interface capabilities, networking capabilities, portability, light-weight design and support for additional module loading and tab-completion for commands. MAVProxy was the primary ground control software used in the experiments; it interfaced with the unmanned aerial vehicle and monitored flight path progress.

- **Mission Planner Ground Control Software:** Mission Planner was developed for ArduPilot [5]. Mission Planner offers some advantages over MAVProxy, especially its flight plan creation and logging features that were leveraged in the experiments. The software also permits flight plans to be saved and a saved flight plan to be loaded into an unmanned aerial vehicle before its flight.

- **Python Analysis Script:** The Python script was designed to parse the log entries related to GPS and waypoint information. When malicious activity is not detected, the data is grouped and organized by run, waypoint and then by log entry. A confidence interval is then created across each run for each log entry on a one-to-one basis. This represents the safe corridor in which the unmanned aerial vehicle can travel while providing high confidence that it will not trigger a logic bomb.

3.4 Logic Bomb Creation

The example logic bomb was designed to be easily identifiable upon activation. It targets the `motors_update()` function and prevents the motors from receiving new inputs from the autopilot. The triggering condition was designed to be a three-dimensional geofence specified by three parameters: (i) latitude; (ii) longitude; and (iii) altitude. Upon activation of the triggering condition, the logic bomb causes the unmanned aerial vehicle to crash.

3.5　Test Missions

Four test missions representing real-world scenarios were employed: (i) transit; (ii) circle; (iii) spline circle; and (iv) free area survey. These four missions involve flight paths that progressively increase in complexity and variance. For each mission, the ArduPilot autopilot desktop executable was compiled with the logic bomb and its associated triggering condition(s). Note that all the missions were carried out autonomously by the autopilot code, apart from arming and performing the takeoff to 5 meters.

The experiments involved the following four test missions:

- **Transit:** The transit mission simulates an unmanned aerial vehicle taking off from a given location, transiting to a destination and then landing. Although the logic bomb was incorporated in all the experiments, the geofence was initially set so that the unmanned aerial vehicle would not intersect it.

  Variations in weather and environmental factors in the ArduPilot SITL simulation meant that, as in the real world, slight variations would exist in the actual path traveled by an unmanned aerial vehicle between the set waypoints. In the experiments, ten runs of the transit mission were executed under these conditions. The results were analyzed and a safety corridor was created within which the unmanned aerial vehicle was expected to remain with 95% confidence. The log entries were used to generate a confidence interval in three dimensions along the entire flight path, accurately representing the predicted position of the unmanned aerial vehicle. The size of the corridor affected the next step, which was to exhaustively fly in the corridor at some minimum resolution or distance between flight tracks. The minimum resolution was set to 1 m due to the accuracy of GPS receivers in typical small unmanned aerial vehicles. Next, the geofence was configured so that the unmanned aerial vehicle would hit it during the course of its mission. The transit mission demonstrates the effectiveness of a logic bomb and provides a real-world scenario that helps validate the logic bomb detection methodology.

- **Circle:** The circle mission involves takeoff, approach to the circular holding area, flying in a circular flight path and landing. This type of flight path has various real-world applications such as surveying disaster areas and critical infrastructure assets.

  As with the transit mission, the logic bomb triggering condition for the first ten mission runs was set to be just outside the flight profile. A confidence interval was created across the runs to generate a flight corridor and the corridor was tested exhaustively at the minimum resolution. A final run was executed where the geofence intersected the circular portion of the flight path, causing the logic bomb to be activated.

- **Spline Circle:** The spline circle mission is very similar to the circle mission, the only difference being that the altitude of the unmanned aerial vehicle increases with each successive circular lap. Applications of this type of flight path include disaster area surveys that require views from different altitudes.

  As in the case of the other missions, the logic bomb triggering condition for the first ten mission runs was set to be just outside the flight profile. Following these runs, a final run was executed where the geofence intersected the circular portion of the flight path, causing the logic bomb to be activated. The spline circle mission is useful because it validates the circular area at a number of altitudes, providing the mission planner with increased flight assurance.

- **Free Area Survey:** The free area survey mission differs from the other three missions in that it surveys an entire area of operation at a given altitude, ensuring that no logic bomb triggers exist within the broad area. This mission is the closest to a pure brute-force approach, but it significantly scales down the input set to only what the unmanned aerial vehicle is expected to experience. The unmanned aerial vehicle performs passes across an area with 1 m of separation, covering the entire area, but without having to consider all possible inputs in the simulation to validate safe unmanned aerial vehicle operation. As a result, the safety corridor was set to the entire region of the survey polygon and a confidence interval was created only for the transit portions of the flight path.

  As in the case of the other missions, the logic bomb triggering condition for the first ten mission runs was set to be just outside the flight profile. Following these runs, a final run was executed where the geofence intersected the free area survey mission flight path, causing the logic bomb to be activated. The free area survey mission provides assurance that the unmanned aerial vehicle will safely transit to the mission area and operate dynamically within the area at the specified altitude.

4.   Experimental Results and Analysis

This section presents the experimental results. Also, it analyzes the effectiveness of a logic bomb on unmanned aerial vehicle missions and validates the logic bomb detection methodology using the transit, circle, spline circle and free area survey missions.

4.1   Logic Bomb Effectiveness

A key goal of this research was to create a logic bomb for the ArduPilot autopilot software and demonstrate its effectiveness using the ArduPilot SITL simulation software. Achieving this goal is important because it proves that a logic bomb can be executed in the autopilot code and that its behavior can be accurately depicted in a simulated environment.

The experiments demonstrate that the logic bomb in the ArduPilot autopilot code was able to successfully use the latitude, longitude and altitude parameters as triggering conditions. The logic bomb is rudimentary, but it was extremely effective at disabling the unmanned aerial vehicle motor and cause a loss of aircraft event. Figure 3(b) shows an example of an unmanned aerial vehicle crash.

4.2   Transit Mission

The transit flight path involved takeoff, transit and landing. Figures 3(a) and 3(b) show the sequences of events without and with logic bomb activation, respectively. Figure 3(b) shows that, when the unmanned aerial vehicle entered the logic bomb triggering area, it began to stray off course and eventually crashed.

Figure 4 shows a sample analysis script output with the confidence interval of the safety corridor created for the transit mission over ten runs. The results reveal that the confidence interval range for safe unmanned aerial vehicle operation has little variance. This is due to the design of the ArduPilot SITL simulator. Although variances such as wind can be introduced, they have moderate effects on unmanned aerial vehicle flight. A simulator that implements advanced weather effects would be needed to produce greater variations between runs. Because the confidence interval is less than the minimum resolution of 1 m, the detection methodology does not require the safe corridor to be tested exhaustively.

(a) Transit mission without logic bomb triggerng event.

(b) Transit mission with logic bomb triggering event.

Figure 3. Transit missions without and with logic bomb triggering events.

4.3 Circle Mission

The circle mission flight path involved takeoff, a brief transit to the edge of the circle, a circular flight path and landing. Figures 5(a) and 5(b) show the sequences of events without and with logic bomb activation, respectively. Note that Figure 5(a) shows the mission plan execution from an angled perspective to illustrate the different phases of flight whereas Figure 5(b) shows a side view of the flight path to illustrate the effect of the logic bomb.

The circle mission area had a diameter of 100 m with an area of approximately 7,854 m². To reduce the complexity, the circular area was assumed to be at a single altitude. Exhaustively searching at the 1 m

```
The confidence interval for the latitude for entry 6 is -35.36326014793303
    through -35.36326051206697
The confidence interval for the longitude for entry 6 is 149.16522861959928
    through 149.16522920040072
The confidence interval for the altitude for entry 6 is 589.0616580587994
    through 589.1243419412006
The distance between the edges of the confidence interval for entry 6 is
    0.0664 meters.

The confidence interval for the latitude for entry 7 is -35.36326014793303
    through -35.36326051206697
The confidence interval for the longitude for entry 7 is 149.165228584783
    through 149.16522919521702
The confidence interval for the altitude for entry 7 is 589.2232957358882
    through 589.3007042641119
The distance between the edges of the confidence interval for entry 6 is
    0.0686 meters.

The confidence interval for the latitude for entry 8 is -35.36326010948
    through -35.36326051052
The confidence interval for the longitude for entry 8 is 149.1652285487848
    through 149.16522915121521
The confidence interval for the altitude for entry 8 is 589.4212129285787
    through 689.5127870714213
The distance between the edges of the confidence interval for entry 6 is
    0.07054 meters.
```

Figure 4.   Sample program output.

resolution required a simulated flight distance of approximately 7,854 m. By utilizing the flight path, the search space was reduced to 314 m per run (circumference of the circular area), with the unmanned aerial vehicle passing through all the relevant points during the mission. Using ten runs to generate the confidence interval increased the total simulated flight distance to 3,140 m, a reduction of 60% from the original 7,854 m. The small variance observed between runs allowed for fewer runs to generate an acceptably small confidence interval, but this may not always be true.

4.4   Spline Circle Mission

The spline circle mission flight path was very similar to the circle mission flight path, except that multiple laps were taken around the circle as the altitude was increased by 5 m per lap. The logic bomb was set to trigger at a specific altitude. Figures 6(a) and 6(b) show the mission runs. Figure 6(b) shows that the unmanned aerial vehicle

(a) Circle mission without logic bomb triggering event.

(b) Circle mission with logic bomb triggering event.

Figure 5. Circle missions without and with logic bomb triggering events.

operated normally for multiple laps around the circle until the triggering longitude, latitude and altitude were reached.

Unlike the circle mission, which was analyzed at one altitude (two dimensions), the spline circle mission was analyzed in three dimensions. The volume of the mission area, which extended from the ground level to a maximum altitude of 25 m, was 196,349 m^3. Exhaustively testing this volume at 1 m latitude and longitude resolutions and 5 m altitude resolution (for fair comparison) resulted in a simulated flight distance of

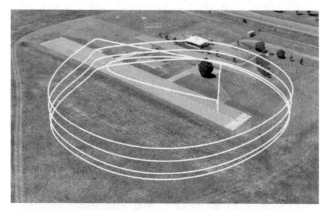

(a) Spline circle mission without logic bomb triggering event.

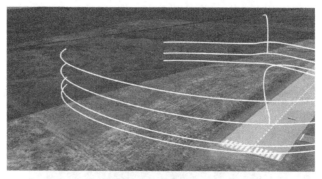

(b) Spline circle mission with logic bomb triggering event.

Figure 6.　Spline circle missions without and with logic bomb triggering events.

39.3 km. Each run for developing the confidence interval required only 1.57 km, a total of 15.7 km over ten runs. As in the case of the circle mission, this reduced the total simulated flight distance by a significant 60% from the original 39.3 km.

4.5　Free Area Survey Mission

The free area survey mission required an approach closest to brute-force detection, but the approach still provided significant benefits over brute forcing an entire area of operation when used in conjunction with the reduction techniques used for the other missions. For the free area survey mission, the confidence interval was generated only for the transit, takeoff and landing portions of the mission. When the unmanned aerial vehicle reached its intended free search area, the flight path called for a

(a) Free area survey mission without logic bomb triggering event.

(b) Free area survey mission with logic bomb triggering event.

Figure 7. Free area survey missions without and with logic bomb triggering events.

sweeping pattern with a distance of 1 m between every sweep of a very specific area of operation at a given altitude. Utilizing this technique, all the theoretical coordinate data that could reliably activate a logic bomb in the area was input, allowing for dynamic flying within an area during a real-world mission. Figures 7(a) and 7(b) show the free area survey flight paths without and with logic bomb triggering events, respectively.

The volume of the operating region in the free area survey mission was approximately $188,000\,\mathrm{m}^3$. A region of this size requires a huge number of inputs to be validated. Utilizing a $1\,\mathrm{m}$ resolution, would have required the unmanned aerial vehicle to traverse a linear flight distance of $188,000\,\mathrm{m}$ in order to validate the entire area of operation. In contrast, utilizing the takeoff, transit and landing portions and then performing $1\,\mathrm{m}$ sweeps in the defined area of operation drastically reduced the amount of inputs required for validation.

5. Conclusions

The methodology for detecting logic bombs hidden in unmanned aerial vehicle autopilot code is novel and promising because it operates without source code access by simulating mission runs in a software-in-the-loop simulator to define safe unmanned aerial vehicle operating areas. By using preplanned mission flight paths as baselines, the methodology drastically reduces the space to be searched to ensure that an unmanned aerial vehicle will not encounter a logic bomb triggering condition during its mission. The search space reduction is very significant because the only alternative to this point was to conduct brute-force testing. Thus, in a real-world scenario, instead of having to process all the inputs corresponding to a large region such as a town or county, the input space would be restricted only to a section of a power line or a field that is of interest. While the focus has been on logic bombs in the ArduPilot autopilot software that are triggered by latitude, longitude and altitude values, the simulation methodology is general enough to be applicable to other unmanned aerial vehicle systems and logic bombs with arbitrary triggering conditions.

Securing unmanned aerial vehicles is vital to ensuring safe critical infrastructure operations. This research is a starting point in an area that has received little attention to date. It is hoped that the proposed simulation methodology will stimulate efforts at securing unmanned aerial vehicles of all types from logic bombs, including logic bombs with more nuanced triggers, as well as from other kinds of malware.

The views expressed in this chapter are those of the authors, and do not reflect the official policy or position of the U.S. Air Force, U.S. Department of Defense or U.S. Government. This document has been approved for public release, distribution unlimited (Case #88ABW-2019-6088).

References

[1] S. Adams and C. Friedland, A survey of unmanned aerial vehicle (UAV) usage for imagery collection in disaster research and management, *Proceedings of the Ninth International Workshop on Remote Sensing for Disaster Response*, 2011.

[2] H. Agrawal, J. Alberi, L. Bahler, J. Micallef, A. Virodov, M. Magenheimer, S. Snyder, V. Debroy and E. Wong, Detecting hidden logic bombs in critical infrastructure software, *Proceedings of the Seventh International Conference on Information Warfare and Security*, pp. 1–11, 2012.

[3] ArduPilot, ArduPilot, New York (`ardupilot.org/about`), 2020.

[4] ArduPilot, MAVProxy, New York (`ardupilot.github.io/MAVProxy/html/index.html`), 2020.

[5] ArduPilot, Mission Planner Home, New York (`ardupilot.org/planner`), 2020.

[6] ArduPilot, SITL Simulator (Software in the Loop), New York (`ardupilot.org/dev/docs/sitl-simulator-software-in-the-loop.html`), 2020.

[7] R. Austin, *Unmanned Aircraft Systems: UAVS Design, Development and Deployment*, John Wiley and Sons, Chichester, United Kingdom, 2010.

[8] Enterprise and Industry Directorate-General of the European Commission, Study Analyzing the Current Activities in the Field of UAV, Report ENTR/2007/065, Brussels, Belgium, 2007.

[9] Y. Fratantonio, A. Bianchi, W. Robertson, E. Kirda, C. Kruegel and G. Vigna, TriggerScope: Towards detecting logic bombs in Android applications, *Proceedings of the IEEE Symposium on Security and Privacy*, pp. 377–396, 2016.

[10] K. Hartmann and K. Giles, UAV exploitation: A new domain for cyber power, *Proceedings of the Eighth International Conference on Cyber Conflict*, pp. 205–221, 2016.

[11] M. Hooper, Y. Tian, R. Zhou, B. Cao, A. Lauf, L. Watkins, W. Robinson and W. Alexis, Securing commercial Wi-Fi-based UAVs from common security attacks, *Proceedings of the IEEE Military Communications Conference*, pp. 1213–1218, 2016.

[12] A. Javaid, W. Sun, V. Devabhaktuni and M. Alam, Cyber security threat analysis and modeling of an unmanned aerial vehicle system, *Proceedings of the IEEE Conference on Technologies for Homeland Security*, pp. 585–590, 2012.

[13] R. Kandala, What are logic bombs and how to detect them, *Techulator Blog*, May 29, 2013.

[14] M. Khan, Different approaches to the black box testing technique for finding errors, *International Journal of Software Engineering and Applications*, vol. 2(4), pp. 31–40, 2011.

[15] M. Khan and F. Khan, A comparative study of white box, black box and grey box testing techniques, *International Journal of Advanced Computer Science and Applications*, vol. 3(6), pp. 12–15, 2012.

[16] B. Madan, M. Banik and D. Bein, Securing unmanned autonomous systems from cyber threats, *Journal of Defense Modeling and Simulation: Applications, Methodology, Technology*, vol. 16(2), pp. 119–136, 2019.

[17] P. Mozur, Drone maker DJI may be sending data to China, U.S. officials say, *New York Times*, November 29, 2017.

[18] S. Nidhra and J. Dondeti, Black box and white box testing techniques – A literature review, *International Journal of Embedded Systems and Applications*, vol. 2(2), pp. 29–50, 2012.

[19] J. Pleban, R. Band and R. Creutzburg, Hacking and securing the AR.Drone 2.0 quadcopter – Investigations for improving the security of a toy, *Proceedings of the SPIE Conference on Electronic Imaging – Mobile Devices and Multimedia: Enabling Technologies, Algorithms and Applications*, vol. 9030, pp. 90300L-1–90300L-12, 2014.

[20] C. Rani, H. Modares, R. Sriram, D. Mikulski and F. Lewis, Security of unmanned aerial vehicle systems against cyber-physical attacks, *Journal of Defense Modeling and Simulation: Applications, Methodology, Technology*, vol. 13(3), pp. 331–342, 2016.

[21] N. Rodday, R. Schmidt and A. Pras, Exploring security vulnerabilities of unmanned aerial vehicles, *Proceedings of the IEEE/IFIP Network Operations and Management Symposium*, pp. 993–994, 2016.

[22] M. Smith, Leaked DHS memo accuses drone maker DJI of spying for China, *CSO Digital Magazine*, December 3, 2017.

[23] J. Sullivan, Evolution or revolution? The rise of UAVs, *IEEE Technology and Society*, vol. 25(3), pp. 43–49, 2006.

[24] U.S. Department of Homeland Security, Critical Infrastructure Sectors, Washington, DC (www.dhs.gov/cisa/critical-infrastructure-sectors), March 24, 2020.

[25] K. Wehrum, Technology: When IT workers attack – How to prevent tech sabotage, *Inc.*, April 1, 2009.

Chapter 3

ASSESSING THE CYBER RISK OF SMALL UNMANNED AERIAL VEHICLES

Dillon Pettit and Scott Graham

Abstract   The growing market for commercial-off-the-shelf unmanned aerial vehicles has brought with it innate rewards and vulnerabilities. Aerial technology presents unique cyber risk characteristics that must be managed in new ways. A key stage of the risk management process is risk assessment – the earlier in the lifecycle the assessment is performed, the more the security that can be designed into the operational environment.

This chapter presents a quantitative risk assessment framework for unmanned aerial vehicles based on qualitative cyber measures and requirements that captures the dynamics of probability and severity. The assessment uses 14 sub-metrics that cover unmanned aerial vehicle security, temporal aspects and mission environments to express the risk as a single score ranging from 0.0 (best) to 10.0 (worst). A case study involving three popular unmanned aerial vehicle models in three mission-environment scenarios demonstrates the breadth and variability, general applicability and ease of use of the risk assessment framework. Performing risk assessments before unmanned aerial vehicle acquisition will enable organizations and individuals to accurately compare and select the best vehicles for their missions and environments.

Keywords: Unmanned aerial vehicles, cyber risk, quantitative assessment

1.   Introduction

Applications of small unmanned aerial vehicles (UAVs) have grown considerably over the last two decades. While the military sector may have had almost exclusive use of these vehicles in the past, the commercial sector has recognized the benefits of small, inexpensive unmanned aircraft to meet a multitude of needs. Infrastructure is defined as "[t]he framework of interdependent networks and systems ... that provide a reliable flow of products and services essential to the defense and eco-

© IFIP International Federation for Information Processing 2020
Published by Springer Nature Switzerland AG 2020
J. Staggs and S. Shenoi (Eds.): Critical Infrastructure Protection XIV, IFIP AICT 596, pp. 45–67, 2020.
https://doi.org/10.1007/978-3-030-62840-6_3

nomic security of the United States..." [2]. Whether the infrastructure is critical or non-critical, it increasingly employs unmanned aerial vehicles. Applications include geospatial surveys, civil surveillance, traffic and crowd management, natural disaster monitoring and control, agriculture and environment management, urban security, big data processing and coordination of heterogeneous systems [15]. Small unmanned aerial vehicles are routinely used for mapping and inspection of buildings, goods distribution and inaccessible terrain monitoring [12]. These small unmanned aerial vehicles are designed as operational aircraft and functional computer systems, which come with combined vulnerabilities. The operational risks include collisions with buildings and other aircraft as well as uncontrolled landings [1].

Cyber risk, on the other hand, arises from the potential of an attacker to compromise cyber components. However, unlike the operational risk arena, there is no lead agency that manages the growing cyber risk to critical infrastructure posed by small unmanned aerial vehicles [17]. With the Federal Aviation Administration (FAA) and other regulatory bodies lagging in efforts focused on mitigating the cyber risk posed by small unmanned aerial vehicles [13], organizations (and individuals) have little guidance in assessing the amount and types of risks incurred when deploying fleets. Acquisition teams are ill-equipped to analyze the complex cyber ramifications of components that may or may not be installed in unmanned aerial vehicles. What is needed is a construct for comparing the risks of the various unmanned aerial vehicle options that could accomplish an organization's mission.

This chapter presents a cyber risk assessment methodology that is tailored to small unmanned aerial vehicles. A risk assessment case study considers common types of unmanned aerial vehicles along with various organizational missions and environments.

2.   Background and Related Work

Historically built for military applications, unmanned aerial vehicles are widely used by civilian organizations and hobbyists. By definition, an unmanned aerial vehicle is a system that can sustain autonomous flight similar to remotely piloted vehicles (RPVs) and drones [6]. Unmanned aerial vehicles are usually able to hover or move entirely via computer navigation whereas remotely piloted vehicles require control instructions throughout their flights; drones have even more limited missions and sophistication. The exact definitions of the sizing tiers are not standardized, but they are typically categorized as very small, small, medium and large. Very small unmanned aerial vehicles are miniaturized devices that operate in very low Reynolds number regimes and are usually less than 20 inches in any dimension. Small unmanned aerial vehicles are popular with hobbyists and have at least one dimension that is greater than 20 inches. Medium and large unmanned aerial vehicles are too massive for an individual to carry; they may even use small runways like light aircraft. These larger vehicles have on-board security functionality and are subject to more regulations than smaller vehicles. Their internal architectures differ greatly and the vehicles are controlled at varying degrees of autonomy by their autopilots [9].

Quantitative risk assessments are not unique to the cyber domain; indeed, such assessments have existed in the military domain as well as the civilian domains of commerce and industry for centuries. The most generalized description of risk is the product of cost and likelihood. Cost is the financial loss or recovery price tag incurred as a result of a failure. Likelihood is the probability of failure over time or the rate of failure during a specific time frame.

Risk management of unmanned aerial vehicles is a multi-dimensional problem. Operational risk assessment of small unmanned aerial vehicles has been delegated to the National Aeronautics and Space Administration (NASA) for development and testing, and subsequently to be fielded by the FAA within the National Airspace System [14]. In response to commercial requests, NASA began the development of the UAV Traffic Management (UTM) System in 2014 with the publication of a 15-year plan, and initial deployment planned within five years [14]. Connections to the new UTM System would involve approximately ten new communications protocols as standard on all unmanned aerial vehicles, enabling receipt of flight plan constraints for individual unmanned aerial vehicle autopilots to navigate around blocked areas in real-time [14]. The UTM risk modeling software is device-agnostic, except for size and weight, which means that the system does not quantify cyber risk threats to unmanned aerial vehicles, although cyber exploits would cause "off-nominal trajectories" [1] that NASA and the FAA seek to reduce. While the regulation of small unmanned aerial vehicle production to meet the communications requirements of the National Airspace System may incidentally provide some cyber risk reduction, the failure to design for cyber objectives implies that any improved cyber risk posture would be undocumented and ineffective.

The Cyber Vulnerability and Scoring System (CVSS) [18], maintained by the Forum of Incident Response and Security Teams (FIRST), is the most commonly used quantitative vulnerability severity assessment tool. As an "open framework for communication of the characteristics and severity of software vulnerabilities" [8], CVSS provides data points to the

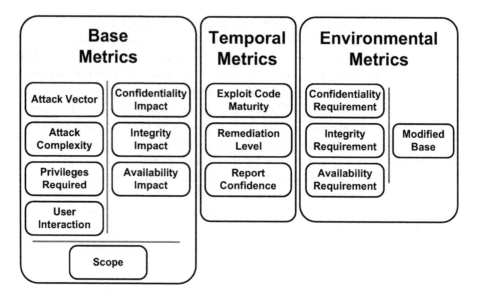

Figure 1. CVSS v3.1 metrics [8].

National Vulnerabilities Database (NVD) and Common Vulnerabilities and Exposures (CVE) database, which are utilized by risk frameworks to define information technology network vulnerabilities.

The current CVSS version (v3.1) computes a final score from 0.0 (best) through 10.0 (worst) using the 15 sub-metrics shown in Figure 1. The base metrics are split into three sub-categories and the environmental metrics are split into two sub-categories based on commonalities and use by algorithms, as will be discussed later. An extensions framework optionally allows for the manual adjustment of constants for specific fields; however, no published framework currently exists for unmanned aerial vehicles. CVSS focuses on component vulnerabilities and, therefore, does not fully define a system, its mission or its environment, all of which are critical to unmanned aerial vehicles [10]. CVSS does however provide the most robust, utilized and, therefore, practical scoring system for cyber devices.

As of 2016, only 61% of organizations in the healthcare sector employed cyber risk management [4]. Recognizing that cyber flaws were only being treated as device flaws to be corrected via long-term regulations by the Food and Drug Administration (FDA), Stine [19] proposed a medical device risk assessment framework that would provide an understanding of risk in hospitals, prioritization of devices requiring additional protection and ease of computation by general healthcare practitioners with limited cyber expertise. Stine created a cyber risk scoring system that considers the severity of the worst-case scenario and the number of security features present. While the cyber risk scoring system satisfies the goals of understandable results, low cost and ease of use, employing manually crafted constants to define the severity of an attribute to the overall risk of a device requires significantly more effort.

Hartmann and Steup [11] have proposed a scoring system for unmanned aerial vehicles that provides a quantifiable cyber risk score, but it has significant shortcomings. They define the general internal network of unmanned aerial vehicles with the most vulnerable components being communications links, sensors, data storage and autopilot configurations. The hardware and software of these components were defined using a market survey, autopilot attributes were limited to the fail-safe state, and sensors were increased to four configurations with three combinations. An environment attribute was considered with the imperative that risk assessments for unmanned aerial vehicles must include the risk inherent to the operational environments and mission sets. However, the system lacks a categorization of risk and does not specify the values that are acceptable. Furthermore, although Hartmann and Steup state that mission sets must be included, no attributes are provided for computing or factoring mission in the cyber risk score.

3. Proposed Risk Assessment Framework

The proposed risk assessment framework is based on CVSS, which provides a common nomenclature for cyber risk managers who administer information technology networks with strong quantification constants in their functions. The proposed framework incorporates base metrics augmented with temporal and environmental metrics. As described above, CVSS does not score risk, but the severity of vulnerabilities; therefore, significant changes are required to shift the focus to device risk and unmanned aerial vehicle risk in particular. A simple extensions framework, as provisioned in CVSS v3.1, would not update the original scoring system to rate any metric outside of the severity of vulnerabilities because the framework merely tweaks constants within the equations. The proposed framework redefines all the sub-metrics to some extent while maintaining as much of the CVSS structure as possible. Figure 2 shows the proposed assessment metrics.

3.1 Base Metrics

The attack vector (AV) sub-metric of the base metrics category evaluates the connection of a unmanned aerial vehicle to potential attackers. Similar to networked information technology devices, the logical location

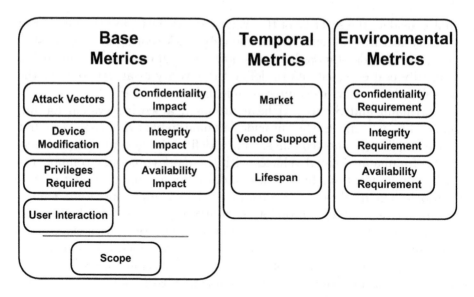

Figure 2.   Proposed risk assessment metrics.

Table 1.   Attack vector (AV) values.

Base Level	Description	Value
Direct	Unmanned aerial vehicle is "remotely exploitable" in that it can be compromised at the protocol level one or more network hops away.	0.85
Ground Controller	Unmanned aerial vehicle is indirectly bound to the Internet via the ground controller.	0.62
Air-Gapped	Unmanned aerial vehicle is not bound to the network, but an attacker can exploit persistent read/write/execute capabilities on the ground controller.	0.55
None	Attacker is physically present to manipulate the vulnerable component; the physical interaction may be brief or persistent.	0.20

of an attacker directly correlates to the risk of the device being attacked due to the size of the audience and automation of scanning and exploitation (Table 1). The greater the logical separation between the set of potential attackers and the unmanned aerial vehicle, the less the risk of cyber compromise. The numerical values of the new sub-metrics are taken directly from CVSS, with higher values indicating greater risk [8].

Table 2. Device modification (DM) values.

Base Level	Description	Value
Low	Specialized modifications or extenuating circumstances do not exist. Attacker can expect repeatable success when attacking the unmanned aerial vehicle.	0.77
High	One or more custom modifications or extenuating circumstances exist, requiring an attacker to invest in a measurable amount of preparation.	0.44

The second sub-metric of the base metrics category is device modification (DM), which evaluates how an unmanned aerial vehicle conforms to its brand advertising or specifications (Table 2). Commercial-off-the-shelf unmanned aerial vehicles have baseline models with few (if any) variations. Less variations induce higher levels of risk because an attacker would expend less discovery effort and would have more confidence in repeatability for the same models. The other extreme is a do-it-yourself or custom-made unmanned aerial vehicle that has no standard configuration and is close to being unique.

Table 3. Privileges required (PR) values.

Base Level	Description	Value
None	Attacker is unauthorized before an attack and therefore does not require any access to settings or files of the vulnerable unmanned aerial vehicle system to carry out the attack.	0.85
Low	Attacker requires privileges that provide basic user capabilities.	0.62[1]
High	Attacker requires privileges that provide access to device-wide settings and files.	0.27[2]

[1] Value of 0.68 is used if the scope is changed.
[2] Value of 0.50 is used if the scope is changed.

The privileges required (PR) sub-metric of the base metrics category is concerned with the software components that implement privilege delineation (Table 3). Unlike common information technology networks, unmanned aerial vehicles typically operate under the assumption that

Table 4. User interaction (UI) values.

Base Level	Description	Value
None	Unmanned aerial vehicle can be exploited without interaction with a user.	0.85
Required	Exploited unmanned aerial vehicle still allows the authorized user to send commands and otherwise control its flight.	0.62

the physically or wirelessly connected user is the administrator with the only other privilege level being kernel access to the operating system. Authentication of communications and commands, and authentication prior to access of data at rest have high levels of separation. If the communications protocol allows received signals to be executed or if valuable flight data and commands are accessible physically by any user with a cable, then the level of privileges required is none.

The user interaction (UI) sub-metric of the base metrics category evaluates the risk associated with not having a human in the loop (Table 4). Unmanned aerial vehicle architectures range from fully autonomous to inject only to full human control. When an unmanned aerial vehicle has complete control of its flight (assuming some preset mission parameters), the user does not have the ability to override incorrect decisions made by the vehicle. User interactions help mitigate errors and compromises, such as countering a Global Positioning System (GPS) spoofing attack with new waypoints or direct human control.

The scope (S) sub-metric of the base metrics category evaluates the risk associated with an attack on the unmanned aerial vehicle spreading to other devices. While many unmanned aerial vehicles are operated under the one user/one device model, ad hoc networking and swarm technologies are gaining traction, resulting in the risk levels shown in Table 5. The addition of trust-connected agents to a targeted unmanned aerial vehicle increases the risk to other devices and increases the likelihood of an attack on the unmanned aerial vehicle, similar to the situation in information technology networks. The connections can vary from command signals to simple navigational directions, but a single vulnerable unmanned aerial vehicle has the potential to infect or otherwise impact other connected devices and compromise a mission. The scope sub-metric switches the equations used in the algorithms to associate all the sub-metrics, increasing the score potential for a changed value.

Table 5. Scope (S) values.

Base Level	Description	Value
Unchanged	An exploited unmanned aerial vehicle can only affect resources local to it or the ground controller.	N/A
Changed	An exploited unmanned aerial vehicle can affect other devices outside the local scope.	N/A

Table 6. Confidentiality impact (C) values.

Base Level	Description	Value
None	No confidentiality protections are in place, enabling an attacker to obtain all the information from the compromised unmanned aerial vehicle.	0.56
Low	Some confidentiality protections are in place; unsecured information does not cause a direct, serious loss to the user.	0.22
High	Strong confidentiality protections are in place; confidentiality of all information at rest and in motion is maintained.	0

The next three sub-metrics of the base metrics category relate to the impacts of attacks on unmanned aerial vehicle confidentiality, integrity and availability. The first is the confidentiality impact (C), which evaluates the security mechanisms that combat confidentiality breaches (Table 6). Security mechanisms include encryption of information at rest and over-the-air. Not all information at rest or in motion is considered to be sensitive, so reduced security mechanisms may be adequate to mitigate the risk.

The integrity impact (I) sub-metric of the base metrics category evaluates the security mechanisms that enforce the integrity of information at rest and in motion (Table 7). Integrity mechanisms such as secure communications protocols with checksums or cryptography, and self-diagnostics prevent an attacker from tampering with information.

The availability impact (A) is the third and final impact sub-metric of the base metrics category (Table 8). Command and control communications with an unmanned aerial vehicle should not be disrupted by an attack or by non-malicious electromagnetic interference. Availability is

Table 7.   Integrity impact (I) values.

Base Level	Description	Value
None	No integrity protections are in place, enabling an attacker to modify any and all information.	0.56
Low	Some integrity protections are in place, but modification of data is possible. However, an attacker is unable to control the consequence of a modification or the amount of modification is limited.	0.22
High	Strong integrity mechanisms are in place; integrity of all information at rest and in motion is maintained.	0

Table 8.   Availability impact (A) values.

Base Level	Description	Value
None	No availability protections are in place, enablng an attacker to deny access to an unmanned aerial vehicle in a sustained or persistent manner.	0.56
Low	Some availability protections are in place. Unmanned aerial vehicle resources are partially available all the time or fully available some of the time, but there are direct or serious consequences.	0.22
High	Strong availability protections are in place; availability of aerial vehicle resources are maintained at all times.	0

commonly ensured via multi-channel communications that may be built into a wireless protocol or provided by hardware.

3.2   Temporal Metrics

A significant aspect of cyber risk is its temporal nature – its ability to change over time. The sub-metrics in the temporal metrics category evaluate various risk aspects that change over time.

The market (M) sub-metric of the temporal metrics category evaluates the ubiquity of an unmanned aerial vehicle brand and its potential value as a target for compromise. As shown in Table 9, based on the attacker's

Table 9. Market (M) values.

Temporal Level	Description	Value
High	One-half (50%) or more of the market share is held by the unmanned aerial vehicle brand or the brand is used by more than one major customer.	1
Medium	More than 25% but less 50% of the market share is held by the unmanned aerial vehicle brand or the brand is used by one major customer.	0.97
Low	Less than 25% of the market share is held by the unmanned aerial vehicle brand or the brand is not used by any major customer.	0.94
None	Close to 0% of the market share is held by the unmanned aerial vehicle, which is non-standard or custom-built.	0.91

motivation, the risk is increased when the reward to effort ratio is high. This sub-metric value constantly changes as the market fluctuates and regulations impact the viability and marketability of unmanned aerial vehicles.

Table 10. Vendor support (VS) values.

Temporal Level	Description	Value
Unavailable	Unmanned aerial vehicle has no vendor support and no active community support.	1
Low	Unmanned aerial vehicle has no vendor support, but there is active community support that provides updates and workarounds to address vulnerabilities.	0.97
Medium	Unmanned aerial vehicle has occasional vendor support and active community support.	0.96
High	Unmanned aerial vehicle has active vendor support and active community support.	0.95

The vendor support (VS) sub-metric of the temporal metrics category evaluates the rate or quality of updating unmanned aerial vehicle software (Table 10). Vendors release code updates that address vulnerabilities and provide new features. Additionally, the user/research community may release patches when vendors do not provide software

Table 11.   Lifespan (L) values.

Temporal Level	Description	Value
High	Expected unmanned aerial vehicle lifespan for missions is longer than the expected vendor support duration or is greater than two years.	1
Normal	Expected unmanned aerial vehicle lifespan for missions is within the expected vendor support duration or is between one and two years.	0.96
Low	Expected unmanned aerial vehicle lifespan for missions is less than one year and the unmanned aerial vehicle is expected to be discontinued soon.	0.92

support or updates. Cyber risk is significantly reduced when software is supported and updates are provided on a regular basis.

The lifespan (L) sub-metric of the temporal metrics category evaluates the expected duration of service (Table 11). The risk increases when an unmanned aerial vehicle has a longer service life because there is more time for vulnerabilities to be discovered and for it to be attacked. Most large organizations determine a lifecycle management plan over the mission life of computing equipment. However, unlike computing equipment, the lifespan of a small unmanned aerial vehicle is typically shorter than the desired lifecycle. Therefore, it is important to consider when new vehicles would have to be purchased.

3.3   Environmental Metrics

Mission risk, which is vital to any unmanned aerial vehicle risk assessment, is evaluated using the environmental metrics. The mission requirements are similar to the original CVSS definition because the entire device or system is rated for the mission requirements, instead of an individual vulnerability. Since an unmanned aerial vehicle may be designed for multiple mission sets, it must be rated for the highest requirement in each sub-metric. The environmental metrics category includes the confidentiality requirements (CR) sub-metric, integrity requirements (IR) sub-metric and availability requirements (AR) sub-metric, which are rated using the values high, medium and low (Table 12). Unlike CVSS, which includes the not-defined value, this framework requires a determination of mission requirements, with the medium (default) value having a neutral modifying effect on the base metric scores.

Table 12. Environmental (CR, IR, AR) values.

Requirement Level	Description	Value
High	Loss of confidentiality, integrity or availability are likely to have catastrophic adverse effects on an organization or its mission.	1.5
Medium	Loss of confidentiality, integrity or availability are likely to have serious adverse effects on an organization or its mission.	1.0
Low	Loss of confidentiality, integrity or availability are likely to have limited adverse effects on an organization or its mission.	0.5

The CVSS environmental score includes the modified base metric scores, which correspond to the base sub-metric scores adjusted for the specific situation of the device in question. The CVSS base sub-metric scores are expected to be network- and mission-agnostic for the vulnerability in question, which means that the metrics would be static for any user who employs a vulnerable device.

In contrast, the proposed approach evaluates the unmanned aerial vehicle mission and environment in the base score, which means that no new risk-related information would be provided by a modified base score. Eliminating the modified base sub-metrics from the scoring system is simple because CVSS by default uses the original base sub-metrics. If it is determined during a future unmanned aerial vehicle risk assessment that it would be beneficial to separate mission and environment, then the modified base sub-metrics rather the base sub-metrics should be used in the environmental score computations.

4. Risk Scoring System

The risk scoring system is designed to incorporate the metrics defined in the previous section to calculate an overall risk score. For ease of use, the score is limited to values between 0.0 (best) and 10.0 (worst), which should provide close to 101 possible risk states based on the 14 sub-metric values. The sub-metric values are drawn directly from the open-source values of CVSS, leveraging the long-term value testing and refining efforts invested in the CVSS vulnerability severity assessment methodology. Since the proposed sub-metrics address the same cyber security fundamentals as the CVSS sub-metrics, the values of severity should be close and directly related to the risk values. The equations

---

Algorithm 1 : Base score computation.

ISS = 1 − [(1 − C) * (1 − I) * (1 − A)]
if S = Unchanged **then**
    Impact = 6.42 * ISS
else
    Impact = 7.52 * (ISS − 0.029) − 3.25 * (ISS − 0.02)^{15}
end if
Exploitability = 8.22 * AV * DM * PR * UI
if Impact ≤ 0 **then**
    BaseScore = 0
else
    if S = Unchanged **then**
        BaseScore = Roundup(Min[Impact + Exploitability, 10])
    else
        BaseScore = Roundup(Min[1.08 * (Impact + Exploitability), 10])
    end if
end if

---

used in the proposed risk scoring system are directly taken from CVSS due to the close connection between the two scoring systems.

4.1   Base Score

The base score is computed from the first eight sub-metrics that consider unmanned aerial vehicle design and security. This score is not necessarily accurate for a future assessment or for a different user because the use case, configuration and payload are considered in the computation. Algorithm 1 specifies the base score computation. Note that scope (S) serves as a modifier to both intermediates via CVSS constants. The influence of each metric has been balanced over time and testing by CVSS for its vulnerabilities and directly relate to the risk metrics in the proposed framework.

4.2   Temporal Score

The temporal score is computed using its three sub-metrics. The temporal score is the new score for an unmanned aerial vehicle because the base score is potentially reduced by factors relating to time. The highest risk values could be considered by default because the worst-case temporal state is assumed for each sub-metric and this does not have an effect on the base score. Algorithm 2 specifies the temporal score computation.

Algorithm 2 : Temporal score computation.

TemporalScore = Roundup(BaseScore * M * VS * L)

Algorithm 3 : Environmental score computation.

//EnvironmentalScore ← {C, I, A Requirements, Modified Base Metrics}
MISS = Min {1 − [(1 − CR * C) * (1 −IR * I) * (1 − AR * A)], 0.915}
if S = Unchanged **then**
   ModifiedImpact = 6.42 * MISS
else
   ModifiedImpact = 7.52 * (MISS − 0.029) − 3.25 * (MISS * 0.9731 − 0.02)^{13}
end if

ModifiedExploitability = 8.22 * AV * DM * PR * UI

if ModifiedImpact ≤ 0 **then**
   EnvironmentalScore = 0
else
   if S = Unchanged **then**
      EnvironmentalScore = Roundup(Roundup[Min([ModifiedImpact + ModifiedExploitability], 10)] * M * VS * L)
   else
      EnvironmentalScore = Roundup(Roundup[Min(1.08 * ModifiedImpact + ModifiedExploitability), 10] * M * VS * L)
   end if
end if

4.3 Environmental Score

The environmental score uses the assessed sub-metrics in relation to the unmanned aerial vehicle mission sets or requirements. The word "modified" is used to separate the terms from the base score and, as explained above, unlike CVSS, the actual modified values are not used. The environmental score is then computed using the temporal sub-metrics and base sub-metrics. Algorithm 3 specifies the environmental score computation.

The environmental score is the final score that expresses the cyber risk for a particular unmanned aerial vehicle and a particular mission-environment set. The scores, which range from 0.0 (best) to 10.0 (worst) with rounding up to the nearest tenth, are designed to be easy to use by non-cyber focused personnel and vary enough based on subtle changes in the sub-metric values.

5.   Case Study

The case study employs three popular unmanned aerial vehicle models in three mission-environment scenarios to demonstrate and analyze the proposed risk assessment framework. The nine individual cases are intended to clarify that the breadth and variability, general applicability and ease of use criteria are satisfied.

5.1   UAV Model 1

The Chinese-made DJI Mavic 2 Pro quad-rotor, which was released in mid-2018, is rated very highly for "camera performance, video transmission, fight time, flight speed, less noise, omnidirectional obstacle sensing, intelligent flight modes and its unique hyperlapse feature" [3]. It has a maximum flight time of 31 minutes, maximum speed of 45 mph, hover control at wind speeds up to 25 mph and is sold for under 2,000 dollars. The Mavic 2 Pro is controlled via the DJI GO 4 app on a smartphone that is connected to a DJI controller, which sends commands and receives data over separate Wi-Fi frequencies by default [5].

The DJI brand is well-known for autopilot obstacle avoidance; in fact, the Mavic 2 Pro boasts 360 degree vision. The user is always in control of the unmanned aerial vehicle per FAA regulations, and the Mavic 2 Pro features multiple control failure protocols, including returning to a home waypoint. The DJI brand employs closed systems and protocols, with the data being encrypted using the AES-256 standard [5]. However, DJI is plagued by rumors of supply chain vulnerabilities. The Department of Homeland Security (DHS) Cybersecurity and Infrastructure Security Agency (CISA) has placed the company on an industry alert [20]. DJI denied all the allegations in a June 2019 hearing of the Subcommittee on Security of the Committee on Commerce, Science and Transportation of the U.S. Senate [20]. Nevertheless, some customers are wary about acquiring unmanned aerial vehicles from DJI.

5.2   UAV Model 2

The U.S.-made Intel Falcon 8+, which was released in 2015, is intended for mapping structures and terrains [12]. The Falcon 8+ has eight rotors and boasts a maximum flight time of 26 minutes, maximum speed of 22 mph and hover control at wind speeds up to 27 mph. Engineered specifically under Intel's FAA waiver to enable the Intel Cockpit (ground controller) to operate upwards of 1,500 unmanned aerial vehicles at one time, the individual price tag of 30,000 dollars is a bit misleading because the vehicles are contracted by mission and are not purchased as single units [7]. The Falcon 8+ is controlled exclusively via the Intel Cockpit, which send commands and receives data over separate Wi-Fi frequencies with manual control of a single vehicle possible during an emergency [12]. The Falcon 8+ has an open-source Linux operating system. Wi-Fi encryption is used for data in motion; data at rest is not encrypted [12]. When multiple unmanned aerial vehicles are operating, mission data is processed by Intel data centers; some missions have been clocked at generating more than 18 TB of data [7].

5.3   UAV Model 3

The French-made Parrot Anafi, is a cheaper (600 dollars) but capable unmanned aerial vehicle model. Its price tag puts it in the professional tier, while still being accessible to hobbyists. The quad-rotor Anafi has a flight time of 25 minutes, 33 mph maximum horizontal speed and hover control at wind speeds of up to 31 mph [16]. It employs a proprietary controller that can be deployed as a smartphone app for navigation; the standard software build requires full control during missions with a few pre-programmable fail-safe controls. The controller utilizes Wi-Fi frequency standards for control and data; transmitted data as well as data at rest are not secured. The controller, which is usually connected to Parrot servers, can also operate away from the network.

5.4   Mission Scenario 1

The simplest mission scenario involves an independent farmer who intends to purchase a single unmanned aerial vehicle to monitor crops and livestock. Since video streaming is the only mission and the user does not have the ability to modify the vehicle, it will be used in the standard out-of-the-box configuration. The terrain is almost completely flat with no buildings and very few trees. The unmanned aerial vehicle will be operated manually only to obtain first-person video capture with no data storage. Any data that is captured is not considered to be confidential. With full access to the area and a low operating ceiling, manual recovery after losing the signal would be easy. A tablet serves as the ground controller and there will be no Internet access during operation. The vehicle will be used for only a single season in order to evaluate its effectiveness.

5.5   Mission Scenario 2

The second mission scenario involves a company that is intending to purchase a fleet of unmanned aerial vehicles for product delivery. The unmanned aerial vehicles will require in-house modification to enable them to carry and deposit small packages. To satisfy regulations, each unmanned aerial vehicle will be controlled by a separate ground controller and the vehicles will not be interfaced. The delivery area is a ten-minute radius around the distribution center that comprises suburban residential communities with no nearby airports. The company plans to utilize the unmanned aerial vehicles for three years, at which point it plans to purchase a new fleet. The flight data stored on the unmanned aerial vehicles is considered sensitive by the company because of the research it has conducted to expedite deliveries. The delivery area has many civilians and homes, so uncontrolled landings are dangerous. The ground controllers are connected directly to the Internet for off-site data processing.

5.6   Mission Scenario 3

The third mission scenario involves a military entity that intends to procure a fleet of unmanned aerial vehicles to map potential enemy positions. The unmanned aerial vehicles require sophisticated camera and sensor technologies, but the software will remain standard. The fleet will be pre-programmed with mission data from a standalone ground controller that manages mission-partnered unmanned aerial vehicles as a swarm, which means that the swarm would be at risk if even a single vehicle is compromised. The military entity plans to operate the fleet for two years before replacing all the unmanned aerial vehicles. All the collected data is stored on the unmanned aerial vehicles and this data is extremely sensitive.

5.7   Risk Assessment Results

Table 13 shows the individual and composite risk scores for all the model-scenario pairs. Note that V1, V2 and V3 correspond to the DJI Mavic 2 Pro, Intel Falcon 8+ and Parrot Anafi unmanned aerial vehicles, respectively. As mentioned above, the environmental score corresponds to the final score.

Table 13 does not include the worst-case scenario, which simply involves setting each individual sub-metric to the highest risk value. This scenario is used for analysis to demonstrate breadth and to compute the loss in the potential scores as a result of using the maximum CVSS values.

Table 13. Mission scenario sub-metrics and scores.

Sub-Metric/Score	Scenario 1			Scenario 2			Scenario 3		
	V1	V2	V3	V1	V2	V3	V1	V2	V3
Base Sub-Metrics									
AV	0.55	0.55	0.55	0.62	0.62	0.62	0.20	0.20	0.20
DM	0.77	0.77	0.77	0.44	0.44	0.44	0.44	0.44	0.44
PR	0.27	0.62	0.62	0.27	0.62	0.62	0.50	0.68	0.68
UI	0.62	0.62	0.62	0.62	0.62	0.62	0.85	0.85	0.85
C	0	0	0.56	0.22	0	0.56	0.56	0	0.56
I	0.22	0.22	0.56	0.22	0.22	0.56	0.56	0.22	0.56
A	0.22	0.22	0.56	0.22	0.22	0.56	0.22	0.22	0.56
Temporal Sub-Metrics									
M	1.00	0.97	0.97	1.00	0.97	0.97	1.00	0.97	0.97
VS	0.95	0.95	0.97	0.95	0.95	0.97	0.95	0.95	0.97
L	0.92	0.92	0.92	1.00	1.00	1.00	0.96	0.96	0.96
Environmental Sub-Metrics									
CR	0.5	0.5	0.5	1.5	1.5	1.5	1.5	1.5	1.5
IR	0.5	0.5	0.5	1.0	1.0	1.0	1.5	1.5	1.5
AR	0.5	0.5	0.5	1.5	1.5	1.5	0.5	0.5	0.5
Base Score	3.1	3.9	7.3	3.8	3.4	6.8	6.8	3.4	7.0
Temporal Score	2.8	3.4	6.4	3.7	3.2	6.4	6.3	3.1	6.4
Final Score	1.7	2.3	4.7	4.4	3.7	6.4	6.4	3.1	6.4

6. Analysis

This section discusses the benefits and challenges related to the proposed cyber risk assessment framework for unmanned aerial vehicles. Specifically, the proposed framework is evaluated against breadth and variability, general applicability and ease of use, which are important criteria for cyber risk assessment methodologies [11, 19]. The analysis does not consider live situations or historical information, which would likely yield different results.

6.1 Benefits

The first observation related to the case study is the spread of scores despite the limited number of model-scenario pairs. With just ten example scenarios (including the worst case), the scores cover 83% of the possible scores. The best-case scenarios were not considered because they convey trivial information that can easily be achieved by a number of vectors. An unmanned aerial vehicle with high security for the confidentiality, integrity and availability impact sub-metrics would force the base, temporal and final (environmental) scores to 0.0 without any variations. Therefore, the breadth sub-objective that mandates maximal variations in the risk scores is achieved.

Across the three scenarios, when the risk to prospective users increased, the risk scores for almost all the models increased as well. Additionally, between models, the more expensive DJI Mavic 2 Pro and Intel Falcon 8+ provide more security than the Parrot, rendering the scores noticeably lower for the vast majority of mission scenarios. The only exception is in Scenario 3, where the rumored supply chain risk of the DJI Mavic 2 Pro is a huge issue for a non-Chinese military entity and this risk manifests itself in a DJI Mavic 2 Pro score that is close to the score for the unsecured Parrot Anafi. In Scenario 2, the company was slightly concerned about this risk, so despite the increased risk, the DJI Mavic 2 Pro has a much better score than the Parrot Anafi. Therefore, the variability sub-objective as well as general risk correlation are achieved.

With regard to the general applicability objective, the framework was able to handle all the unmanned aerial vehicles and mission scenarios without having a sub-metric being inapplicable. This is in sharp contrast to CVSS, where several sub-metrics are inapplicable based on the component scope versus system-level view in conventional information technology network environments. However, since all the unmanned aerial vehicles considered in the case study were limited to similar copter designs, broader research is required to validate the general applicability objective.

The ease of use objective is more subjective that the other two objectives. Nevertheless, it appears to be achieved based on the documentation required to obtain the risk assessment scores. For the three unmanned aerial vehicle models considered, all the sub-metric values were determined by reviewing their published (online) specifications and advertisements. This means that practically any organization or individual could determine the personal risk scores with good accuracy. Testing and forensic investigations were not conducted to rate any of the sub-metrics, but research on vulnerabilities can still be considered as in the case of the DJI Mavic 2 Pro supply chain risk.

6.2   Drawbacks and Challenges

The spread of risk scores appears to be limited by the built-in caps instituted by CVSS to prevent scores from going above 10.0, which can occur in the worst case. An investigation of the worst case revealed that a number of possible high-range risk values were lost, such as 10.8 for the base score (no values were lost when scope was unchanged) and 10.9 for the environmental (final) score. Capping scores to the maximum of 10.0 reduces the variability of the scores at the top end of the risk spectrum. CVSS accepts this anomaly loss under the assumption that a user who conducts a risk assessment would take strong measures to reduce the glaring vulnerability of the information technology network [8]. The same assumption can be made with regard to the proposed framework – few unmanned aerial vehicles would score above 10.0 and users would reduce the scores by implementing security measures or choosing a different unmanned aerial vehicle.

Another drawback of the proposed assessment framework is the actual level of usability due to its application during the acquisition phase. Acquisition personnel typically have limited cyber expertise, but the translation done by the assessment of cyber principles is expected to bridge the gap. Validating usability would involve human studies and live production level results, both of which are outside the scope of this research. The analysis of documentation required to perform a risk assessment shows promise, but it would not prove that the usability objective is met.

7. Conclusions

Small unmanned aerial vehicles are used to perform vital mapping and surveillance tasks throughout the critical infrastructure, but few, if any, robust methodologies are available for assessing their risk. The risk assessment framework described in this chapter, which is grounded in the well-known CVSS model for network vulnerabilities, engages 14 sub-metrics covering unmanned aerial vehicle security, temporal aspects and mission environments to express the risk as a single score ranging from 0.0 (best) to 10.0 (worst). The case study involving three popular unmanned aerial vehicle models in three mission-environment scenarios demonstrates the breadth and variability, general applicability and ease of use of the framework, especially during the acquisition phase of unmanned aerial vehicles.

Quantitative risk assessments are preferred over qualitative assessments, but a true quantitative risk assessment of unmanned aerial vehicles requires further investigation in a number of areas. Future research will examine the sub-metric definitions and weights to ensure that they comprehensively cover the requirements specific to unmanned aerial vehicles. Additionally, it will attempt to validate the breadth and variability claims using market data, and the ease of use objective using human studies.

The views expressed in this chapter are those of the authors, and do not reflect the official policy or position of the U.S. Air Force, U.S. Department of Defense or U.S. Government. This document has been approved for public release, distribution unlimited (Case #88ABW-2019-6089).

References

[1] E. Ancel, F. Capristan, J. Foster and R. Condotta, Real-time risk assessment framework for unmanned aircraft system (UAS) traffic management (UTM), *Proceedings of the Seventeenth AIAA Aviation Technology, Integration and Operations Conference*, 2017.

[2] B. Clinton, Executive Order 13010: Critical Infrastructure Protection, The White House, Washington, DC (www.hsdl.org/?abs tract&did=1613), 1996.

[3] F. Corrigan, DJI Mavic 2 Pro and Zoom Review of Features, Specs with FAQs, *DroneZon* (www.dronezon.com/drone-reviews/dji-mavic-2-pro-zoom-review-of-features-specifications-wit h-faqs), April 20, 2020.

[4] Dimensional Research, Trends in Security Framework Adoption: A Survey of IT and Security Professionals, Sunnyvale, California (static.tenable.com/marketing/tenable-csf-report.pdf), 2016.

[5] DJI, Mavic 2 Pro/Zoom User Manual v2.0, Shenzen, China (dl.djicdn.com/downloads/Mavic_2/20190417/Mavic_2_Pro_Zoom_User_Manual_v2.0_en.pdf), 2019.

[6] P. Fahlstrom and T. Gleason, *Introduction to UAV Systems*, John Wiley and Sons, Chichester, United Kingdom, 2012.

[7] J. Feist, Intel's drone business explained – Falcon 8+, Shooting Star and Insight, *Drone Rush* (www.dronerush.com/intel-drone-business-12568), May 8, 2018.

[8] Forum of Incident Response and Security Teams (FIRST), Common Vulnerability Scoring System SIG, Cary, North Carolina (www.first.org/cvss), 2020.

[9] J. Gray, Design and Implementation of a Unified Command and Control Architecture for Multiple Cooperative Unmanned Vehicles Utilizing Commercial-off-the-Shelf Components, M.S. Thesis, Department of Systems Engineering and Management, Air Force Institute of Technology, Wright-Patterson Air Force Base, Ohio, 2015.

[10] K. Hartmann and K. Giles, UAV exploitation: A new domain for cyber power, *Proceedings of the Eighth International Conference on Cyber Conflict*, pp. 205–221, 2016.

[11] K. Hartmann and C. Steup, The vulnerability of UAVs to cyber attacks – An approach to risk assessment, *Proceedings of the Fifth International Conference on Cyber Conflict*, 2013.

[12] Intel, Intel Falcon 8+ System, Santa Clara, California (`www.intel.com/content/www/us/en/products/drones/falcon-8`), 2020.

[13] P. Kopardekar, Unmanned Aerial System (UAS) Traffic Management (UTM): Enabling Civilian Low-Altitude Airspace and UAS Operations, Technical Report NASA/TM-2014-218299, NASA Ames Research Center, Moffett Field, California, 2014.

[14] P. Kopardekar, Unmanned Aircraft Systems Traffic Management, U.S. Patent No. 0275801 A1, September 22, 2016.

[15] F. Mohammed, A. Idries, N. Mohammed, J. Al-Jaroodi and I. Jawhar, UAVs for smart cities: Opportunities and challenges, *Proceedings of the International Conference on Unmanned Aircraft Systems*, pp. 267–273, 2014.

[16] Parrot, Anafi, Paris, France (`www.parrot.com/global/drones/anafi`), 2020.

[17] D. Pettit, R. Dill and S. Graham, Zero stars: Analysis of cybersecurity risk of small COTS UAVs, *Proceedings of the Thirteenth International Conference on Emerging Security Information, Systems and Technologies*, pp. 90–95, 2019.

[18] K. Scarfone and P. Mell, An analysis of CVSS version 2 vulnerability scoring, *Proceedings of the Third International Symposium on Empirical Software Engineering and Measurement*, pp. 516–525, 2009.

[19] I. Stine, A Cyber Risk Scoring System for Medical Devices, M.S. Thesis, Department of Electrical and Computer Engineering, Air Force Institute of Technology, Wright-Patterson Air Force Base, Ohio, 2017.

[20] Subcommittee on Security, Drone Security: Enhancing Innovation and Mitigating Supply Chain Risks, Hearing, Committee on Commerce, Science and Transportation, U.S. Senate, Washington, DC (`www.commerce.senate.gov/2019/6/drone-security-enhancing-innovation-and-mitigating-supply-chain-risks`), June 18, 2019.

Chapter 4

CYBER STATE REQUIREMENTS FOR DESIGN AND VALIDATION OF TRUST IN THE CRITICAL TRANSPORTATION INFRASTRUCTURE

Tim Ellis, Michael Locasto and David Balenson

Abstract   The National Transportation Safety Board is charged with investigating transportation-related accidents and incidents in the aviation, railroad, highway, marine and pipeline infrastructure. The increasing integration of traditional information technology systems with operational technology systems increases the cyber vulnerabilities and risk. National Transportation Safety Board investigations require trustworthy data to determine accident and incident causes and remedies. This chapter explores the requirements for trust in the critical transportation infrastructure due to operational technology and information technology integration. The focus is on internal aircraft systems and their data in accident investigations. While commercial avionics systems employ very reliable serial bus architectures, these systems and their components were not designed with cyber security in mind. Cyber state mechanisms such as software attestation and data protection must be designed into systems and validated to support trust requirements for accident investigations. Additionally, it is important to ensure the secure collection of data used in investigations, employ anomaly detection techniques to detect potential cyber attacks and establish a vulnerability registry and risk assessment system as in the information technology domain to share information and address potential cyber security problems.

Keywords: Transportation infrastructure, investigations, trustworthy data

1.   Introduction

The National Transportation Safety Board (NTSB) investigates accidents and incidents in the critical transportation infrastructure, which includes aviation, railroad, highway, marine and pipeline systems, and

© IFIP International Federation for Information Processing 2020
Published by Springer Nature Switzerland AG 2020
J. Staggs and S. Shenoi (Eds.): Critical Infrastructure Protection XIV, IFIP AICT 596, pp. 69–83, 2020.
https://doi.org/10.1007/978-3-030-62840-6_4

plays a crucial role in maintaining and improving the safety and security of systems over time [21, 24]. Thorough investigations restore and bolster public confidence in the reliability and safety of the transportation infrastructure. The conclusions and recommendations of these investigations are seen as impartial and carry weight precisely because the investigations are undertaken in a deliberate, forensic manner. Investigations proceed on the assumption that operational data related to computer and communications equipment in the system under investigation is trustworthy. However, the validity of this assumption may be questioned, especially as the critical transportation infrastructure integrates information technology components in operational technology systems.

Operational technology systems used in industrial operations, energy distribution and control, and aircraft operations are rapidly evolving in sophistication and automation. These systems, many of them based on old technology, are increasingly vulnerable to accidents and intentional attacks via cyber means. Minimizing these problems and distinguishing between normal component wear or failure and malicious cyber activities are increasingly important to operators and incident investigators.

This chapter assesses the requirements space for acquiring trustworthy data so that investigations into the causes of accidents and incidents in the critical transportation infrastructure can be conducted reliably and the findings and safety recommendations are accurate and trustworthy. The focus is on the internal aviation data systems (avionics) of commercial aircraft. The operational and investigative support capabilities of these systems and the cyber considerations involved in their design and implementation are examined. Guidelines and recommendations are provided for the commercial aviation industry, standards authorities and incident investigation entities to improve the cyber-resilient posture of onboard avionics systems and the trustworthiness of system data used in accident and incident investigations.

A review of recent NTSB aviation accident and incident reports [22] reveals that, while none of the commercial aviation accidents over the last ten years were likely due to cyber causes, vital data collected and used for investigations was potentially vulnerable to cyber interference. However, there is a high degree of implicit trust in the validity and integrity of the data sources, and the only recognized vulnerabilities appear to be fire and physical damage. While storage media and the data and software they contain are protected from damage, they are not necessarily secured from attacks by active cyber adversaries. As a result, there is a need for better attestation of data and software used in operations as well as mechanisms to preserve them for forensic investigations.

Additionally, promising data analysis opportunities such as advanced machine learning techniques can be employed to monitor aviation and operational technology bus traffic and detect anomalies and protect the systems from cyber attacks.

2. Aviation Data Challenges

Aircraft systems, like most operational technology systems, employ a complex mix of components to sense, control, automate, communicate and monitor their operations. These components include hardware and software-based programmable logic, memory and communications devices. Investigating the potential cause(s) of a system malfunction or anomalous incident necessitates the inspection and assessment of the operational states and associated data of each relevant component before, during and after the incident. Standard information technology networking and data collection or extraction tools may be applicable to some extent, but many need to be adapted or redesigned to provide data in accident and incident investigations.

The procedures for investigating components are well established and often augmented by vendor-provided tools, procedures and guidance. Vendors may also collaborate directly with accident investigators as in the case of the Air France 447 crash, where flight data was extracted from mangled storage devices [8]. However, when considering a system as a whole and the potential for intentional cyber causes, it is also necessary to monitor and assess the inter-component communications in networks and buses. Understanding these protocols and what constitutes normal and abnormal communications patterns can help identify malicious traffic introduced into the communications fabric by direct injection or via compromised components. Analysis of the traffic could be performed in real-time for incident detection and possible prevention provided that adequate onboard processing and analytic models are available. Alternatively, the analysis could be conducted forensically in an incident investigation or response mode to recreate the actual sequences of messages and events from stored traffic data.

Operational technology systems typically communicate using standard serial interfaces and buses, but they require specialized equipment to effectively monitor and extract traffic data. In the ARINC 429 standard used in commercial aircraft [1], each bus has a transmitter component node or line replaceable unit (LRU) and up to 20 receiver line replaceable units. Bidirectional communications between line replaceable units require a transmit and receive bus for each line replaceable unit. The buses may be interconnected by line replaceable units designed to pass messages from their input ports to their output ports. Thus, a typical aircraft has many interconnected buses connecting dozens of line replaceable units. These include controllers, managers, monitors and recorders in aircraft subsystems such as flight management and controls, communications, engine and fuel controls, landing systems and environmental controls. Collecting coherent communications sessions often requires traffic captures on multiple bus segments simultaneously with synchronized and secure timestamps to accurately reconstruct all the elements of an accident or incident.

The ARINC 429 protocols have evolved to incorporate new capabilities and enhance performance by overloading existing functions to maintain backward compatibility. Consequently, message interpretation must capture the precise context of the data and line replaceable units involved in the communications. The high level of context dependence can expose vulnerabilities that induce problematic or anomalous machine behaviors. Language-theoretic security analysis [14] is a promising approach for determining potential vulnerabilities introduced by context dependencies and for message handling and implementing mitigation strategies for the ARINC 429 protocol.

3.   Data Trustworthiness

In order to conduct reliable and accurate investigations, system software and data must have verifiable levels of trust. For software-based components to operate reliably, it is important to ensure that only certified, trusted software is loaded, maintained and executed on each component. This requirement is addressed in the information technology domain via secure methods that ensure software integrity before installation and during execution. The attestation techniques include the use of cryptographic hashing and timestamps on "gold" releases of firmware and supporting data, software attestation checks of hashes every time a system is started and the use of trusted platform module (TPM) [31] hardware in line replaceable units for automated attestation on the devices. Hashed message authentication codes (HMACs) [13] for inter-node communications can provide additional assurance that a code segment or update comes from a reliable source and has not been tampered with either through fabrication at its source or modification in transit, especially when the message codes are combined with code signing techniques. It is worthwhile to examine how such code and updates can take advantage of The Update Framework (TUF) for securing software update systems [15] and its Uptane variant for securing automobile software updates [16].

Table 1. Example cyber state requirements checklist.

Statement	Assurance (Binary/ Continuous)	Protection Mechanism	Specific Procedures/ Equipment	Initial Priority
Recorded data is unmodified	True	Hash and timestamp of all the data in the flight data recorder	Digitally sign and hash all the data in the flight data recorder	1
All the bits of the critical firmware are gold	True	Firmware attestation, TPM, paper logs	Attest firmware boot/load, check for TPM in hardware	2
No LRU code corruption	True	Hash of the gold code copy	Compare code hash against the gold hash	2
No messages of abnormal origin	Prob(X>.99)	HMAC of each message	Attest the ability of the origin to send the messages	3
No injected messages	True	HMAC of each message	Verify message HMAC against trusted codes	4

A collaborative process is needed to ensure that an investigative entity has access to trusted data. Table 1 illustrates a common, cyber state checklist approach that covers the system requirements for trusted operations as well as trusted state data for post-operational analyses. Only a few items are presented to give an indication of the overall structure of the checklist. A real checklist would greatly expand the number of options and define the flows between the assurance statements. The checklist could be used to define, review and verify that NTSB investigation trustworthiness needs are met by avionics systems designs and implementations. A set of truth statements provides assertions that must be satisfied definitively or to a high probability as indicated in the assurance column of Table 1 (e.g., True or False, and Prob(X)). The protection mechanisms that ensure these statements are met and the pro-

Table 2.   SPC × CIA matrix.

Subsystem	Confidentiality	Integrity	Availability
Storage			
Persistent	Encryption[a]	Hash,[c] Timestamp[c]	Redundancy[b]
Volatile	Access Control[a]	Hash,[c] Timestamp[c]	Backup[c]
Processing			
Static Code	Encryption[a]	Trusted Boot,[b] Hash,[c] Timestamp,[c] TPM Trusted Boot[a]	Backup[c]
Dynamic Behavior	Access Control[b]	Dynamic Behavior Measurement[b]	Heartbeat[b]
Communications			
Individual Messages	Firewall,[a] Access Control[a]	Hash,[b] Timestamp,[b] Hashed Content,[a] Hashed Timestamp,[a] Trustworthy Time Source[a]	Firewall,[a] Redundancy[b]
Multi-Message Patterns	Chaff,[a] Privacy[a]	Trustworthy Time Source[a]	Pattern Detection[a]

cedures or equipment needed for implementation must be provided by equipment manufacturers and system integrators. These entities must also prioritize the requirements to achieve the greatest impact given the available resources and schedules.

4. Data Protection

Building trust in the operational data used in forensic investigations requires the data to be protected throughout its lifetime. Table 2 provides a notional assessment of the current state of data protection in terms of confidentiality, integrity and availability (CIA) of digital data in storage, processing and communications (SPC) subsystems.

In this assessment, confidentiality means that only authorized entities and devices can access data and services, integrity means that the data has not been tampered with and can be trusted to be accurate, and availability means that the data can be accessed when it is needed.

The data domains are further divided into two subtypes, corresponding to static and dynamic properties. Storage is divided into persistent and volatile storage, processing is divided into static code and dynamic behavior, and communications is divided into individual messages and multi-message patterns.

The table entries correspond to typical mechanisms that provide data protection. Each entry has a superscript that indicates its use in aircraft data systems – infrequent use (superscript *a*), some or limited use (superscript *b*) and common use (superscript *c*). The assessment, which is not intended to serve as a rigorous or comprehensive evaluation, is based on publicly-available vendor and standards information and background knowledge of the authors. However, the table shows a number of areas where improved protection mechanisms could be used to better safeguard critical data. In avionics operational technology, as in much of information technology today, there are limited protections in place for the dynamic aspects of storage, processing and multi-message communications monitoring and threat detection. A rigorous assessment of these risk states should be conducted and the recommended data protection improvements should be implemented. This would lead to an enhanced cyber standard reference for NTSB investigations as well as a guide for improving avionics component data protection levels.

5. Data Collection and Analysis

Capturing network and bus traffic is an effective means for monitoring system health via pattern analysis and detection. This data store of accurately-timestamped messages is useful for predictive maintenance and for analyzing potential anomalies postflight. Given the large volumes of data flowing in avionic networks and buses, it would be necessary to be store data selectively based on pattern analysis. Naturally, down-selection or sampling of messages pose the risk of losing data related to attacks and malfunctions. This is an area that could evolve over time as more knowledge is gained about normal and abnormal message traffic and as technology advances.

Functional data collection requirements include the ability to connect to multiple data buses at multiple points and collect traffic flows along with associated time synchronization data in order to analyze temporally-dependent messages and events. The collected data must be hashed to protect the data from modification and tampering. A secure data collection regime must employ authentication and encryption to protect sensitive data while ensuring operational safety. Additionally, it could be advantageous if the collected data, or some relevant subset or metadata, is transmitted over the air or via an available network to a ground-based repository to support extensive investigation and analysis if the aircraft or system is damaged or otherwise unavailable for onboard data extraction.

Data analysis requirements include the ability to integrate time-synchronized data collected from multiple buses for event replays and simulation analyses. Further, if sufficient processing capabilities are available onboard an aircraft or operational system, traffic analysis could be performed to detect potentially anomalous activities. For efficiency, only data pertaining to traffic patterns in key operational regimes (e.g., taxi, takeoff, departure, climb, cruise, descent, approach and landing) may be stored for subsequent analysis.

In addition to timestamped command, control and monitoring data related to flight, propulsion, power, communications and environmental systems collected and maintained by a flight data recorder [20, 23], relevant cyber data should be collected for later analyses. This data includes:

- Relevant addressed (labeled) messages to key devices. These include communications between specific line replaceable units, and not just specific commanded states and sensed states of aircraft components.

- Software attestation log data (at load/startup and at periodic intervals) to record and ensure that proper software and firmware are being executed.

- Heartbeat hashed messages from select line replaceable units to monitor or recreate component health. These messages could include lower-level health status and content pattern data pertaining to the processor, communications hardware, memory and other storage components of specific line replaceable units to ensure consistency with baseline models and support forensic analyses.

- Anomalous data generated by line replaceable units such as malformed messages received by line replaceable units that would otherwise be discarded as non-compliant. This type of data could constitute attack signatures vital to post event analysis as well as future investigations and model development.

Additionally, to effectively track vulnerabilities in operational technology systems, a registry like the MITRE Common Vulnerabilities and Exposures (CVE) catalog for information technology systems and software [19] should be created. This would enable the community to share information about vulnerabilities and address them in a timely manner. Similarly, a risk evaluation system such as the Risk Scoring System developed by QED Secure Solutions [26] would provide a reliable means for establishing the criticality and potential severity of a given risk as it relates to the safe operation of an aircraft or its operational technology systems.

6.   Recommendations

The NTSB should mandate robust aviation data systems to ensure that the intended avionics functions are being executed properly in commercial aircraft. It should also ensure that, in the event of an accident or incident, the investigation into the causes can be reliably conducted using the collected data and that the findings and safety recommendations are accurate and trustworthy.

The following recommendations could improve the safety and security of operational avionics systems in commercial aircraft, and also improve data access and trustworthiness in accident and incident investigations:

- Improve data collection and protection to increase trust in accident and incident investigations. Storing more of the data flowing on aircraft data buses by extending the flight data recorder approach would support more detailed cyber-related analyses of events leading up to, during and immediately following an accident. Storing all the data associated with a typical commercial aircraft may be infeasible. Therefore, a focused data collection approach should be used that starts with the most critical subsystems and leverages anomaly detection techniques.

- Apply attestation techniques to the firmware running on avionics devices. Digitally sign all device firmware to provide a reliable means for aircraft maintenance personnel to ensure that only certified software is used. Attestation should be designed into device hardware and software architectures to ensure that every time a device is powered up, a trusted attestation process ensures that the correct firmware is loaded and executed.

- Establish a cyber state issue tracker to collect and share findings about potential vulnerabilities in devices and firmware. Implement an effective information technology practice that captures salient information about vulnerabilities and associated information such as component models and version numbers, configuration settings and relevant details related to integration with other devices. Each vulnerability should be scored to express its potential impact on safe and secure flight operations, and not merely its potential to disrupt component operations. This would assist manufacturers, operations and maintenance personnel in prioritizing remedial actions.

- Develop advanced data analytics to detect anomalies and potential attacks. Consider in-flight and post-flight analytic approaches. Apply machine learning techniques to discover message traffic patterns in various flight and operational regimes and use the trained models for anomaly detection in real-time if adequate onboard processing capability exists, or in post-flight evaluations to detect and address potential anomalies, and continually improve the anomaly detection model.

- Review the ARINC protocols for potential security risks related to the advanced functions that are being added to the latest avionics devices and the increased use of traditional information technology in these historically operational technology systems. Conduct language-theoretic security analyses [14] of protocols and messages to identify potential protocol vulnerabilities and ensure context-free and valid message processing.

- Incorporate cyber state requirements in equipment designs to support NTSB investigations. Avionics vendors and the NTSB should work together to define core cyber state assertions to conduct reliable investigations and obtain trustworthy results. Ensure that the requirements are implemented in the next generation of equipment.

7.   Related Work

This chapter focuses on the cyber aspects of NTSB investigations of transportation accidents and incidents, and the requirements that ensure trustworthy cyber-related data is available to support NTSB investigations. While some suggested actions and approaches may be under consideration by the avionics industry and regulators, the authors of this chapter were unable to discern any such efforts.

A November 2017 Atlantic Council report on aviation cyber security [9] explores the increased digitalization in the aviation industry, including aircraft, air traffic management, airports and their supply chains. The report seeks to increase awareness about cyber security and initiate public discussion around the need for increased security. The recommendations include improving the agility of security updates; designing systems and processes that capture cyber security data; and incorporating cyber perspectives in accident and incident investigations. However, the report stops short of enumerating detailed requirements.

In contrast, this chapter suggests a method that structures the cyber security problem space by introducing the matrix of confidentiality, integrity and availability for avionics storage, processing and communications subsystems. This structure provides a means for the aviation and cyber security communities to understand the boundaries of the cyber security problem. The two communities need to limit the problem scope so that they can prioritize the gaps that must be addressed using cyber security technologies (e.g., cryptographic-integrity mechanisms) in aircraft systems and integrating the resulting data in investigation procedures. The structure also identifies new requirements for securely storing measurements of network provenance (i.e., message origin authentication and message path validation similar to routing security) and dynamic device behavior (i.e., runtime behavior of embedded device code, not just its firmware hash). In doing so, this work assists the ongoing discussion reflected in [9] about the requirements needed to ensure trust in the cyber aspects of investigations.

Sabatini [29] has examined the reliance of information and communications technologies in aircraft systems, challenges associated with airborne data networks and the need for increased cyber security in civil aviation. A significant body of work has focused on cyber resilience, resilient systems and resilient trust (see, e.g., [5–7, 18]) that can be leveraged to protect critical data in aircraft storage, processing and communications subsystems. Similarly, there is a large body of work in digital forensics [2, 12], including the preservation of evidence and chain of custody that can be applied to cyber data needed for aircraft accident and incident investigations.

Several organizations provide cyber security and incident response services, including the Cybersecurity and Infrastructure Security Agency (CISA) [10] of the U.S. Department of Homeland Security, which houses the National Cybersecurity and Communications Integration Center and subsumes the former US-CERT and ICS-CERT. Many commercial organizations offer security consulting and incident response services as well. Meanwhile, there is a growing body of academic research on incident response technologies and tools, and operating effective incident response teams [3, 11, 17, 25].

A number of individuals have argued for an NTSB-like organization that would investigate cyber security incidents [4, 27, 28, 30]. While such an organization may be necessary to spearhead investigations of accidents and incidents involving the critical infrastructure across the board, the new organization as well as the NTSB would need – as discussed in this chapter – appropriate means for ensuring the confidentiality, integrity and availability of trustworthy cyber data to support their investigations.

8.   Conclusions

The critical transportation infrastructure must support the proper functional execution, reliable capture and protection of operational data in order to support trustworthy investigations in the event of accidents, failures and other incidents. However, operational technologies employ specialized architectures and technologies that may not support the direct use of established data protection mechanisms routinely employed in information technology systems. Therefore, it is necessary for the operational technology community to review data protection postures and identify areas for improvement where traditional information technology protection mechanisms can be adapted and employed and where completely new tools and techniques are needed due to the unique properties and constraints of operational technology systems.

This chapter has reviewed data protection mechanisms for internal aviation data systems (avionics) as an exemplar critical transportation infrastructure system. It recommends areas of improvement to ensure that the intended functions are executed properly and to provide the NTSB, the organization responsible for investigating aviation accidents and incidents, with trustworthy data to produce trustworthy findings. The areas include improved and increased data collection and protection to enhance trust in post-event investigations, use of attestation techniques on avionics device firmware, creation of a cyber vulnerability tracker that collects and shares information about vulnerabilities in devices and firmware, development of data analytics to detect anomalies and potential attacks, language-theoretic security analyses of protocols and messages to ensure context-free and valid message processing, and addition of cyber state design requirements to support accident and incident investigation needs.

Avenues for future research include developing enhanced flight data recorder requirements and prototypes, implementing attestation techniques for avionics devices, creating machine learning models for message patterns and anomaly detection, applying language-theoretic security techniques to the ARINC 429 protocol and specifying NTSB cyber state requirements in coordination with avionics manufacturers and stakeholders.

Any opinions, findings, conclusions or recommendations expressed in this chapter are those of the authors and do not necessarily reflect the views of the U.S. Department of Homeland Security, and should not be interpreted as necessarily representing the official policies or endorsements, either expressed or implied, of the U.S. Department of Homeland Security, National Transportation Safety Board or the U.S. Government.

Acknowledgements

This research was sponsored by the U.S. Department of Homeland Security Science and Technology Directorate (DHS S&T) under Contract No. HSHQDC-16-C-00034. The authors thank DHS S&T Program Manager, Mr. Gregory Wigton, for his guidance and support. The National Transportation Safety Board did not sponsor this research nor did it participate in the research.

References

[1] Actel, ARINC 429 Bus Interface, Mountain View, California (www.actel.com/ipdocs/CoreARINC429_DS.pdf), 2006.

[2] D. Aitel, Daily Dave Mailing List (seclists.org/dailydave), 2020.

[3] J. Arthorne, Expect the unexpected: Preparing SRE teams for responding to novel failures, presented at the *Site Reliability Engineering Conference Europe, Middle East, Africa,* 2019.

[4] S. Bellovin, The Major Cyberincident Investigations Board, *IEEE Security and Privacy,* vol. 10(6), p. 96, 2012.

[5] D. Bodeau and R. Graubart, Cyber Resiliency and NIST Special Publication 800-53 Rev.4 Controls, MITRE Technical Report MTR 130531, MITRE Corporation, Bedford, Massachusetts, 2013.

[6] D. Bodeau and R. Graubart, Cyber Resiliency Design Principles: Selective Use Throughout the Lifecycle and in Conjunction with Related Disciplines, MITRE Technical Report MTR 170001, MITRE Corporation, Bedford, Massachusetts, 2017.

[7] D. Bodeau, R. Graubart, W. Heinbockel and E. Laderman, Cyber Resiliency Engineering Aid – The Updated Cyber Resiliency Engineering Framework and Guidance on Applying Cyber Resiliency Techniques, MITRE Technical Report MTR 140499R1, MITRE Corporation, Bedford, Massachusetts, 2015.

[8] Bureau d'Enquetes et d'Analyses pour la Securite de l'Aviation Civile, Final Report on the Accident on 1st June 2009 to the Airbus A330-203 Registered F-GZCP Operated by Air France Flight AF 447 Rio de Janeiro – Paris, Le Bourget, France (www.bea.aero/docspa/2009/f-cp090601.en/pdf/f-cp090601.en.pdf), 2012.

[9] P. Cooper, Aviation Cybersecurity: Finding Lift, Minimizing Drag, Atlantic Council, Washington, DC (`www.atlanticcouncil.org/in-depth-research-reports/report/aviation-cybersecurity-finding-lift-minimizing-drag`), November 7, 2017.

[10] Cybersecurity and Infrastructure Security Agency (CISA), Washington, DC (`www.cisa.gov`), 2020.

[11] Forum of Incident Response and Security Teams (FIRST), CSIRT Framework Development SIG, Cary, North Carolina (`www.first.org/global/sigs/csirt`), 2020.

[12] S. Garfinkel, Digital forensics research: The next 10 years, *Digital Investigation*, vol. 7(S), pp. S64–S73, 2010.

[13] H. Krawczyk, M. Bellare and R. Canetti, HMAC: Keyed-Hashing for Message Authentication, RFC 2104, 1997.

[14] LangSec, LangSec: Language-Theoretic Security (`langsec.org`), 2020.

[15] Linux Foundation, The Update Framework: A Framework for Securing Software Update Systems, San Francisco, California (`theupdateframework.github.io`), 2020.

[16] Linux Foundation, Uptane: Securing Software Updates for Automobiles, San Francisco, California (`uptane.github.io`), 2020.

[17] M. Locasto, M. Burnside and D. Bethea, Pushing boulders uphill: The difficulty of network intrusion recovery, *Proceedings of the Twenty-Third Conference on Large Installation System Administration*, article no. 1, 2009.

[18] R. McQuaid, R. Graubart and D. Bodeau, Designing for Resilience, MITRE Corporation, Bedford, Massachusetts (`www.mitre.org/capabilities/cybersecurity/overview/cybersecurity-blog/designing-for-resilience`), July 24, 2017.

[19] MITRE Corporation, Common Vulnerabilities and Exposures (CVE), Bedford, Massachusetts (`cve.mitre.org`), 2020.

[20] National Transportation Safety Board, Safety Recommendation Report: Extended Duration Cockpit Voice Recorders, ASR18-04, Washington, DC, 2018.

[21] National Transportation Safety Board, About the National Transportation Safety Board, Washington, DC (`www.ntsb.gov/about/pages/default.aspx`), 2020.

[22] National Transportation Safety Board, Aviation Accident Reports, Washington, DC (`www.ntsb.gov/investigations/AccidentReports/Pages/aviation.aspx`), 2020.

[23] National Transportation Safety Board, Cockpit Voice Recorders (CVR) and Flight Data Recorders (FDR), Washington, DC (`www.ntsb.gov/news/pages/cvr_fdr.aspx`), 2020.

[24] National Transportation Safety Board, The Investigative Process, Washington, DC (`www.ntsb.gov/investigations/process/Pages/default.aspx`), 2020.

[25] L. Nolan, Practical incident response, presented at the *Site Reliability Engineering Conference Europe*, 2016.

[26] QED Secure Solutions, Risk Scoring System for Aviation Systems, Coppell, Texas (`www.riskscoringsystem.com/aviation`), 2019.

[27] N. Robinson, The Case for a Cyber Security Safety Board: A Global View on Risk, *The RAND Blog*, Santa Monica, California, June 18, 2012.

[28] P. Rosenzweig, The NTSB as a Model for Cyber Security, R Street Shorts No. 58, R Street Institute, Washington, DC (`2o9ub0417ch12 1g6m43em6psi2i-wpengine.netdna-ssl.com/wp-content/uploads/2018/05/Final-Short-No.-58.pdf`), 2018.

[29] R. Sabatini, Cyber security in the aviation context, presented at the *First Cyber Security Workshop*, 2016.

[30] S. Shackelford, The U.S. needs an NTSB for cyber attacks, *Wall Street Journal*, June 4, 2019.

[31] Trusted Computing Group, Trusted Platform Module (TPM) Summary, White Paper, Beaverton, Oregon (`trustedcomputinggroup.org/wp-content/uploads/Trusted-Platform-Module-Summary_04292008.pdf`), 2008.

II

VEHICLE INFRASTRUCTURE SECURITY

Chapter 5

AN EFFICIENT BLOCKCHAIN AUTHENTICATION SCHEME FOR VEHICULAR AD-HOC NETWORKS

Matthew Wagner and Bruce McMillin

Abstract   Autonomous vehicles cooperate to perform many life-saving and cost-saving applications such as advanced collision warning, tailgating and traffic routing. As the use of autonomous vehicles increases, the transportation infrastructure as a whole becomes highly susceptible to cyber attacks due to the number of components that communicate with each other over wireless networks and the Internet.

This chapter presents an efficient blockchain scheme for ad-hoc networks of autonomous vehicles, helping reduce the risk to the transportation infrastructure. In the proposed scheme, every vehicle maintains blocks generated by its platoon containing transactions that evaluate the actions of every vehicle. A central blockchain is not maintained and the vehicles have different blocks and blockchains as they join and leave platoons. The blocks are used as tokens by the vehicles to gain access to future platoons. The proposed scheme, which uses a variant of Schnorr multi-signatures to reach consensus in a platoon, is proven to be secure under reasonable assumptions.

Keywords: Vehicular ad-hoc networks, blockchain, authentication

1.   Introduction

Critical infrastructure assets include telecommunications networks, electric power grids, oil and gas facilities, banking and finance systems, water supply systems, emergency services and transportation systems [8] that are vital to modern society. Unfortunately, they are increasingly becoming targets of cyber attacks [13]. The attacks have been limited to systems with large cyber components or central control systems such as the supervisory control and data acquisition systems that manage electrical power systems. However, it is only a matter of time before the

© IFIP International Federation for Information Processing 2020
Published by Springer Nature Switzerland AG 2020
J. Staggs and S. Shenoi (Eds.): Critical Infrastructure Protection XIV, IFIP AICT 596, pp. 87–109, 2020.
https://doi.org/10.1007/978-3-030-62840-6_5

attacks expand to other critical infrastructures, including the national transportation infrastructure.

With autonomous vehicles on the rise, national transportation systems are primed to become key cyber attack targets. This is a concern due to the push towards vehicular ad-hoc networks (VANETs) to increase safety, efficiency and cost savings in the national transportation system. The U.S. Department of Transportation [1] projects the annual savings provided by vehicular ad-hoc networks to be approximately 202 billion dollars from crash-prevention alone [1]. This does not include the reduced fuel costs brought about by large-scale deployments of tailgating maneuvers and traffic rerouting applications. Unfortunately, the infrastructure required for vehicular ad-hoc networks is estimated to be 2.5 trillion dollars in capital costs with approximately 121.5 billion dollars for annual maintenance [15]. Thus, low cost solutions are needed to secure national transportation systems.

This chapter proposes a formal scheme for securing autonomous transportation systems without the infrastructure needed by a typical vehicular ad-hoc network. The scheme leverages blockchain technology for its useful properties such as immutability, verifiability, non-repudiation and ability to reach consensus in distributed systems.

2.   Background

A distributed blockchain is employed to secure a vehicular ad-hoc network with minimal infrastructure. Multiple security domain nondeducibility (MSDND) is employed to prove that the cyber-physical blockchain is secure compared with other blockchain versions. This section discusses vehicular ad-hoc networks, blockchains, digital signatures and MSDND.

2.1   Vehicular Ad-Hoc Networks

A vehicular ad-hoc network is a platoon of vehicles that communicate with each other and cooperate for a specific purpose, such as to perform a tailgating maneuver [4]. It is assumed that the vehicular ad-hoc network comprises autonomous vehicles that can monitor the actions of each another via sensor readings. Additionally, each autonomous vehicle has a secure GPS device that it uses to navigate and synchronize with the processors of all the vehicles in the platoon.

Vehicular ad-hoc networks typically involve an infrastructure comprising a certificate authority (CA), road-side units (RSUs) and vehicles driving on roadways. Road-side units act as interaction points between the centralized certificate authority and vehicles, enabling high-speed verification of messages, identities and other information. These units cost 51,600 dollars each and are required to cover all roadways [1]. Due to the massive capital costs, a vehicular ad-hoc network architecture without road-side units is considered in this work. Additionally, the certificate authority is only involved when a vehicle initially registers to participate in a vehicular ad-hoc network.

A vehicular ad-hoc network platoon typically has a leader that is tasked with issuing commands to platoon members and managing the platoon. The proposed security solution covers the entire vehicular ad-hoc network during platoon joining and leaving, and other platoon operations.

2.2   Blockchains

A blockchain is a state agreement mechanism that enables an untrusted distributed network to reach consensus and create a computationally-immutable ledger. The basic components of a blockchain include a consensus mechanism, digital signature scheme, transactions, blocks and a network. Transactions are the raw data that is stored in the blockchain; they are signed by the participants using a digital signature scheme that ensures non-repudiation and immutability. A verification mechanism is needed to check the veracity of the data in each transaction. A consensus mechanism is used to create blocks that signify the ordering of transactions. The consensus mechanism should be hard or impossible to replicate by a single participant, resulting in an immutable ordering of events.

Blockchains are widely used to implement cryptocurrencies and they have many other applications. This work addresses the four main challenges that arise when applying blockchain technology to vehicular ad-hoc networks: (i) cyber-only transactions; (ii) system-wide ledger in a disconnected network; (iii) real-time transaction requirements; and (iv) no registration for participants [14].

2.3   Digital Signatures

The proposed scheme employs asymmetric digital signatures and multi-digital signatures. An asymmetric digital signature scheme involves a public key and a private key that is owned by the signer. The signer can sign a message using the private key, which can be verified using the associated public key. The protocols specified in this work are not restricted to a specific asymmetric digital signature scheme.

A digital signature scheme has a key generation function, signing function and verification function. The key generation function is $(Key_{Pub},$

$Key_{Priv}) \leftarrow KeyGen(X)$, where Key_{Pub} is the public key, Key_{Priv} is the private key and $KeyGen(X)$ is the key generation algorithm given inputs X. The signing function is $M' \leftarrow Sign(Key_{Priv}, M)$, where M' is the signed messaged and $Sign(Key_{Priv}, M)$ is the signature creation function given an input private key Key_{Priv} and message M. The verification function is $Output \leftarrow Verify(Key_{Pub}, M')$, where $Output$ is either accept or reject and the verification algorithm is $Verify(Key_{Pub}, M')$ with key Key_{Pub} and signed message M' as inputs.

A multi-digital signature scheme is a protocol that enables a group of signers to produce a short, joint signature on a common message. The message can be verified using the group public key generated when signing the message [7]. This work uses an adaptation of the Schnorr multi-signature scheme.

2.4   MSDND

MSDND employs modal logic to evaluate information flows in order to formally analyze trust in cyber-physical systems [5]. MSDND is formally defined as:

$$\text{MSDND(ES)}: \exists w \in W \vdash [(S_x \vee S_y)] \wedge \neg (S_x \wedge S_y)$$
$$\wedge [w \models (\nexists V_{S_x}^i(w) \wedge \nexists V_{S_y}^i(w))] \quad (1)$$

where W is a set of worlds, w is a world, S_x and S_y are state variables, i is an entity, $V_{S_x}^i(w)$ and $V_{S_y}^i(w)$ are valuation functions of entity i with respect to state variables S_x and S_y, respectively, $\vdash$ is the logical satisfies operator and $\models$ is the logical models operator.

This can be simplified using Boolean logic and the definition of exclusive-or operator ($\oplus$) to yield:

$$\text{MSDND(ES)}: \exists w \in W \vdash [(S_x \oplus S_y)] \wedge [w \models (\nexists V_{S_x}^i(w) \wedge \nexists V_{S_y}^i(w))] \quad (2)$$

It is important to note that, if a system or information flow path is MSDND secure, then it is vulnerable to a Stuxnet-like attack in a model that attempts to maintain high integrity. However, if the system or information flow path is MSDND secure, then it is secure under a privacy model.

MSDND proofs are presented to demonstrate the security of the proposed scheme. Specifically, they are used to show that cyber-only and physical-only blockchains are insecure in the face of attacks, but that the cyber-physical blockchain presented in this chapter is secure from attacks.

Certificate Authority   **Vehicle**

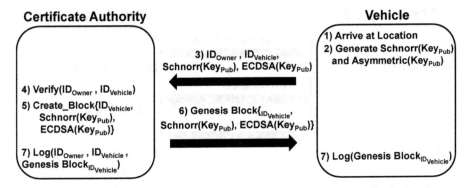

Figure 1. Vehicle registration protocol.

3. Proposed Scheme

This section presents the protocols used by participants in a vehicular ad-hoc network. In particular, the vehicle registration, block creation, platoon join, intra-platoon communications and platoon leave protocols are presented. The initial vehicle registration is the only protocol that involves the certificate authority or any other infrastructure component.

3.1 Vehicle Registration Protocol

The proposed scheme uses private blockchains, which require all the vehicles to register with the certificate authority in order to participate. The certificate authority is charged with inspecting each vehicle, collecting fees and taxes, and creating a certification for the vehicle. The certification, which is considered to be the genesis block of a vehicle's blockchain, enables the vehicle to participate in the vehicular ad-hoc network and accrue its safety, efficiency and cost-saving benefits. Figure 1 outlines the vehicle registration protocol.

After the vehicle registration protocol is complete, the vehicle can join its first platoon. It does not need to register again unless it is kicked out of the platoon for possessing a bad block. A good block denotes that a vehicle that has behaved correctly while a bad block indicates that it has not. This notion of correctness is explained in more detail below.

3.2 Block Creation Protocol

Blocks are generated whenever there is a change in the state of a platoon. The block creation protocol is adapted from the Schnorr multi-signature scheme and applied to a platoon. The protocol must be executed and a platoon signature is created for a vehicle to join another platoon upon leaving the platoon. If a vehicle does not have a valid block

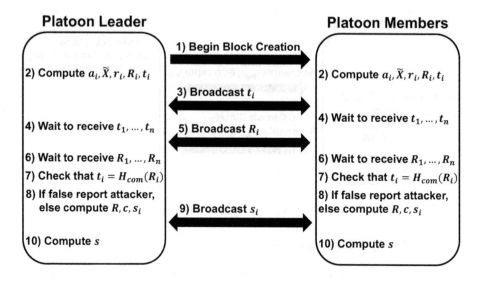

Figure 2. Block creation protocol.

when it leaves, it cannot join future platoons. The block generated by the protocol certifies that the vehicle behaved correctly in the platoon during all its cyber and physical actions.

Figure 2 outlines the block creation protocol. The protocol has the following steps:

1. The platoon leader indicates to the platoon that they will begin the block creation protocol by broadcasting a signed message.

2. Every platoon member i in the n-vehicle platoon computes $a_i = H_{agg}(L, X_i)$. The aggregated public key for the platoon is $\tilde{X} = \prod_{i=1}^{n} X_i^{a_i}$. Each platoon member also generates a random $r_i \leftarrow \mathbb{Z}_p$ and computes $R_i = g^{r_i}$ and $t_i = H_{com}(R_i)$. Note that L is the multiset of the public keys in the block creation process and g is the associated public key; this corresponds to the Schnorr signature scheme presented in [7].

3. Each platoon member broadcasts its t_i value to all the other platoon members.

4. The platoon waits until every platoon member receives the t_i values from all the other platoon members.

5. Each platoon member broadcasts its R_i value to all the other platoon members.

6. The platoon waits until every platoon member receives the R_i values from all the other platoon members.

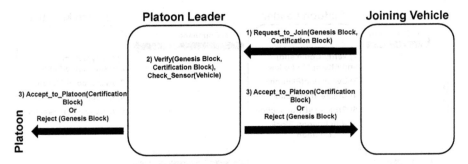

Figure 3. Platoon join protocol.

7. Each platoon member checks that $t_i = H_{com}(R_i)$ for all the other platoon members.

8. If a check fails, then the platoon aborts the computation and creates a transaction evaluating the faulty vehicle. Otherwise, every platoon member computes $R = \prod_{i=1}^{n} R_i$, $c = H_{sig}(\tilde{X}, R, M)$ and $s_i = r_i + c a_i x_i \bmod p$. Note that M is the message to be signed by the platoon, x_i is the private key of a platoon member and p is the prime order of the cyclic group G presented in [7].

9. Each platoon member broadcasts its s_i value to all the other platoon members.

10. After every platoon member receives the s_i values from all the other platoon members, it computes $s = \sum_{i=1}^{n} s_i \bmod p$. The signature for the message is $\sigma = (R, s)$.

Algorithm 2 in [3] is applied in Steps 3, 5, and 9 to reach consensus in the broadcasted values in the face of Byzantine faults under partially synchronous communications and synchronous processors when authentication is present. The proposed protocol uses the digital signature when sending messages. Additionally, all the vehicles have a secure GPS device that is used for navigation and to synchronize the processors of all the vehicles in the platoon.

3.3   Platoon Join Protocol

Whenever a vehicle attempts to join a platoon, its last certification block must be verified by the platoon. When a vehicle joins a platoon, its secure GPS device reports the total distance it has traveled. The platoon trusts that the previous platoon behaved correctly and gave the vehicle the appropriate designation of good or bad. The correctness of this assumption is proven in Section 4. Figure 3 outlines the platoon join protocol.

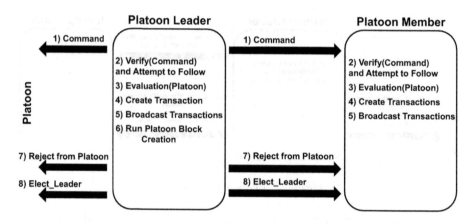

Figure 4. Intra-platoon communications protocol.

3.4   Intra-Platoon Communications Protocol

Every time a command is issued by the platoon leader, the intra-platoon communications protocol is executed to disseminate transactions and detect faults in vehicles in the platoon. Figure 4 outlines the intra-platoon communications protocol. It has the following steps:

1. The platoon leader issues a command to the platoon.

2. Every vehicle in the platoon receives the command, verifies that it is from the platoon leader and attempts to follow the command assuming that the result will not end in a bad state.

3. As the platoon members follow the command, they monitor each other according to the system invariants. After the platoon maneuver is complete, every vehicle creates transactions for all the other vehicles in the platoon.

4. Every vehicle in the platoon broadcasts its transactions to the other vehicles in the platoon.

5. The platoon executes the block creation protocol to reach consensus on the actions of the vehicles in the platoon.

6. If any vehicles behaved inappropriately during the maneuver, they are deemed untrustworthy and are kicked out of the platoon.

7. If the platoon leader is kicked out, a new platoon leader is elected from the remaining vehicles.

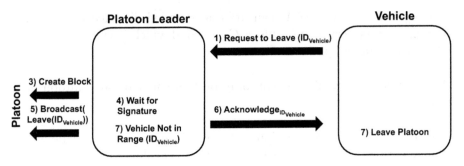

Figure 5. Platoon leave protocol.

3.5 Platoon Leave Protocol

In order to leave the platoon, a vehicle must receive a certification block from the platoon. Otherwise, it will not be allowed to join any future platoons. Figure 5 outlines the platoon leave protocol. After a vehicle leaves the platoon, it uses the last signed leave platoon request to join the next platoon.

4. Security Proofs

This section proves several theorems that formally establish the security of the proposed scheme. First, seven assumptions underlying the model are listed. Next, some basic definitions are provided. Finally, the theorems that establish the security of the protocols are proven.

Assumption 1. The central authority that generates certificates for vehicles is a trusted entity and does not reveal any information about a vehicle V to an attacker A.

Assumption 2. A vehicle V does not reveal its private signing information.

Assumption 3. There are a limited number of attackers A. This number is strictly less than $\frac{n-1}{3}$ where n is the number of vehicles in a platoon. This assumption is based on previous work by Dwork et al. [3] that discusses the maximum number of attackers that enables consensus to be reached under partial synchronicity in the face of Byzantine faults with authentication.

Assumption 4. Each vehicle V has a tamperproof GPS device.

Assumption 5. A vehicle V can drive a bounded distance D_B without receiving a new certification block C_V beyond which it will no longer be allowed to join the platoon.

Assumption 6. A vehicle V can only be a member of one platoon at a time.

Assumption 7. For every action in the blockchain, there must be a certifiable action, either cyber or physical, that is evaluated by the platoon.

Throughout this section, correctness refers to a vehicle's actions in the cyber and physical domains. This description of correctness follows directly from Assumption 7.

Definition 1. A vehicle V is behaving correctly if it passes the evaluation and certification of its actions by other vehicles in the platoon; the actions are stored in its blockchain.

The description of correctness is purposely left vague to avoid detailed and lengthy proofs. The following definitions clarify the notions of a platoon in a vehicular ad-hoc network, the requirements for joining a platoon and the result of leaving a platoon.

Definition 2. A platoon P is a group of n vehicles (n is bounded) that drive in proximity to each other and cooperate for an application. The vehicles in the platoon execute communications protocols as needed when vehicles join or leave and when a physical action is conducted by the platoon.

Definition 3. In order to join a platoon P, a vehicle V must possess a valid certification block C_V, move in the same direction as the platoon and be physically sensed by the platoon.

Definition 4. When a vehicle V leaves a platoon P, it receives a valid certification block C_V that denotes whether it behaved correctly based on Definition 1.

The following theorems establish the security of the protocols.

Theorem 1. A vehicle V may be a part of only one block creation event at a time.

Proof: This theorem is proved by contradiction. Assume that vehicle V created two blocks at the same time. Blocks are generated by joining a platoon and subsequently leaving the same platoon (Definition 4) or by participating in a platoon maneuver as mentioned above. Thus, V would have had to join two platoons and participate in maneuvers in both platoons or left both platoons. To join a platoon, a vehicle must have a valid certification block that shows it behaved correctly and was physically a part of the platoon (Definition 3). Since V could never be in two places at the same time, it could not be a part of two platoons. Hence, it could not create two blocks at the same time. $\qquad\qquad\square$

Theorem 2. A vehicle V is not able to change the contents of its certification block C_V when it is not a part of a platoon.

Proof: This theorem is proved by contradiction. Assume that vehicle V is able to change its certification block C_V when it was not in a platoon. In order to change C_V, one of two cases should have occurred. Either V reverted to a previous certification block or V changed the contents of C_V

Case 1: Assume that vehicle V reverted to a previous certification block. Assume that V traveled more than the bounded distance D_B since receiving the previous certification block. In this case, the certification block would contain the GPS reading D_0. According to Assumption 4, a GPS device is tamperproof. If the current GPS reading is D_C, then $D_C - D_0 > D_B$, which means that V could not have joined the platoon due to Assumption 5.

Now assume that vehicle V traveled less than D_B since receiving the previous certification block. Since it traveled less than D_B, V either did not move since leaving the last platoon or it did move. If the current GPS device reading is D_C and the GPS reading in the certification block is D_0, then $D_C - D_0 < D_B$. If vehicle V did not move, it would be unable to participate in the platoon because all the platoon members had to move with the platoon and be physically sensed by the platoon in order to join the platoon (Definition 3).

Vehicle V is unable to use C_V to participate in the platoon because it could not have joined due to the physical constraints imposed by the platoon join requirements. Thus, due to Assumption 5, V would be unable to use the previous certification block to participate. If V did move then it would have a period before it traveled D_B until the previous certification block became invalid. Thus, V would eventually be caught using a false certification block and would not be allowed to join a platoon.

Case 2: Assume that vehicle V changed the contents of C_V. If V changed C_V, then it would have possessed the private signing information of all the vehicles in the previous platoon that was used to create C_V or a fork was created in the platoon's blockchain. However, according to Assumption 2, a vehicle never reveals its private signing information. Furthermore, according to Theorem 1, a vehicle cannot create two blocks simultaneously. Therefore, V could not have changed the contents of C_V.

Thus, V could not revert to a previous certification block or change the contents of C_V. This contradicts the assumption that V changed its certification block C_V when it was not in a platoon.   □

Theorem 3. A vehicle V will always have a valid certification block C_V when it attempts to join a platoon.

Proof: This theorem is proved by induction.

Base Step: Prove that vehicle V had a valid certification block C_V^1 when it attempted to join its first platoon P_1. In this case, the certification block would have been created by the certificate authority. By Assumption 1, this certification block is valid. Additionally, according to Theorem 2, V could not change C_V^1. Since V received a valid certification block from the certificate authority and was unable to change it, V would have had to use the certification block to join P_1. Thus, V would be allowed to join the P_1 if C_V^1 said it behaved correctly or V would be denied admission if it had behaved incorrectly.

Inductive Step: Assume that vehicle V had a valid certification block C_V^n when it joined platoon P_n. Prove that V has a valid certification block C_V^{n+1} when it attempts to join platoon P_{n+1}. According to Theorem 1 and Assumption 6, V must leave platoon P_n before it can join P_{n+1}. When V left platoon P_n, a secure certification block would have been created for V. According to Assumption 3, if there are x vehicles in the platoon not including V, then there are a maximum of y attackers where $\frac{x-1}{3}$. In the block creation protocol, vehicles exchange their evaluations of other vehicles with each other and the majority score for a vehicle is taken as the cumulative trust value. Thus, when the cumulative trust value for a vehicle is computed, the honest portion of the platoon always wins because the number of honest vehicles $h = x - y$ is never less than $\frac{2x+1}{3}$. Thus, V would have received a valid certification block when it left the platoon.

By Theorem 2, vehicle V could not have altered C_V^{n+1} after it left platoon P_n. Therefore, it would have to use C_V^{n+1} to join platoon P_{n+1}. Thus, V would be allowed to join the platoon P_{n+1} if C_V^{n+1} said it

Table 1. Symbols used in the MSDND proofs.

Symbol	Description
CP	Consensus protocol of the platoon.
LB_2	Local blockchain of vehicle V_2.
VC_1, VC_2	Vehicle controllers of vehicles V_1 and V_2, respectively.
VO_2	Physical vehicle operations of vehicle V_2.
CC_1, CC_2	Cyber communications of vehicles V_1 and V_2, respectively.
S_1	Sensor unit of vehicle V_1.
FP_2	Future platoon of vehicle V_2.

behaved correctly or V would be denied admission if it had behaved incorrectly.

Theorem 3 holds because the base step and inductive step hold. $\square$

Theorem 4. The cyber-physical blocks created in the form of certification blocks encapsulate the cyber and physical domains.

Proof: This theorem is proved by contradiction. Assume that the certification blocks do not encapsulate the cyber and physical domains. This means that the certification blocks either do not encapsulate the cyber system or do not encapsulate the physical system. According to Assumption 7, every transaction in the blockchain used to evaluate a vehicle V will have a cyber representation of some action by V. The actions of V are cyber or physical. Cyber actions are those that do not result in direct physical actions; these include evaluating other vehicles and replying to messages from the platoon within the specified time interval. Physical actions include braking, accelerating and turning. Thus, by Assumption 7, the blockchain includes cyber and physical actions because they are verifiable actions. $\square$

Having proven some basic properties of the proposed protocols, additional theorems that point to the benefits of the proposed scheme in evaluating the cyber and physical portions of a system (instead of just one or the other) are proven. These proofs use MSDND to demonstrate the security properties of the proposed scheme. In MSDND, $IBT_{1,2}\,val$ is a macro that describes the information flow from one entity to another in a system model [11]. It means that Entity 2 reported to Entity 1 that the value val is true and that Entity 1 believes Entity 2. Table 1 describes the symbols used in the MSDND proofs.

Figure 6 shows that a physical-only blockchain has no information flow path from VO_2 to S_1. Let φ_1 be the statement: "Vehicle 2 is maneuver-

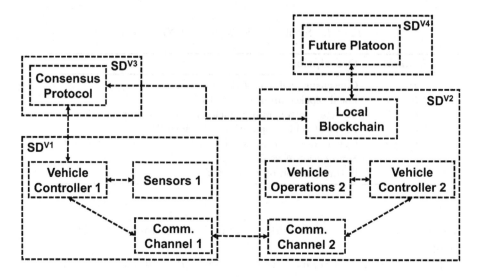

Figure 6.   Information flows in a cyber-only blockchain.

ing correctly." Let φ_2 be the statement: "Vehicle 2 is communicating correctly with other vehicles." Definition 1 specifics the notion of correctness. Either φ_1 or $\neg\varphi_1$ must be true at all times. Similarly, either φ_2 or $\neg\varphi_2$ must be true at all times. Finally, $\varphi = \varphi_1 \wedge \varphi_2$ means that the vehicle is behaving correctly. Repeated evaluations of other vehicles recorded in the local blockchains are used by future platoons to evaluate the trust of vehicles. Thus, there is an information flow path from the consensus protocol of the platoon to the local blockchain of a vehicle and a path from the local blockchain of a vehicle to future platoons of the vehicle.

Theorem 5. A cyber-only blockchain is not MSDND secure under an attack on the cyber communications of a vehicle.

Proof: Assume that in a cyber-only blockchain, the consensus protocol CP has a function f that determines whether φ_2 is true or false. This follows from Assumption 7. According to Assumption 3, CP is always honest due to the bounded number of attackers. The following statements hold:

- $\neg\varphi_2 = true$; V_2 is not sending correct cyber communications.
- $w \vDash V_{\varphi_2}^{VC_2}(w) = \text{true}$; VC_2 observes that they are communicating correctly.
- $IBT_{CC_2,VC_2}\varphi_2$; VC_2 lies to CC_2 that the cyber communications are correct.

- $w \vDash V_{\varphi_2}^{CC_2}(w) = \text{true}$; CC_2 observes that V_2 is sending correct cyber communications.

- $IBT_{CC_1, CC_2}\,\varphi_2$; CC_2 is sending correct cyber communications to CC_1.

- $w \vDash V_{\varphi_2}^{CC_1}(w) = \text{true}$; CC_1 observes that V_2 is sending correct cyber communications.

- $IBT_{VC_1, CC_1}\,\varphi_2$; CC_1 tells VC_1 that V_2 is sending correct cyber communications.

- $w \vDash V_{\varphi_2}^{VC_1}(w) = \text{true}$; VC_1 observes that V_2 is sending correct cyber communications.

- $IBT_{CP, VC_1}\,\varphi_2$; VC_1 tells CP that V_2 is sending correct cyber communications.

- $w \vDash V_{\varphi_2}^{CP}(w) = \text{true}$; CP observes that V_2 is sending correct cyber communications.

- $\neg\varphi_2 \Rightarrow \neg f$; since $\neg\varphi_2 = \text{true}$, then function $\neg f = \text{true}$.

- $IBT_{CP, f}\,\neg\varphi_2$; f tells CP that V_2 is sending incorrect cyber communications.

- $w \vDash V_{\neg\varphi_2}^{CP}(w) = \text{true}$; CP deduces that V_2 is sending incorrect cyber communications.

- $w \vDash V_{\neg\varphi_2}^{CP}(w) = \text{true} \implies w \vDash V_{\neg\varphi_2}^{FP_2}(w) = \text{true}$; since a valuation function exists at CP to evaluate φ_2, it follows that there also exists a valuation function at FP_2 to evaluate φ_2.

- $IBT_{LB_2, CP}\,\neg\varphi_2$; CP tells LB_2 that V_2 is sending incorrect cyber communications.

- $w \vDash V_{\neg\varphi_2}^{LB_2}(w) = \text{true}$; LB_2 observes that V_2 is sending incorrect cyber communications.

- $IBT_{FP_2, LB_2}\,\neg\varphi_2$; LB_2 tells FP_2 that V_2 is sending incorrect cyber communications.

- $w \vDash V_{\neg\varphi_2}^{FP_2}(w) = \text{true}$; FP_2 observes that V_2 is sending incorrect cyber communications.

- $\neg\text{MSDND(ES)}$: $\exists w \in W \vdash [(\varphi_2 \oplus \neg\varphi_2)] \wedge [w \vDash (\exists V_{\varphi_2}^{FP_2}(w))]$.

The future platoon FP_2 has a valuation of φ_2. Therefore, the cyber action readings are not MSDND secure to FP_2. This means that FP_2 knows the truth whether vehicle V_2 behaved correctly at the cyber level in previous platoons. $\qquad\square$

Theorem 6. A cyber-only blockchain is MSDND secure under an attack on the physical maneuvers of a vehicle.

Proof: This proof is similar to that for Theorem 5, except for the valuation function f. Thus, the future platoon FP_2 believes the false physical action reading reported by local blockchain LB_2. Therefore, the physical action readings are MSDND secure to FP_2. This means that FP_2 does not know the truth whether vehicle V_2 behaved correctly at the physical level in previous platoons. $\qquad\square$

Lemma 1. Since the consensus protocol CP is the only entity with an information flow to local blockchain LB_2 and LB_2 is the only entity with information flow to future platoon FP_2, it follows that a world w exists such that $w \vDash V^{CP}_{\neg\varphi_2}(w) = true \implies w \vDash V^{FP_2}_{\neg\varphi_2}(w) = true$.

Proof: This lemma follows from the fact that the history of the local blockchain LB_2 of vehicle V_2 cannot be changed because it is a read-only ledger belonging to V_2. Thus, since LB_2 cannot be malicious, it follows that it passes on the same information that it receives from the consensus protocol CP. Thus, if CP has a valuation function that can evaluate the truth of φ_2, then so does FP_2. $\qquad\square$

Lemma 2. The future platoon FP_2 receives correct information regardless of whether vehicle V_1 is malicious or not.

Proof: The key is understanding that the future platoon FP_2 participates in the agreement protocol of Dwork et al. [3] yielding IC1 – all non-malicious and non-faulty platoon members receive the same physical sensor readings and IC2 – if a vehicle is maneuvering correctly, then every platoon member that is non-malicious and non-faulty will report that it is maneuvering correctly. Since the number of attackers (malicious vehicles) is bounded by Assumption 3, the consensus protocol CP will always have a valuation function that satisfies both the adapted IC1 and IC2. Thus, it will reach the correct valuation regardless of the presence of a bounded number of malicious vehicles. $\qquad\square$

Corollary 1. It follows that, in a cyber-only blockchain, the physical actions of vehicle V_2 can be successfully altered while the cyber actions of V_2 cannot be successfully altered to deceive future platoon FP_2.

Proof: The state variables φ_1 and φ_2 are independent of one each other. This means that a vehicle can behave incorrectly at the cyber level or physical level without forcing incorrect actions at the other level. $\qquad\square$

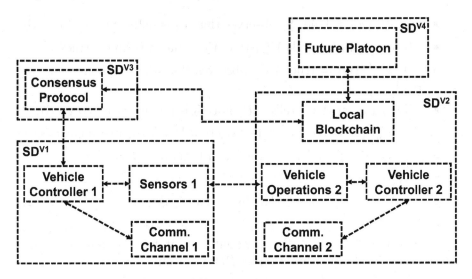

Figure 7. Information flows in a physical-only blockchain.

This proof shows the inherent weakness of a cyber-only blockchain applied to a cyber-physical system. If a future platoon can be deceived about a vehicle's actions in past platoons, then the cyber-only blockchain is insecure because it cannot ensure a joining vehicle is trusted.

Theorem 7 below proves the security of a physical-only blockchain in the proposed scheme. Figure 7 shows that a physical-only blockchain has no information flow path from CC_2 to CC_1.

Theorem 7. A physical-only blockchain is not MSDND secure under an attack at the physical level.

Proof: Assume that in a cyber-only blockchain, the consensus protocol CP has a function f that determines whether φ_1 is true or false. This follows from Assumption 7. According to Assumption 3, CP is always honest due to the bounded number of attackers. The following statements hold:

- $\neg\varphi_1 = $ true; V_2 is not maneuvering correctly.
- $w \vDash V_{\varphi_1}^{VC_2}(w) = $ false; VC_2 observes that V_2 is not maneuvering correctly.
- $IBT_{VO_2,VC_2} \varphi_1$; VO_2 lies to VO_2 that V_2 is maneuvering correctly.
- $w \vDash V_{\varphi_1}^{VO_2}(w) = $ true; VO_2 observes that V_2 is maneuvering correctly.
- $IBT_{S_1,VO_2} \varphi_1$; VO_2 tells S_1 that V_2 is maneuvering correctly.

- $w \vDash V_{\varphi_1}^{S_1}(w) = \text{true}$; S_1 observes that V_2 is maneuvering correctly.
- $IBT_{VC_1,S_1}\,\varphi_1$; S_1 tells VC_1 that V_2 is maneuvering correctly.
- $w \vDash V_{\varphi_1}^{VC_1}(w) = \text{true}$; VC_1 observes that V_2 is maneuvering correctly.
- $IBT_{CP,VC_1}\,\varphi_1$; VC_1 tells CP that V_2 is maneuvering correctly.
- $w \vDash V_{\varphi_1}^{CP}(w) = \text{true}$; CP observes that V_2 is maneuvering correctly.
- $\neg\varphi_1 \Rightarrow \neg f$; since $\neg\varphi_1 = \text{true}$, then function $\neg f = \text{true}$.
- $IBT_{CP,f}\,\neg\varphi_1$; f tells CP that V_2 is maneuvering incorrectly.
- $w \vDash V_{\neg\varphi_1}^{CP}(w) = \text{true}$; CP deduces that V_2 is maneuvering correctly.
- $w \vDash V_{\neg\varphi_1}^{CP}(w) = \text{true} \implies w \vDash V_{\neg\varphi_1}^{FP_2}(w) = \text{true}$; since a valuation function exists at CP to evaluate φ_1, it follows that there also exists a valuation function at FP_2 to evaluate φ_1.
- $IBT_{LB_2,CP}\,\varphi_1$; CP tells LB_2 that V_2 is maneuvering correctly.
- $w \vDash V_{\varphi_1}^{LB_2}(w) = \text{true}$; LB_2 observes that V_2 is maneuvering correctly.
- $IBT_{FP_2,LB_2}\,\varphi_1$; LB_2 tells FP_2 that V_2 is maneuvering correctly.
- $w \vDash V_{\varphi_1}^{FP_2}(w) = \text{true}$; FP_2 observes that V_2 is maneuvering correctly.
- $\neg\,\text{MSDND(ES)}$: $\exists w \in W \vdash [(\varphi_1 \oplus \neg\varphi_1)] \wedge [w \vDash (\exists V_{\varphi_1}^{FP}(w))]$.

The future platoon FP_2 has a valuation of φ_2. Therefore, the physical action readings are not MSDND secure to FP_2. This means that FP_2 knows the truth whether vehicle V_2 behaved correctly at the physical level in previous platoons. $\qquad\square$

Theorem 8. A physical-only blockchain is MSDND secure under an attack at the cyber level.

Proof: This proof is similar to that for Theorem 7, except for the valuation function f. The future platoon FP_2 does not have a valuation of φ_2. Therefore, the cyber action readings are MSDND secure to FP_2. This means that FP_2 does not know the truth whether vehicle V_2 behaved correctly at the cyber level in previous platoons. $\qquad\square$

Lemma 3. Since the consensus protocol CP is the only entity with an information flow to local blockchain LB_2 and LB_2 is the only entity with information flow to future platoon FP_2, it follows that a world w exists such that $w \vDash V_{\neg\varphi_1}^{CP}(w) = \text{true} \implies w \vDash V_{\neg\varphi_1}^{FP_2}(w) = \text{true}$.

Corollary 2. This lemma follows from the fact that, in a physical-only blockchain, the cyber actions of vehicle V_2 can be successfully altered while the physical actions of V_2 cannot be successfully altered to deceive future platoon FP_2.

Proof: The proof is similar to that of Corollary 1. $\square$

Theorem 9. A cyber-physical blockchain is not MSDND secure to an attack at the cyber or physical levels. This model is similar to Figures 6 and 7, except that there are information flow paths from VO_2 to S_1 and CC_2 to CC_1.

Proof: Assume that in a cyber-physical blockchain, consensus protocol CP has a function f_1 that determines whether φ_1 is true or false and a function f_2 that determines whether φ_2 is true or false. This follows from Assumption 7. According to Assumption 3, CP will always be honest due to the bounded number of attackers. Thus, since CP is the only entity with an information flow to LB_2 and LB_2 is the only entity with information flow to FP_2, it follows that a world w exists such that $w \vDash V_{\neg\varphi_1}^{CP}(w) = \text{true} \implies w \vDash V_{\neg\varphi_1}^{FP_2}(w) = \text{true}$ and $w \vDash V_{\neg\varphi_2}^{CP}(w) = \text{true} \implies w \vDash V_{\neg\varphi_2}^{FP_2}(w) = \textit{true}$. It follows from Theorems 7 and 8 that, in a cyber-physical blockchain, neither the cyber nor physical actions of vehicle V_2 can be successfully altered to deceive future platoon FP_2. $\square$

Lemma 4. A blockchain is only secure against an attack if it has a verification mechanism for attacks that come from a component in the system.

This lemma shows the inherent weakness of many previous approaches that apply blockchains to cyber-physical systems.

5. Related Work

Considerable research has focused on using blockchains in vehicular ad-hoc networks. Lu et al. [6] have proposed a blockchain-based anonymous reputation system that preserves privacy by removing the linkability between real identities and public keys in vehicular ad-hoc networks. They employ different blockchains to store information such as messages, certificates and revoked public keys. In their architecture, road-side units are used to reach consensus on the blockchains using proofs of work.

Yang et al. [17] have specified a proof-of-event consensus algorithm for validating traffic events in vehicular ad-hoc networks. The algorithm, which is executed by road-side units, collects state information from passing vehicles. Once a threshold value is reached, the event is claimed to be true and broadcast to the rest of the vehicular ad-hoc network.

All valid traffic events are published in a blockchain with the proof used to validate them.

Xie et al. [16] have proposed a trust management scheme for vehicular messages that uses road-side units to collect state information about roadways from reporting vehicles. The road-side units use proofs of work to reach consensus on the state of roadways across the entire network. Having collected the state information, individual reports can be used to compute the trust and accuracy of vehicles, determine their credibility and identify malicious vehicles.

Singh and Kim [12] have proposed branch-based blockchains that enable a single ledger to be maintained across a large geographic area for intelligent vehicle networks. Branches of the blockchain that represent subsections of the geographic area are maintained by the infrastructure. The architecture enables vehicles to communicate with each other without compromising their private information.

The U.S. Department of Transportation has also proposed a non-blockchain solution for securing vehicular ad-hoc networks. However, the limitation of this solution as well as most others is that they are heavily reliant on a large and costly infrastructure, which is not required by the proposed scheme.

6.   Conclusions

As the use of autonomous vehicles increases, the transportation infrastructure becomes highly susceptible to cyber attacks. This chapter has presented a secure and efficient blockchain scheme for ad-hoc networks of autonomous vehicles, helping reduce the risk to the transportation infrastructure. The scheme employs private blockchains representing vehicle history that are used by vehicles as tokens to join future platoons. The blocks use a variation of the Schnorr digital signature scheme to create a group signature that is signed by the entire platoon. The proposed scheme is formally proven to be secure under a bounded number of attackers. The consensus mechanism uses basic Byzantine fault tolerance algorithms to reach an agreement by the platoon during block creation. This scheme provides significant cost savings over other solutions by using a minimal infrastructure; in fact, a certificate authority is only involved when a vehicle initially registers to participate in a vehicular ad-hoc network.

An earlier approach by Wagner and McMillin [15] satisfies the real-time requirements of vehicular ad-hoc networks. In the approach, the entire blockchain of a vehicle is transmitted so that it can be verified. However, this takes too much time and forces vehicles to re-register with the certificate authority. The scheme proposed in this chapter outperforms the earlier approach and satisfies the same real-time requirements because it leverages a group digital signature. The group signature enables all the vehicles in a platoon to agree on a single block. Thus, only a single block is required to join the next platoon, which saves considerable time.

This chapter also demonstrates the need for physical-level verification mechanisms when applying blockchains to cyber-physical systems. The verification mechanism presented here determines if the actions of a vehicle are correct or incorrect by employing sensor data from other vehicles. Future work will focus on developing additional verification mechanisms and blockchain applications for cyber-physical systems that accrue the benefits of blockchains.

Acknowledgement

This research was partially supported by the Missouri University of Science and Technology Chancellor's Distinguished Fellowship and by the National Science Foundation under Grant Nos. CNS-1505610 and CNS-1837472.

References

[1] American Association of State Highway and Transportation Officials, National Connected Vehicle Field Infrastructure Footprint Analysis – Final Report, Report No. FHWA-JPO-14-125, Washington, DC, 2014.

[2] M. Amoozadeh, H. Deng, C. Chuah, H. Zhang and D. Ghosal, Platoon management with cooperative adaptive cruise control enabled by VANETs, *Vehicular Communications*, vol. 2(2), pp. 110–123, 2015.

[3] C. Dwork, N. Lynch and L. Stockmeyer, Consensus in the presence of partial synchrony, *Journal of the ACM*, vol. 35(2), pp. 288–323, 1988.

[4] H. Hartenstein and L. Laberteaux, A tutorial survey on vehicular ad-hoc networks, *IEEE Communications*, vol. 46(6), pp. 164–171, 2008.

[5] G. Howser and B. McMillin, A modal model of Stuxnet attacks on cyber-physical systems: A matter of trust, *Proceedings of the Eighth International Conference on Software Security and Reliability*, pp. 225–234, 2014.

[6] Z. Lu, Q. Wang, G. Qu and Z. Liu, BARS: A blockchain-based anonymous reputation system for trust management in VANETs, *Proceedings of the Seventeenth IEEE International Conference on Trust, Security and Privacy in Computing and Communications and the Twelfth IEEE International Conference on Big Data Science and Engineering*, pp. 98–103, 2018.

[7] G. Maxwell, A. Poelstra, Y. Seurin and P. Wuille, Simple Schnorr multi-signatures with applications to Bitcoin, *Designs, Codes and Cryptography*, vol. 87(9), pp. 2139–2164, 2019.

[8] J. Moteff, C. Copeland and J. Fischer, Critical Infrastructures: What Makes an Infrastructure Critical? Report for Congress, Report RL31556, Congressional Research Service, Washington, DC, 2003.

[9] S. Nakamoto, Bitcoin: A Peer-to-Peer Electronic Cash System (`bitcoin.org/bitcoin.pdf`), 2008.

[10] Office of the Assistant Secretary for Research and Technology, Security Credential Management System (SCMS), U.S. Department of Transportation, Washington, DC (`www.its.dot.gov/resources/scms.htm`), 2020.

[11] P. Palaniswamy and B. McMillin, Cyber-physical security of an electric microgrid, *Proceedings of the Twenty-Third IEEE Pacific Rim International Symposium on Dependable Computing*, pp. 74–83, 2018.

[12] M. Singh and S. Kim, Branch based blockchain technology in intelligent vehicles, *Computer Networks*, vol. 145, pp. 219–231, 2018.

[13] D. Wagner and B. Schweitzer, The growing threat of cyber-attacks on critical infrastructure, *The Huffington Post*, May 24, 2016.

[14] M. Wagner and B. McMillin, Cyber-physical transactions: A method for securing VANETs with blockchains, *Proceedings of the Twenty-Third IEEE Pacific Rim International Symposium on Dependable Computing*, pp. 64–73, 2018.

[15] M. Wagner and B. McMillin, Formal Verification of Cyber-Physical Blockchain Transactions in VANETs, Department of Computer Science, Missouri University of Science and Technology, Rolla, Missouri (`drive.google.com/file/d/1RwZLG6kjbGsbO7eDVu_vgQtO3ybHktJl/view?usp=sharing`), 2019.

[16] L. Xie, Y. Ding, H. Yang and X. Wang, Blockchain-based secure and trustworthy Internet of Things in SDN-enabled 5G-VANETs, *IEEE Access*, vol. 7, pp. 56656–56666, 2019.

[17] Y. Yang, L. Chou, C. Tseng, F. Tseng and C. Liu, Blockchain-based traffic event validation and trust verification for VANETs, *IEEE Access*, vol. 7, pp. 30868–30877, 2019.

Chapter 6

ENGAGING EMPIRICAL DYNAMIC MODELING TO DETECT INTRUSIONS IN CYBER-PHYSICAL SYSTEMS

David Crow, Scott Graham, Brett Borghetti and Patrick Sweeney

Abstract   Modern cyber-physical systems require effective intrusion detection systems to ensure adequate critical infrastructure protection. Developing an intrusion detection capability requires an understanding of the behavior of a cyber-physical system and causality of its components. Such an understanding enables the characterization of normal behavior and the identification and reporting of anomalous behavior.

This chapter explores a relatively new time series analysis technique, empirical dynamic modeling, that can contribute to system understanding. Specifically, it examines if the technique can adequately describe causality in cyber-physical systems and provides insights into it serving as a foundation for intrusion detection.

Keywords: Intrusion detection systems, empirical dynamic modeling

1.   Introduction

Intrusion detection systems are commonly used to defend against cyber-physical system attacks and protect critical infrastructure assets. These systems monitor computer systems and networks, and report malicious activity to system administrators. In the cyber-physical system domain, an intrusion detection system can identify attempts by attackers to modify or misrepresent physical processes.

Consider an automobile as an example of a cyber-physical system. If an attacker intends to have the driver receive a speeding ticket, the attacker could inject packets that specify a lower speed to cause the speedometer to display incorrect information. In this case, an effective intrusion detection system would notice that the speed data does not conform to the expected behavior indicated by the related physical pro-

© IFIP International Federation for Information Processing 2020
Published by Springer Nature Switzerland AG 2020
J. Staggs and S. Shenoi (Eds.): Critical Infrastructure Protection XIV, IFIP AICT 596, pp. 111–133, 2020.
https://doi.org/10.1007/978-3-030-62840-6_6

cess data such as engine and wheel rotational velocities, throttle position and fuel efficiency. In other words, the intrusion detection system would notice that the speedometer readings are anomalous.

In another example, if an intrusion detection system knows that a substantial increase in the automobile's brake pressure likely precedes a relative decrease in velocity, it could assert that no change, a small change or an increase in velocity (after the application of significant brake pressure) are anomalous. Of course, this requires the intrusion detection system to determine the expected behavior and identify anomalies.

Designing an effective intrusion detection system for a vulnerable cyber-physical system requires insights into the system dynamics or patterns, including how the current system state enables predictions about future states. An adequate quantity of data obtained under normal operating conditions is required to establish normal behavior. A process is needed to determine whether new traffic conforms to normal behavior. Also, an alerting system is necessary to report abnormal traffic behavior.

Intrusion detection architects need a strong understanding of cyber-physical systems or powerful computational resources to model system dynamics. However, the latter is often infeasible because many cyber-physical systems have limited hardware or are constrained by standards and regulations. Modern automobiles, for example, utilize small network packets and fairly simple hardware. For this reason, the former is often more attainable. A solid understanding of system dynamics – specifically, causality, such as how one signal affects another and how a current state predicts future states – is required to identify anomalous traffic, assuming that an ample quantity of normal data is available.

This research examines empirical dynamic modeling, an emerging technique that supports sophisticated time series analyses. Empirical dynamic modeling can contribute to the understanding of cyber-physical systems, and this research evaluates the feasibility of using the technique to detect intrusions in cyber-physical systems.

Two datasets are employed in the evaluation. The first is based on a simple linear model of the relationship between the steering wheel of an automobile and the relative velocities of its two front wheels. The second dataset was generated using a nonlinear flight simulator called the avionics vulnerability and assessment system (AVAS).

2.   Background

This section discusses cyber-physical systems and time series, along with empirical dynamic modeling, an emerging technique for nonlinear forecasting and causality analysis.

2.1 Cyber-Physical Systems and Time Series

The journal *ACM Transactions on Cyber-Physical Systems* [1] defines cyber-physical systems as:

> "... systems where the cyber parts, i.e., the computing and communications parts, and the physical parts are tightly integrated, both at the design time and during operation. Such systems use computations and communications deeply embedded in and interacting with physical processes to add new capabilities to physical systems ... There is an emerging consensus that new methodologies and tools need to be developed to support cyber-physical systems."

Analyses of cyber-physical systems require high-fidelity models. However, the models are often difficult to articulate and replicate. For this reason, it is necessary to analyze the inputs and outputs of a cyber-physical system to develop a model of the system.

Often, the output of a cyber-physical system is time series data that expresses the values of its processes over time. An example time series in the case of an aircraft is the instantaneous revolutions per minute (rpm) of the propeller over time as measured by the aircraft sensors. The National Institute of Standards and Technology (NIST) [9] observes that "[t]ime series analysis accounts for the fact that data points taken over time may have an internal structure (such as autocorrelation, trend or seasonal variation) that should be accounted for."

Kotu and Deshpande [6] differentiate between time series analysis and time series forecasting. Time series analysis involves the extraction of meaningful non-trivial information and patterns from time series. Time series forecasting involves the prediction of future time series data based on past observations and other inputs.

Most time series analysis and forecasting techniques require data stationarity for the time series in question. A stationary process has the property that the mean, variance and autocorrelation do not change over time; the time series data is flat without trends, and has constant variance over time, constant autocorrelation over time and no periodic fluctuations (seasonality) [9].

Figure 1 presents examples of time series plots [5]. Figure 1(a) shows Google stock prices over 200 consecutive days. Figure 1(b) shows the annual numbers of labor strikes in the United States. Figure 1(c) shows the annual prices of a dozen eggs in the United States (constant dollars). Figure 1(d) shows the monthly totals of pigs slaughtered in Victoria, Australia. Figure 1(e), which represents a stationary time series, shows the annual totals of lynx trapped in the McKenzie River District of Northwestern Canada. Figure 1(f) shows the monthly electricity

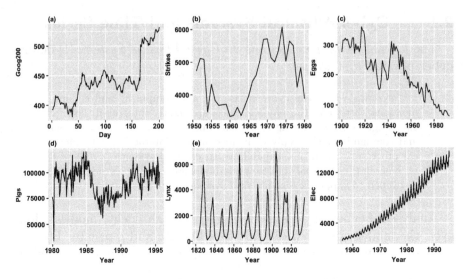

Figure 1.   Example time series plots [5].

production in Australia. These plots demonstrate the diversity of time series models.

Time series data generated by the cyber-physical systems of an aircraft are non-stationary, so analysis and forecasting techniques that require stationarity are not viable. However, empirical dynamic modeling supports non-stationary time series analyses and forecasting.

2.2   Empirical Dynamic Modeling

Takens [16] introduced the delay embedding theorem in 1981. The theorem deals with mathematical attractors, where an attractor is the value or set of values that a system settles towards over time. Empirical dynamic modeling is an application of the delay embedding theorem. Sugihara et al. [15] state that empirical dynamic modeling "is based on the mathematical theory of reconstructing system attractors from time series data." In practice, empirical dynamic modeling is used to capture nonlinear dynamical systems with observational time series data.

Figure 2 provides visual representations of the main ideas underlying Taken's delay embedding theorem and empirical dynamic modeling [15, 19]. Figure 2(a) shows a Lorenz attractor, a set of solutions to a Lorenz dynamical system that is modeled as a set of ordinary differential equations [8]. The attractor manifold M is the set of states that the system progresses through time. The figure shows that a time series for a given dimension can be identified by recording observations in the dimension over time.

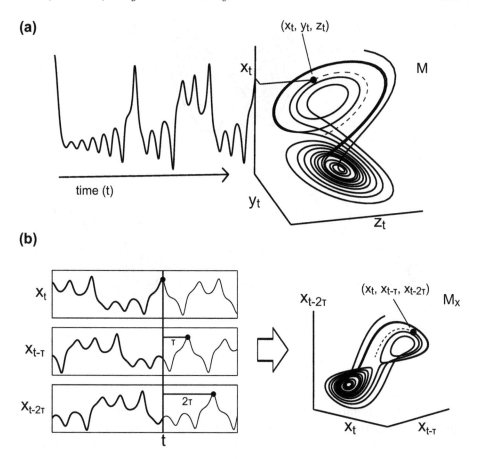

Figure 2. Lorenz attractor and shadow manifold [15, 19].

Figure 2(b) shows how a univariate time series can be converted to a higher dimensional representation using time-lagged versions of itself as additional dimensions [15, 19]. Projecting the system states from M to the coordinate axis X generates a time series. The time series is not the manifold, but it is used to create it using lags. The figure shows how lags of the time series X are used as coordinate axes to construct the shadow manifold M_X. The visual similarity between M_X and M is apparent. Takens [16] showed that the shadow manifold M_X is diffeomorphic (maps one-to-one) to its original attractor manifold M.

Sugihara et al. [14] have also shown that the diffeomorphic property between M and its shadow manifolds – one for each dimension – implies that the shadow manifolds are diffeomorphic with respect to each other; the opposite is also true. Thus, if two shadow manifolds are diffeomorphic with respect to each other, it can be assumed that they belong

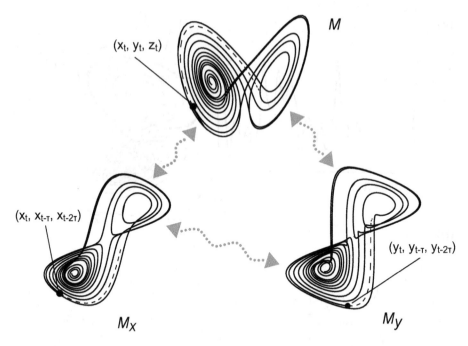

Figure 3. Convergent cross-mapping.

to the same dynamical system. Convergent cross-mapping (CCM), a mathematical technique developed by Sugihara et al. [14], can then be used to identify and quantify the causality between the two original time series. In short, convergent cross-mapping seeks to determine whether an arbitrary point and its nearest neighbors in one shadow manifold can accurately predict a point and its neighbors in another shadow manifold.

Figure 3 summarizes these concepts. Convergent cross-mapping tests the correspondence between shadow manifolds. The figure shows the attractor manifold of the original Lorenz system in three-dimensional space and two shadow manifolds, M_X and M_Y, constructed via lagged coordinate embeddings of X and Y, respectively. The arrows between the manifolds represent the diffeomorphic properties of the attractors. Because X and Y are dynamically coupled, nearby points in M_X correspond temporally to nearby points in M_Y. This enables the estimation of states across manifolds using Y to estimate the state of X, and vice versa, using the nearest neighbors. In the case of longer time series, the shadow manifolds become denser and the neighborhoods (ellipses of the nearest neighbors) shrink, allowing more precise cross-mapping estimates [14, 19]. Sugihara et al. [14] have shown that increasing the sample sizes of shadow manifolds improves the predictive power of convergent cross-mapping and that the predictive power converges to some maximum as the sample size increases to infinity.

2.3 Related Work

A survey of the literature reveals that no published research has focused on applying empirical dynamic modeling to automobile or aircraft time series data, or even cyber security problems in general. The vast majority of applications are in the areas of economics and natural sciences. For example, the Sugihara Lab [15], where empirical dynamic modeling originated, primarily applies the technique to problems in ecology. This research explores the application of empirical dynamic modeling to intrusion detection in cyber-physical systems.

3. Proposed Methodology

The proposed methodology employs empirical dynamic modeling, a relatively new statistical analysis tool, to obtain insights into the characteristics of cyber-physical systems, including their nonlinearity, deterministic chaos and causality. This section discusses the nature and origins of the experimental data. Additionally, it describes the techniques used to analyze the data.

3.1 Datasets

This research has employed datasets generated from two simulated cyber-physical systems, an automobile and an aircraft. The two datasets are employed to evaluate empirical dynamic modeling techniques on linear and nonlinear cyber-physical systems.

The first dataset is based on simple relationships between the steering wheel of an automobile and the relative velocities of its two front wheels. The steering dataset is considered to be linear because the relationships between the pairs of time series are linear or nearly linear. Specifically, the relationship between the velocities of the two front wheels is linear and the relationships between the steering input and the velocity of each of the two wheels are almost linear. The latter two relationships are linear for steering wheel angles of small magnitude, but grow in nonlinearity as the steering wheel angle increases.

The second dataset was generated using the AVAS nonlinear flight simulator that employs real-world physics and flight dynamics for research purposes. Since the focus was on airplane airspeed, altitude and pitch, simulated data pertaining to airspeed, angle of attack, position, heading and wind angle was collected. The dataset is nonlinear because the relationships between the time series are nonlinear.

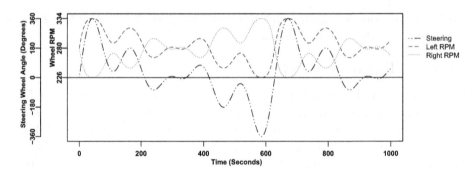

Figure 4.   Plots of the steering system time series.

Linear Data.   Linear data corresponding to the steering wheel angle and front wheel velocities of a passenger vehicle was employed to assess empirical dynamic modeling techniques. The time series were generated for a vehicle with 30-inch wheel radius including the tires, 72-inch wheelbase, 60-inch track, maximum steering wheel turning angle of 360°, steering ratio of 8:1 (maximum wheel angle of 45°) and constant forward speed of 25 mph.

Under the assumptions, a sum of sines function loosely represents a hypothetical driving scenario. That is, the steering line in Figure 4 serves as a potential steering wheel angle time series, and the inside and outside wheel velocities (in rpm) are computed using the following equations:

$$
rpm_{inside} = \frac{60sb}{\pi r \left(b + \cos\left(90 - \frac{\theta}{t}\right) \sqrt{b^2 + \left(k + b\tan\left(90 - \frac{\theta}{t}\right)\right)^2} \right)} \tag{1}
$$

$$
rpm_{outside} = \frac{60s \sqrt{b^2 + \left(k + b\tan\left(90 - \frac{\theta}{t}\right)\right)^2}}{\pi r \left(b\sec\left(90 - \frac{\theta}{t}\right) + \sqrt{b^2 + \left(k + b\tan\left(90 - \frac{\theta}{t}\right)\right)^2} \right)} \tag{2}
$$

Note that, when the steering wheel angle θ is less than zero, the left wheel corresponds to the inside wheel; otherwise, the right wheel corresponds to the inside wheel.

Table 1 describes the variables used in Equations (1) and (2) and specifies their values.

The automobile steering system model is rather rudimentary. It does not account for the physical properties of the real system and the effects of other relevant variables. Despite its simplicity, it is possible to draw

Table 1. Automobile steering system variables.

Variable	Description	Defined Value
r	Wheel radius	15 in
b	Wheelbase	12 in
k	Track	60 in
t	Steering ratio	8:1
s	Forward speed	25 mph
θ	Current steering wheel angle	NA

conclusions about the applicability of empirical dynamic modeling to linear cyber-physical systems.

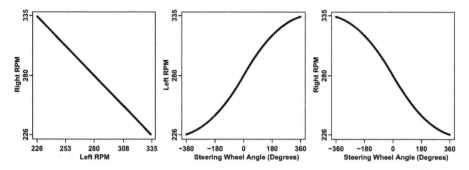

Figure 5. Scatter plots of the relationships between steering system variables.

Figure 5 shows the scatter plots of the relationships between the steering system variables, confirming that the time series are fairly linearly related. The somewhat nonlinear behavior between the steering wheel and each front wheel is due to the mechanics of the standard Ackermann automobile steering mechanism. The values of the variables cover significantly different ranges. For this reason, all the variables were standardized using the `scale` function in the R programming language to ensure that each variable would be equally important in the analysis. Given a time series as input, the `scale` function z-scales it by subtracting its mean and dividing by its standard deviation.

Nonlinear Data. The second dataset was created by guiding an AVAS-simulated aircraft through takeoff, low-altitude cruising and multiple shallow banked turns. The data collection yielded 7,582 observations from a 14-minute flight. Each observation included eight flight metrics with a timestamp relative to the start of the simulation. The metrics

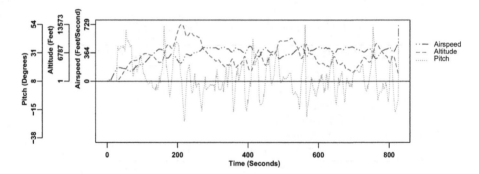

Figure 6.   Plots of the selected AVAS time series.

included roll (deg) and pitch (deg), altitude (ft) and airspeed, vertical velocity and velocity along each of the three coordinate axes (ft/s). The roll and pitch values ranged from $-180°$ to $180°$. Altitude, airspeed and the directional velocities were floating point values (airspeed and altitude were nonnegative values). Note that yaw was excluded because, in the simulator, it is simply a measurement of aircraft heading relative to north, not a characteristic of aircraft dynamics.

The variables in the nonlinear dataset were also z-scaled using the `scale` function in R. A subset of variables – airspeed, altitude and pitch – were selected before conducting the analysis. Other subsets of the eight variables likely exhibit the desired dynamics, but the three selected variables were expected to best demonstrate a tightly-coupled system.

Figure 6 presents the three time series prior to scaling. Figure 7 shows the scatter plots of the relationships between each pair of AVAS variables, clearly demonstrating that the system is highly nonlinear.

3.2   Empirical Dynamic Modeling Techniques

Ye et al. [19] suggest that the following empirical dynamic modeling techniques be applied in sequence to best interpret the characteristics of a dataset:

1. Conduct nearest neighbor forecasting via simplex projection to identify the embedding dimension E that maximizes the forecast skill ρ [13].

2. Use simplex projection and E to determine whether the system exhibits deterministic chaos.

3. Employ sequential locally-weighted global linear maps (S-maps) to characterize the nonlinearity of the data [12].

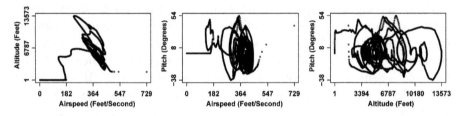

Figure 7. Scatter plots of the relationships between each pair of AVAS variables.

4. Use convergent cross-mapping to generate shadow manifolds, evaluate predictive accuracy and quantify causality [14].

A simplex is a generalization of a triangle or tetrahedron to an arbitrary number of dimensions. Simplex projection iteratively selects a point Y_t in a shadow manifold and b other points whose histories over time t are most similar to the selected point [7, 11, 13]. The weighted averages of the future values of the b other points are used to make predictions about future values of Y_t. The differences between these predictions and the actual future values give the forecast skill ρ. By repeating this process with shadow manifolds of different dimensionalities, the embedding dimension E that optimizes ρ is determined [3].

The (strong) Whitney embedding theorem states [17]:

Theorem 1. Any m-manifold of class C^r ($r \geq 1$ finite or infinite) may be embedded by a regular C^r-map in E^{2m} and by such a map in a one-one manner in E^{2m+1}.

Stated simply, the embedding dimension E of an attractor manifold has an upper bound of $2D + 1$ where D is the true dimension (number of variables) of the system [3, 11]. Thus, simplex projection can be used to definitively identify the optimal E in a finite amount of time.

S-map projection is also an iterative process, but it uses all the neighboring points to create linear regression vectors. Aggregating the regression vectors yields an approximation of an n-dimensional spline. This spline is compared against the shadow manifold attractor to obtain ρ [3, 7, 12]. When generating the regression estimates, a nonlinear tuning parameter θ is used to weigh the neighbors with respect to their distances to the current focal point Y_t. Finally, the time series is determined to belong to a simple linear system if ρ is maximized when $\theta = 0$; otherwise, it is a nonlinear system [3, 11, 12].

Stone et al. [11] claim that this process provides insights into the true dimensionality of the system that generates the observational data without having a complete understanding of the system itself. Accurate knowledge of E is a prerequisite to effectively applying convergent cross-mapping to multiple time series to detect causality. Alternatively, a proper S-map analysis of time series relationships may indicate whether the relationships correspond to a simple linear system. If so, computationally simpler methods such as Granger causality or autoregressive linear models could replace the more complex convergent cross-mapping technique in order to detect causality [4, 12, 19]. Finally, knowledge of the dimensionality of a system may assist in creating a high quality model of the system. Such a model – and the results of causality analysis – could enable the development of an effective intrusion detection capability for a cyber-physical system.

The analysis was conducted using the rEDM repository on GitHub [18, 19]. The codebase enables empirical dynamic modeling analysis using the R programming language. It includes the following functions (among others):

- Function `simplex`, which corresponds to the first and second empirical dynamic modeling techniques.

- Function `s_map`, which corresponds to the third empirical dynamic modeling technique.

- Functions `ccm` and `ccm_means`, which correspond to the fourth empirical dynamic modeling technique.

These functions, along with some helper functions, facilitate effective empirical dynamic modeling analyses.

Interested readers are referred to [10] for a detailed presentation of empirical dynamic modeling, including the mathematics underlying simplex projection, S-map analysis and convergent cross-mapping.

4.   Analysis Results

This section presents the results of the empirical dynamic modeling analyses of the linear and nonlinear datasets.

4.1   Linear Data

Knowledge of the optimal embedding dimension E for each time series of a system is required to effectively apply convergent cross-mapping to make predictions and quantify causality. The optimal value is identified by iteratively utilizing simplex projection to quantify the predictive accuracy at different values of E.

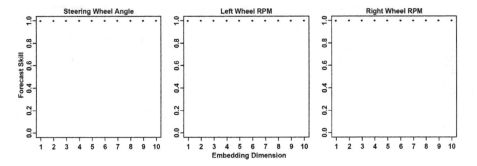

Figure 8.   Optimal embedding dimensions for the steering system time series.

Figure 8 illustrates the results of applying this process to each steering system time series. The plots show that the forecast skill (ability to forecast future values of a time series) is maximized when E is greater than one. The value of E is fixed at two for the empirical dynamic modeling techniques in this section because a lower dimensionality reduces complexity and processing time. To be clear, setting $E = 2$ means that the techniques construct a two-dimensional shadow manifold where each dimension is a time series lagged by some multiple of τ. When predicting the steering wheel angle, for example, the technique constructs a shadow manifold using the steering wheel angle and one copy of the steering wheel angle where the copy is lagged by τ. The lag τ is assumed to be equal to one second in the analysis.

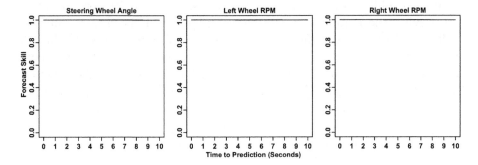

Figure 9.   Deterministic chaos present in each steering system time series.

If E is kept constant and the time to prediction tp is varied, simplex projection enables an analysis of the deterministic chaos of the system. Figure 9 shows the deterministic chaos present in each steering system time series. Specifically, it shows how ρ decreases as tp increases for

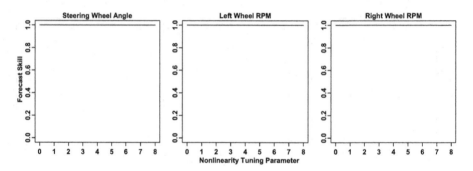

Figure 10.   Nonlinearity of each steering system time series.

each of the three time series. In other words, predictions further in the future are much worse than those closer in time, which indicates chaotic behavior of the three variables. This is due to the nature of driving – without knowledge of the route taken by an automobile, it is practically impossible to predict the steering wheel angle. The simulated data conforms to this interpretation of driving behavior. However, the difference in the values of ρ at $tp = 0$ and $tp = 10$ is only about 0.0008; thus, the chaotic behavior in the system is minuscule. Empirical dynamic modeling does not support a deeper analysis of the chaos of the system.

S-map analysis fits local linear maps to a system to describe its non-linearity. This is different from simplex projection, which analyzes the nearest neighbors of each point. The plots in Figure 10 were obtained by varying the nonlinearity tuning parameter θ in the S-map function call and plotting the value of ρ. When $\theta = 0$, S-map equally weights all the points – as θ increases, the function places more weight on points close to the point under analysis. Thus, when θ is higher, the function assumes that the system has more nonlinearity. For all three time series, ρ is the greatest when θ is high, which indicates the presence of nonlinearity in each time series; however, the trends are minuscule. Indeed, it appears that nonlinearity analysis using empirical dynamic modeling is not particularly useful for a linear system.

Empirical dynamic modeling also enables next-point predictions. Figure 11 overlays the predictions on each time series. Clearly, the predictions are extremely accurate, which indicates that the three variables do not change significantly from one observation to the next. Each plot also shows the prediction variance using a shaded polygon, but the variances are so low that the polygons are all but invisible. In fact, the plots in Figure 9 have already implied this – when tp is small, ρ is very high.

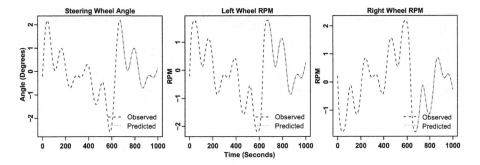

Figure 11. Next-point predictions for each steering system time series.

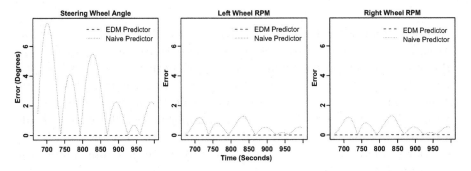

Figure 12. Next-point prediction errors for each steering system time series.

Additionally, a naive prediction model was created that simply predicts that a point at time $t + 1$ has the same value as the point at time t. In other words, the model predicts no change in the next value. Figure 12 shows the next-point prediction errors (residuals) for the naive model and empirical dynamic model. The majority of the errors are small, especially for the empirical dynamic model.

Table 2. Root-mean-square errors for each steering system time series.

Time Series	Naive Model	Empirical Dynamic Model
Steering wheel angle	0.009424	0.003351
Left wheel rotational velocity	0.005742	0.003893
Right wheel rotational velocity	0.005742	0.003893

Table 2 compares the root-mean-square errors for the naive and empirical dynamic models. Note that the root-mean-square error was used

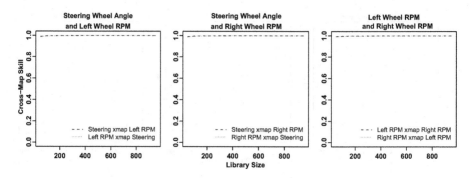

Figure 13.   Causality between each pair of steering system time series.

in order to penalize large mispredictions heavily because such errors strongly affect intrusion detection system performance. As the table illustrates, the empirical dynamic model outperforms the baseline predictor for each time series. The time series are incapable of large, instantaneous changes, so accurately predicting the next point is not impressive nor it is very useful in practical applications. However, it could still assist in designing intrusion detection systems with low complexity. Of course, methods other than empirical dynamic modeling would also suffice for linear systems.

Figure 13 shows the inter-variable dynamics in the automobile steering system. Specifically, it plots the cross-mapping skill ρ against the library size (number of points) used to compute ρ for each pair of variables. The cross-mapping skill quantifies the ability to use one shadow manifold to identify values in another. Each plot has two lines, one for X xmap Y and one for Y xmap X. X xmap Y refers to the convergent cross-mapping analysis technique, which uses the shadow manifold of X to forecast the shadow manifold of Y. The value of ρ obtained for a given library size indicates this predictive capability. The three plots show that ρ is equivalent across library sizes and in both directions for every pair of time series. This means that the steering angle data is encoded in the wheel velocity data and the wheel velocity data is similarly encoded in the steering angle data, which in turn imply an expected causal effect in both directions. Unfortunately, it appears that empirical dynamic modeling does not provide insights about pairwise causality for this linear dataset.

Figure 14 shows the system causality over time. The plots again show the results of using X to forecast Y, but ρ is plotted against tp. According to Ye [18], negative values of tp indicate that past values of Y are best cross-mapped from the reconstructed state of X. Ye also

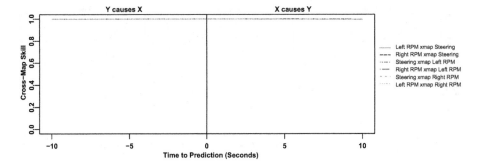

Figure 14. Causality predictions for selected pairs of steering system time series.

suggests that a signal appearing first in Y and later in X is consistent with Y causing X. The opposite is true when tp is positive. In the case of the automobile steering system, regardless of tp and the variables in question, ρ is approximately equal to one. Thus, according to empirical dynamic modeling, each variable has a strong causal effect on every other variable regardless of the time to prediction. This is unlikely and it bolsters the claim that empirical dynamic modeling does not support sophisticated analyses of linear system causality.

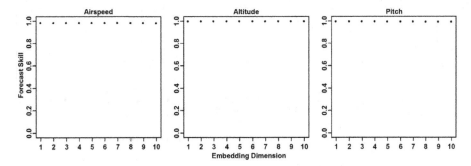

Figure 15. Optimal embedding dimensions for selected AVAS time series.

4.2   Nonlinear Data

Figure 15 presents the forecast skill ρ for various embedding dimensions E for three AVAS time series. The visual differences in ρ are minuscule, but the optimal embedding dimension was two for each series. Thus, $E = 2$ was used in the empirical dynamic modeling techniques in this section. Additionally, the time interval τ between two observations in a given time series was set to one second.

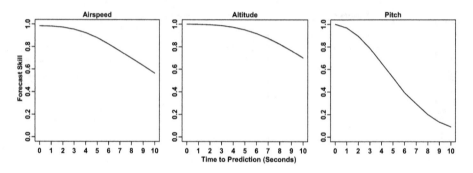

Figure 16. Deterministic chaos present in each selected AVAS time series.

Figure 16 plots the forecast skill ρ against the time to prediction tp to illustrate the deterministic chaos in the system. For each time series, predictions further in the future are much less accurate than earlier predictions. The effects are strongest for pitch and weakest for altitude. Regardless, this is evidence of chaotic behavior for all three variables.

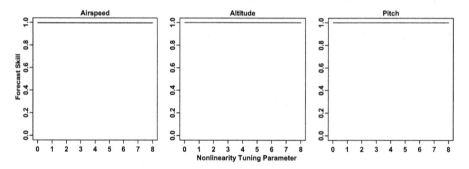

Figure 17. Nonlinearity of each selected AVAS time series.

Figure 17 plots ρ against θ to characterize the nonlinearity of each variable. In the case of airspeed and pitch, ρ is greatest when the function assumes the most nonlinearity; this is indicative of nonlinear dynamics. In the case of altitude, the S-map analysis implies the absence of nonlinear dynamics in the time series, but it is important to note that the change in ρ in all three plots is extremely small regardless of θ. For this reason, it is not possible to definitively claim the presence or absence of nonlinear dynamics.

Figure 18 presents the next-point predictions of empirical dynamic modeling for each time series. Unsurprisingly, the variances of the predictions – as exemplified by the nearly imperceptible shaded polygons –

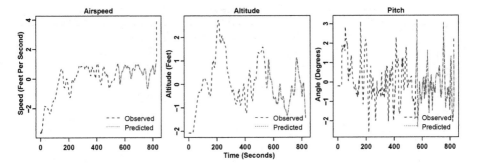

Figure 18. Next-point predictions for each selected AVAS time series.

are small. As Figure 16 strongly indicated, none of the variables change significantly between a pair of observations.

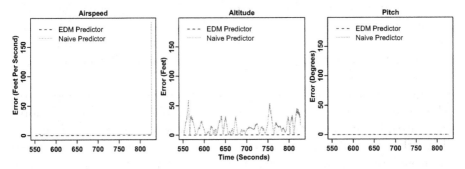

Figure 19. Next-point prediction errors for each selected AVAS time series.

Figure 19 shows the next-point prediction errors (residuals) for the naive and empirical dynamic models. The results confirm that the empirical dynamic model is highly accurate and once again outperforms the naive model.

Table 3. Root-mean-square errors for each AVAS time series.

Time Series	Naive Model	Empirical Dynamic Model
Airspeed	3.907005	0.070161
Altitude	18.192201	0.001535
Pitch	0.013749	0.019748

Table 3 compares the root-mean-square errors for the naive and empirical dynamic models. The empirical dynamic model vastly outper-

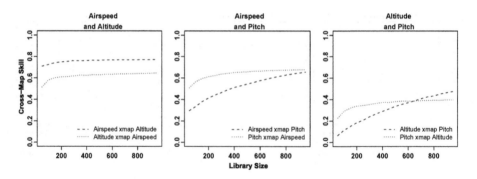

Figure 20.   Causality between selected pairs of AVAS time series.

forms the naive model for two of the three time series. Although the
naive model is a better predictor of the remaining pitch variable, the
difference in root-mean-square errors is insignificant. Once again, it is
possible that even these short-term predictions could assist in intrusion
detection. However, the empirical dynamic model has a clear limitation
– it cannot foresee values that are not in the library. This explains the
large outlier predictions.

Figure 20 shows the cross-mapping skill for each pair of time series.
The leftmost plot shows that the airspeed manifold can effectively forecast altitude but the opposite is noticeably weaker. The middle plot
shows that the difference in cross-mapping skills between airspeed xmap
pitch and pitch xmap airspeed decreases as the library size increases.
The rightmost plot shows a more extreme case – above a certain library
size, an inversion occurs in the difference in cross-mapping skills. In all
three cases, the results indicate diminishing returns when attempting to
improve ρ by increasing the library size. However, it is still possible that
the analysis can improve intrusion detection system design.

Finally, Figure 21 plots the cross-mapping skill against time to prediction. Consider, for example, airspeed xmap pitch. When tp is slightly
less than zero, ρ is maximized. This implies that airspeed best predicts pitch when lagged by about one second. In other words, pitch
strongly affects airspeed after about one second. This behavior is expected. When tp is positive, ρ quickly decreases, and it can be asserted
that airspeed does not have a strong causal effect on pitch. This is
consistent with the standard interpretation of airplane mechanics.

5.   Conclusions

The study of empirical dynamic modeling demonstrates that it can
quantify the behavior of linear systems, but the results are limited and

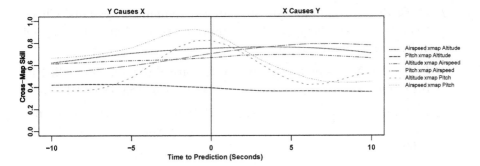

Figure 21. Causality predictions for selected pairs of AVAS time series.

may not assist in developing intrusion detection systems. In contrast, empirical dynamic modeling provides easy-to-use techniques that yield detailed insights about the behavior of nonlinear systems, which could advance intrusion detection efforts.

While empirical dynamic modeling may not be well suited to linear systems, it is important to note that cyber-physical systems are often highly nonlinear. Moreover, the linear system considered in this work is not fully representative of a real-world linear system. For this reason, future research should verify the applicability of empirical dynamic modeling to robust linear systems.

The nonlinear system analysis provided by empirical dynamic modeling is clearly useful for intrusion system design. In particular, it effectively quantifies causality in nonlinear systems. However, realizing the true potential of empirical dynamic modeling requires analyses of more realistic and complex datasets covering a variety of cyber-physical systems. It is hoped that this research will stimulate further investigations into the applicability of empirical dynamic modeling to intrusion detection and cyber security problems in general.

The views expressed in this chapter are those of the authors, and do not reflect the official policy or position of the U.S. Air Force, U.S. Department of Defense or U.S. Government. This document has been approved for public release, distribution unlimited (Case #88ABW-2020-049).

References

[1] Association for Computing Machinery, ACM Transactions on Cyber-Physical Systems, New York (`tcps.acm.org/about.cfm`), 2020.

[2] G. Boeing, Visual analysis of nonlinear dynamical systems: Chaos, fractals, self-similarity and the limits of prediction, *Systems*, vol. 4(4), article no. 37, 2016.

[3] C. Chang, M. Ushio and C. Hsieh, Empirical dynamic modeling for beginners, *Ecological Research*, vol. 32(6), pp. 785–796, 2017.

[4] C. Granger, Investigating causal relations by econometric models and cross-spectral methods, *Econometrica*, vol. 37(3), pp. 424–438, 1969.

[5] R. Hyndman and G. Athanasopoulos, *Forecasting: Principles and Practice*, OTexts, Melbourne, Australia, 2018.

[6] V. Kotu and B. Deshpande, *Data Science: Concepts and Practice*, Morgan Kaufmann, Cambridge, Massachusetts, 2019.

[7] J. Lee, *Introduction to Topological Manifolds*, Springer-Verlag, New York, 2011.

[8] E. Lorenz, Deterministic nonperiodic flow, *Journal of the Atmospheric Sciences*, vol. 20(2), pp. 130–141, 1963.

[9] National Institute of Standards and Technology, Introduction to time series analysis, in *NIST/SEMATECH e-Handbook of Statistical Methods*, Gaithersburg, Maryland (`www.itl.nist.gov/div898/handbook/pmc/section4/pmc4.htm`), 2012.

[10] N. Rennie, Empirical Dynamic Models: A Method for Detecting Causality in Complex Deterministic Systems (`docplayer.net/156079632-Empirical-dynamic-models-a-method-for-detecting-causality-in-complex-deterministic-systems.html`), 2018.

[11] B. Stone, Enabling Auditing and Intrusion Detection of Proprietary Controller Area Networks, Ph.D. Dissertation, Department of Computer Science, Air Force Institute of Technology, Wright-Patterson Air Force Base, Ohio, 2018.

[12] G. Sugihara, Nonlinear forecasting for the classification of natural time series, *Philosophical Transactions of the Royal Society of London, Series A: Physical and Engineering Sciences*, vol. 348(1688), pp. 477–495, 1994.

[13] G. Sugihara and R. May, Nonlinear forecasting as a way of distinguishing chaos from measurement error in time series, *Nature*, vol. 344(6268), pp. 734–741, 1990.

[14] G. Sugihara, R. May, H. Ye, C. Hsieh, E. Deyle, M. Fogarty and S. Munch, Detecting causality in complex ecosystems, *Science*, vol. 338(6106), pp. 496–500, 2012.

[15] Sugihara Lab, Empirical Dynamic Modeling, Scripps Institution of Oceanography, University of California at San Diego, La Jolla, California (`deepecoweb.ucsd.edu/nonlinear-dynamics-research/edm`), 2020.

[16] F. Takens, Detecting strange attractors in turbulence, in *Dynamical Systems and Turbulence*, D. Rand and L. Young (Eds.), Springer, Berlin Heidelberg, Germany, pp. 366–381, 1981.

[17] H. Whitney, Differentiable manifolds in Euclidean spaces, *Proceedings of the National Academy of Sciences*, vol. 21(7), pp. 462–464, 1935.

[18] H. Ye, Using rEDM to Quantify Time Delays in Causation (`ha0ye.github.io/rEDM/articles/rEDM-time-delay-ccm.html`), 2019.

[19] H. Ye, A. Clark, E. Deyle and G. Sugihara, rEDM: An R Package for Empirical Dynamic Modeling and Convergent Cross-Mapping (`ha0ye.github.io/rEDM/articles/rEDM.html`), 2019.

III

TELECOMMUNICATIONS SYSTEMS SECURITY

Chapter 7

MULTI-CHANNEL SECURITY THROUGH DATA FRAGMENTATION

Micah Hayden, Scott Graham, Addison Betances and Robert Mills

Abstract   This chapter presents a novel security framework developed for a multi-channel communications architecture that achieves security by distributing messages and their authentication codes across multiple channels at the bit level. This method of transmission provides protection from confidentiality and integrity attacks without relying on encryption. The two communicating parties utilize existing key exchange mechanisms to pass initialization information. The framework operates by assigning to each message bit a fragment identifier using a hardware-based stream cipher as a pseudorandom number generator, and transmitting specific message fragments across each channel. This prevents the entirety of a message from being transmitted over a single channel and spreads the authentication across the available channels, enabling the sender and receiver to identify a compromised channel even in the presence of a sophisticated man-in-the-middle attack where the adversary forces message acceptance at the destination, perhaps by altering the message error detecting code. Under some conditions, the receiver can recover the original message without retransmission. The holistic framework is attractive for critical infrastructure communications because it provides availability while defending against confidentiality and integrity attacks.

Keywords: Multi-channel communications, security, data fragmentation

1.   Introduction

Traditional communications frameworks rely on information traveling over a single communications link. Methods exist for communicating administrative information separately from message data; however, if an adversary gains access to the communications link carrying the message data, he/she can obtain the entire message content. This forces the use of encryption to protect the confidentiality of the transmissions. Typi-

© IFIP International Federation for Information Processing 2020
Published by Springer Nature Switzerland AG 2020
J. Staggs and S. Shenoi (Eds.): Critical Infrastructure Protection XIV, IFIP AICT 596, pp. 137–155, 2020.
https://doi.org/10.1007/978-3-030-62840-6_7

cally, these systems use a hashed message authentication code (MAC) to check the integrity of each message and retransmit a message if necessary. However, such methods are susceptible to adversarial action that fools a receiver to accept an invalid message. The guarantees of confidentiality and integrity are of paramount importance in critical infrastructure communications due to the operational and physical impacts of successful attacks.

This chapter extends the research of Wolfe et al. [12], which proposed the use of two channels to defeat various adversarial actions. The effort, which targeted low-power devices, addressed each type of attack with an individual security policy. In contrast, this chapter proposes a tunable framework for multi-channel communications, enabling a user to address multiple types of attacks simultaneously. The architecture utilizes data fragmentation and duplication to provide increased security and reliability. By splitting the data into fragments at the bit level and distributing the fragments over a channel set, information leakage is reduced in the presence of adversarial actions. Additionally, man-in-the-middle attacks can be detected and defeated even if an adversary is able to modify the error correcting code to fool the receiver. As expected, there is an overhead associated with these services. However, due to the tunable nature of the architecture, a trade-off can be struck between the services provided and the overhead involved.

The proposed secure communications framework is intended to serve as a road map for network designers to create multi-channel communications systems for specific use cases. Indeed, security protocols such as Transport Layer Security (TLS) could reasonably incorporate multi-channel communications to provide security when multiple lines of communication are available.

2.   Background

This section describes security developments that are relevant to multi-channel communications systems. As customary, Alice and Bob are the communicating entities and Eve is the adversary.

Wolfe et al. [12] have proposed multi-channel communications as a viable security alternative for low-power devices. They describe how multiple channels can thwart eavesdropping attacks by splitting the data across the channels and defeat integrity attacks by duplicating the data across two or more channels. However, they do not mention specific mechanisms for splitting and duplicating the data, nor do they perform the two tasks simultaneously. This research extends the work of Wolfe and colleagues by proposing a mechanism for splitting messages across multiple channels. Also, it identifies several tunable characteristics that can meet the security requirements.

2.1 CIA Triad

The confidentiality, integrity and availability (CIA) triad covers the key security requirements. User-specific confidentiality, integrity and availability needs dictate the level and type of security required for a given application:

- **Confidentiality:** The confidentiality requirement specifies that only the sender and intended recipient(s) may correctly decode/decrypt the transmitted data.

- **Integrity:** The integrity requirement specifies that the received data is correct and unmodified.

- **Availability:** The availability requirement specifies that the data arrives within a certain time or latency window. This is typically quantified using traditional quality of service (QoS) metrics.

2.2 Transport Layer Security

Transport Layer Security 1.0, which was specified in RFC 2246, provides communications privacy over the Internet – it "[allows] client/server applications to communicate in a way that is designed to prevent eavesdropping, tampering or message forgery" [4]. It is a widely-used protocol for protecting communications. RFC 2246 specifies the following four goals for the Transport Layer Security Protocol in order of priority:

- **Cryptographic Security:** The protocol should be used to establish a secure connection between two parties.

- **Interoperability:** Independent programmers should be able to develop applications using the protocol that will successfully exchange cryptographic parameters without any knowledge of each other's code.

- **Extensibility:** The protocol should provide a framework into which new public key and bulk encryption methods can be incorporated as necessary.

- **Relative Efficiency:** Since cryptographic – especially key – operations tend to be very computationally intensive, the protocol must incorporate an optional session caching scheme to reduce the number of connections that need to be established from scratch.

The Transport Layer Security Protocol achieves these four goals by relying on the TLS Record Protocol for connection security and the TLS Handshake Protocol to authenticate the two parties.

The TLS Record Protocol client specifications list two basic properties [4]:

- **Private Connections:** Symmetric cryptography is used for data encryption. A unique symmetric key is generated for each connection and key transfer is accomplished using a secret negotiated by another protocol (e.g., TLS Handshake Protocol).

- **Reliable Connections:** Message transport includes a message integrity check using a keyed message authentication code.

The TLS Record Protocol allows the encapsulation of various higher-level protocols. One of these protocols is the TLS Handshake Protocol, which guarantees authentication, confidentiality, integrity and availability.

Deprecation of Secure Sockets Layer. Transport Layer Security became the *de facto* protocol for securing transport layer communications after the deprecation of Secure Sockets Layer Version 3 (SSLv3) described in RFC 7568 [1]. The SSLv3 key exchange mechanism and cipher suites were attacked over several years, leading to the creation of Transport Layer Security 1.0 and 1.1 specified in RFC 2246 [4] and RFC 4346 [5], respectively. However, there was no widespread support of these replacement protocols, which led to the continued use of SSLv3 [1].

Starting with Transport Layer Security 1.2 in RFC 5246 [6], backwards compatibility with SSL was eliminated to ensure that sessions would not support the negotiation and use of SSL security. In fact, RFC 7568 [1] states that "SSLv3 is comprehensively broken." Specifically, it has flaws in its cipher block chaining (CBC) modes and weaknesses in its stream ciphers. Key exchange is vulnerable to man-in-the-middle attacks through two methods – renegotiation and session resumption. Moreover, it relies on SHA-1 and MD5 hashing, which are considered weak and are being replaced with stronger hash functions. Transport Layer Security 1.2 addresses all these weaknesses using new cryptographic methods and features. RFC 7568 states that SSLv3 must not be used, indicating a complete shift to Transport Layer Security 1.2.

Transport Layer Security Development. Transport Layer Security 1.0, which was defined in 1999 [4], did not indicate significant shifts from SSL. Specifically, it allowed for the negotiation of SSL connections.

The first major shift was made in Transport Layer Security 1.1, which addressed several SSL vulnerabilities. The changes were [5]:

- Replacement of the implicit initialization vector with an explicit initialization vector for protection against cipher block chain attacks.

- Handling padding errors to protect against cipher block chain attacks.

The principal goals and properties of the Transport Layer Security Protocol remained the same from Transport Layer Security 1.0 through 1.2. However, Transport Layer Security 1.2 incorporates several changes from Transport Layer Security 1.1. It allows for improved flexibility, specifically in negotiating cryptographic algorithms and specifying cipher-suite-specific pseudorandom functions. There is support for authenticated encryption and additional data modes. Transport Layer Security 1.2 eliminates support for cipher suites such as IDEA and DES. Finally, it lowers the support for SSLv2 backwards-compatibility from a "should" to a "may," under the assumption that it will become a "should not" in the future [6].

As the security environment continued to develop, written standards were required to ensure that entities communicate security parameters via the same language to ensure clarity and efficient communication. These guidelines were specified in RFC 3552: "The Guidelines for Writing RFC Text on Security Considerations" [11]. Transport Layer Security 1.3 incorporates the security updates from Transport Layer Security 1.2 and a change in the protocol goals to align with the language specifications in RFC 3552. The updated goals are [10]:

- **Authentication:** The server side of a channel is always authenticated whereas the client side is optionally authenticated. Authentication can occur via asymmetric cryptography or a symmetric pre-shared key.

- **Confidentiality:** Data sent over a channel after establishment is only visible to the endpoints. Transport Layer Security does not natively hide the length of the data it transmits, although endpoints are able to pad Transport Layer Security records in order to obscure lengths and enhance protection against traffic analysis.

- **Integrity:** Data sent over a channel after establishment cannot be modified by attackers without detection.

The major changes incorporated in Transport Layer Security 1.3 reflect significant research in secure communications [10]. The protocol modifies the cipher suite concept to separate the authentication and key exchange mechanisms from the record protection algorithm. It prunes the list of allowable cipher suites by removing legacy algorithms and eliminating the static RSA and Diffie-Hellman cipher suites, instead allowing only public-key mechanisms that provide forward secrecy – the assurance of the secrecy of past sessions even if future sessions are compromised. It requires handshake messages to be encrypted and restructures the handshake state machine to be more consistent and remove overhead.

Transport Layer Security 1.0 has been adapted to the current Transport Layer Security 1.3 to keep up with new vulnerabilities and attacker capabilities. The pattern demonstrates the willingness to adapt to an ever-changing security environment by developing new methods and protocols that maintain secure communications. The adaptation is expected to continue, including providing support for multi-channel communications in the coming years.

2.3   Data Fragmentation

An efficient and cryptographically secure method should be used to fragment messages. A linear feedback shift register (LFSR) provides an elegant way of realizing long, pseudorandom sequences with minimal software/hardware requirements, making it an ideal candidate for data fragmentation. An LFSR has a series of flip flops and a feedback path that outputs a single bit of output during each clock cycle.

The maximum output length of an m-bit LFSR is given by [9]:

$$Length = 2^m - 1 \tag{1}$$

After $2^m - 1$ values, the sequence repeats itself; this length is the period of the LFSR.

Paar and Pelzl [9] provide a proof that an LFSR can be broken with $2m$ key stream bits due to the linear progression of its internal state. This leads to the Trivium hardware-oriented synchronous stream cipher [3]. By chaining three LFSRs, the internal state of each LFSR does not evolve in a linear fashion.

De Canniere and Preneel [3] describe the construction of the Trivium cipher and its hardware requirements at the gate level, and provide a brief security analysis. The stream cipher has an output period of 2^{64} bits. It also has low-power hardware implementations. For these reasons, the proposed framework leverages the Trivium cipher to generate pseudorandom sequences to map each message bit to a corresponding fragment identifier.

2.4 Diffie-Hellman Key Exchange

A communications system must guarantee security as long as its initialization/key information are kept secret. Thus, a secure method is needed to exchange the system initialization parameters over an insecure channel.

The Diffie-Hellman Key Exchange algorithm is a one-way function that relies on the commutative property of exponentiation. The algorithm, which incorporates setup and key exchange phases, guarantees that only Alice and Bob can obtain the session key from the transmitted information, even if Eve is able to access all communications. Details about the algorithm and a proof of its security are provided in [9]. The Diffie-Hellman Key Exchange algorithm is used to exchange initialization information in the proposed data fragmentation scheme. Alice and Bob both compute the session key k_{AB} and utilize the most significant bits to generate the key and initialization vector for the Trivium cipher.

2.5 Regulatory Standards

The North American Electric Reliability Council (NERC) created the Critical Infrastructure Protection (CIP) Security Standards CIP-002-014 [8] to formalize security requirements for the entire energy sector, ranging from personnel and training requirements in CIP-004-6 to information protection outlined in CIP-011-2, which is the standard adopted in this work. CIP-011-2 seeks to prevent unauthorized access to information about the bulk electric system and specifies requirements for protecting cyber systems against compromises that could lead to misoperation or instability.

Fries and Falk [7] reference the International Electrotechnical Commission IEC 62443-3-3 Standard that imposes two requirements directly related to secure communications:

- **Requirement 3.3.1 Communications Integrity:** The control system shall provide the capability to protect the integrity of transmitted information.

- **Requirement 4.4.1 Communications Confidentiality:** The control system shall provide the capability to protect the confidentiality of information at rest and in remote access sessions traversing an untrusted network.

2.6 Summary

There is clearly a vested interest in developing mechanisms that ensure the confidentiality and integrity of communications, specifically in the critical infrastructure. Certain regulatory standards specify the requirements for secure communications. The Transport Layer Security protocol is one of the primary methods for securing networked communications. The protocol has gone through several iterations to accommodate the changing security needs as reflected in the three main goals of Transport Layer Security 1.3, namely authentication, confidentiality and integrity. Other ongoing work addresses the emerging field of multi-channel communications. This research proposes a data fragmentation scheme based on the Trivium cipher that distributes message content across multiple channels.

3.   Proposed Framework

This section discusses the proposed framework, including its goals, tunability and operation,

3.1   Goals

The proposed framework is designed to accomplish two goals: (i) explore the challenges in a multi-channel security system; and (ii) investigate the potential security services obtained through its use. A full communications session from initialization through message receipt is completed across a user-specified number of channels. Adversarial actions can occur on any of the available channels to demonstrate resilience. This gives an increased understanding of the effort required to field an operational system. Abstractions are used to reflect issues that are yet to be resolved, but developmental paths or guides are provided for future research. The information an adversary gains from a given attack against a single channel in an unencrypted scenario is specified; in an encrypted scenario, the proposed multi-channel framework would likewise use encryption. The comparison demonstrates how a multi-channel architecture can identify, mitigate and even defeat several adversarial attacks.

3.2   Tunability

A user of the framework would determine several parameters based on a set of security requirements. The parameters include the number of channels, duplication factor, number of fragments and a fragment-to-channel mapping. Each of these parameters identifies a trade-off between the elements of the confidentiality, integrity and availability triad and the associated overhead.

A channel requires a handshake to initialize its connection and an associated network interface. As the number of channels increases, more

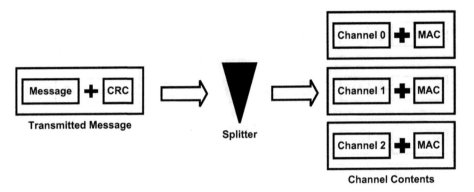

Figure 1.   Three-channel message transmission.

channels are available for an adversary to target, but the defender also gains the ability to increase obfuscation.

The duplication factor strictly refers to the duplication of information. No duplication indicates that only a single copy of each bit of message is sent; this provides the maximum level of confidentiality because all messages on all channels must be intercepted in order to fully recreate the message. Full duplication indicates that the entire message is sent across each of the available channels, providing the maximum level of availability but with reduced confidentiality. As the duplication factor increases, there is a corresponding increase in the amount of information sent.

A single fragment could represent a single bit of a message while the maximally-sized fragment could contain the entire message. As the number of fragments increases, greater data obfuscation is provided by spreading the fragments across the channel set. However, there is additional overhead because more key bits are required to map a message bit to a fragment. This illustrates the complex environment of a multi-channel communications architecture as well as the unique advantage it presents to users. A user of the framework may specify the desired services but, and in doing so, would accept the incurred overhead.

Figure 1 shows the basic mechanism for a three-channel transmission. To transmit a message, the system computes a cyclic redundancy code (CRC), appends it to the end of the message and then assigns each bit to a channel. Each channel transmits its own set of data with a corresponding channel CRC.

Figure 2 shows the receiving side of the communications session. Each channel CRC is checked to verify the channel contents. Next, each bit

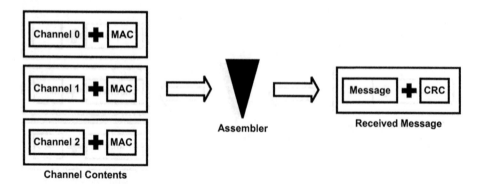

Figure 2. Three-channel message reception.

is reassembled to obtain the message and message CRC. The message CRC is used to verify the accurate transmission of the message.

3.3　Operation

The proposed framework has three phases of operation:

- **Initialization:** Alice and Bob predetermine the number of channels, number of fragments and fragment-channel mapping, and whether error detection or error correction is to be used. During a simulation, the modeler must also indicate the adversarial actions to be applied in the scenario. Before Alice can send a message, both Alice and Bob must compute the session key using the Diffie-Hellman Key Exchange algorithm. They each extract the most significant 160 bits of the shared key. The first 80 bits are used as the Trivium key and the next 80 bits are used as the Trivium initialization vector.

- **Sending:** In order to send a message, Alice assigns each individual bit of the message to a fragment based on the output of the Trivium cipher. After all the message (data and message CRC) bits have been assigned to fragments and the fragments have been assigned to one or more channels, appropriate error detection/correction bits are computed for each channel for transmission of its assigned fragments. If forward error correction is used, Alice computes a Reed-Solomon code for each channel output and appends the code instead of a channel CRC.

- **Receiving:** The receiver Bob begins by assuming that each channel is valid. If a channel is unavailable due to network degradation or adversarial action, the channel is marked as invalid. Bob then checks the contents of each channel using the CRC or Reed-Solomon code. If the channel CRC indicates an error or the channel Reed-Solomon code indicates an error that cannot be corrected, then the corresponding channel is marked as invalid. Otherwise, Bob recombines the message using the channel mapping. For a given bit, if there are differences between channels carrying the bit (i.e., Channel 1 and 2 both transmit a specific bit, but their contents differ), the particular fragment is flagged as having been modified. After the recombination process is completed, the message CRC is checked to see if it was received properly. In the event of a failure, the protocol goes into the recovery mode. If the modified fragments are isolated to a single channel, then a "smart recovery" is attempted by marking the channel carrying the fragments as invalid. If the smart recovery succeeds, Bob flags the channel modified by the adversary as being insecure.

Consider an example involving a three-channel communications session between Alice and Bob. Alice sends a message M, which is divided into three fragments, f_1, f_2 and f_3, with the following fragment-channel mapping:

$$C_1 = \{f_1, f_2\}$$
$$C_2 = \{f_2, f_3\}$$
$$C_3 = \{f_3, f_1\}$$

Eve conducts a man-in-the-middle attack on channel C_2 that changes f_2 to f_2' and f_3 to f_3'. This causes Bob to receive the following information on the three channels:

$$C_1 = \{f_1, f_2\}$$
$$C_2 = \{f_2', f_3'\}$$
$$C_3 = \{f_3, f_1\}$$

When Bob attempts to recombine the message, he detects differences between the two copies of both f_2 and f_3, indicating a potential adversary in channel C_2. He proceeds to accurately and correctly determine message M from only the contents of channels C_1 and C_3, and reports the adversarial presence in channel C_2.

If Bob was unable to isolate the modified channel, which could occur if Eve modified multiple channels, he could attempt to recover M by iterating through all the channel combinations that carried the entire message. This is possible because the message authentication code is spread across the channels, so even if a message in a compromised channel is accepted by Bob, the message authentication code would indicate the modification of the message. This recovery is computationally very expensive, but may be acceptable in some cases.

4.   Insights

This section discusses the implementation challenges related to the proposed multi-channel framework, along with its complexity and effectiveness at mitigating attacks.

4.1   Implementation Challenges

The most glaring implementation challenge is to define the communications channels used by the sender and receiver. The challenge is addressed in this work by using a predefined channel set, but it limits the flexibility. Similarly, since the splitting mechanism relies on the communicated session parameters, the parameters must be transmitted via a key exchange mechanism over one or multiple channels in the channel set or be transmitted out of band. The transmission of session parameters is a design choice based on the security needs. Also, dynamic operation/channel configuration are required to address the possibility that a channel can become unresponsive or experience degraded performance. These challenges would likely be resolved as protocols such as Transport Layer Security are enhanced to support multi-channel systems.

Error detection and correction also pose challenges. Given a cryptographically secure splitting mechanism, if a bit is lost (and not recovered using forward error correction), then the joining mechanism would be unable to piece together the final message without knowing which bit was lost. Thus, error detection or correction must be implemented for every channel. The current solution relies on the message CRC and Reed-Solomon code for error detection and correction, respectively.

The other main challenge relates to security configuration. Relationships exist between the overhead of a security scheme and its resilience, confidentiality and integrity. The duplication of information increases the overhead while enhancing confidentiality and integrity. Confidentiality and integrity requirements do not need to be specified; instead, they are achieved by selecting an appropriate error correction mechanism and amount of duplication.

4.2   Time and Storage Complexity

The operation of the framework involves: (i) initialization and key exchange; (ii) message fragmentation and sending; (iii) message transmission; and (iv) receipt and recombination. The most computationally intensive part is the Diffie-Hellman key exchange. The security of key exchange relies on the discrete logarithm problem, which is discussed in [2]. Yakymenko et al. [13] have shown that the temporal complexity of modular exponentiation, which is required to compute a Diffie-Hellman key, is $O(b^2 \cdot \ln^2 b)$, where b is the size in bits of the modulus p used in the algorithm.

Fragmenting and sending a message M requires $\log_2(n)$ operations to generate a fragment for a message bit, where n is the number of channels. These operations must be performed m times, where m is the number of bits in message M. As each byte is processed, the error correction code for the message is computed, which requires $O(1)$ time. After fragmenting the entire message, an error correction code is computed for each channel, which requires $O(\frac{m}{8}) = O(m)$ time. Thus, fragmenting and sending a message requires $O(m \cdot \log_2(n))$ time. However, since the number of channels n is much less than the number of message bits m, the time complexity becomes $O(m)$. This also accounts for the inclusion of the message and channel error correction codes.

Message transmission is not included in the complexity analysis because it depends entirely on the transmission time and end-to-end delay of a communications link/interface.

Receiving and recombining a message operates similarly to message sending, with the exception that the system must recover from a message modified by an adversary. If each channel transmits securely, then message recombination requires $O(m \cdot \log_2(n)) = O(m)$ time. However, the recombination of a modified transmission depends on the allowed attempts. The system can attempt to recover from errors in x channels, where $0 \le x \le n - 1$ because there must be at least one correct transmission. Each recombination requires m operations and, in the worst case, it would require the full nested structure. Thus, the recombination would require $O(m^x)$ time.

The storage requirement depends primarily on the amount of duplication. The Trivium cipher was selected because its implementation requires minimal hardware, just 180 bits of state. System operation requires the ability to recombine a message from some of its parts (if there are errors), which means that the contents of each channel must be stored in a buffer. Because each channel could potentially carry the entire message, the buffers would require $\frac{m \cdot n}{8}$ bytes. Once again, because

$m >> n$, the storage requirement in practice would be $O(m)$, which is reasonable.

4.3   Attack Mitigation

As stated above, RFC 3552 clarifies the terminology for writing security considerations in future RFCs. Additionally, RFC 3552 specifies the following attack environment [11]:

> "We assume that the attacker has nearly complete control of the communications channel over which the end-systems communicate. This means that the attacker can read any PDU (protocol data unit) on the network and undetectably remove, change, or inject forged packets onto the wire. This includes being able to generate packets that appear to be from a trusted machine. Thus, even if the end-system with which you wish to communicate is itself secure, the Internet environment provides no assurance that packets which claim to be from that system in fact are."

This section discusses the effectiveness of the proposed framework in mitigating eavesdropping, jamming and man-in-the-middle attacks that target a single communications channel. As stated above, the attacker can access protocol data units in a channel if desired (except in the case of a jamming attack).

In an eavesdropping attack, an adversary only intercepts the portion of the message carried on the targeted channel. However, the adversary does not know which bits have been intercepted and how many bits are missing from the actual message. This significantly reduces the usable information obtained by the attacker.

A jamming attack seeks to undermine the availability of a targeted message. Let df denote the number of times each fragment is duplicated across the available channels. For example, if there are three channels, $df = 0$ means no duplication (each fragment is sent once), $df = 1$ means each fragment is sent twice and $df = 2$ means full duplication (each fragment is sent on all three channels). The adversary would certainly succeed if the duplication factor df is zero because the loss of a single channel would prevent message receipt. However, when $df \geq 1$, the receiver can recreate the message if no more than df channels are lost.

The most sophisticated man-in-the-middle attack involves an adversary who successfully modifies the information in a channel, including the channel CRC, so that the channel information is accepted at the destination. However, due to the recombination mechanism, the adversary only succeeds if more than df channels are modified. In addition, the receiver can determine which channel(s) have been affected while still receiving the message without retransmission. This mitigation is possible because the message CRC is interleaved in all the available channels.

In the implementation, no logical relationships exist between fragments in different channels. System resilience stems from the strict duplication of information and the dispersion of the message authentication code across the available channels. Methods exist for reducing the overhead involved in operating a multi-channel system while maintaining the same level of resilience. However, as the dependencies and relationships of the data in different channels increase, so does the amount of information that an adversary can gain. An example is a system with three channels C_1, C_2 and C_3, where each channel transmits equal length fragments. If $C_3 = C_1 \oplus C_2$, then even if an adversary compromises any one channel, the message can be recovered from the remaining two channels. However, a drawback of this approach is that all the channels are forced to carry information of equal lengths instead of probabilistically-equal lengths as implemented.

5.   Discussion

This section discusses the implementation of the proposed framework in the TCP/IP architecture and in the critical infrastructure.

5.1   TCP/IP Implementation

A key issue is how the proposed framework would fit within the TCP/IP architecture. An argument could be made to include it as a session layer protocol because it relies on several channels, each of which would have its own TCP/UDP connection. However, the Transport Layer Security protocol was specifically designed to be flexible to accommodate a changing cyber security paradigm. Clearly, there is a need to develop multi-channel communications systems that provide security even if attacks outpace encryption schemes. Thus, there is a high likelihood that Transport Layer Security or another protocol would provide multi-channel security support.

The proposed system would work with a protocol that allows the creation and synchronization of multiple channels. Given a set of channels between a client and server, the framework would function as a cipher suite for the Transport Layer Security Protocol. Relying on the current Transport Layer Security nomenclature, it would merely be necessary to specify the method of key exchange as in the following examples:

- **TLS_RSA:** RSA.

- **TLS_DH:** Diffie-Hellman.

- **TLS_DHE:** Ephemeral Diffie-Hellman.

- **TLS_ECDH:** Elliptic curve Diffie-Hellman.

It is also necessary to specify the message authentication code to be used. Transport Layer Security currently utilizes hash-based message authentication codes (HMACs) with stream ciphers; these special message authentication codes provide message integrity and authenticity. They are currently denoted as follows:

- **HMAC-MD5.**

- **HMAC-SHA1.**

- **HMAC-SHA256/384.**

To match the Transport Layer Security nomenclature, the message authentication codes would be denoted as:

- **HMAC-CRC-32.**

- **HMAC-RS.**

This only leaves the session parameters for the fragmentation factor and duplication factor based on the number of available channels n. Thus, the client would offer the following items:

- **FF-X:** Number of message fragments $(X \leq n)$.

- **DF-Y:** Session duplication factor $(Y < n)$.

By modifying the proposed multi-channel system as a cipher suite for a future version of Transport Layer Security, the following session parameters would be communicated by the client at system initialization:

- **TLS_DH_CRC-32_FF-X_DF-Y.**

- **TLS_DH_RS_FF-X_DF-Y.**

5.2 Critical Infrastructure Implementation

The encryption and authentication methods utilized in the proposed framework would not immediately meet the security requirements for widespread implementation in critical infrastructure communications. However, the framework demonstrates several concepts that must be considered and addressed prior to an implementation. Also, it showcases the benefits of using multiple channels, especially when data is split at the bit level in a nonpredictable/pseudorandom manner. Even if an adversary could break the encryption used in a channel, the adversary would not know which bits have been decrypted and how the bits fit into the overall message. Thus, the adversary would have to intercept/compromise several channels to gain any meaningful information. This matches the confidentiality requirement specified in RFC 3552 for network communications [11]. Similarly, because the message authentication code is distributed across multiple channels, changes to a particular channel can be detected even if the adversary modifies the information so that it passes the channel-specific message authentication code. This matches the integrity requirement specified in RFC 3552 [11].

The proposed framework can thus be applied to existing critical infrastructure communications, where the primary concerns are message confidentiality and integrity. By fragmenting data across multiple channels for infrastructure communications, the adversarial actions needed to defeat the security mechanisms increase considerably. Specifically, multiple channels have to be intercepted and modified, and even if multiple channels are compromised, the adversary would still have to break the data splitting mechanism at the endpoints.

It is possible that the Trivium cipher may not provide adequate security for the splitting mechanism in some critical infrastructure scenarios. In such cases, the cipher may be replaced with a more secure alternative. Also, encryption can be applied to messages or individual channels or both, depending on the timing and overhead constraints.

6. Conclusions

Secure communications protocols should support multi-channel communications to leverage the security services that can be provided by multiple channels. The proposed multi-channel communications framework relies on data fragmentation in order to secure transmissions – it uses existing key exchange mechanisms to communicate initialization information, a splitting mechanism to map data to channels, and error detection and correction mechanisms. The framework also provides tunable parameters, namely the number of channels, duplication factor and number of fragments per message, which can accommodate user-specific security requirements. An important feature of the framework is its resilience to adversarial actions, including eavesdropping, jamming and man-in-the-middle attacks. For example, the framework can detect and defeat man-in-the-middle attacks without retransmission while reporting the channels that were compromised. However, some challenges need to be resolved prior to implementation, including securely determining the channel set prior to initializing communications sessions.

The framework can serve as a roadmap for developing secure, multi-channel communications systems because it demonstrates what is necessary to meet key security requirements and illustrates the challenges that must be addressed before implementation. The framework would dovetail nicely with future implementations of Transport Layer Security and other protocols. The resulting multi-channel communications system could be tailored to user needs, gaining corresponding increases in confidentiality, integrity and availability even in the presence of adversarial actions. Indeed, the multi-channel system would significantly increase the overhead required by attackers to gain meaningful information (confidentiality), modify transmitted information (integrity) and prevent information from being used (availability).

The views expressed in this chapter are those of the authors, and do not reflect the official policy or position of the U.S. Air Force, U.S. Department of Defense or U.S. Government. This document has been approved for public release, distribution unlimited (Case #88ABW-2019-6022).

References

[1] R. Barnes, M. Thomson, A. Pironti and A. Langley, Deprecating Secure Sockets Layer Version 3.0, RFC 7568, 2015.

[2] I. Blake and T. Garefalakis, On the complexity of the discrete logarithm and Diffie-Hellman problems, *Journal of Complexity*, vol. 20(2-3), pp. 148–170, 2004.

[3] C. De Canniere and B. Preneel, Trivium Specifications, Computer Security and Industrial Cryptography Group, Department of Electrical Engineering, Catholic University of Leuven, Heverlee, Belgium (www.ecrypt.eu.org/stream/p3ciphers/trivium/trivium_p3.pdf), 2006.

[4] T. Dierks and C. Allen, The TLS Protocol Version 1.0, RFC 2246, 1999.

[5] T. Dierks and E. Rescorla, The Transport Layer Security (TLS) Protocol Version 1.1, RFC 4346, 2006.

[6] T. Dierks and E. Rescorla, The Transport Layer Security (TLS) Protocol Version 1.2, RFC 5246, 2008.

[7] S. Fries and R. Falk, Ensuring secure communications in critical infrastructures, *Proceedings of the Sixth International Conference on Smart Grids, Green Communications and IT Energy-Aware Technologies*, pp. 15–20, 2016.

[8] North American Electric Reliability Corporation, United States Mandatory Standards Subject to Enforcement, Atlanta, Georgia (`www.nerc.com/pa/stand/Pages/ReliabilityStandardsUnited States.aspx`), 2020.

[9] C. Paar and J. Pelzl, *Understanding Cryptography: A Textbook for Students and Practitioners*, Springer, Berlin Heidelberg, Germany, 2010.

[10] E. Rescorla, The Transport Layer Security (TLS) Protocol Version 1.3, RFC 8446, 2018.

[11] E. Rescorla and B. Korver, Guidelines for Writing RFC Text on Security Considerations, RFC 3552, 2003.

[12] C. Wolfe, S. Graham, R. Mills, S. Nykl and P. Simon, Securing data in power-limited sensor networks using two-channel communications, in *Critical Infrastructure Protection XII*, J. Staggs and S. Shenoi (Eds.), Springer, Cham, Switzerland, pp. 81–90, 2018.

[13] I. Yakymenko, M. Kasianchuk, S. Ivasiev, A. Melnyk and Y. Nykolaichuk, Realization of RSA cryptographic algorithm based on vector-module method of modular exponentiation, *Proceedings of the Fourteenth IEEE International Conference on Advanced Trends in Radioelectronics, Telecommunications and Computer Engineering*, pp. 550–554, 2018.

Chapter 8

SECURING AN INFINIBAND NETWORK AND ITS EFFECT ON PERFORMANCE

Lucas Mireles, Scott Graham, Patrick Sweeney, Stephen Dunlap and Matthew Dallmeyer

Abstract   The InfiniBand network architecture, which delivers very high bandwidth and low latency, is one of the leading interconnects used in high performance computing. As its popularity increases, applications of InfiniBand in the critical infrastructure are growing, which creates the potential of new security risks.

This chapter addresses some open security issues related to InfiniBand. It demonstrates that common traffic analyzing tools are unable to capture or monitor InfiniBand traffic transmitted between hosts. Due to the kernel bypass nature of InfiniBand, many host-based network security systems cannot be executed on InfiniBand applications and, unfortunately, those that can impose significant network performance penalties. The principal takeaways are that Ethernet security practices do not translate to InfiniBand networks and securing InfiniBand networks requires a hardware offload strategy.

Keywords: InfiniBand networks, security, performance

1.   Introduction

InfiniBand is a powerful interconnect architecture that is quickly becoming the standard for input/output connectivity in servers and high performance computing clusters. In fact, 28% of the top 500 supercomputers in the world use InfiniBand as their interconnects, accounting for more than 35% of the total performance, second only to Gigabit Ethernet (Table 1). The popularity of InfiniBand stems from its ability to provide higher bandwidth and lower memory latency than Ethernet networks. InfiniBand engages a copy-avoidance architecture that reduces CPU utilization. As the demand for high bandwidth and low latency

© IFIP International Federation for Information Processing 2020
Published by Springer Nature Switzerland AG 2020
J. Staggs and S. Shenoi (Eds.): Critical Infrastructure Protection XIV, IFIP AICT 596, pp. 157–179, 2020.
https://doi.org/10.1007/978-3-030-62840-6_8

Table 1.   Top five supercomputer interconnects.

Interconnect	Count	Share
Gigabit Ethernet	259	51.8%
InfiniBand	140	28%
Omnipath	50	10%
Custom Interconnects	45	9%
Proprietary Networks	5	1%

increase, InfiniBand is seeing applications outside of high performance computing in all areas of computer communications [5].

Computer communications are essential in an information-based society [14]. As its popularity increases, InfiniBand may well become the interconnect standard that underlies communications in the critical infrastructure that are vital to the provision of goods and services in modern society. It is therefore essential to explore and evaluate the security of InfiniBand networks and address the risk of potential cyber attacks. Although some researchers have investigated InfiniBand security issues [3, 4, 11, 12, 15], the work focuses heavily on protocol security instead of applications.

This chapter focuses on some open security issues related to Infini-Band. It evaluates whether or not InfiniBand traffic can be monitored by common traffic analyzers used in Ethernet networks. Also, it assesses the impacts of network security solutions on InfiniBand performance. Three case studies are employed to frame the issues involved in securing InfiniBand networks.

2.   InfiniBand Architecture

The InfiniBand network protocol architecture is becoming the *de facto* standard for server input/output and server-to-server communications in large high performance computing clusters and storage area networks. While it is comparable to Ethernet in some ways, InfiniBand was designed for data centers with high performance clusters that would be logically separated from the Internet [11]. The design and development of the InfiniBand architecture was driven by the inability of existing protocols to provide sufficient network bandwidth and reduced memory latency to keep up with processing performance. InfiniBand improves input/output bandwidth by employing (non-bus) point-to-point connections and channel (message) semantics, where commands and data are transferred between hosts and devices as messages instead of via memory operations [10]. Unlike a bus architecture, the point-to-point connections support the scaling of large switched networks and fault isolation. To achieve this, InfiniBand has moved away from the traditional network topology and implements point-to-point switched input/output fabric that uses cascading switches as shown in Figure 1. This enables Infini-Band to explicitly treat input/output as a form of communication, giving input/output units the same communications capabilities as processor nodes [2, 10].

2.1 InfiniBand Components

From a high-level perspective, InfiniBand is an interconnect for processors, input/output units and routers, all of which are considered to be end nodes. The smallest complete InfiniBand network is an InfiniBand subnet comprising end nodes, switches, links and a subnet manager [10]. InfiniBand subnets can be connected to other InfiniBand subnets using routers. Furthermore, end nodes that are part of a subnet can be connected to multiple switches to create a switched fabric network.

- **Channel Adapters:** Every end node in an InfiniBand network must have a channel adapter (CA) that generates and consumes InfiniBand packets [2]. A channel adapter can be defined as a host channel adapter (HCA) or target channel adapter (TCA). A host channel adapter provides a collection of features specified by InfiniBand verbs whereas a target channel adapter does not have a defined software interface.

  A channel adapter is essentially a programmable direct memory access (DMA) engine that provides local and remote direct memory access and constructs packets in hardware. Channel adapters communicate using work queues consisting of send, receive and completion queues. Each host channel adapter is assigned a globally unique identifier (GUID) by the chip manufacturer. Additionally, each of its ports is assigned a port GUID that identifies each port globally (within a subnet and between subnets).

- **Subnet Manager:** InfiniBand implementations of routing and forwarding are similar to software-defined networking (SDN) [7]. The routing and forwarding tables of InfiniBand switches and routers are not decided by each device. Instead, a subnet manager (SM) is responsible for configuring and managing all switches, routers and channel adapters in a subnet [2, 7]. The subnet manager actively communicates with each switch, channel adapter and router subnet manager agent to ensure that all the routing and for-

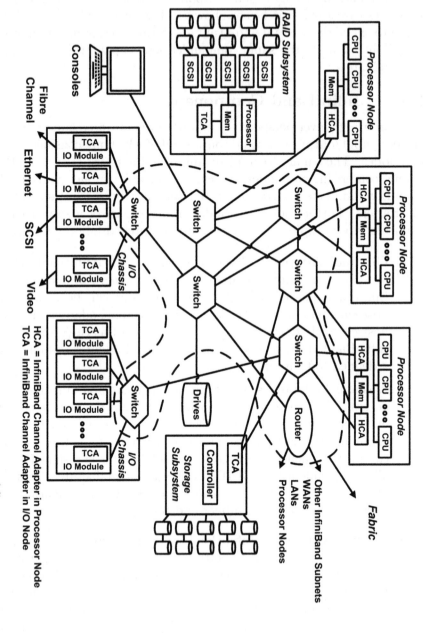

Figure 1. InfiniBand network with fabric highlighted (adapted from [2]).

warding tables are correct [11]. InfiniBand allows multiple subnet managers in a subnet for resilience; one subnet manager is active and the others are in a standby mode. During subnet initialization, a polling algorithm is executed by a state machine that enables all the subnet managers to agree on a single master subnet manager based on the highest priority.

- **Switch:** Similar to Ethernet, where forwarding decisions are based on MAC addresses, InfiniBand switches make forwarding decisions based on local identifiers (LIDs). Every destination port in a subnet is assigned a local identifier by the subnet manager. Destination local identifiers represent paths along which a switch forwards packets. Every switch is configured with forwarding tables that include paths for local identifiers in the subnet. Multiple paths to destinations may exist for redundancy and load sharing. The subnet manager should be configured to handle multiple paths when link failures occur or load sharing is desired. InfiniBand supports unicast and multicast functions, enabling Internet Protocol (IP) applications to operate normally over InfiniBand fabric.

2.2 Software Architecture

In order to maintain independence of the host operating system and processor, the InfiniBand Trade Association [6] has defined a software architecture that is compatible with all major operating systems. The software architecture comprises kernel modules and protocols that exist solely in kernel space. Applications in user space need not be aware of the underlying InfiniBand architecture, enabling them to operate using InfiniBand just as they would using Ethernet [2, 6].

Figure 2 shows the InfiniBand software stack. The kernel space is divided into three major layers: (i) host channel adapter drivers; (ii) mid-layer core; and (iii) upper layer protocols [6]. The role of a host channel adapter driver is no different than that of any other input/output device driver. An input/output driver allows applications executing in user space to control hardware by calling a set of character strings that identify the input/output protocol supported by the driver. These calls are interpreted by the device driver and mapped to the specific device operations called upon by the applications [1]. Per the InfiniBand architecture specification, each host channel adapter driver must be compatible with the mid-layer core kernel modules [2].

The kernel modules located in the InfiniBand mid-layer core allow access to multiple host channel adapters and provide a common set of shared services. Some of the notable functions in the mid-layer core

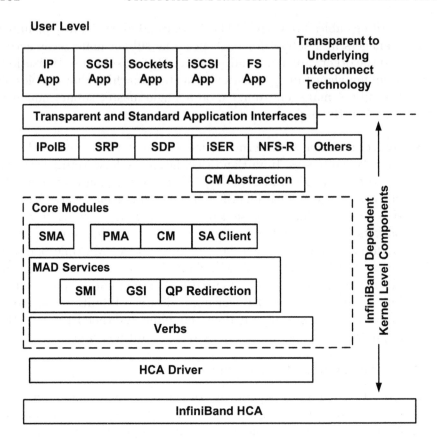

Figure 2. InfiniBand software stack [6].

include the management datagram (MAD) interface, connection manager (CM) interface and access to InfiniBand verbs. InfiniBand verbs are abstract descriptions of operations that take place between a host channel adapter and host [2]. The mid-layer core provides an interface to these functions for user applications via the InfiniBand VPI (Verbs API). This API allows users to directly craft packets in hardware using functions/methods to bypass the kernel completely, enabling high bandwidth and low latency. Additionally, the mid-layer core implements mechanisms that enable user applications to interact with InfiniBand hardware [6].

The final layer of the kernel space comprises the upper layer protocols. These protocols enable applications that employ standard data networking and filesystem access to operate in the InfiniBand architecture.

Thus, no changes are required to the applications and the applications can benefit from InfiniBand's high bandwidth and low latency.

2.3   IPoIB, RDMA and RoCE

IP over InfiniBand (IPoIB) is an upper layer protocol that implements a network interface over the InfiniBand architecture. Specifically, IPoIB encapsulates IP datagrams over an InfiniBand transport service [6], enabling any application or kernel module with a standard Linux network interface to operate in the InfiniBand architecture without modification. However, applications running IPoIB still have to traverse the TCP/IP call stack in the kernel.

InfiniBand provides a remote direct memory access (RDMA) capability, which enables data to be transferred between two servers or between a server and storage without any involvement of the host processor. In traditional networks, applications request resources from the processor which, in turn, fulfills the resource requests. This requires significant processor overhead and leads to large CPU utilization every time a request is made. With remote direct memory access, the processor is only used to initialize the communications channel that enables applications to directly communicate and share resources without processor involvement. Remote direct memory access devices allow applications to directly read and write to virtual memory. This provides low latency through stack bypass and copy avoidance, reduces CPU utilization and provides high bandwidth utilization [9]. The combination of the Infini-Band link layer and software stack comprise the remote direct memory access messaging service over InfiniBand.

In addition to the InfiniBand protocol, remote direct memory access can be supported over Ethernet. This usage is referred to as RDMA over converged Ethernet (RoCE) [9]. It is the most efficient low latency Ethernet solution today, requiring much less CPU overhead than other remote direct memory access solutions such as iWARP. Like remote direct memory access over InfiniBand, RoCE uses InfiniBand verbs to craft packets for its applications.

2.4   Communications Model

A work queue is created when an end user wishes to communicate with another node in the network or queue up a series of requests that need to be completed by hardware. Work queues, which are typically created in pairs, hold the service requests made by consumers. A queue pair (QP) comprises a send queue and a receive queue. A send queue is used to send operations that specify the data to be sent and its destination. The receive queue holds operations that inform the hardware where to place the data received from a consumer. After the host channel adapter has executed the queue pair, a completion queue event that holds information about the completion of the work queue is created and eventually sent to the host. Queue pairs can be viewed as a virtual interface used by a consumer to communicate with the hardware. InfiniBand supports up to 2^{24} queue pairs per host channel adapter. Queue pairs are independent of each another; this provides isolation and protection from operations associated with other queue pairs.

2.5   InfiniBand Security Features

InfiniBand can be viewed as a layer 2 protocol much like Ethernet. Thus, layer 3-7 application security mechanisms built on top of Ethernet are implemented the same way with InfiniBand [8]. It is the developer's responsibility to implement encryption, authentication, integrity and authorization of applications.

InfiniBand claims that it overcomes known Ethernet vulnerabilities by providing advanced enforcement mechanisms that secure physical devices and resources. One enforcement mechanism is partitioning, which provides private access to private devices and allows access to shared resources [10]. To prevent unauthorized access to shared resources, a hardware mechanism called partition keys (P_Keys) is employed. The P_Keys mechanism enforces membership in a partition by requiring queue pairs to be in the same partition in order to communicate. Every data packet carries a P_Key to prevent unauthorized access to shared resources [2]. Furthermore, partitions are controlled centrally from the subnet manager, preventing nodes from determining their own partitions. This eliminates potential hacking and security holes because a host cannot manipulate its access to shared resources [8].

InfiniBand also claims to prevent attackers from accessing unauthorized destinations, sniffing unintended traffic and impersonating other entities [8]. The subnet manager implements switching tables that are strictly defined at every node and can only be updated by the subnet manager. Because the switching tables are determined by the subnet manager at a central location, a host cannot manipulate its own switching table, preventing traffic from arriving at unintended destinations.

InfiniBand's unreliable and reliable transport services have security mechanisms that mitigate session hijacking and unauthorized access [8]. In the case of unreliable communications, queue pairs are created to send and receive traffic. A queue pair key (Q_Key) is sent with each packet. When a packet arrives at its destination, the Q_Key sent with the packet must match the Q_Key held by the receiver; otherwise, the packet is dropped. In the case of reliable communications, Q_Keys as well as sequence numbers and CRCs are employed to ensure message security. If any of these do not match, the fabric manager is informed and the corresponding packets are dropped [8].

Memory protection is required because remote direct memory access enables nodes to directly access virtual memory belonging to other nodes. InfiniBand implements memory protection by issuing an L_Key and R_Key with every remote direct memory access communication. The L_Key defines the local region of memory that can be accessed by a queue pair and the R_Key is passed to a remote node. When a remote node executes a remote direct memory access operation, it passes the R_Key that it was given to validate the remote node's right to access the destination node's memory. This security mechanism cannot be disabled or changed, ensuring memory protection for all InfiniBand devices [2, 8].

3. InfiniBand Security

Research on InfiniBand security began shortly after the InfiniBand Trade Association was formed in 1999. Early studies discovered significant vulnerabilities in InfiniBand and presented solutions to address them. Additional research went beyond the InfiniBand architecture and evaluated the security of InfiniBand network implementations, identifying vulnerabilities that were not found in earlier studies.

3.1 Vulnerabilities

Lee and colleagues [3, 4] identified InfiniBand security gaps and suggested that the associated vulnerabilities could be exploited with modest effort. Two major vulnerabilities were related to authentication.

First, InfiniBand's use of partitioning keys to prevent unauthorized network traffic does not fully mitigate the risk of an attack. All the partitioning keys are sent plaintext over the network, allowing easy access to an attacker. The solution is to use partition level and queue pair level key management/distribution methods. The partition level key management scheme ensures that all communications in a partition are done using the same shared secret key. Because the queue pair is the smallest communications entity, the queue pair level key management scheme guarantees confidentiality and integrity in a partition using temporary session keys between queue pairs.

The second authentication vulnerability is addressed by providing another method for authentication using an invariant CRC (ICRC). The ICRC is normally used as an end-to-end error detection method. However, Lee et al. propose using it as an authentication tag to further harden InfiniBand security for two reasons. One is that the ICRC does not change from end to end and the other is that it does not require changes to the InfiniBand packet format.

Lee and colleagues concluded that implementing these two authentication methods strengthen InfiniBand security without hindering network performance.

3.2   GUID Spoofing

Ethernet MAC spoofing has been used by attackers for years. The GUID used by InfiniBand to uniquely specify a host channel adapter is similar to an Ethernet MAC address. In order to address spoofing attacks [8], InfiniBand packets are crafted in hardware with the GUID residing in firmware and are changed only by reprogramming the host channel adapter (by flashing the firmware). However, Warren [15] has successfully exploited an InfiniBand network through GUID spoofing. The attack is mitigated by relying on a monitoring system that captures an initial link state configuration. After system startup, the monitoring system sends alerts to an administrator when link state changes occur and LID-GUID matches change because these two changes are necessary for the attack to be successful.

3.3   Protocol Implementation Security

Sebedi et al. [12] have conducted static and dynamic code analyses for potential vulnerabilities in the InfiniBand protocol implementation. The static code analysis employed various tools to inspect InfiniBand code and identified potentially vulnerable functions. The dynamic analysis involved "fuzz testing" that used carefully-crafted inputs and monitored the outputs to discover vulnerabilities. The study concluded that no significant vulnerabilities exist in the protocol itself, but recommended that three potentially-vulnerable functions should be replaced.

3.4   Vulnerability Assessment

Schmitt et al. [11] have conducted a cyber vulnerability assessment of an InfiniBand network and concluded that some security aspects of InfiniBand have yet to be investigated thoroughly. The InfiniBand architecture was designed as a data center technology that would be logically separated from the Internet, rendering defensive mechanisms such as packet encryption unnecessary. To date, malicious actors do not appear to have taken a significant interest in InfiniBand, but this is likely to change as the technology proliferates. Schmitt and colleagues suggest

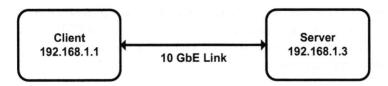

Figure 3. Network diagram of the Ethernet 10 GbE with Connect-X 5 adapters.

some mitigation techniques and tools that could be adapted to Infini-Band; the most interesting technique involves a software-defined networking approach to fabric management. As mentioned above, GUID spoofing in an InfiniBand network can be mitigated using a monitoring system [15]. Schmitt et al. suggest that the monitoring functionality could be implemented via a software-defined networking approach. Interestingly, Schmitt et al. observe that, although cyber security was not a high priority when InfiniBand was developed, it is inherently resistant to many cyber attacks.

4. Case Studies

This research has sought to explore how an InfiniBand network can be secured and to analyze the potential effects that a security implementation might have on the architecture/network. Case studies were conducted to examine the difficulties in implementing well-known network security systems on multiple types of InfiniBand applications to demonstrate the security limitations. Additionally, effects on network bandwidth were examined to determine the performance implications of securing InfiniBand and understand how alternate methods may be used to achieve the desired speeds.

4.1 Testbed Setup

The InfiniBand architecture allows Ethernet and InfiniBand protocols to coexist on the same network or device without changing the application software. This is largely due to the InfiniBand verb construct that enables applications to communicate directly with the hardware that crafts the traffic. As a result, the case studies used the Ethernet and InfiniBand interconnect protocols. Mellanox was chosen as the primary hardware vendor because it is largest provider of InfiniBand technology solutions and services, some of which support Ethernet.

Ethernet 10 GbE with Connect-X 5 Adapter. Figure 3 shows the network configuration used in this study. The configuration incorporated two host machines, each with a Connect-X 5 adapter. The two Connect-X 5s were connected "back-to-back" via a 10 GbE active optical cable. A switch was not required and the Ethernet protocol was used for interconnect traffic.

IPsec Configuration.   The following configuration was used in all the tests that implemented IPsec:

- **Encryption Algorithm:** AES-GCM 128/256-bit key and 128-bit integrity check value.

- **IPsec Operation Mode:** Transport mode.

- **IPsec Protocol:** Encapsulating Security Protocol (ESP).

- **IP Version:** IPv4.

IProute2, a user application that controls TCP/IP network flows, was used in the study. It implemented the IPsec configuration specified above.

Kernel Bypass and Network Security System Implementation. Kernel bypass facilitates low latency and high bandwidth communications in InfiniBand networks. A program that uses InfiniBand verbs will always bypass the host machine kernel, regardless of whether remote direct memory access or raw Ethernet packets are used. A custom program was written to demonstrate the effects that a security implementation might have on an InfiniBand network. The program implemented the following actions:

1. Get the InfiniBand device list.
2. Open the requested device.
3. Query the device capabilities.
4. Allocate a protection domain to contain the resources.
5. Register a memory region.
6. Create a completion queue.
7. Create a queue pair.
8. Bring up a queue pair.
9. Post work requests and poll for completion.
10. Perform cleanup.

The InfiniBand program demonstrated kernel bypass using a raw Ethernet client/server model, where the client sent pre-formatted TCP/IP packets to the server and the server received packets destined to its MAC address. Although the program sent raw Ethernet packets, it simply described the type of queue pair established between the two devices and conformed to the InfiniBand architecture specification because it was written with InfiniBand verbs.

The InfiniBand program was used in two of the three case studies conducted in this research. Case Study 1 was conducted to demonstrate the ability to monitor traffic while bypassing the kernel on a host machine. Case Study 2 explored the implications of bypassing the kernel with network security in place, specifically IPsec. Case Study 3 examined the performance impact of executing IPsec on a program that did not bypass the kernel.

4.2 Case Study 1: Traffic Monitoring

The first case study demonstrates the ability of an InfiniBand application to bypass a kernel by executing the client/server program. Wireshark and `tcpdump` were used to explore the possibility of monitoring InfiniBand traffic with common network tools, both of them are packet analyzers that use `libpcap` to sniff packets entering a host machine. The `libpcap` API enables applications to capture and analyze link layer packets traversing the kernel. Because its implementation occurs in the kernel and the raw Ethernet client/server program was written to demonstrate kernel bypass, another tool, namely Mellanox's Offloaded Traffic Sniffer, was used to capture traffic that bypassed the kernel. The Offloaded Traffic Sniffer used the standard capabilities of the `ethtool` utility to capture packets in hardware. The captured packets were then analyzed using `tcpdump`. A kernel bypass was confirmed when the packets sent with the program could only be captured with the Offloaded Traffic Sniffer.

The case study used the Ethernet 10 GbE with Connect-X 5 adapter network configuration to conduct two tests. The first test used `tcpdump` to capture the TCP/IP packets being transmitted. The second test enabled the Offloaded Traffic Sniffer to determine if the packets bypassed the kernel. The raw Ethernet client/server program incorporated two executables – a receiver program that represented the server and a sender program that represented the client. During execution, both the programs reported every successful message transmission by polling the completion queue. If the client/server program was unsuccessful in bypassing the kernel, then TCP/IP packets could be captured by `tcpdump`, and opened and analyzed with Wireshark without a hardware offload.

Test without the Offloaded Traffic Sniffer:

1. Configure the server and client host machines to enable IPoIB. This enables queue pairs to be established based on IP addresses instead of GUIDs.

2. Start the receiver program on the server (192.168.1.3). The receiver must run as root to create queue pairs.

3. Initiate `tcpdump` on the server and specify the appropriate interface on which to capture packets.

4. Run the sender program on the client (192.168.1.1) to send pre-formatted TCP/IP packets to the receiver.

5. After ten seconds of capture, terminate `tcpdump` and save the packets in a PCAP file.

6. Terminate the programs on the server and client machines.

Test with the Offloaded Traffic Sniffer Enabled:

1. Enable the Offloaded Traffic Sniffer by entering the command `ethtool --set-priv-flags enp9s0f0 sniffer on`, where `enp9s0f0` is the desired interface.

2. Repeat Steps 2 through 6 in the previous test.

When the raw Ethernet client/server program bypassed the kernel successfully, the pre-formatted TCP/IP packets were only captured with the Offloaded Traffic Sniffer enabled.

4.3   Case Study 2: Security Implementation

This case study examined the impact of implementing a network security system on an InfiniBand program. Conventional Ethernet networks employ a variety of techniques and systems to monitor and control network traffic on hosts. These include:

- **Firewalls:** Firewalls establish a barrier between trusted and untrusted networks by monitoring and controlling packets that enter and leave hosts.

- **Host-Based Intrusion Detection Systems:** Host-based intrusion detection systems use signatures to analyze network traffic at hosts and dynamically monitor system state.

- **Deep Packet Inspection:** Deep packet inspection filters network traffic by examining payload content instead of only traffic headers.

- **Secure Network Protocols:** Secure network protocols protect data in transit to prevent unauthorized access by users and programs. Examples include IPsec, SSL and SFTP.

The security systems listed above are commonly implemented as kernel modules that enforce security policies based on information within the kernel. The second case study attempted to evaluate how these systems could enforce security on packets that bypassed the kernel.

Specifically, the case study explored the implications of implementing IPsec on an InfiniBand application. IPsec was selected because of its ability to secure communications between and within networks. It is a secure network protocol that provides confidentiality, integrity and authentication between devices and is implemented as a kernel module. Based on the IPsec security policy configured by a user, an IPsec module is forwarded packets based on the source and destination IP addresses and encrypts the packets using an algorithm implemented in the TCP/IP stack kernel layer.

The case study determined whether or not IPsec could be executed on an InfiniBand program that sent TCP/IP packets. The Ethernet 10 GbE with Connect-X 5 adapter network configuration was used. The InfiniBand program used was the raw Ethernet client/server program. Additionally, the case study assumed that the Offloaded Traffic Sniffer was enabled to capture packets.

The following steps were involved:

1. Configure the server and client host machines to enable IPoIB. This enables queue pairs to be established based on IP addresses instead of GUIDs.

2. Start the receiver program on the server (192.168.1.3). The receiver must run as root to create queue pairs.

3. Initiate tcpdump on the server with the Offloaded Traffic Sniffer enabled and specify the appropriate interface on which to capture packets.

4. Run the sender program on the client (192.168.1.1) to send pre-formatted TCP/IP packets to the receiver.

5. After ten seconds of capture, terminate tcpdump and save the packets in a PCAP file.

6. Terminate the programs on the server and client machines.

7. Implement the IPsec configuration described above using the IProute2 utility.

8. Repeat Steps 2 through 6

9. Compare the PCAP files to determine if IPsec was executed.

If IPsec executed on the InfiniBand program, then the second set of packets captured would be in the form of encapsulated security packets and packet examination would reveal the encryption. This would demonstrate the successful execution of IPsec because the TCP/IP packets were encrypted by the configured algorithm.

4.4 Case Study 3: Performance

The third case study examined the effects of implementing a security system on an application that does not bypass the kernel. As mentioned earlier, IPoIB encapsulates TCP/IP packets after they have traversed the TCP/IP stack in the kernel. Thus, a program that uses IPoIB does not bypass the kernel and would allow IPsec to be executed on its packets.

The Iperf program was used to evaluate the performance of IPsec in an InfiniBand network. Iperf is a network performance application that tests the maximum throughput that a device can handle. It was selected in the case study because it replicates the client/server model and sends TCP/IP packets like the raw Ethernet client/server program used in the previous two case studies. When used with a 10 GbE cable, Iperf produced a bandwidth slightly under 10 Gbps.

Because the high computing power requirement imposed by IPsec can limit network throughput, it was essential to measure the bandwidth with and without IPsec. Ten tests were performed in random order, five with Ipsec and five without Ipsec. Each test recorded 300 samples. Each sample corresponded to the average bandwidth during a one-second interval.

The tests involved the following steps:

1. Reboot the server and client host machines.

2. Configure the server and client host machines to enable IPoIB with the correct IP configurations.

3. If IPsec is used, implement it according to the configuration in the experimental setup.

4. Run Iperf on the server (192.168.1.3) specifying the server IP address.

5. Run Iperf on the client (192.168.1.1) specifying the client IP address, server IP address and transmission time.

6. Capture 310 samples and discard the first ten samples to account for ramp-up.

7. Terminate the Iperf programs on the server and client machines after the specified time interval is reached.

The results of this case study were analyzed to determine the effects of executing IPsec on the InfiniBand network.

5.   Results

This section presents the results of the three case studies and discusses how they affect the overall security of an InfiniBand network.

5.1   Case Study 1 Results

This case study explored the security implications of bypassing the kernel with an InfiniBand program. In particular, it evaluated the ability of common network traffic analyzers to monitor kernel bypass traffic.

The first test in the case study used the `tcdump` network analyzer in an attempt to capture packets on the server machine. No packets were captured on the specified interface using `tcpdump`/Wireshark with the Offloaded Traffic Sniffer disabled. The test successfully registered message completions back to the server and client sides of the program, indicating successful packet transmission. This strongly suggests that the InfiniBand program did indeed bypass the kernel completely because messages were successfully transmitted, but were not captured in the kernel (`tcpdump` uses `libpcap`, which is implemented as a kernel module). Therefore, monitoring InfiniBand traffic must be executed outside the host machine kernel (subject of the second test).

In the second test, the Offloaded Traffic Sniffer was enabled and the InfiniBand client/server program was run again. Unlike the first test, the PCAP file recorded by `tcpdump` contained the captured packets.

Figure 4 shows a screenshot of the first five packets analyzed using Wireshark. The screenshot shows that the exact pre-formatted TCP/IP packets created by the InfiniBand client/server program were captured. This result has two implications. First, InfiniBand programs can successfully send Ethernet TCP/IP packets without traversing the TCP/IP stack in the kernel, suggesting a potential vulnerability of security applications executed in the kernel. Second, monitoring InfiniBand traffic is possible with the assistance of the Offloaded Traffic Sniffer, implying the need for a hardware implementation of traffic monitoring.

5.2   Case Study 2 Results

Case Study 2 sought to determine whether IPsec could be implemented on an InfiniBand program that sent TCP/IP packets.

The first test in Case Study 2 executed the InfiniBand client/server program without IPsec as in Case Study 1. Accordingly, the results in the first test were identical to those shown in Figure 4 for Case Study 1, illustrating the successful transmission of TCP/IP packets. Note that the highlighted data section of the packet was sent in plaintext.

The second test in Case Study 2 ran the InfiniBand client/server program again with IPsec implemented. IPsec was executed within the IP layer of the kernel stack when TCP/IP packets were formed.

Figure 5 shows that IPsec was not executed on the InfiniBand Program. If IPsec was executed correctly, the protocol of the captured packets would no longer be TCP, but would be encapsulated security payload protocol packets, and the payloads of the packets would be encrypted using the AES-GCM algorithm instead of being in plaintext. The conclusion is that, because IPsec was executed in the kernel stack and the InfiniBand client/server program bypassed the kernel, IPsec could not be implemented on a program that used InfiniBand verbs. Therefore, a

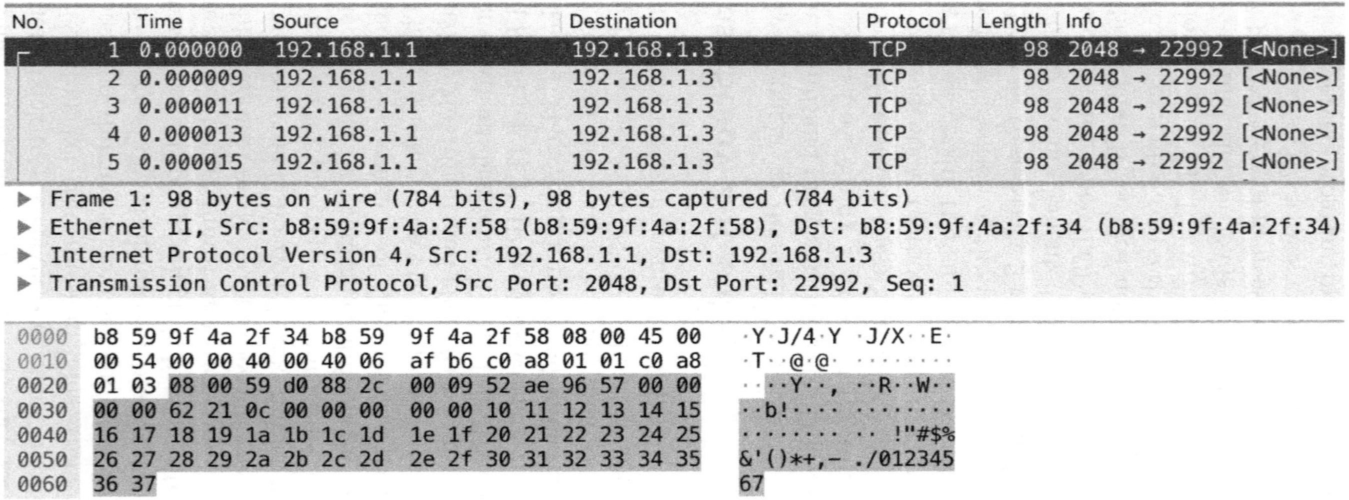

No.	Time	Source	Destination	Protocol	Length	Info
1	0.000000	192.168.1.1	192.168.1.3	TCP	98	2048 → 22992 [<None>]
2	0.000009	192.168.1.1	192.168.1.3	TCP	98	2048 → 22992 [<None>]
3	0.000011	192.168.1.1	192.168.1.3	TCP	98	2048 → 22992 [<None>]
4	0.000013	192.168.1.1	192.168.1.3	TCP	98	2048 → 22992 [<None>]
5	0.000015	192.168.1.1	192.168.1.3	TCP	98	2048 → 22992 [<None>]

▼ Frame 1: 98 bytes on wire (784 bits), 98 bytes captured (784 bits)
▼ Ethernet II, Src: b8:59:9f:4a:2f:58 (b8:59:9f:4a:2f:58), Dst: b8:59:9f:4a:2f:34 (b8:59:9f:4a:2f:34)
▼ Internet Protocol Version 4, Src: 192.168.1.1, Dst: 192.168.1.3
▼ Transmission Control Protocol, Src Port: 2048, Dst Port: 22992, Seq: 1

```
0000  b8 59 9f 4a 2f 34 b8 59   9f 4a 2f 58 08 00 45 00   ·Y·J/4·Y ·J/X··E·
0010  00 54 00 40 00 40 06 af   b6 c0 a8 01 01 c0 a8       ·T·@·@·· ········
0020  01 03 08 00 59 d0 88 2c   00 09 52 ae 96 57 00 00   ····Y··, ··R··W··
0030  00 00 62 21 0c 00 00 00   00 00 10 11 12 13 14 15   ··b!···· ········
0040  16 17 18 19 1a 1b 1c 1d   1e 1f 20 21 22 23 24 25   ········ ·· !"#$%
0050  26 27 28 29 2a 2b 2c 2d   2e 2f 30 31 32 33 34 35   &'()*+,- ./012345
0060  36 37                                                67
```

Figure 4.   Wireshark analysis of captured InfiniBand packets.

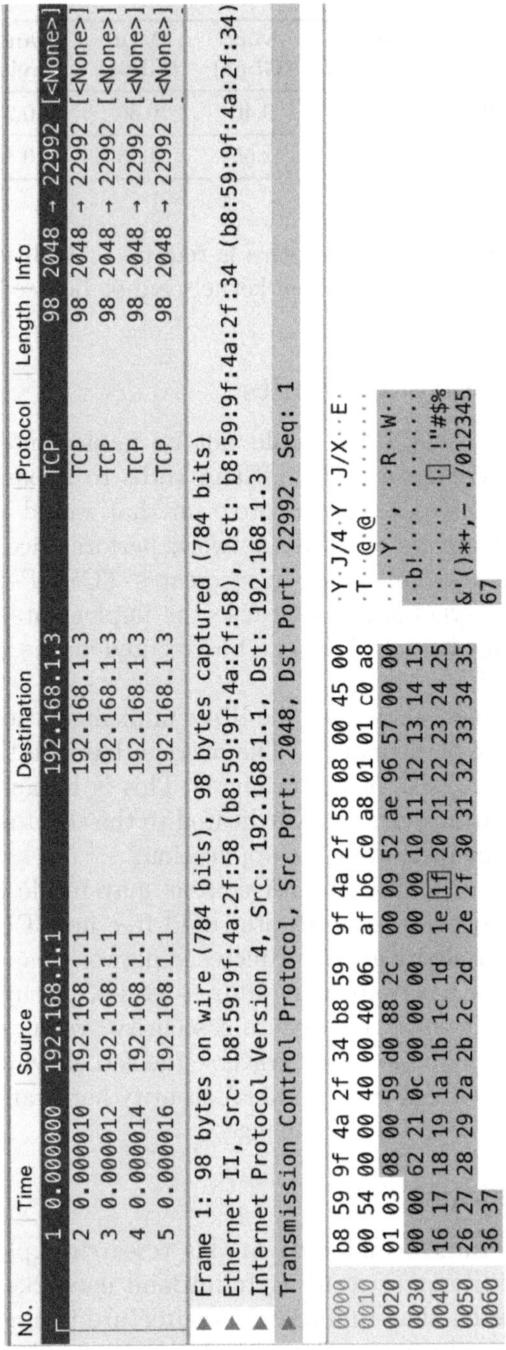

No.	Time	Source	Destination	Protocol	Length	Info
1	0.000000	192.168.1.1	192.168.1.3	TCP	98	2048 → 22992 [<None>]
2	0.000010	192.168.1.1	192.168.1.3	TCP	98	2048 → 22992 [<None>]
3	0.000012	192.168.1.1	192.168.1.3	TCP	98	2048 → 22992 [<None>]
4	0.000014	192.168.1.1	192.168.1.3	TCP	98	2048 → 22992 [<None>]
5	0.000016	192.168.1.1	192.168.1.3	TCP	98	2048 → 22992 [<None>]

▲ Frame 1: 98 bytes on wire (784 bits), 98 bytes captured (784 bits)
▲ Ethernet II, Src: b8:59:9f:4a:2f:58 (b8:59:9f:4a:2f:58), Dst: b8:59:9f:4a:2f:34 (b8:59:9f:4a:2f:34)
▲ Internet Protocol Version 4, Src: 192.168.1.1, Dst: 192.168.1.3
▲ Transmission Control Protocol, Src Port: 2048, Dst Port: 22992, Seq: 1

```
0000  b8 59 9f 4a 2f 34 b8 59  9f 4a 2f 58 08 00 45 00   ·Y·J/4·Y ·J/X··E·
0010  00 54 00 00 40 06 40 06  af b6 c0 a8 01 01 c0 a8   ·T··@·@· ·······
0020  01 03 08 00 59 d0 88 2c  00 09 52 ae 96 57 00 00   ····Y··, ··R··W·
0030  00 00 62 21 0c 00 00 00  00 10 11 12 13 14 15      ··b!···· ·······
0040  16 17 18 19 1a 1b 1c 1d  1e 20 21 22 23 24 25      ········ · !"#$%
0050  26 27 28 29 2a 2b 2c 2d  2e 2f 30 31 32 33 34 35   &'()*+,- ./012345
0060  36 37                                              67
```

Figure 5. Wireshark analysis of captured InfiniBand packets with IPsec.

Table 2. Case Study 3 results.

Test	Mean (Gbps)	Max (Gbps)	Min (Gbps)	Standard Deviation
IPerf without IPsec	8.636	9.40	6.30	0.247
IPerf with IPsec	2.359	2.65	1.93	0.112

solution that does not involve software is required. Additionally, many security systems implemented in the kernel cannot be used with Infini-Band programs.

5.3 Case Study 3 Results

After determining that IPsec could not be implemented on an InfiniBand program written with InfiniBand verbs to bypass the kernel, the next logical step was to find a program that would permit IPsec execution and evaluate its effect on network performance. Unlike the InfiniBand client/server program, Iperf creates TCP/IP packets and, thus, traverses the kernel stack. Because the implementation of IPsec takes place within the kernel, IPsec can be executed on the packets being transmitted by Iperf.

The results in Table 2 show that the IPsec implementation drastically reduced the network performance. The average bandwidth with IPsec implementation was 27.3% of the original. This is because significant resources and CPU utilization were dedicated to the cryptographic tasks associated with IPsec instead of the application.

A solution to combat CPU intensive tasks may reside in hardware. Offloading IPsec processes to hardware could free up CPU utilization, speed up encryption algorithms and increase network bandwidth. Additionally, the use of hardware may address issues encountered in the other case studies. In order to execute a security system on an InfiniBand network, the application must traverse the kernel, which eliminates the performance benefits of InfiniBand. A security hardware offload may be able to overcome both these challenges.

6. Conclusions

The three case studies conducted in this research explored the implications and limitations of securing InfiniBand networks. Schmitt et al. [11] have suggested that InfiniBand architecture is inherently resistant to tampering and attack. However, InfiniBand relies not only on its architecture for security, but also on application developers for security in the higher layers [8]. As a result, many InfiniBand applications are built on the same principles and assumptions as Ethernet networks. Therefore, it was worthwhile to explore the implications of using network security systems designed for Ethernet networks to secure InfiniBand networks.

Case Study 1 showed that InfiniBand traffic cannot be monitored or captured with traditional network analysis tools due to hardware packet generation that bypasses the kernel completely. Case Study 2 demonstrated the impact of bypassing the kernel, suggesting that any network security system implemented in software (specifically the operating system) would be ineffective when employed with an InfiniBand program that uses InfiniBand verbs. Case Study 3 revealed that using a network security system has a negative performance impact on InfiniBand.

The case studies demonstrate the need for network security systems that are targeted for InfiniBand. Specifically, a hardware device is required to monitor and capture InfiniBand traffic due to the nature of InfiniBand verbs. Traditional applications residing in a host kernel are unable to inspect InfiniBand traffic. Furthermore, the CPU utilization required by a host-based security system running in an InfiniBand network yields a significant performance penalty. The solution is to offload the security system to hardware to reduce CPU utilization and improve network performance. Conventional network security systems developed for Ethernet networks do not directly translate to InfiniBand networks. Indeed, InfiniBand networks require a new class of hardware-offloaded security systems.

The views expressed in this chapter are those of the authors, and do not reflect the official policy or position of the U.S. Air Force, U.S. Department of Defense or U.S. Government. This document has been approved for public release, distribution unlimited (Case #88ABW-2019-6098).

References

[1] J. Corbet, A. Rubini and G. Kroah-Hartman, *Linux Device Drivers*, O'Reilly Media, Sebastopol, California, 2005.

[2] InfiniBand Trade Association, InfiniBand Architecture Specification, Volume 1, Release 1.3, Beaverton, Oregon (`cw.infinibandta.org/document/dl/7859`), 2015.

[3] M. Lee and E. Kim, A comprehensive framework for enhancing security in the InfiniBand architecture, *IEEE Transactions on Parallel and Distributed Systems*, vol. 18(10), pp. 1393–1406, 2007.

[4] M. Lee, E. Kim and M. Yousif, Security enhancement in the InfiniBand architecture, *Proceedings of the Nineteenth IEEE International Parallel and Distributed Processing Symposium*, 2005.

[5] Mellanox Technologies, Introduction to InfiniBand, White Paper, Document No. 2003WP, Santa Clara, California (www.mellanox. com/pdf/whi tepapers/IB_Intro_WP_190.pdf), 2003.

[6] Mellanox Technologies, InfiniBand Software and Protocols Enable Seamless Off-the-Shelf Applications Deployment, White Paper, Sunnyvale, California (www.mellanox.com/pdf/whitepapers/WP_ 2007_IB_Software_and_Protocols.pdf), 2007.

[7] Mellanox Technologies, InfiniBand: The Production SDN, White Paper, Document No. 3987WP Rev. 1.0, Sunnyvale, California (www.mellanox.com/related-docs/whitepapers/WP_InfiniBan d_Production_SDN.pdf), 2012.

[8] Mellanox Technologies, Security in Mellanox Technology's InfiniBand Fabrics, Technical Overview, White Paper, Document No. 3861WP Rev. 1.0, Sunnyvale, California (www.mellanox. com/related-docs/whitepapers/WP_Secuirty_In_InfiniBand_ Fabrics_Final.pdf), 2012.

[9] Mellanox Technologies, RDMA Aware Networks Programming User Manual, Rev. 1.7, Sunnyvale, California (www.mellanox.com/ related-docs/prod_software/RDMA_Aware_Programming_user_ manual.pdf), 2015.

[10] G. Pfister, An introduction to the InfiniBand architecture, in *High Performance Mass Storage and Parallel I/O: Technologies and Applications*, R. Buyya and T. Cortes (Eds.), John Wiley and Sons, New York, pp. 617–632, 2001.

[11] D. Schmitt, S. Graham, P. Sweeney and R. Mills, Vulnerability assessment of InfiniBand networking, in *Critical Infrastructure Protection XIII*, J. Staggs and S. Shenoi (Eds.), Springer, Cham, Switzerland, pp. 179–205, 2019.

[12] K. Subedi, D. Dasgupta and B. Chen, Security analysis of InfiniBand protocol implementations, *Proceedings of the IEEE Symposium Series on Computational Intelligence*, 2016.

[13] TOP500, List Statistics, Sinsheim, Germany (top500.org/ statistics/list), 2019.

[14] U.S. Department of Homeland Security, Communications Sector-Specific Plan: An Annex to the NIPP 2013, Washington, DC (www. hsdl.org/?view&did=796518), 2015.

[15] A. Warren, InfiniBand Fabric and Userland Attacks, Information Security Reading Room, SANS Institute, North Bethesda, Maryland, 2012.

IV

INDUSTRIAL CONTROL
SYSTEMS SECURITY

Chapter 9

CYBER-RESILIENT SCADA SYSTEMS VIA SECURE STATE RESTORATION

Zachary Birnbaum, Matthew Davis, Salman Salman, James Cervini, Lanier Watkins, Saikiran Yamajala and Shruti Paul

Abstract   Supervisory control and data acquisition (SCADA) systems are widely used in the critical infrastructure. These systems are high risk targets for cyber attacks due to their criticality, interconnectedness and Internet accessibility. SCADA systems employ programmable logic controllers to monitor and issue control instructions to other devices. Unfortunately, programmable logic controllers are typically configured in a persistent manner – they are configured once and designed to operate continuously. They are, therefore, ill-suited to operate in virtual, dynamic and cyber-resilient environments. SCADA systems must employ cyber-resilient architectures to enable them to endure and recover from cyber attacks.

   This chapter describes a secure methodology for storing SCADA system states that can be used by redundant, non-persistent devices during operations and recovery. The proposed methodology realizes a non-persistent, Byzantine fault-tolerant, virtual industrial control system architecture whose state and function can be stored and restored securely, contributing to its cyber resilience. Implementation of the methodology in a SCADA environment incorporating non-persistent programmable logic controllers reveals that cyber attacks are identified quickly and secure restoration can occur without loss of state or functionality. Mathematical and timing analyses demonstrate the applicability and efficacy of the methodology in creating cyber-resilient SCADA systems.

Keywords: SCADA systems, non-persistence, fault tolerance, cyber resilience

1.   Introduction

Supervisory control and data acquisition (SCADA) systems are essential to monitoring and controlling industrial operations across the critical infrastructure. Unlike many enterprise computing systems, these com-

---

The original version of this chapter was revised: the name of the fourth author was changed. The correction to this chapter is available at https://doi.org/10.1007/978-3-030-62840-6_17

© IFIP International Federation for Information Processing 2020, corrected publication 2022
Published by Springer Nature Switzerland AG 2020
J. Staggs and S. Shenoi (Eds.): Critical Infrastructure Protection XIV, IFIP AICT 596, pp. 183–207, 2020.
https://doi.org/10.1007/978-3-030-62840-6_9

plex cyber-physical systems have tight real-time constraints due to their interactions with the physical world.

The critical and interconnected nature of SCADA systems makes them attractive targets for cyber attacks. The Stuxnet attacks [19] demonstrated the vulnerabilities of SCADA systems and the irreparable damage that can be caused. Stuxnet, a self-replicating computer virus, infected programmable logic controllers (PLCs) used in Iran's nuclear program, destroying more than 1,000 uranium enrichment centrifuges and significantly impacting Iranian nuclear ambitions.

Securing SCADA systems from cyber attacks is challenging. Classical defensive techniques such as encryption, firewalls, anomaly detection and patching are difficult to apply in SCADA environments. Something as simple as applying a system update, which occurs with regularity in enterprise environments, is challenging due to the high availability demands of SCADA systems. Additionally, many SCADA systems were designed and integrated years ago and, therefore, have limited computing, memory and networking resources that hinder the ability to implement modern security mechanisms.

Applying conventional cyber defense and attack prevention solutions such as encryption, authentication and anomaly detection to SCADA systems may not be enough to deter skilled and determined adversaries. Therefore, SCADA systems must rapidly recover their functionality after they are degraded or disrupted. Cyber resilience is the ability to continuously deliver the intended outcomes despite adverse cyber events – it goes beyond attack prevention by ensuring continuity of operations. A National Institute of Standards and Technology special publication [24] lists 14 resilience techniques, including diversity, unpredictability, non-persistence and redundancy.

Virtualization is a promising technology for implementing defensive and cyber resilience techniques in SCADA environments. Many vendors and integrators now offer virtual SCADA and industrial control system components. In fact, during new integrations and upgrades, older SCADA components are increasingly being replaced by their virtual counterparts. Due to the increased computing power, memory and network bandwidth, virtualization enables security techniques to be applied in SCADA environments. Unlike physical systems, virtual systems can be rebooted on demand. Rebooting a system, a simple cyber-resilient (and defensive) action that manifests non-persistence, is effective against certain types of malware [15].

Unfortunately, applying cyber resilience techniques in SCADA environments is challenging, primarily due to their real-time nature, high availability requirements and criticality. For example, when manifesting non-persistence via a system reboot, it is important to minimize the downtime. Applying non-persistence techniques to SCADA systems is also challenging; rapidly regaining positive control is vital, but positive control often requires knowledge of the current inputs as well as past inputs and outputs. The reliance on historical data directly conflicts with non-persistence. Other resilience techniques, such as redundancy and heterogeneity, are easily integrated in cyber-resilient solutions for SCADA systems without this concern.

Novel solutions must be developed to imbue cyber resilience in SCADA systems. This chapter describes a secure methodology for storing system states that can be used by redundant, non-persistent devices during operation and recovery. The methodology realizes a non-persistent, Byzantine fault-tolerant, virtual industrial control system architecture whose state and function can be stored and restored securely, contributing to its cyber resilience.

2. Background

This section briefly discusses important aspects of control theory, SCADA system virtualization and cyber resilience.

2.1 Control Theory

The primary objective of a SCADA system is to produce outputs (control commands to actuators) in the face of input disturbances [26]. Outputs are computed via feedforward or feedback mechanisms. Feedforward control reduces the effects of measured input disturbances by adjusting the control effort based on the input disturbances [21]. Feedback control measures the difference between the true and desired system states and uses the error to adjust the control effort [2]. This section considers feedback systems, but a similar treatment can be applied to feedforward systems.

Control systems are typically designed in the Laplace domain that transforms hard-to-solve continuous time-domain differential equations to their simple frequency domain equivalents [26]. The designed solutions are then converted to discrete time difference equations for implementation in modern controllers.

For example, a third-order continuous time-domain controller can be represented in the Laplace domain $\mathcal{L}$ as:

$$H(s) = \frac{a_2 s^2 + a_1 s + a_0}{b_3 s^3 + b_2 s^2 + b_1 s + b_0} \tag{1}$$

where a_i and b_i are constants, and s is a complex number frequency parameter.

Assuming a constant time step Δt and adjusting for causality, the equivalent representation in the discrete time domain $\mathcal{Z}$ is:

$$H(z) = \frac{\alpha_2 z^{-1} + \alpha_1 z^{-2} + \alpha_0 z^{-3}}{1 + \beta_2 z^{-1} + \beta_1 z^{-2} + \beta_0 z^{-3}} \qquad (2)$$

where α_i and β_i are constants, and z is the discrete complex time parameter.

The corresponding $\mathcal{Z}$ domain controller is represented by the following difference equation:

$$y(k) = -\beta_2 y(k-1) + -\beta_1 y(k-2) + -\beta_0 y(k-2) + \\ \alpha_2 x(k) + \alpha_1 x(k-1) + \alpha_0 x(k-2)$$

where α_i and β_i are constants, and $y(k)$ is the output at the discrete time step k.

This difference equation is easily implemented by a controller that transforms inputs to outputs consistent with the system design. Even in this fairly simple control system example, previous input and output states are key to computing the new output. The controller can then be integrated in a standalone physical control device or virtualized in a modern industrial control system architecture.

2.2   SCADA System Virtualization

The concept of a virtual SCADA environment is still novel and its utility is actively discussed in the industrial community. In a virtual SCADA system deployment, a single hypervisor typically contains multiple virtual programmable logic controller instances.

Johansson [18] discusses the benefits and disadvantages of SCADA system virtualization. The benefits include:

- **Number of Physical Devices:** Co-locating multiple virtual programmable logic controllers and human-machine interfaces reduces the physical footprints of SCADA systems.

- **Software Development and Disaster Recovery:** Virtual machine snapshots facilitate quick system rollbacks to saved copies after failures due to software errors, cyber attacks and catastrophes.

- **Security Architecture Testing:** Virtual security solutions are readily deployed in SCADA environments. Security can be integrated in hypervisors and standard host-based solutions can be incorporated directly in virtual programmable logic controllers.

- **System Updates:** Virtual systems are easier to update and patch compared with their physical counterparts. A patch can be tested and integrated in a virtual environment upon verification of functionality and the system can be rolled back to a saved image in the event of a failure.

The disadvantages of SCADA system virtualization include:

- **System Complexity:** Adding new technology to a system makes it more difficult to identify the origin of a system problem or failure.

- **Non-Standard Physical Interfaces:** Many SCADA environments use proprietary or outdated physical devices to interface with sensors and actuators. Interfacing these devices with commodity server equipment is challenging.

- **Cyber Attack Surface:** Hypervisors increase the attack surface. Successfully compromising a hypervisor may provide an attacker with root privileges to all the running virtual machines [4]. Developing cyber secure hypervisors with reduced attack surfaces is an active area of research [27].

The proposed methodology is designed for virtual SCADA systems. The benefits of virtualization outweigh the disadvantages, which can be mitigated by technical maturity and careful adoption [25]. Additionally, advancements have been made in virtual SCADA devices and testbeds [22, 23]. The application of virtualization to SCADA systems enhances cost savings and the ease of integration. This chapter demonstrates that SCADA system virtualization increases cyber resilience.

2.3 Cyber Resilience

Cyber resilience is a relatively new concept in the cyber security field. It involves several key characteristics [6]:

- **Inhibit:** While inhibit capabilities are technically not an official characteristic of cyber resilience, they prevent an adversary from having a cyber impact on a system. Traditional security techniques are often employed to enhance the overall cyber resilience.

- **Endure:** Endure capabilities enable a system to provide a minimum level of functionality when it is under cyber attack.

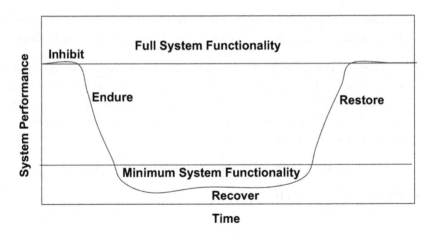

Figure 1.   Cyber resilience capabilities timeline.

- **Recover:** Recover capabilities enable actions to be undertaken to respond to degraded system performance.

- **Restore:** Restore capabilities help regain complete system functionality.

- **Improve:** Improve capabilities support enhanced cyber resilience design and implementation to mitigate anticipated threats.

Figure 1 shows the placement of the five cyber resilience characteristics in an operational timeline. Inhibit technologies keep a system fully functional. However, if a cyber effect is realized despite the defenses, endure capabilities ensure that the system can still provide minimum functionality. Recover capabilities ensure that, even if the system functionality falls below an acceptable threshold, adequate functionality will become available in an acceptable timeframe. Finally, restore capabilities ensure that the system will regain full functionality.

Cyber resilience capabilities are realized through the application of several techniques. Bodeau and Graubart [6] have identified the following cyber resilience techniques:

- **Applied Analytics and Monitoring:** This refers to the continual collection and analysis of system data to identify possible vulnerabilities, adversarial activities and negative system impacts.

- **Heterogeneity:** This refers to the utilization of diverse cyber technologies to minimize the impacts of attacks and force an adversary to attack different technologies with different vulnerabilities.

- **Distributed Allocation:** This refers to the positioning of critical assets to provide an unpredictable attack surface to an adversary.

- **Non-Persistence:** This refers to the retention of systems for a limited time, reducing the ability of an adversary to act maliciously and establish a persistent foothold. A persistent system is generally configured once and accessed only if troubleshooting or maintenance is required. A non-persistent system is designed to support repeated shutdown, destruction, re-creation and initialization.

- **Redundancy:** This refers to the presence of multiple protected instantiations of a system, forcing an adversary to achieve cyber effects on multiple targets simultaneously.

3. Related Work

Cardenas et al. [7] have provided an overview of the challenges involved in securing SCADA systems. Many challenges arise from the unique properties of SCADA systems compared with enterprise environments, namely their legacy nature and real-time operational constraints.

Melin et al. [20] have demonstrated that traditional cyber security techniques can be applied to SCADA systems, but the systems must be designed to be cyber resilient. Their work focuses on a framework and testing criteria for system resilience. A key finding is that resilience is greatly increased by eliminating the ability to remotely program individual programmable logic controllers. This is because an attacker is limited to adjusting only the system reference, which is easily detected.

Cox et al. [10] have demonstrated that heterogeneity provides cyber resilience. Their framework executes heterogeneous system variants with the same inputs and monitors their behavior to detect anomalies; this technique forces an attacker to compromise multiple system variants to achieve the desired effects. Gearheart et al. [14] have specified diversity metrics and have demonstrated that text-based features can effectively differentiate software diversity strategies implemented in open-source diversifying compilers.

Byzantine fault-tolerant systems, which employ a form of distributed allocation or redundancy, are also effective at enhancing cyber resilience. Considerable work has been done in this area, especially coupled with virtualization and other resilience enabling technologies.

Ahmed and Bhargava [1] have demonstrated that Byzantine fault avoidance can be implemented in cloud environments using OpenStack and software defined networking by allowing replicas to live for a short time on computing platforms (hypervisors, hardware and operating systems) as a form of moving target defense. They present a fault avoidance architecture that leverages cloud platform technologies, providing replica refresh algorithms to control the exposure of platforms to attacks, and a scheme that preserves state while undergoing failure avoidance.

A Byzantine architecture employs a set of replicas for failure avoidance. Within the replicas, a primary node exchanges consensus messages with a specific replica. The replica node then prepares a reply and commits the response. The node is selected from a pre-prepared virtual machine pool, which is refreshed after a set amount of time or after completing a specific number of transactions. The primary benefit is that the time advantage to a potential attacker is eliminated by not having a virtual machine operate indefinitely. By dynamically using a cloud software stack, Ahmed and Bhargava [1] were able to minimize the virtual machine attack exposure window and boot new virtual machines in under 12 seconds. Unfortunately, while the approach has its benefits, a 12-second recovery time is often unacceptable in real-time SCADA environments.

Babay et al. [3] have created an intrusion-tolerant SCADA system that is resilient to system-level compromises and network attacks. Their approach uses the Spines messaging framework, which provides automatic reconfiguration and network flexibility [12]. Core SCADA functionality is distributed across $3f + 2k + 1$ heterogeneously-compiled (multicompiler) replicas, where f is the number of simultaneous acceptable failures and k is the number of proactive recoveries (with no failures detected). The replicas themselves are distributed across multiple cloud servers. The SCADA system was employed in a power grid experiment, where it met all the power and latency requirements. However, Babay and colleagues do not address how programmable logic controller failures are detected and how the system state can be transitioned correctly to new environments.

Yamamoto et al. [29] have employed a customized intrusion detection solution and virtualization technologies to enable SCADA system recovery. Running multiple virtual programmable logic controllers simultaneously supports seamless transition from an anomalous virtual programmable logic controller to another virtual controller. Regions of acceptable behavior are defined to enable anomaly detection and trigger a transition to the backup virtual programmable logic controller. However, Yamamoto and colleagues do not address the inherent issues associated with homogeneity and cyber attacks – if the primary and backup systems are homogeneous (because they use the same baseline virtual image), an attack launched against the primary system would also impact the backup system. Additionally, Yamamoto et al. do not

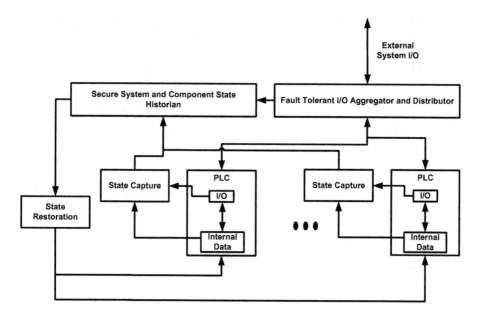

Figure 2. Proposed cyber-resilient architecture.

address state restoration directly; they simply assume it will be maintained by the failover system.

Cyber-resilience techniques have been developed for enterprise and SCADA system applications in standard and virtual environments. However, the proposed cyber resilience methodology is unique in that it focuses on SCADA system endurance and restoration in non-persistent, redundant virtual environments.

4. Proposed Methodology

This section describes the methodology for achieving cyber resilience in SCADA systems using state restoration.

4.1 Overview

Rapid and reliable state restoration are important requirements for cyber-resilient SCADA system architectures with non-persistence. Employing redundancy further increases cyber resilience. The proposed cyber resilience methodology involves state storage and restoration in a non-persistent, redundant SCADA environment.

Figure 2 shows the key features of the proposed cyber-resilient architecture. These include:

- **State Capture:** The system state is identified and captured without negatively impacting performance.

- **State Storage:** After the state has been captured, it is stored in a secure, immutable and decentralized manner.

- **State Recovery:** When a new, non-persistent SCADA device is added to the system, the state is pushed promptly to the new device to ensure continued operation.

- **I/O Aggregation and Distribution:** The inputs and outputs to and from the redundant, non-persistent SCADA components are processed securely.

- **Non-Persistence:** Non-persistent redundant programmable logic controllers and other devices are started, stopped and restarted with relatively little effort.

Implementing these features requires a complex and capable architecture. The proposed architecture enables continuity of normal operations due to component redundancy and ensures rapid state recovery of SCADA components when required. To simplify the presentation, but without any loss of generality, it is assumed that programmable logic controllers are the only SCADA devices that have non-persistent and redundant capabilities.

The new architecture functions as follows during normal operations:

1. Input is sent to the I/O aggregator and distributor via normal communications paths. Communications in a SCADA environment may use a point-to-point serial protocol, Ethernet or wireless.

2. The I/O distributor sends inputs to multiple programmable logic controllers for processing. Ideally, these programmable logic controllers would be heterogeneous, further enhancing cyber resilience.

3. After a programmable logic controller completes its scan and computes its output, the internal programmable logic controller data structures and memory are saved to a state storage database (blockchain) [28].

4. The I/O aggregator processes the output from each programmable logic controller using a Byzantine fault-tolerant algorithm to determine consensus [3].

5. The I/O aggregator stores the input data, consensus and associated metadata in the blockchain.

6. The resulting consensus state is converted to an output, which the I/O aggregator transmits to an actuator to implement a control action.

A state restoration procedure is executed when any of the following conditions hold:

- An intrusion or cyber attack is detected on a non-persistent programmable logic controller.

- A programmable logic controller does not agree with the output of the consensus voting scheme.

- A programmable logic controller is randomly selected to be restarted based on another factor (e.g., random sampling, time-alive or pre-determined schedule). In order to prevent an adversary from obtaining access to all the programmable logic controllers prior to launching an attack (which would not be detected by the fault-tolerant voting scheme), the virtual programmable logic controllers should be destroyed and restored at irregular, but operationally-small, time intervals to ensure non-persistence.

The state restoration procedure, which is executed on every programmable logic controller, has the following steps:

1. The virtual programmable logic controller is destroyed, a trivial task in a virtual environment.

2. A new programmable logic controller is initialized to a default state containing no internal data. Ideally. the new programmable logic controller should be heterogeneous compared with the previous version, limiting the likelihood that a previous cyber attack would be successful.

3. The last known good state of the system is identified using the state database and the corresponding programmable logic controller internal memory and data are pushed by the state restoration engine to the new programmable logic controller.

The remainder of this section describes how the system state is captured, determined, stored and restored in a secure manner.

4.2 Capturing State

Before capturing the complete SCADA system state, it is necessary to identify the locations where the data resides. Figure 3 shows the

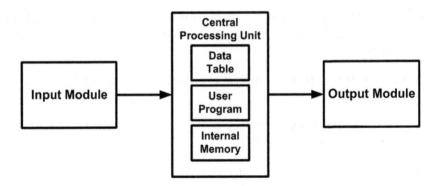

Figure 3. Programmable logic controller components.

components of a standard programmable logic controller. In order to capture the system state, it is necessary to collect input data, output data and data residing in internal memory structures.

Since modern SCADA systems employ enterprise components for communications [16], the costs of capturing input and output information are minimal. If standard Ethernet is used, a physical network tap or modified switch can be used to monitor data going to and from devices. If the device is virtual, equivalent software solutions are available to capture network data. Regardless of the approach used, it is important that state capture does not negatively impact SCADA system operations.

The process for capturing internal programmable logic controller data varies according to the vendor hardware. For example, if the Modbus communications protocol is used and internal data is mapped to holding registers, it is straightforward to request internal programmable logic controller data over a network connection [9].

Programmable logic controllers have very predictable scan cycles, with each cycle taking several milliseconds. Each scan cycle has input, program and output stages [28]:

- **Input Stage:** Input is read by the programmable logic controller CPU from the input modules.

- **Program Stage:** Input and current internal data and memory structures are modified as necessary.

- **Output Stage:** Required changes to the output modules are made.

The state capture must operate after every scan cycle without degrading system performance.

4.3   Determining State

After the I/O and internal state of each device have been captured, the overall system state is computed for each device and anomalous states and devices are identified. The Byzantine fault tolerance algorithm of Castro and Liskov [8] with $3f + 1$ replicas is employed to determine consensus (f is the maximum number of possible faulty nodes).

The following procedure computes the consensus state and identifies anomalous devices for destruction and restoration:

1. Collect the output information state from $3f + 1$ devices.

2. Determine the consensus state as the state common to at least $f + 1$ devices.

3. Identify the non-consensus devices for restoration.

4. Save the consensus state in the blockchain.

4.4   Storing State

After the system state has been determined via secure means, it must be stored in a secure manner. Specifically, it is necessary to ensure that the stored system state can be recovered at any future point in time with the assurance that it was not modified.

A blockchain can be used to ensure non-repudiation and immutability [11]. Each iteration involving state capture, consensus determination and metadata addition results in a data block. Decentralized operation prevents an attacker from modifying the shared history from a single location, which enhances security. Different blockchains are used for the I/O aggregator and distributor, and for each programmable logic controller. If the programmable logic controllers are heterogeneous, then a separate blockchain must be maintained for each programmable logic controller. If the programmable logic controllers are homogeneous, then all the internal data structures and memory are identical, and a single blockchain may be used.

Each I/O aggregator data block contains the following information: (i) input value; (ii) consensus state; (iii) time; (iv) iteration number; (v) hash value of the previous block; (vi) hash value of all the current block data; (vii) programming logic controllers that agree with the consensus; and (viii) programming logic controllers that disagree with the consensus (i.e., devices that have to undergo state restoration).

Each programmable logic controller data block contains the following information: (i) input value; (ii) output value; (iii) internal data and memory; (iv) time; (v) iteration number; (vi) hash value of the previous block; and (vii) hash value of all the current block data.

After the block information has been computed, the block is appended to the corresponding blockchain that contains all the preceding blocks. At this point, the system state is securely stored in an immutable manner and is ready to be restored when required.

4.5   Restoring State

After each data block is appended to the I/O aggregator chain, the virtual programmable logic controllers that were identified as having disagreed with the consensus are destroyed. Such destruction is a routine and timely procedure in virtual environments.

A new virtual programmable logic controller is then initialized. However, before it can process any input, the blank internal structures are updated with historical consensus data. Note that the restored state is independent of the specific programmable logic controller instance; instead, it represents the consensus of all the participating programmable logic controllers.

The following steps are involved in initializing a new programmable logic controller:

1. Identify the last several consensus states required for successful programmable logic operation.

2. For each identified state, select a random programmable logic controller with an output equal to the consensus state.

3. For each identified state, pull the appropriate internal information from the blockchain of the selected programmable logic controller and save the information in the internal data structures of the new programmable logic controller.

These steps assume that the programmable logic controllers are homogenous. Depending on the programmable logic controller vendor, virtualization technology and other factors, writing to the internal programmable logic controller structures has a varying degree of difficulty. If the Modbus protocol is used, it is possible to write directly to the programmable logic controller data structures via normal communications protocols; this task can be more challenging for other programmable logic controllers.

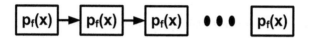

Figure 4. Iteration flow of the architectures.

5. Experimental Verification

The experimental verification involved two types of analyses. The first was a mathematical analysis to verify that the proposed methodology increases cyber resilience. The second involved a timing analysis to determine the overhead induced by the architecture.

5.1 Mathematical Analysis

Three SCADA system architectures were analyzed to assess the efficacy of the proposed methodology:

- Single standard programmable logic controller without redundancy and state restoration.

- Byzantine fault-tolerant architecture without state restoration.

- Byzantine fault-tolerant architecture with state restoration.

Each architecture was analyzed as a process over time to determine when a failure threshold of $p_t(x)$ was reached. Each iteration of the architecture assessed the ability to produce a correct output while assuming a constant failure probability of $p_f(x)$. Assuming that the probability of architecture failure $p_f(x)$ was greater than zero meant that, at some point in time t or after a certain number of iterations, the overall process failure probability would be greater than the failure threshold $p_t(x)$.

Figure 4 shows the iteration flow of the architectures. As an architecture becomes more resilient, the probability of an iteration being successful increases, which increases the expected longevity of the architecture. The overall process can be analyzed using the following equation:

$$p_t(x) < 1 - (1 - p_f(x))^i \tag{3}$$

where i is the number of expected iterations until system failure.

In the case of the Byzantine architectures, at least $f + 1$ of the $3f + 1$ individual programmable logic controller operations had to succeed in order for an overall iteration to be successful. Therefore, the following

Table 1.   Expected iterations to failure for various architectures ($p_t(x) = 0.99$).

Architecture	Failure Probability	Redundant PLCs	Expected Iterations to Failure
Single PLC	0.1	0	44
Single PLC	0.2	0	21
Single PLC	0.4	0	10
Byzantine	0.1	1	1,243
Byzantine	0.2	1	167
Byzantine	0.4	1	24
Byzantine	0.1	3	504,862
Byzantine	0.2	3	5,326
Byzantine	0.4	3	82
Byzantine	0.1	5	170,381,911
Byzantine	0.2	5	141,198
Byzantine	0.4	5	239

modified computation of $p_f(x)$ was performed:

$$p(\text{at least } m \text{ out of } n) = \sum_{i=m}^{n} \binom{n}{i} p^i (1-p)^{n-i} \qquad (4)$$

where f is the number of tolerable failures, $m = f + 1$, $n = 3f + 1$, $p = 1 - p_f(x)$ and i is the number of expected iterations until system failure.

Two variables were analyzed while also varying the architectures: (i) probability of architecture failure $p_f(x)$ during a single iteration; and (ii) number of redundant programmable logic controllers in a Byzantine fault-tolerant architecture.

Table 1 shows the results. As the probability of an individual iteration failure increased, the expected system longevity decreased. Furthermore, the Byzantine architectures without state restoration were more resilient than the single programmable logic controller architectures without redundancy and state restoration.

It is important to note that the expected iterations until failure for the Byzantine architectures with state restoration could not be computed. This is because every programmable logic controller failure was corrected after an interaction and the architecture was restored to the correct state before it received any subsequent inputs. Therefore, each iteration was effectively independent and the overall probability of system failure as inputs were processed was never greater than $p_f(x)$ regardless of the number of iterations or system uptime. Additionally, the overall system probability was less than $p_t(x)$.

However, the increased resilience using state restoration did not come without a cost. Additional computing resources and time were required to successfully identify and restore the anomalous programmable logic controllers.

5.2 Timing Analysis

A timing analysis of the architectures was conducted to assess the impact of the cyber resilience methodology. Three components were instantiated using Python programs: (i) programmable logic controllers; (ii) fault-tolerant I/O aggregator and distributor; and (iii) secure system and component state historian. The individual components communicated using the Flask micro web framework [17].

The environment did not adhere strictly to real-world SCADA system and programming logic controller restrictions, but it did incorporate the same building blocks used in real systems. The simulated programmable logic controllers processed difference equations much like their real-world counterparts. The other virtual components had no readily-available industry equivalents, so simulated Python representations were utilized.

Architecture Complexity. The complexity of the architecture was assessed using three variables:

- **Programming Logic Controller Complexity:** The length of the difference equation used by a programmable logic controller was used as a pseudo-approximation of its complexity.

- **System Redundancy:** The number of tolerable programmable logic controllers in a Byzantine fault-tolerant system was used to approximate system redundancy.

- **Blockchain State Storage Enabled:** A Boolean value indicated if the states of a programmable logic controller and I/O aggregator and distributor were committed to a blockchain.

The first timing analysis experiment examined the timing impacts of the programmable logic controller complexity variable. The other two variables were held constant. Table 2 shows the results – as the programmable logic controller complexity increased, so did the expected execution time.

The second timing analysis experiment assumed a Byzantine fault-tolerant architecture with a variable number of tolerable failed programmable logic controllers. All the other variables were held constant.

Table 2.   Execution times of a single programmable logic controller.

PLC Coefficients	Execution Time (seconds)
1	0.011806
10	0.012572
100	0.013346
1,000	0.022429

The number of coefficients (i.e., programmable logic controller complexity) was set to 100 and blockchain state storage was not employed.

Table 3.   Execution times of the I/O aggregator and distributor.

Tolerable PLC Failures	Execution Time (seconds)
0	0.020581
1	0.040104
2	0.061726
4	0.105565
8	0.186051

Table 3 shows that, as the number of nodes required for the Byzantine fault-tolerant system increased, so did the time required to process a single input. Also, a Byzantine fault-tolerant system with zero tolerable failures had an overhead of 54.2% compared with a single programmable logic controller of equal complexity.

The third timing analysis experiment examined the impact of state restoration. The single programmable logic controller and Byzantine fault-tolerant architectures were assessed with and without state saving after every scan cycle. In the experiment, the number of programmable logic controller coefficients was fixed at 100 and the number of tolerable failures was set to zero.

Table 4 shows that committing the system state to the blockchain after every iteration caused significant overhead. The overhead for a single programmable logic controller was 44.2% whereas the overhead was 88.8% for the Byzantine architecture. The increased overhead of the Byzantine architecture was caused by two commits to the blockchain, once for the programmable logic controller in the architecture and once after consensus was reached.

Table 4. Execution times of the secure state storage.

Experiment	Secure Storage (Blockchain) Used	Execution Time (seconds)
PLC	No	0.009254
PLC	Yes	0.013346
Byzantine	No	0.020581
Byzantine	Yes	0.038867

Restoration Analysis. The previous experiments assessed the architectural complexity, not resilience in the face of failures. This section discusses the experiments conducted to assess the timing impacts of restoration where the Byzantine fault-tolerant and state capture systems were enabled. When simulating an attack against a single programmable logic controller, it was assumed that the attack probability was constant and that each programmable logic controller iteration was equally likely to be attacked. Since the goal was not to determine when an architecture would fail, but to assess the timing impacts, it was assumed that only a maximum of f programmable logic controllers could fail where f is the number of tolerable programmable logic controller failures. Because at most only f programmable logic controllers failed, every architecture always returned the correct result.

Each architecture in the experiments had a predetermined probability of failure that was propagated to the programmable logic controllers. To determine if a programmable logic controller failed during each iteration, f programmable logic controllers generated a random value between zero and one. If the value was less than the probability of failure, the (anomalous) programmable logic controller yielded an incorrect result, forwarding the wrong answer to the I/O aggregator. After each iteration, the anomalous programmable logic controllers were restored.

Table 5 shows the results obtained when the number of tolerable programmable logic controller failures was varied while keeping the probability of a single failure constant at 40%. As expected, the greater the number of redundant devices, the greater the expected execution time. This was due to the increased number of queries that the I/O aggregator had to issue in order to achieve consensus and the increased number of commits to the blockchain.

Table 6 shows the results obtained when the probability of f programmable logic controllers failing was varied while holding all the other variables constant. The number of tolerable programmable logic controller failures was set to four and the number of programmable logic

Table 5.   Execution times of the I/O aggregator and distributor with secure storage.

Tolerable PLC Failures	Execution Time (seconds)
1	0.076437
2	0.100038
4	0.165552
8	0.297060

Table 6.   Execution times of the I/O aggregator and distributor with secure storage.

PLC Failure Rate	Execution Time (seconds)
0	0.151104
0.05	0.152491
0.1	0.153756
0.2	0.156992
0.4	0.165552
0.8	0.190867
1	0.194210

controller coefficients was 100. The table reveals that the expected execution time increased with the probability of failure, but the failure rate did not incur as much overhead as the other variables. These results indicate that the timing cost to restore a programmable logic controller was fairly low. Comparing the results for the architecture with 0% failure probability to the one with 100% failure probability reveals that restoring all f programmable logic controllers required only 28.5% overhead.

5.3   Summary

The mathematical analysis demonstrated that incorporating two redundant programmable logic controllers in a Byzantine fault-tolerant scheme along with state storage and restoration capabilities rendered each system iteration independent. This is important because programmable logic controllers use difference equations, so past computations are important for present and future computations. A key benefit of the cyber resilience methodology is that past failures cannot propagate to future operations.

The timing analysis demonstrated that implementing redundancy and blockchain state storage increased overhead. However, the overhead involved in restoring state to failed programmable logic controllers was comparatively fast.

6.   Discussion

This section discusses the strengths and limitations of the proposed cyber resilience methodology.

6.1   Strengths

The primary strength of the methodology is that it realizes a cyber-resilient SCADA architecture that can mitigate the negative effects of a number of common cyber attacks. Due to non-persistence, redundancy and state restoration, an attack against a single programmable logic controller would not cause irreparable damage. The methodology supports the endurance and recovery phases of cyber resilience. Moreover, the architecture is simple to implement and could easily be retrofitted to existing SCADA systems. Additionally, the use of blockchain technology and fault-tolerant consensus ensures that the system state is computed and stored in a secure manner, which enhances cyber resilience.

Experimental evaluations of the methodology suggest that the implementation impact is fairly minimal given virtualization and modern computing resources, provided that the infrastructure exists in the SCADA environment. Most deployed industrial control systems have outdated physical hardware. As new systems are designed and integrated, transitions to modern virtual environments are likely to occur due to their reduced physical footprints, ease of upgrade and service co-location compared with physical environments. Thus, the proposed cyber resilience methodology is expected to see increased applications in future SCADA environments.

6.2   Limitations

The proposed methodology eliminates the reliance on single programmable logic controllers to enhance cyber resilience, but this increases the cyber attack surface. Instead of targeting a programmable logic controller, an attacker could target the consensus algorithm, blockchain and virtual programmable logic controller destruction and restoration procedures. Therefore, it is vital that all the additional components in a cyber-resilient SCADA architecture incorporate cyber security best practices to the extent possible. Certain improvements can be made to mitigate the increased cyber attack surface. For example, the blockchain could be distributed and made non-persistent, ensuring that it could be restored from a distributed replica if it was attacked.

Creating virtual programmable logic controllers and other SCADA devices is by no means easy. Not all SCADA devices can be virtualized at this time and additional research is required. The proposed methodology was implemented and tested using standard enterprise equipment (i.e., laptops running Python code); the experiments did not engage industry-grade physical or virtual programmable logic controllers, let alone an industrial control system testbed. Further research is needed to evaluate the methodology in realistic SCADA environments. State restoration for virtual programmable logic controllers would vary greatly from vendor to vendor. Additional research is required to evaluate data writing to industry-grade programmable logic controllers.

While the experimental results indicate that the overhead of implementing cyber resilience is modest, a realistic SCADA testbed implementation may exhibit increased latency. SCADA environments have rigid time constraints, so the methodology would have to scale to large real-world systems. Also, limited computing resources in industrial SCADA environments would require additional computing equipment to be installed for virtualization. The utilization of Byzantine fault tolerance, which is known for its overhead in terms of communications bandwidth and number of replicas, would exacerbate the implementation challenges in real SCADA environments.

The proposed methodology focuses on a small subset of cyber resilience techniques and improves some characteristics. Moreover, non-persistence introduces new risks. For example, a device that has been repeatedly re-initialized could fail permanently; this risk could be mitigated by having redundant non-persistent devices. Additionally, if virtualization is utilized, the hypervisor should assume the role of monitoring and verifying the successful initialization of non-redundant devices. Layering additional techniques such as distributed allocation and heterogeneity would increase the overall effectiveness. For example, instead of using homogeneous programmable logic controllers, heterogeneous equivalents could be used that would further limit the likelihood of successful cyber attacks. Future research will explore the integration of these and other novel techniques in the cyber resilience methodology.

7. Conclusions

Cyber-resilient systems are becoming increasingly important in the current threat environment. Several resilience techniques are available that can provide useful capabilities in SCADA environments. However, some techniques, such as non-persistence, are challenging to implement given the tight real-time constraints imposed on SCADA systems. The proposed methodology addresses this challenge by securely storing SCADA system state for use by redundant, non-persistent devices during operation and recovery. The methodology realizes a non-persistent, Byzantine fault-tolerant, virtual industrial control system architecture whose state and function can be stored and restored securely, contributing to its cyber resilience. Implementation of the methodology in a SCADA environment incorporating non-persistent programmable logic controllers reveals that cyber attacks can be identified quickly and secure restoration can occur without loss of state or functionality. The mathematical and timing analyses demonstrate the applicability and efficacy of the methodology in creating cyber-resilient SCADA systems.

Future research will focus on integrating additional resilience techniques such as heterogeneity. Successful application of resilience techniques is vital to mitigating threats to SCADA systems and the critical infrastructure assets they operate.

References

[1] N. Ahmed and B. Bhargava, From Byzantine fault-tolerance to fault-avoidance: An architectural transformation to attack and failure resiliency, to appear in *IEEE Transactions on Cloud Computing*.

[2] K. Astrom and R. Murray, *Feedback Systems: An Introduction for Scientists and Engineers*, Princeton University Press, Princeton, New Jersey, 2008.

[3] A. Babay, J. Schultz, T. Tantillo and Y. Amir, Toward an intrusion-tolerant power grid: Challenges and opportunities, *Proceedings of the Thirty-Eighth IEEE International Conference on Distributed Computing Systems*, pp. 1321–1326, 2018.

[4] J. Barrowclough and R. Asif, Securing cloud hypervisors: A survey of the threats, vulnerabilities and countermeasures, *Security and Communication Networks*, article no. 1681908, 2018.

[5] F. Bjorck, M. Henkel, J. Stirna and J. Zdravkovic, Cyber resilience – Fundamentals for a definition, in *New Contributions in Information Systems and Technologies, Volume 1*, A. Rocha, A. Correia, S. Costanzo and L. Reis (Eds.), Springer, Cham, Switzerland, pp. 311–316, 2015.

[6] D. Bodeau and R. Graubart, Cyber Resiliency Engineering Framework, MITRE Technical Report MTR 110237, MITRE Corporation, Bedford, Massachusetts, 2011.

[7] A. Cardenas, S. Amin, B. Sinopoli, A. Giani, A. Perrig and S. Sastry, Challenges for securing cyber-physical systems, presented at the *Workshop on Future Directions in Cyber-Physical Systems Security*, 2009.

[8] M. Castro and B. Liskov, Practical Byzantine fault tolerance, *Proceedings of the Third Symposium on Operating Systems Design and Implementation*, pp. 173–186, 1999.

[9] Control Solutions Minnesota, Modbus 101 – Introduction to Modbus, St. Paul, Minnesota (`www.csimn.com/CSI_pages/Modbus101.html`), 2020.

[10] B. Cox, D. Evans, A. Filipi, J. Rowanhill, W. Hu, J. Davidson, J. Knight, A. Nguyen-Tuong and J. Hiser, N-variant systems: A secretless framework for security through diversity, *Proceedings of the Fifteenth USENIX Security Symposium*, article no. 9, 2006.

[11] M. Crosby, Nachiappan, P. Pattanayak, S. Verma and V. Kalyanaraman, Blockchain technology: Beyond Bitcoin, *Applied Innovation Review*, vol. 2016(2), pp. 6–10, 2016.

[12] Distributed Systems and Networks Laboratory, Spines, Department of Computer Science, Johns Hopkins University, Baltimore, Maryland (`www.spines.org`), 2020.

[13] G. Engel and M. Mumcouglu, Method for Detecting Anomaly Action within a Computer Network, U.S. Patent No. 0165207 A1, June 12, 2014.

[14] A. Gearhart, P. Hamilton and J. Coffman, An analysis of automated software diversity using unstructured text analytics, *Proceedings of the Forty-Eighth Annual IEEE/IFIP International Conference on Dependable Systems and Networks Workshops*, pp. 79–80, 2018.

[15] D. Goodin, FBI tells router users to reboot now to kill malware infecting 500K devices, *Ars Technica*, May 25, 2018.

[16] K. Gordon, M. Davis, Z. Birnbaum and A. Dolgikh, ACE: Advanced CIP evaluator, *Proceedings of the Workshop on Cyber-Physical Systems Security and Privacy*, pp. 90–101, 2018.

[17] M. Grinberg, *Flask Web Development: Developing Web Applications with Python*, O'Reilly Media, Sebastopol, California, 2018.

[18] E. Johansson, Virtualization in control systems: Possibilities and challenges, presented at the *SANS European Community SCADA and Process Control Summit*, 2009.

[19] D. Kushner, The real story of Stuxnet, *IEEE Spectrum*, vol. 50(3), pp. 48–53, 2013.

[20] A. Melin, E. Ferragut, J. Laska, D. Fugate and R. Kisner, A mathematical framework for the analysis of cyber-resilient control systems, *Proceedings of the Sixth International Symposium on Resilient Control Systems*, pp. 13–18, 2013.

[21] P. Nachtwey, Feed forwards augment PID control, *Control Engineering*, vol. 52, pp. 42–45, March 31, 2015.

[22] T. Rodrigues Alves, M. Buratto, F. de Souza and T. Rodrigues, OpenPLC: An open-source alternative to automation, *Proceedings of the IEEE Global Humanitarian Technology Conference*, pp. 585–589, 2014.

[23] T. Rodrigues Alves, R. Das and T. Morris, Virtualization of industrial control system testbeds for cyber security, *Proceedings of the Second Annual Industrial Control System Security Workshop*, pp. 10–14, 2016.

[24] R. Ross, M. McEvilley and J. Oren, Systems Security Engineering: Considerations for a Multidisciplinary Approach in the Engineering of Trustworthy Secure Systems, NIST Special Publication 800-160, Volume 1, National Institute of Standards and Technology, Gaithersburg, Maryland, 2016.

[25] J. Sahoo, S. Mohapatra and R. Lath, Virtualization: A survey of concepts, taxonomy and associated security issues, *Proceedings of the Second International Conference on Computer and Network Technology*, pp. 222–226, 2010.

[26] V. Skormin, *Introduction to Automatic Control, Volume I*, Linus Publications, Ronkonkoma, New York, 2009.

[27] J. Szefer, E. Keller, R. Lee and J. Rexford, Eliminating the hypervisor attack surface for a more secure cloud, *Proceedings of the Eighteenth ACM Conference on Computer and Communications Security*, pp. 401–412, 2011.

[28] Technology Transfer Services, The Basics of PLC Operation, *Technology Transfer Blog*, Tampa, Florida (`www.techtransfer.com/blog/basics-plc-operation`), September 9, 2014.

[29] S. Yamamoto, T. Hamaguchi, S. Jing, I. Koshijima and Y. Hashimoto, A hot-backup system for backup and restore of ICS to recover from cyber attacks, in *Advances in Human Factors, Software and Systems Engineering*, B. Amaba (Ed.), Springer, Cham, Switzerland, pp. 45–53, 2016.

Chapter 10

VULNERABILITY ASSESSMENTS OF BUILDING MANAGEMENT SYSTEMS

Raymond Chan, Forest Tan, Ulric Teo and Brandon Kow

Abstract   A building management system enables the remote monitoring and control of the infrastructure within a smart building. The elevator system, power meters, and gas and water supply systems can be monitored and administered by a building management system. A building management system is essentially an industrial control system that directly impacts the quality of life of the occupants of a building. As in the case of industrial control systems, building management systems are vulnerable to cyber attacks. Therefore, it is important to assess their vulnerabilities and understand the risks and impacts of cyber attacks. This chapter describes vulnerability assessments of two important components of a smart building management system, the building energy metering system and smart lighting system.

Keywords: Building management systems, cyber security, vulnerability assessments

1.   Introduction

Smart cities have become a popular trend around the world. The concept incorporates industrial control networks, Internet of Things devices and other advanced computing technologies to conveniently monitor, control, administer and analyze physical assets and environments. An example is a smart building with an advanced automation system that manages the power control system, water and gas supply systems, elevator system and fire alarm system, all of which are critical to safe, secure and efficient operations of the building infrastructure.

The integration of cyber components in the physical infrastructure of a smart building means that cyber vulnerabilities may be targeted maliciously or accidentally to disrupt vital building operations, potentially impacting the comfort and well-being, even the lives of the occupants.

© IFIP International Federation for Information Processing 2020
Published by Springer Nature Switzerland AG 2020
J. Staggs and S. Shenoi (Eds.): Critical Infrastructure Protection XIV, IFIP AICT 596, pp. 209–220, 2020.
https://doi.org/10.1007/978-3-030-62840-6_10

Therefore, it is important to assess the vulnerabilities of building management systems and understand the risks and impacts of cyber attacks. This chapter describes vulnerability assessments of two important components of a smart building management system, the building energy metering system and smart lighting system.

2.   Related Work

Khatoun and Zeadally [5] have discussed security and privacy concerns pertaining to smart cities and have proposed several countermeasures. AlDairi and Tawalbeh [1] have provided an overview of the major security problems and influencing factors related to smart cities. They note that the emergent integration of technologies in a smart city leads to an unbounded attack surface.

Baig et al. [2] have discussed the cyber security and digital forensic challenges with regard to smart cities, and smart buildings in particular. They note that building automation system protocols are inherently insecure due to the trust given to sensors and controllers. Building automation systems must be protected to the maximal extent and it is important to implement digital forensic readiness to investigate malicious acts as well as accidents.

Wang et al. [9] have specified a threat model for a smart city infrastructure and have proposed assessment and mitigation approaches. Mundt and Wickboldt [7] have conducted security analyses of building automation systems and have identified potential attacks. Paridari et al. [8] have proposed a cyber-physical security framework for a building energy management system and a security information analytics algorithm for resilient recovery after attacks. Chan and Chow [4] have conducted a threat analysis of an elevator control system, which demonstrates the possibility of attacks on key building management subsystems. They also proposed a methodology for conducting a forensic analysis of a programmable logic controller of the type used in building automation [3].

Minoli et al. [6] have reviewed the technical challenges posed by integrating Internet of Things devices in smart buildings, and note that the fragmented nature of the industry acerbates the security challenges. Wang et al. [10] have proposed an approach for securing a microkernel-based controller, which is commonly used in building automation systems.

A review of the literature reveals that no studies have been conducted that assess the vulnerabilities of a real smart building management system and how it could be attacked. This chapter addresses the gap by

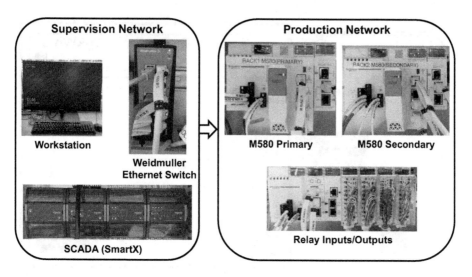

Figure 1. Building energy metering system.

describing the results of vulnerability assessments of two important components of a smart building management system, the building energy metering system and smart lighting system. Experimental cyber attacks conducted on the building energy metering and smart lighting systems, and their impacts are discussed.

3. Building Energy Metering System

This section describes a vulnerability assessment of a building energy metering system. The system is located in the Advanced Cyber Security Laboratory at Singapore Institute of Technology. The assessment focused on the Modicon M580 programmable logic controller and the Unity Pro XLS that programs the Modicon 580 device and industrial control system. Penetration tests were performed on the Modicon M580 programmable logic controller to assess its vulnerabilities.

3.1 System Components

Figure 1 shows the network architecture of the building energy metering system. The supervision network incorporates a SmartX supervisory control and data acquisition (SCADA) system, supervisory workstation that enables an operator to manage the system and Ethernet switch. The production network incorporates Modicon M580 primary and secondary programmable logic controllers and relay input/output drops that facil-

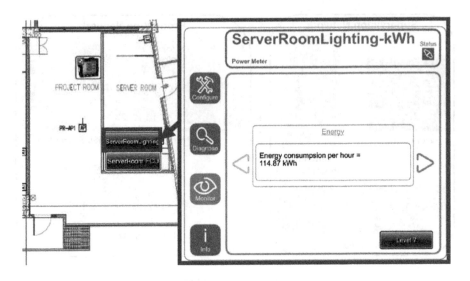

Figure 2. Server room lighting status.

itate communications between the programmable logic controllers and physical energy metering components (sensors and actuators).

The SmartX supervisory control and data acquisition system is a key component of the supervision network. The SmartX AS-P server supports important functionality such as logic control, trend logging, alarm supervision, communications support and connectivity to the input/output and field buses via the EcoStruxure software. The intelligent EcoStruxure software supports fault tolerance and provides a full-featured operator interface via the workstation and web stations.

Floor plans were created to observe the status of the electric power meters in various rooms in the building. An operator can check the status of fans, lights and other electrical appliances in each room and perform supervisory control in the building. Figure 2 shows the floor plan of the server room.

A Modicon M580 hot standby system serves as the programmable logic controller in the building energy metering system. The system is designed to eliminate downtime by incorporating primary and secondary (backup) programmable logic controllers. The two programmable logic controllers have identical hardware, software and configurations.

The primary M580 programmable logic controller communicates with sensors and actuators via the relay input/output drops. The primary M580 updates the standby M580 at the start of every scan and checks the health of the relay input/output Ethernet network links and the hot standby connection between the primary and backup CPUs. The standby M580 checks the health of the primary M580 and identifies the modules in the primary and standby racks, the applications running in the primary and standby M580 controllers, firmware versions executing in the primary and standby CPUs, and the health of the links between the primary and standby CPUs. The standby M580 controller takes control within one scan if the primary M580 controller stops prematurely or breaks down.

3.2 Vulnerability Assessment

Several penetration testing experiments were conducted on the M580 programmable logic controller system.

The first step in the penetration tests was to identify the IP addresses of the M580 programmable logic controllers. Various methods were used to perform the device scans; the most effective ones involved the use of Nmap and PLCSCAN.

The Nmap scan detected two IP addresses: `192.168.10.1` corresponding to the primary M580 and `192.168.10.2` corresponding to the standby M580. The scan also identified the open HTTP and FTP ports on the programmable logic controllers that could be exploited by an attacker.

Unlike an Nmap scan, which identifies open ports on devices in a computer network, PLCSCAN identifies industrial control system ports such as port 102 (Siemens programming logic controller) and port 502 (Modbus protocol). PLCSCAN was used to detect the M580 programmable logic controllers. A range of IP addresses was entered on a Raspberry Pi 3B+ installed with Kali Linux that executed the PLCSCAN software; this resulted in the discovery of the Modbus port 502. PLSCAN was also able to extract information about the programmable logic controller module and the firmware version.

The Simple Network Management Protocol (SNMP) is a standard Internet protocol that is used to collect and organize data about managed devices in IP networks, and to change the data to modify device behavior. After obtaining the host IP address, it was possible to obtain the default network name of the remote SNMP server. This enables an attacker to acquire information about the remote server and even change its configuration.

After obtaining the IP addresses of the programmable logic controllers, Nmap and PLCSCAN were used to gather information about the network configurations of the programmable logic controllers, network route configurations, and TCP and UDP listening ports.

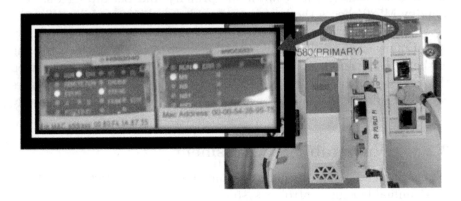

Figure 3.   M580 programmable logic controller after the denial-of-service attack.

Denial-of-service attacks were performed on the M580 programmable logic controllers. Function codes were exploited to send "kill switch" messages to the controllers. Figure 3 shows the result of the attack – the M580 programmable logic controller was disabled and all connectivity and communications with it were terminated.

3.3   Smart Lighting System

This section describes the vulnerability assessment of a smart lighting system. The system is located in the Advanced Cyber Security Laboratory at Singapore Institute of Technology.

The smart lighting system models a common smart office lighting setup. It incorporates 15 lights and seven multi-function sensors organized in a wireless local area network. Figure 4 shows the placement of lights and sensors in the smart lighting system.

3.4   System Components

The smart lighting system comprises the following components:

- **Supervisory System/Web Application:** This system provides services such as web server hosting and a representational state transfer application programming interface (REST API). It also doubles up as a client that accesses the web interface hosted by the supervisory system to control the lights.

- **Zigbee Gateway:** This gateway relays data packets from the router to Zigbee drivers via Zigbee wireless transmission.

Figure 4. Placement of lights and sensors.

- **Zigbee Drivers/Controllers:** These components control the lights based on the data packets received from the gateway and transmit data packets from the lights and multi-function sensors back to the supervisory system.

- **Multi-Function Sensors:** The multi-function sensors include infra-red photo sensors that measure room occupancy and thermal sensors that measure light intensity and temperature, and transmit the data to the supervisory system via the Zigbee drivers/controllers and Zigbee gateway.

Data travels through the system in a specific order upon which the web interface enables the operator to control the lighting. The web interface uses Apache Tomcat, an open-source Java servlet container that runs web applications written in JavaScript, and can be used as an HTTP server. The instructions are sent via the Ethernet cable to the Internet router, which sends them to the correct IP address (i.e., Zigbee gateway). The gateway transmits the instructions via Zigbee wireless to the Zigbee drivers/controllers that direct the hardware to execute the instructions.

3.5   Communications Protocol Analysis

An extensive analysis was conducted to determine system vulnerabilities. The effort leveraged the Wireshark open-source packet analyzer to capture incoming and outgoing data packets in the network. A vulnerability was discovered in the manner in which the system used HTTP, an application layer protocol sent over TCP/IP with the default port number of 80. HTTP has three phases: initialization, data exchange and termination. It uses a request-response API, where the HTTP request contains the host URL and request verb. The response sent by the host contains the requested data and status code.

3.6   Vulnerability Assessment

This section discusses three types of attacks that were executed on the smart lighting system: (i) man-in-the-middle attacks; (ii) packet tampering attacks; and (iii) denial-of-service attacks.

A Raspberry Pi 3B+ installed with Kali Linux and equipped with a Wi-Fi antenna was used to attack the smart lighting system. Figure 5 shows the smart lighting system and the targets of the attacks. In the experiments, it was assumed that the attacker has access to the WLAN network that houses the smart lighting system.

- **Man-in-the-Middle Attacks:** Active man-in-the-middle attacks involving ARP poisoning/spoofing were conducted. Each attack intercepted a communications channel between the gateway and client, and leveraged the access to read, modify and/or inject data.

  The experiment demonstrated that data packets were successfully routed through an attacker, who was able to capture the data sent by the system to the gateway. The HTTP API commands and host IP addresses were reverse engineered to obtain the commands sent by the system.

  Other HTTP commands such as POST, GET, OPTIONS, PUT and DELETE were captured, enabling an attacker to know the HTTP request parameters that were employed. As a result, the

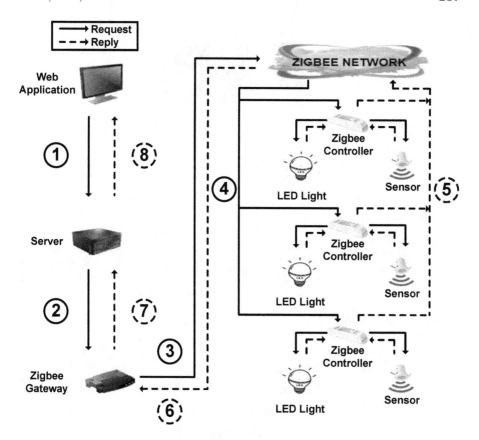

Figure 5. Smart lighting system.

attacker could craft and issue a DELETE request that permanently deleted the targeted resources.

All requests for data were transmitted in plaintext. Since the supervisory system sent requests over a fixed period, the total number of lights and sensors, and the HTTP API commands in the requests were determined. If an HTTP request was sent in the correct format, no authorization was needed to request data from the gateway. Indeed, the HTTP vulnerability enabled any number of man-in-the-middle attacks to be used to spy on the smart lighting system and disrupt its operations.

- **Packet Tampering Attacks:** Web parameter tampering attacks manipulate the parameters in data packets as they are transmitted between two components. These attacks can be executed using tools such as WebScarab and Burp Suite. The tools can also be

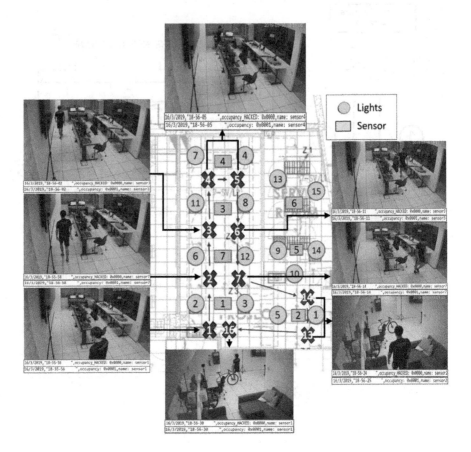

Figure 6.   Result of a packet tampering attack.

used to launch cross-site scripting (XSS) and Structured Query Language (SQL) injection attacks.

The experimental packet tampering attack sought to modify the room occupancy data so that the sensor would incorrectly report that the room was empty.

Figure 6 shows that the attack successfully modified the room occupancy data in the packet. The keyword and value in the system data log were changed to the attacker-inserted values and displayed. Comparison of the occupancy values revealed that the system received 0x0000, indicating that the room was empty, whereas the attacker received 0x0001, indicating that a person was in the room as confirmed by the CCTV footage in Figure 6. The person kept moving in the room for the duration of the attack, but the system continued to receive the modified data indicating that the room was empty.

This type of attack is not limited to altering parameters. Indeed, it can be used to inject viruses or malware that create backdoors to other devices in the network.

■ **Denial-of-Service Attacks:** The information obtained from the man-in-the-middle attacks was used to conduct denial-of-service attacks. These attacks were directed from a single device to targets over Ethernet and wireless connections. One attack flooded the network with packets to prevent requests from being sent or received, resulting in complete denial-of-service of the smart lighting system. These attacks could be easily expanded to distributed denial-of-service attacks launched from multiple devices.

An HTTP unbearable load king (HULK) attack was used to target the application layer. This type of attack sends legitimate requests such as GET and POST that exploit Apache or Windows vulnerabilities to crash the server. The use of legitimate requests makes the attacks harder to detect than other types of denial-of-service attacks. However, the HULK attack was only able to achieve a partial denial of service because the system was able to send some requests. The number of successful requests made by the system varied over the five executions of the attack, each of which lasted 30 seconds. The variations could be due to the latency in the transmission of attack packets, which enabled the smart lighting system to send some of its requests.

4. Conclusions

The vulnerability assessments demonstrate that it is relatively easy to attack and seriously impact two key components of a smart building management system, the energy metering system and smart lighting system. The results underscore the need to conduct periodic vulnerability assessments of smart building management systems immediately after the initial deployment and after every major technology upgrade to understand the nature of the potential attacks and help implement appropriate mitigations.

Future research will leverage a smart living laboratory at Singapore Institute of Technology. Risk assessments will be performed on a number of smart building management system components. Also, security methodologies will be developed and implemented to mitigate attacks and ensure system resilience.

References

[1] A. AlDairi and L. Tawalbeh, Cyber security attacks on smart cities and associated mobile technologies, *Procedia Computer Science*, vol. 109, pp. 1086–1091, 2017.

[2] Z. Baig, P. Szewczyk, C. Valli, P. Rabadia, P. Hannay, M. Chernyshev, M. Johnstone, P. Kerai, A. Ibrahim, K. Sansurooah, N. Syed and M. Peacock, Future challenges for smart cities: Cyber security and digital forensics, *Digital Investigation*, vol. 22, pp. 3–13, 2017.

[3] R. Chan and K. Chow, Forensic analysis of a Siemens programmable logic controller, in *Critical Infrastructure Protection X*, M. Rice and S. Shenoi (Eds.), Springer, Cham, Switzerland, pp. 117–130, 2016.

[4] R. Chan and K. Chow, Threat analysis of an elevator control system, in *Critical Infrastructure Protection XI*, M. Rice and S. Shenoi (Eds.), Springer, Cham, Switzerland, pp. 175–192, 2017.

[5] R. Khatoun and S. Zeadally, Cybersecurity and privacy solutions in smart cities, *IEEE Communications*, vol. 55(3), pp. 51–59, 2017.

[6] D. Minoli, K. Sohraby and B. Occhiogrosso, IoT considerations, requirements and architectures for smart buildings – Energy optimization and next-generation building management systems, *IEEE Internet of Things Journal*, vol. 4(1), pp. 269–283, 2017.

[7] T. Mundt and P. Wickboldt, Security in building automation systems – A first analysis, *Proceedings of the IEEE International Conference on Cyber Security and Protection of Digital Services*, 2016.

[8] K. Paridari, A. El-Din Mady, S. La Porta, R. Chabukswar, J. Blanco, A. Teixeira, H. Sandberg and M. Boubekeur, Cyber-physical security framework for building energy management systems, *Proceedings of the Seventh ACM/IEEE International Conference on Cyber-Physical Systems*, 2016.

[9] P. Wang, A. Ali and W. Kelly, Data security and threat modeling for smart city infrastructure, *Proceedings of the IEEE International Conference on Cyber Security of Smart Cities, Industrial Control Systems and Communications*, 2015.

[10] X. Wang, R. Habeeb, X. Ou, S. Amaravadi, J. Hatcliff, M. Mizuno, M. Neilsen, S. Rajagopalan and S. Varadarajan, Enhanced security of building automation systems through microkernel-based controller platforms, *Proceedings of the Thirty-Seventh IEEE International Conference on Distributed Computing Systems Workshops*, pp. 37–44, 2017.

Chapter 11

FORENSIC INVESTIGATION OF A HACKED INDUSTRIAL ROBOT

Yanan Gong, Kam-Pui Chow, Yonghao Mai, Jun Zhang and Chun-Fai Chan

Abstract   Industrial robots are playing a key role in the Fourth Industrial Revolution (Industry 4.0). This latest generation of robots incorporates smart technologies and networking to support machine-to-machine and machine-to-human communications, and Internet of Things integration for advanced automation. The enhanced connectivity increases the attack surface of industrial robots, providing hackers with more attack options. Cyber attacks on industrial robots not only bring about economic losses to manufacturers, such as damage to production lines, but they can also cause injuries to workers, even deaths.

This chapter describes a digital forensic investigation of a hacked Universal Robots UR3 collaborative robot. Network and physical attacks were executed, following which a digital forensic investigation of the hacked robot was conducted, including forensic image acquisition and detailed data analysis.

Keywords: Industrial robots, UR3 robot, hacking, digital forensic investigation

1.   Introduction

Applications of robot technology are proliferating across the critical infrastructure, especially in the manufacturing sector. Indeed, the massive use of advanced industrial robots in smart factories is heralding the Fourth Industrial Revolution (Industry 4.0). The International Federation of Robotics [10] predicts that, by 2022, the number of industrial robots in the world's factories will increase to about four million units [10].

The new generation of robots incorporate smart technologies and networking to support machine-to-machine and machine-to-human communications, and Internet of Things integration for advanced automation.

© IFIP International Federation for Information Processing 2020
Published by Springer Nature Switzerland AG 2020
J. Staggs and S. Shenoi (Eds.): Critical Infrastructure Protection XIV, IFIP AICT 596, pp. 221–241, 2020.
https://doi.org/10.1007/978-3-030-62840-6_11

The enhanced connectivity increases the attack surfaces of industrial robots, providing hackers with more attack options and significantly increasing the cyber risk [12]. Cyber attacks on industrial robots not only bring about economic losses to manufacturers, such as damage to production lines, but they can also cause injuries to workers, even deaths. While serious robot hacking incidents are rare, robot-related accidents have occurred. In 2016, a 20-year-old worker at an automotive parts factory in Cusseta, Georgia was crushed to death by a stalled robot at an assembly line that suddenly resumed operations [2]. Clearly, such an incident could easily be replicated by hacking a robot, disabling its safety features and commanding it to suddenly move at an unsafe speed and acceleration with workers in proximity.

The increasing likelihood of cyber attacks on industrial robots requires the development of robust investigative capabilities to understand the nature of incidents, and acquire and analyze evidence of malicious activities. Indeed, forensic investigations of robots is a new sub-area of digital forensics [1]. This chapter describes a digital forensic investigation of a hacked Universal Robots UR3 collaborative robot. Network and physical attacks were executed, following which a digital forensic investigation of the hacked robot was conducted, including forensic image acquisition and detailed data analysis.

2.   Universal Robots UR3 Robot

Industrial robots perform repetitive tasks that are dangerous or unsuitable for workers in manufacturing and production environments. Therefore, they operate in isolation from humans and other machines [3]. However, vendors have introduced collaborative robots (cobots) that work with humans in common workspaces [22]. To facilitate programming and maintenance by humans, these robots are required to comply with safety standards and are connected to computer networks. The robots typically include multiple mechanical actuators, controllers, sensors and human interaction devices [11].

Universal Robots, based in Odense, Denmark, manufactures flexible industrial collaborative robot arms. Its UR3 cobot is a small collaborative table-top robot that is perfect for light assembly tasks and automated workbench activities. The robot has 360° rotation at all its wrist joints and infinite rotation at its end joint. These unique features make the UR3 robot the most flexible, lightweight collaborative table-top robot that can work side-by-side with employees in the market today. UR3 robots are used to manufacture numerous products, including medical devices, electronic components and circuit boards [9].

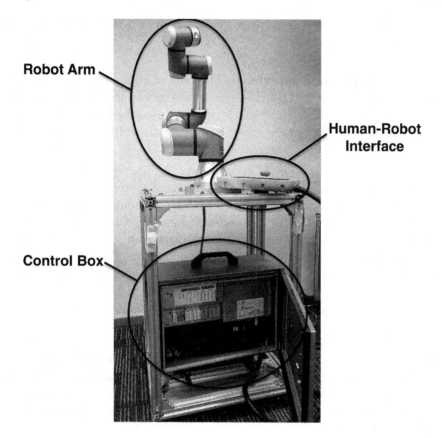

Figure 1. UR3 collaborative robot (version 3.5.1.10661).

Figure 1 shows the UR3 collaborative robot considered in this work. The robot has the following components:

- **Robot Arm:** The multi-purpose robot arm is composed of extruded aluminum tubes and joints, terminated by an end effector such as pliers or a laser beam welder that interacts with the environment. The arm is automatically controlled on three or more axes and moves flexibly based on its instructions [20].

- **Control Box:** The control box primarily contains the physical electrical inputs/outputs that connect the robot arm, human-machine interface and peripherals [19]. It also includes computer systems and multiple interconnected subsystems. The control box is a critical component because it supervises the activities of the robot. The user must turn on the control box to power up the robot arm.

- **Human-Robot Interface:** The human-robot interface, called a teach pendant, is a touch-sensitive screen connected to the control box via a wired connection. It incorporates the PolyScope graphical user interface that is used to operate the robot arm and control box, and execute programs [20].

The UR3 robot has a Linux-based operating system. The URControl low-level robot controller runs on a Mini-ITX personal computer housed in a controller cabinet [18]. The controller has eight input/output ports on the controller board and two input/output ports at the tool point, all of which can control external equipment [23]. When the personal computer boots up, URControl executes as a daemon (like a service), the PolyScope user interface connects as a client using a local TCP/IP connection and a process named URControl automatically executes on the robot system.

The UR3 cobot was selected for the case study because its manufacturer, Universal Robots, is a major player in the global robotics industry [17]. Additionally, most robotic systems now run a Linux operating system or a POSIX-compliant Unix operating system variant [21]. In fact, the trend, as exemplified by UR3, is to run an embedded Linux operating system.

3. Attacking the UR3 Robot

The threat model is based on a typical Industry 4.0 scenario, where an industrial robot is connected to a dedicated subnet and isolated from other endpoints. Depending on the level of attacker access, two types of attacks were considered: (i) network attacks; and (ii) physical attacks.

3.1 Network Attack

DeMarinis et al. [7] have demonstrated that numerous robots can be identified by scanning the public Internet. Even if industrial robots are not directly connected to the Internet, they may be connected to factory local area networks or remote service facilities that may have misconfigurations or vulnerabilities that can be exploited to access them over the Internet. Attackers often make use of various entry points to compromise computers in factory networks. Quarta et al. [13] have shown that Industry 4.0 factory subnets and their connected robots are easy targets.

The network attack on the UR3 robot leveraged a network connection. Many functions in the PolyScope user interface, such as programming the robot and modifying safety settings, are password protected. However, after compromising a computer in the same network as the UR3 robot, it was possible to bypass the authentication process, change the safety configuration of the robot and send malicious scripts that moved its joints remotely.

Network Attack Steps. The network attack involved the following steps:

- **Attack Step 1:** The first step in the attack was to find the IP address of the robot. As described by Cerrudo and Apa [5], the default host could be queried to announce the existence of the robot.

- **Attack Step 2:** The second step in the attack was to change the safety configuration of the robot. Different safety configurations are saved as installation files and URScript programs are saved as URP files on a UR3 robot. The `netcat` command was used to bypass the password protection of the robotic arm and connect to the Dashboard server on port 29999 at the robot IP address. Following this, several commands were sent to the PolyScope user interface over a TCP/IP socket to obtain various information (including real-time status) about the UR3 robot.

  Figure 2 shows the commands that were sent to the PolyScope user interface:

  - The command `PolyScopeVersion` was used to obtain the version number of the robot.
  - The command `Robotmode/running` was used to check the current status of the robot.
  - The two commands `programState` and `get loaded program` were used to obtain the state and path of the program loaded by the robot, respectively.
  - The two commands `unlock protective stop` and `brake release` were used to close the current pop-up window of PolyScope and unlock the protective stop and then release the brakes.
  - The command `load installation/programs/default.installation` was used to load the default installation file that specified the initial status of the robot with no safety boundaries, speed limits, etc.

Figure 2.   Commands sent to the Dashboard server.

- The command `close popup` was used to close the PolyScope pop-up window so as not to attract the attention of an operator.

- The command `power on` was used to turn the robot on.

- **Attack Step 3:** The UR3 robot has three ports 30001, 30002 and 30003 that can be used to receive raw scripts from an external device [15]. These ports could be accessed without authentication by any user on the network. After changing the safety settings of the robot to the default state, random URScript commands shown in Figure 3 were sent to these ports.

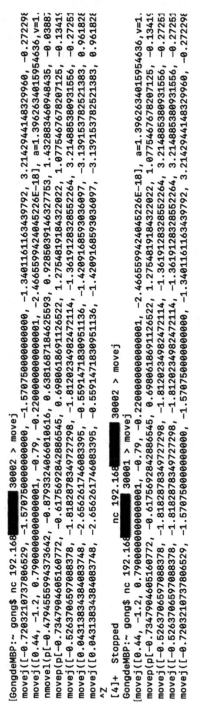

Figure 3. URScript commands.

Network Attack Results. The network attack changed the safety configuration of the robot to the default initial status with no safety limits and sent random URScript commands to the robot. Clicking the start button on the PolyScope after the random commands were sent caused the robot arm to suddenly move at an unsafe speed and acceleration. The uncontrolled robot could cause damage to the work environment and possibly injure people who are nearby.

3.2   Physical Attack

Since industrial robots interact with workers, physical access is expected and acceptable. A physical attack is possible when an attacker can access the robot hardware or mechanical devices to change its behavior or set up persistent threats. A programmer writes robot task programs and a human operator starts, monitors and stops robot operations. The programs may be written by recording action sequences through a joystick or using simulators or text editors.

The programmer and operator usually interact with the robot via the PolyScope user interface. The simplest and most common scenario involves an insider (programmer or operator) who uses the PolyScope user interface to enter a malicious program.

A slightly more sophisticated scenario involves an attacker who inserts an external device into one of the robot's exposed ports [13]. The UR3 robot has several accessible ports and the PolyScope has one open port. The control box has two USB ports and the box itself can be easily opened with a key. A mouse and keyboard are also supported by the USB interfaces of the UR3 controller [14]. A special USB device that acts as a keyboard can be used to modify the robot configurations and actions.

Industrial robots often can be accessed from remote computers to facilitate control and maintenance. The UR3 robot allows SSH access and no enforcement measures are implemented to force users to change the default password. The default username **root** is fixed and the default password can be easily searched for on the Internet.

If a physical attacker wishes to create trouble, he could simply stop an operating robot. The easiest way is to kill the URControl process, which would prevent the URControl controller from running normally. To avoid suspicion, the attacker can return the robot back to normal operation after stopping it. In fact, an attacker can do multiple things to the robot in a single physical attack such as inserting an external device, uploading a malicious file and deleting files.

Physical Attack Steps. The physical attack involved the following steps:

- **Attack Step 1:** The first step of the physical attack was to insert a USB device to an exposed USB port on the UR3 robot.

- **Attack Step 2:** The second step was to use a computer to connect to the robot via the free SSH tool `SmarTTY`. Next, a Python file named `restartp.py` was uploaded from the computer to the robot to start a new URControl process after a preset time.

- **Attack Step 3:** The third step was to execute the `restartp.py` file and kill the running URControl process. A directory called `programs` stores all the safety configuration files and URScript programs. Some files from this directory were downloaded to the plugged USB. After the Python file `restartp.py` executed to completion, it was deleted from the robot.

Physical Attack Results. The log screen in the PolyScope user interface showed that the URControl controller was disconnected and the robot stopped operating. After a while, the controller was connected automatically and the robot returned to normal operations. Examination of the process identifier of the URControl process before and after the execution of the `restartp.py` file revealed that the process identifier of the URControl process was changed.

3.3 Discussion

The attacks were enabled by the fact that considerable details about the UR3 robot were available in technical documentation that is freely available on the Internet. The vendor's website also provides controller software that is available for download. Additionally, an attacker could perform reverse engineering and discover vulnerabilities without access to insider technical knowledge. Moreover, even if an attacker is unable to test exploits on a real robot, it is possible to use a simulator provided by the vendor to run robot controller software and create attack payloads.

4. Digital Forensic Investigation

Digital forensics covers the identification, acquisition, analysis, documentation and preservation of electronic evidence, primarily for incident investigations and courtroom proceedings. This section discusses the acquisition and analysis of digital evidence from the UR3 robot after the network and physical attacks. Robot systems such as UR3 sacrifice functionality to ensure safety, as a result they do not have full-fledged operating systems (e.g., Linux). This makes it more difficult to extract evidence in forensic investigations.

4.1   Image Acquisition

The hacked robot was the direct source of evidence. The `fdisk` command was used to examine the hard drive in the UR3 robot. All the data was stored on the drive `/dev/sda`. The total size of the drive was 2,059,403,264 bytes with a Linux operating system in use.

Several tools can be used to create a forensic image. The `dd` command is available on all Linux distributions and can be used to read from and write to an unmounted drive because it is not bound by a logical filesystem. The `dd` command captures all the files, unallocated data and slack space [6].

A byte-to-byte cloned image of the drive was acquired by connecting a computer to the robot and typing the command: `dd if = /dev/sda of = /media/USB/ursda.img conv=noerror, sync` in a terminal window. Note that `/dev/sda` corresponds to the drive name and `ursda.img` the chosen name and extension of the acquisition file. Using `conv=noerror` ensured that `dd` would not skip over any sectors or blocks on the source device. The second part of the switch `sync` provided zero padding and aligned the sectors on the target device with those on the source device, ensuring an accurate replication of the original media [8]. The UR3 robot did not support remote file transfer. Since the robot had limited storage, there was not enough space to store the image file; thus, the image file was stored on a plugged USB device. After the image was acquired, its hash value was computed to maintain the integrity of the collected data.

4.2   Image Analysis

Image analysis is the process of examining a forensic image in a forensically-sound manner. The robot image had a Linux EXT3 filesystem. Forensic Toolkit (FTK) version 4.2.0.13 running on Windows 10 and Autopsy version 2.24 running on Kali Linux were employed for image analysis.

Network Attack Analysis The log screen in the PolyScope user interface provides useful information about the real-time status of the robot and URControl controller (Figure 4). The information includes the controller temperature, power consumption, power supply output and joint status [16]. However, the log entries disappear from the screen when the UR3 robot is restarted. Fortunately, all the entries were recorded in

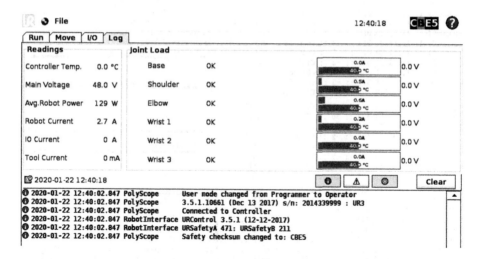

Figure 4. PolyScope log screen.

the log file `log_history.txt` located in the `root` directory of the robot. The only difference is that the information presented by the PolyScope user interface is in human-readable form.

The safety configuration of the UR3 robot was recorded in the `safety.conf` file. The UR3 robot uses the CRC (STM-32) algorithm to generate a checksum that ensures the integrity of the safety configuration file. The first four digits of the CRC checksum value correspond to the safety checksum value, which is displayed in the upper-right corner of the PolyScope user interface. The `safety.conf` file also maintains a safety parameter.

Analysis of the `log_history.txt` file with FTK revealed that the safety checksum recorded was CBE5 when the robot was initially started on January 17, 2020. A short while later (at 11:40:54), the safety checksum was changed to CCCC. After a few minutes, the programs `movej` and `movep` executed successfully (Figure 5).

The `safety.conf` file located in the `/root/.urcontrol` directory saved the safety settings of the robot. The safety parameter recorded was the initial default value 1216962, which corresponded to the default safety checksum CCCC (Figure 6). Therefore, it was certain that the safety settings were changed to the initial status at 11:40:54 on January 17, 2020.

The `programs` directory saves all the installation files and URScript programs. Checking the image revealed that there were no programs named `movej` and `movep` in the robot, nor were they listed as deleted files. Under normal circumstances, when an existing program is executed

```
2020-01-17 11:13:20.015 ..  -5 .. COAO:0 .. null .. 1 .. 3.3.1.10001 (Dec 13 2017) s/n. 2018333070 . 0
2020-01-17 11:13:20.015 ::  -5 :: COAO:7 :: null :: 1 ::    :: Connected to Controller :: null
2020-01-17 11:13:20.015 ::  -2 :: COAO:3 :: null :: 1 :: URControl 3.5.1 (12-12-2017) ::    :: null
2020-01-17 11:13:20.015 ::  -2 :: COAO:12 :: null :: 1 :: URSafetyA 3.5.0: URSafetyB 3.5.0 ::    :: null
2020-01-17 11:13:20.015 ::  -5 :: COAO:7 :: null :: 1 ::    :: Safety checksum changed to: CBE5 :: null
2020-01-17 11:13:21.048 ::  -2 :: C100A2:6 :: null :: 1 ::    ::    :: 0
2020-01-17 11:13:21.048 ::  -1 :: COAO:5 :: 1 :: 1 ::    ::    :: 0
2020-01-17 11:13:21.511 ::  -5 :: COAO:7 :: null :: 1 ::    :: Safety checksum changed to: CBE5 :: null
2020-01-17 11:13:25.552 ::  -2 :: C100A3:6 :: null :: 1 ::    ::    :: 0

2020-01-17 11:40:54.424 ::  -2 :: C101A0:6 :: null :: 1 ::    ::    :: 0
2020-01-17 11:40:54.423 ::  -2 :: C50A83:6 :: null :: 1 ::    ::    :: 0
2020-01-17 11:40:54.415 ::  -5 :: COAO:7 :: null :: 1 ::    :: Safety checksum changed to: CCCC :: null
2020-01-17 11:40:54.592 ::  -2 :: C100A2:6 :: null :: 1 ::    ::    :: 0
2020-01-17 11:40:54.607 ::  -5 :: COAO:7 :: null :: 1 ::    :: Safety checksum changed to: CCCC :: null
2020-01-17 11:40:59.320 ::  -2 :: C100A3:6 :: null :: 1 ::    ::    :: 0
2020-01-17 11:41:49.727 ::  30 :: C4A92:6 :: null :: 2 ::    ::    :: 0
2020-01-17 11:41:49.895 ::  20 :: C4A90:6 :: null :: 2 ::    ::    :: 0

2020-01-17 11:49:13.408 ::  -2 :: C100A7:6 :: null :: 1 ::    ::    :: 0
2020-01-17 11:50:08.560 ::  -3 :: COAO:7 :: null :: 1 :: movej :: Program movej started :: null
2020-01-17 11:50:12.656 ::  -3 :: COAO:7 :: null :: 1 :: movej :: Program movej stopped :: null
2020-01-17 11:50:22.944 ::  -3 :: COAO:7 :: null :: 1 :: movej :: Program movej started :: null
2020-01-17 11:50:26.072 ::  -3 :: COAO:7 :: null :: 1 :: movej :: Program movej stopped :: null
2020-01-17 11:50:42.664 ::  -3 :: COAO:7 :: null :: 1 :: movej :: Program movej started :: null
2020-01-17 11:50:44.768 ::  -3 :: COAO:7 :: null :: 1 :: movej :: Program movej stopped :: null
2020-01-17 11:50:55.984 ::  -3 :: COAO:7 :: null :: 1 :: movej :: Program movej started :: null
2020-01-17 11:50:57.304 ::  -3 :: COAO:7 :: null :: 1 :: movej :: Program movej stopped :: null
2020-01-17 11:51:10.792 ::  -3 :: COAO:7 :: null :: 1 :: movej :: Program movej started :: null
2020-01-17 11:51:12.752 ::  -3 :: COAO:7 :: null :: 1 :: movej :: Program movej stopped :: null
2020-01-17 11:51:47.952 ::  -3 :: COAO:7 :: null :: 1 :: movep :: Program movep started :: null
2020-01-17 11:51:48.552 ::  -3 :: COAO:10 :: null :: 1 :: trajectory_is_scaled:movep: ::    ::
2020-01-17 11:51:48.560 ::  -3 :: C204A3:5 :: 3 :: 1 ::    ::    :: 0
2020-01-17 11:51:48.560 ::  -3 :: COAO:7 :: null :: 1 :: movep :: Program movep stopped :: null
2020-01-17 11:51:48.520 ::  -3 :: C204A3:6 :: null :: 2 ::    ::    :: 0
2020-01-17 11:52:32.152 ::  -3 :: COAO:7 :: null :: 1 :: movej :: Program movej started :: null
2020-01-17 11:52:32.176 ..  -3 .. COAO:7 .. null .. 1 .. movej .. Program movej stopped .. null
```

Figure 5.   Contents of file `log_history.txt`.

safety.conf	3 Regular File	2020/1/17 11:09:02
server.conf	1 Regular File	2020/1/17 10:13:07
touch_calibration.properties	1 Regular File	2018/1/17 15:55:07
urcontrol.conf	1 Symbolic Link	2018/1/17 23:50:44
urcontrol.conf.UR10	3 Regular File	2017/12/13 15:24:22
urcontrol.conf.UR3	3 Regular File	2017/12/13 15:24:22
urcontrol.conf.UR5	3 Regular File	2017/12/13 15:24:22

```
## SafetyParameters ##
[Checksum]
safetyParameters = 121691621
majorVersion = 3
```

Figure 6.   Safety parameter in file `safety.conf`.

```
2020-01-16 18:25:23.559 :: -5 :: COAO:7 :: null :: 1 ::    :: Program goodpunch starting...  (Last saved: 2018-08-27 19:47:36)
2020-01-16 18:25:23.040 :: -3 :: COAO:7 :: null :: 1 :: goodpunch :: Program goodpunch started :: null
2020-01-16 18:25:39.120 :: -3 :: COAO:7 :: null :: 1 :: goodpunch :: Program goodpunch stopped :: null
```

Figure 7.   Execution records of program `goodpunch` in file `log_history.txt`.

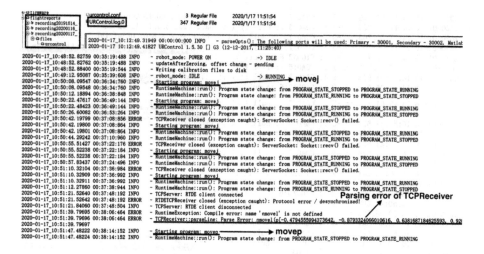

Figure 8. Contents of file `URControl.log.0`.

via the PolyScope user interface, the last saved time of the program would also be displayed in the log file. This implies that no program that existed on the robot was executed by the attacker.

Figure 7 shows the execution records of the robot program named `goodpunch`. When the program began to execute, its last saved time was recorded (shown in parentheses on the right-hand side of the figure).

The folder `flightreports` in the `root` directory contained five compressed files saved at five different times. When the safety settings are modified, the robot automatically saves such compressed files. Each compressed file contains key information and the status of the robot at the specific time. The data includes the controller state, safety settings, loaded program and log.

The compressed file `recording20200117_11_51_54.zip` contained a file named `summary.log` that recorded detailed information about the operating system, memory, thread dump, etc. From the PolyScope Probe information portion contained in this file, it was determined that the name of the installation file at that time was `default` and the loaded program was still `a.urp`. This implied that programs `movej` and `movep` were not executed like regular robot programs and the safety settings were changed to the initial status.

The compressed file `recording20200117_11_51_54.zip` also contained a file named `URControl.log.0` (Figure 8). A TCPReceiver parsing error was found in this file, which contained suspicious URScript `nmovel` commands such as the URScript `nmovel(p [ -0.4794555994373642, -0.8793324066010616, 0.6381687184625593, 0.9285039146327753,`

```
2020-01-16 14:17:00.703 :: -5 :: C0A0:7 :: null :: 1 :: :: Connected to Controller :: null
2020-01-16 14:17:00.703 :: -2 :: C0A0:3 :: null :: 1 :: URControl 3.5.1 (12-12-2017) :: :: null
2020-01-16 14:17:00.703 :: -2 :: C0A0:12 :: null :: 1 :: URSafetyA 3.5.0: URSafetyB 3.5.0 :: :: null
2020-01-16 14:17:00.703 :: -5 :: C0A0:7 :: null :: 1 :: :: Safety checksum changed to: CBE5 :: null
2020-01-16 14:17:01.720 :: -2 :: C100A2:6 :: null :: 1 :: :: :: 0
2020-01-16 14:17:01.720 :: -1 :: C0A0:5 :: 1 :: 1 :: :: :: 0
2020-01-16 14:17:01.903 :: -5 :: C0A0:7 :: null :: 1 :: :: Safety checksum changed to: CBE5 :: null
2020-01-16 14:17:05.224 :: -2 :: C100A3:6 :: null :: 1 :: :: :: 0

2020-01-16 16:49:01.184 :: -5 :: C0A0:7 :: null :: 1 :: :: Disconnected from Controller :: null
2020-01-16 16:50:47.535 :: -5 :: C0A0:7 :: null :: 1 :: :: Connected to Controller :: null
2020-01-16 16:50:47.535 :: -2 :: C0A0:3 :: null :: 1 :: URControl 3.5.1 (12-12-2017) :: :: null
2020-01-16 16:50:47.535 :: -2 :: C0A0:12 :: null :: 1 :: URSafetyA 3.5.0: URSafetyB 3.5.0 :: :: null
2020-01-16 16:50:47.535 :: -5 :: C0A0:7 :: null :: 1 :: :: Failed to activate real robot :: null
2020-01-16 16:50:47.535 :: -5 :: C0A0:7 :: null :: 1 :: :: Failed to activate real robot :: null
2020-01-16 16:50:48.544 :: -2 :: C100A0:6 :: null :: 1 :: :: :: 0
2020-01-16 16:50:48.544 :: -2 :: C101A0:6 :: null :: 1 :: :: :: 0
2020-01-16 16:50:48.552 :: -2 :: C100A1:6 :: null :: 1 :: :: :: 0
2020-01-16 16:50:48.080 :: -2 :: C100A0:6 :: null :: 1 :: :: :: 0
2020-01-16 16:50:48.080 :: -2 :: C100A1:6 :: null :: 1 :: :: :: 0
2020-01-16 16:50:48.088 :: -2 :: C101A0:6 :: null :: 1 :: :: :: 0
2020-01-16 16:50:48.087 :: 30 :: C50A83:6 :: null :: 1 :: :: :: 0
2020-01-16 16:50:47.535 :: -5 :: C0A0:7 :: null :: 1 :: :: Safety checksum changed to: CBE5 :: null
2020-01-16 16:50:48.247 :: -5 :: C0A0:7 :: null :: 1 :: :: Safety checksum changed to: CBE5 :: null
2020-01-16 16:50:48.168 :: -2 :: C100A2:6 :: null :: 1 ::
```

Figure 9. Contents of file log_history.txt.

1.432883460948435,-0.03887073268881964], a=1.2, v=0.25, r= 0.0). URScript commands can only be sent to ports 30001, 30002 and 30003, following which they are executed. Also, before the TCPReceiver parsing error, multiple movej programs were executed. After the parsing error, the program movep was executed. This indicates that the URScript commands sent to ports 30001, 30002 and 30003 were executed successfully. Therefore, movej and movep were in the form of URScript commands and were received by the robot via open socket ports.

The presence of file default.installation in recording20200117_11_51_54.zip means that the default installation file was loaded by the robot at the recorded time. The safety parameter in the safety.conf file in the compressed file was 1216962, which corresponds to the default safety checksum value CCCC. This proves again that the safety settings were changed to the initial status.

Thus, the forensic investigation revealed that the safety configuration of the robot was definitely changed to the initial default status at 11:40:54 on January 17, 2020. This change meant that the robot would not operate within its safety limits. After the change was made, URScript movej and movep commands were sent to ports 30001, 30002 and 30003. The execution of these commands caused the robot arm to suddenly move at an unsafe speed and acceleration.

Physical Attack Analysis   Figure 9 shows the contents of file log_history.txt. The contents reveal that the URControl controller was disconnected at 16:49:01 and, after a while, the controller was connected

.bash_history	15	Regular File	2020/1/17 11:23:30
.profile	1	Regular File	2014/9/23 13:46:14
~~.~~ ~~file~~	~~1~~	~~Regular File~~	~~2018/2/16 16:49:04~~

```
ls
cd /media/urmountpoint_oeWvAZ
ls
cd ..
ls
python restartp.py
killall URControl
```

Figure 10. Records in file `.bash_history`.

automatically and the robot was set back to normal. The safety checksum value recorded in the log file was CBE5. Checking all the other safety-related items, such as file `safety.conf`, safety parameter and files in the folder `flightreports` revealed that the safety checksum value was the same as that when the robot started operation on January 16, 2020 (the loaded installation file and loaded robot program at that time were not changed).

Examination of the file `.bash_history` in the `root` directory revealed that the device `urmountpoint_oeWvAZ` was mounted on the robot. A Python file named `restartp.py` that did not initially belong to the robot was executed, following which the running URControl process was killed (Figure 10).

Current Directory: /1/ /media/					

Del.	Type dir / ln	Name	Written	Accessed	Changed	Si
	d / d	../	2019-12-10 21:19:43 (HKT)	2017-03-22 21:28:56 (HKT)	2019-12-10 21:19:43 (HKT)	4(
	d / d	./	2020-01-17 19:26:10 (HKT)	2016-08-30 20:12:02 (HKT)	2020-01-17 19:26:10 (HKT)	4(
✔	r / r	restartp.py	2020-01-17 00:05:30 (HKT)	2020-01-16 23:42:37 (HKT)	2020-01-17 00:05:30 (HKT)	0

Figure 11. Deleted file `restartp.py`.

The Autopsy tool revealed that file `restartp.py` was deleted from the `media` directory in the robot system (Figure 11).

When SSH is used, the authorization keys configured for each user are recorded in a file named `authorized_keys`. The keys specify which users are allowed to log into a server using public key authentication in SSH. The `authorized_keys` file was located upon searching the `.ssh` folder in the `root` directory. As shown in Figure 12, two users, WU and Gong Yanan, had been connected to the robot (Figure 12). WU is an unknown user whereas Gong Yanan is a known user who remotely controlled the robot.

Del.	dir / in	Name	Written	Accessed	Changed	Size	UID	GID	Meta
r / r		root/.ssh/authorized_keys	2020-01-16 23:38:46 (HKT)	2019-06-11 18:24:24 (HKT)	2020-01-16 23:38:46 (HKT)	808	0	0	97651

Contents Of File: /1/root/.ssh/authorized_keys

ssh-rsa AAAAB3NzaC1yc2EAAAADAQABAAAABAQDQo4lyrFuTJQb7MzbeLU7g9YAk7TvFwBgn1G9Zcck9+cE47pCVlc909nDfYvOic+/A+hNjUHwR
/z8xBPtbTyhNXdWzChn+2KyLPuKH5B1t7/JN0oyqB63IxYNcnQaiT+RaESgMoTrtwn0KR1dcIlsWy
/iKaJ2EQuGj7gdetdGVBT5bWjU2Y2h046kjnXVpiO7IUizSZXHfYiH4AWnv5YKezXxDVQIEMHHQd3hDiBimMUFXEMnLTU/xYv8cyenaxoaot1/+erKydXZfCwbfBDjR7L7Sih
/rTHJ/I/V2HfAZgmCHiUcldt78SgjWFq1ZAt/0WC5JdJJLBFBStRE/jIJJ WU@DESKTOP-OGQ3S4I
ssh-rsa
AAAAB3NzaC1yc2EAAAADAQABAAAABAQCt2RkSMGh62urDDhHGyjzvK+FHsIaQ2sIoxAPD1Xkmk3ngn87piVNv2R5+vZV3rsaGksiCQgbWqCwjzb3p5s5y2owgqEAsidUfy07ymIn
YmfYPKbURjNj9x1kQihc6R172R6LV8uAQEpHoKlnX5c2NGd7RUVmEDlCcFzsthNQl7lCAhOqOgWOcGfbMddtnVFcINTRRrR9lBoqay3Q/U+l
/WpFkC0QnRibqDAIQ9SsyCo4eukxovrrOLNSrjKKCwf/aJ4mfj5rzwe/OA+OLtj0MMM9HuEznQ0f9bJpkW8D6I9d3BMpskJdKJQyT2xGWZHICfJtpPgGQNwz2Q3qCbuJt Gong
Yanan@DESKTOP-CENHIDQ

Figure 12.   Contents of file `authorized_keys`.

The forensic investigation revealed that the unknown user WU connected as `root` without authorization via SSH and inserted the `urmount point_oeWvAZ` device in the robot. The Python file `restartp.py` from the device was then uploaded to the `media` directory in the robot; the file was deleted after it executed. The URControl process was killed by the attacker at 16:49:01 on January 16, 2020, but the controller automatically returned to normal operation at 16:50:47. The execution of the suspicious file `restartp.py` restored the URControl controller connection.

Forensic Investigation Conclusions   After completing the forensic analyses of the network and physical attacks on the robot, FTK and Autopsy were used separately to recompute the MD5 hash value of the image. The hash values matched the original hash values, verifying that the image was not modified during the forensic analyses. This step ensured the reliability of the forensic investigation.

5.   Discussion

This section summarizes the results and provides recommendations for robot security and robot forensics.

5.1   Network Attack

Log history files generated by robots are crucial to forensic investigations. The `log_history.txt` file in the UR3 robot contains various event codes and other symbols. Whereas the raw data in the file is difficult to read, the PolyScope user interface presents the log entries in a human-readable format.

It is also necessary to check other essential information about the robot status, such as the safety settings. In the case of the network attack, compressed files stored at `/root/flightreports` provided valuable information related to the modification of the safety configuration.

When attacks on the robot target the open ports, the specific commands sent over TCP/IP sockets are difficult to find in a forensic investigation. For example, the commands used to get feedback from the Dashboard server cannot be obtained; put simply, all the commands sent to port 29999 are not recorded by the robot. Even when SSH is used to connect to the robot in advance of setting up a connection to the Dashboard server, the `.bash_history` file only saves the first command used to establish the TCP connection with port 29999. Furthermore, raw URScript commands can be transmitted from an external device to the robot using ports 30001, 30002 and 30003. However, the specific URScript content and the exact ports used to transmit the script were not known.

5.2 Physical Attack

SSH tools such as SmarTTY that support the SCP protocol enable files to be uploaded or downloaded between a connected computer and the robot. These tools provide functionality, such as uploading a directory, without having to type commands, just with mouse clicks. No records are maintained about these operations, although the `.bash_history` file preserves all the instructions entered over an SSH connection.

When conducting the physical attack, SmarTTY was used to establish the SSH connection. The Python file `restartp.py` was uploaded from the computer and deleted from the robot after execution. The Autopsy tool revealed that this file was deleted from the robot. However, no records of uploading or deleting the file were found in the `.bash_history` file.

The `.bash_history` file was also tested to see if it recorded commands sent to open ports. SSH was used to connect to the robot remotely and `netcat` was employed to establish connections with the ports. When connecting to the Dashboard server, the `.bash_history` file only saved the `netcat` command sent to port 29999; there was no record of the command that requested feedback from the server. In the case of the interface ports 30001, 30002 and 30003, not even the first `netcat` command that established a TCP connection was recorded, let alone the URScript commands that followed. Only when `echo` and `netcat` were both used to transmit URScript commands to the robot did the `.bash_history` file save records of the commands.

5.3   Recommendations

Industrial robots have long lifetimes [13] and it is difficult to patch all their vulnerabilities. However, some measures can be adopted to enhance cyber security and support digital forensic investigations of security breaches.

- **Authentication and Authorization:** It is important to identify the users who are authorized to access robots [4]. Weak authentication enables an attacker to gain access to and control a robot. Vendors must incorporate multiple password locks to ensure that only valid users have access to robot functionality and services. Implementing code signing mechanisms with strong authentication can control the execution of custom code. An operator must be able to sign code for a specific robot. Thus, even if an attacker could upload code files to a robot, the code would not be executed without a valid signature.

- **Security Audits:** A comprehensive security assessment must be conducted before a robot can become operational. Robot manufacturers should develop and disseminate standard safety procedures for operating robots. Factories should provide safe robot operations training to operators and maintenance personnel. Safety and security awareness should be priorities over the entire lifetimes of robots.

- **Forensic Standards and Best Practices:** A comprehensive forensic investigation framework must be developed for robots. The framework must adhere to the standards and employ best practices to ensure that investigations are forensically sound.

- **Forensic Tools:** Unlike traditional information technology components, robot systems are diverse and often have proprietary hardware and software, and modified (embedded device) operating systems and filesystems, often with very limited documentation. This makes it difficult to employ traditional digital forensic tools or even to modify existing tools to acquire and analyze digital evidence. Dedicated forensic tools for robots should be developed by vendors or in collaboration with vendors.

6.   Conclusions

The use of advanced industrial robots in smart factories is transforming the critical manufacturing sector. The new generation of robots incorporate smart technologies and networking to support machine-to-machine and machine-to-human communications, and Internet of Things integration for advanced automation. The enhanced connectivity increases the attack surface of industrial robots, providing hackers with more attack options and significantly increasing the cyber risk [12]. Cyber attacks on industrial robots bring about economic losses to manufacturers; they can also cause injuries to workers, even deaths.

The digital forensic investigation of the Universal Robots UR3 collaborative robot after network and physical attacks focused on the important image acquisition and image analysis phases. It applied standard techniques and tools in a forensically-sound manner to extract and process evidence related to the attacks and create a forensic narrative about the attacks and the perpetrators. It is hoped that this work will stimulate interest in industrial robot forensics, a new sub-area of digital forensics.

The views expressed in this chapter are those of the authors and do not reflect the official policy or position of HKSAR Logistics and Supply Chain Multi-Tech R&D Centre, Hong Kong.

Acknowledgement

The authors are grateful to HKSAR Logistics and Supply Chain Multi-Tech R&D Centre in Hong Kong for permitting them to conduct research on the UR3 robot.

References

[1] I. Abeykoon and X. Feng, A forensic investigation of the Robot Operating System, *Proceedings of the IEEE International Conference on Internet of Things, Green Computing, Communications, Cyber, Physical and Social Computing, and Smart Data*, pp. 851–857, 2017.

[2] Achieng, 15 most savage deaths caused by robots, *TheRichest*, July 27 2017.

[3] L. Apa, Exploiting Industrial Collaborative Robots, IOActive, Seattle, Washington (`www.ioactive.com/exploiting-industrial-co llaborative-robots`), August 22, 2017.

[4] C. Cerrudo and L. Apa, Hacking Robots before Skynet, IOActive, Seattle, Washington (`ioactive.com/pdfs/Hacking-Robots-Befo re-Skynet.pdf`), 2017.

[5] C. Cerrudo and L. Apa, Hacking Robots before Skynet: Technical Appendix, IOActive, Seattle, Washington (`ioactive.com/pdfs/Ha cking-Robots-Before-Skynet-Technical-Appendix.pdf`), 2017.

[6] V. Codispot, Data Dump (dd) to create a forensic image with Linux, *Threat Analysis Blog* (`vcodispot.com/data-dump-dd-create-fo rensic-image-linux`), July 4, 2017.

[7] N. DeMarinis, S. Tellex, V. Kemerlis, G. Konidaris and R. Fonseca, Scanning the Internet for ROS: A view of security in robotics research, *Proceedings of the IEEE International Conference on Robotics and Automation*, pp. 8514–8521, 2019.

[8] Forensic Focus, Linux dd Basics (`www.forensicfocus.com/arti cles/linux-dd-basics`), July 14, 2011.

[9] Innovative Total Solutions, UR3 Robot, Midleton, Ireland (`itsl. ie/shop/universal-robots/ur3`), 2020.

[10] International Federation of Robotics, Industrial robots: Robot investment reaches record 16.5 billion USD, Press Release, Frankfurt, Germany (`ifr.org/ifr-press-releases/news/robot-investme nt-reaches-record-16.5-billion-usd`), September 18, 2019.

[11] F. Maggi, D. Quarta, M. Pogliani, M. Polino, A. Zanchettin and S. Zanero, Rogue Robots: Testing the Limits of an Industrial Robot's Security, Trend Micro, Milan, Italy (`documents.trendmicro.com/ assets/wp/wp-industrial-robot-security.pdf`), 2017.

[12] I. Priyadarshini, Cyber security risks in robotics, in *Cyber Security and Threats: Concepts, Methodologies, Tools and Applications*, Information Resources Management Association (Ed.), IGI Global, Hershey, Pennsylvania, pp. 1235–1250, 2018.

[13] D. Quarta, M. Pogliani, M. Polino, F. Maggi, A. Zanchettin and S. Zanero, An experimental security analysis of an industrial robot controller, *Proceedings of the IEEE Symposium on Security and Privacy*, pp. 268–286, 2017.

[14] L. Skovsgaard, Training Manual: Hint and Tips, Version 1.4, Zacobria, Singapore (`www.zacobria.com/universal_robots_zac obria_hints_and_tips_manual_1_4_3.htm`), 2012.

[15] L. Skovsgaard, Introduction to Universal-Robots Script Programming, Zacobria, Singapore (`www.zacobria.com/universal-rob ots-knowledge-base-tech-support-forum-hints-tips/unive rsal-robots-script-programming`), 2015.

[16] L. Skovsgaard, Log Window Tab, Zacobria, Singapore (`www.zacob ria.com/universal-robots-zacobria-forum-hints-tips-how -to/log-%20window-tab`), 2017.

[17] Technavio, Top 21 industrial robotics companies in the world 2019, *Technavio Blog*, London, United Kingdom (`blog.technavio.com /blog/top-21-companies-in-the-industrial-robotics-mark et`), February 5, 2019.

[18] Universal Robots, The URScript Programming Language for Version 1.2, Odense, Denmark (`s3-eu-west-1.amazonaws.com/ ur-support-site/18407/UR-Scriptmanual_en_1.2.pdf`), 2010.

[19] Universal Robots, Universal Robots e-Series User Manual: UR10e, Version 5.2, Odense, Denmark (`s3-eu-west-1.amazonaws.com/ ur-support-site/46114/UR10e_User_Manual_en_US.pdf`), 2018.

[20] Universal Robots, User Manual: UR3/CB3, Version 3.5.5, Odense, Denmark (`s3-eu-west-1.amazonaws.com/ur-support-site/323 40/UR3_User_Manual_en_Global-3.5.5.pdf`), 2018.

[21] V. Vilches, L. Kirschgens, E. Gil-Uriarte, A. Hernandez and B. Dieber, Volatile Memory Forensics for the Robot Operating System, *arXiv:* 1812.09492v1, 2018.

[22] Wikipedia, Cobot (`en.wikipedia.org/wiki/Cobot`), 2020.

[23] Zacobria, Linux OS on Industrial Robot, Singapore (`www.zac obria.com`), 2020.

V

CYBER-PHYSICAL
SYSTEMS SECURITY

Chapter 12

DISTRIBUTED BIAS DETECTION IN CYBER-PHYSICAL SYSTEMS

Simon Thougaard and Bruce McMillin

Abstract   An attacker can effectively publish false measurements in distributed cyber-physical systems with noisy measurements. These biased false measurements can be impossible to distinguish from noise and enable the attacker to gain a small but persistent economic advantage. The residual sum, a fundamental measurement of bias in cyber-physical systems, is employed to develop a detection scheme for bias attacks. The scheme is highly efficient, privacy preserving and effectively detects bias attacks.

Keywords: Cyber-physical systems, security, privacy, bias attacks, smart grid

1.   Introduction

False data injection attacks on power systems have been the subject of intense study since they were introduced by Liu et al. [4]. The attack model assumes that an adversary knows the power system configuration and has the ability to send corrupted measurements to a control entity (i.e., bad data injection). Liu and colleagues have also shown that such attacks can be undetectable by standard methods.

False data injection attacks pose a fundamental challenge to cyber-physical systems: if a node in a cyber-physical system is compromised by an attacker and the attacker knows what security measures are in place, the attacker can always inject bad data into a control system while avoiding detection. This chapter proves this result for any cyber-physical system that is tolerant to measurement error.

The effectiveness and limitations of false data injection attacks were discussed in the original paper by Liu et al. [4]. Subsequent papers have proposed defense schemes and variations of false data injection attacks. However, some proposed defense schemes suffer from a simple

© IFIP International Federation for Information Processing 2020
Published by Springer Nature Switzerland AG 2020
J. Staggs and S. Shenoi (Eds.): Critical Infrastructure Protection XIV, IFIP AICT 596, pp. 245–260, 2020.
https://doi.org/10.1007/978-3-030-62840-6_12

lack of imagination. The question is, if an attacker knows the defense schemes, can the attacker still circumvent them? After all, Liu et al. [4] assumed that the attacker knows the system configuration and bad data thresholds.

This research approaches the problem in a more general manner. Sound defense schemes result from specific criteria. The proposed scheme confronts economic attacks specifically and meets the relevant criteria. A novel queue-based approach to attack detection is employed to optimally trade-off the false positive and false negative rates. Attacks on the smart grid are considered. Conventional state estimation assumes the presence of a central system operator who may be able to counteract an attack if it is properly identified. Under a distributed electric grid architecture, a centralized entity may still exist, but it is relevant to consider privacy issues as well as the practical applicability of any defense scheme. The literature on false data injection attacks represents the systems as matrices of data, but for any individual node, only a slice of the data is available.

2.   Related Work

Liu et al. [4] introduced the concept of false data injection attacks in power system state estimation and proved the existence of zero-residual attacks. This chapter does not propose a solution, but derives expressions for optimal attack vectors under different conditions. While the zero-residual attack is the most impressive version of a false data injection attack, it is not considered in this work. Zero-residual attacks can be considered to be unsolvable as they result from an attacker with complete power to arbitrarily inject bad data. However, good system design may make such attacks difficult to conduct. An attacker has to compromise every measurement related to a state variable – this is comparable to the attacker purchasing a bank in order to access the vault. It is theoretically possible, but perhaps not a practical security concern. Therefore, the focus is on attacks whose residuals are below a tolerable threshold.

Liang et al. [3] have conducted a thorough review of the literature on false data injection attacks on power systems. Much of the work focuses on variations of the attacks and systems under attack, as well as defense schemes. However, preference is given to attack scenarios that are easy to define mathematically instead of attack scenarios that capture the rational behavior of attackers. This stems no doubt from the academic norms of the control theory and power systems communities. As a result, an attacker who simply behaves in a sub-optimal or nonconforming manner may go perfectly undetected by schemes that assume optimal or conforming behavior.

Xie et al. [8] have introduced economic attacks on electricity markets that leverage false data injection. Jia et al. [2] have proposed a solution for detecting such attacks. Economic attacks differ from most attacks in the literature by considering attackers with known and quantifiable goals. These attacks may be designed to go undetected at the expense of the magnitudes of the attacks. If an entity gains a small but reliable amount of value from a persistent subtle attack, the entity would want to conduct the attack for as long as possible. However, it is not critical to quickly uncover such attacks because they pose no security threats. It would be sufficient to guarantee eventual detection.

The smart grid presents many new opportunities and challenges given the ability of nodes to coordinate the production, consumption and distribution of electricity. Mengelkamp et al. [5] present a comprehensive approach for implementing such coordination in a decentralized manner. Molina-Markham et al. [6] discuss privacy attacks on smart meters. Specifically, how smart meter data may be used to infer private information about a home. The work is a reminder of how secondary data sources can reveal private sensitive information.

3.   Problem Definition

This chapter considers false data injection attacks on power systems. In power system control, a central operator collects system measurements and decides whether or not to take action. In a decentralized grid, these activities may be carried out in a distributed manner, where local nodes collaborate on decision making and control.

Since measurements may have errors, state estimation is employed to compute the most probable real state of the system. State estimation relies on the relations between states. This can be expressed using the model:

$$z = h(x) + e \qquad (1)$$

where z is a measurement, x is a system state, $h(x)$ is a function relating states to measurements and e is the error.

State estimation is the problem of estimating the state $\hat{x}$ from z when there are multiple interrelated states. The state estimate SE is expressed as a function of the measurement z:

$$\hat{x} = SE(z) \qquad (2)$$

The computation of state estimates is inconsequential to the rest of this chapter. It suffices to say, that given noisy measurements, estimates of the system state can be obtained. This is especially useful in the smart grid where the coordination between nodes may be distributed and traditional state estimation does not apply.

Bad measurement detection is the problem of determining if measurements are abnormal or anomalous. It is computed using the residual r:

$$r = z - \hat{x} \tag{3}$$

which is simply the difference between the measurement and estimate. The residual is tested against a threshold value $r \leq \tau$ to determine if the measurement is credible or not.

3.1 Attack Model

In a traditional false data injection attack, the attacker is assumed to have control over one or several measurements and have detailed knowledge of the system. The attack is modeled by:

$$z_a = h(x) + e + \alpha \tag{4}$$

where α is a non-zero value. The assumption is that an undetected value of α will yield a gain to the attacker whereas $-\alpha$ will yield a loss.

The goal of the attack has two parts: (i) avoid any detection scheme deployed by the controller; and (ii) effect some changes to the estimated states.

Avoiding detection is a matter of keeping the residual r below some threshold. Liu et al. [4] have proved the existence of zero-residual attacks that change $\hat{x}$ without changing r. These attacks are only possible if an attacker controls every measurement related to some state. Liu and colleagues have also identified another type of attack where r may change, but is kept under a threshold τ. These attacks have less impact on $\hat{x}$, but can be carried out with just one corrupt measurement. This work only considers the latter type of attack where there is some change to the residual.

Thus, the goal of the attacker is to maximize the change in $\hat{x}$ while satisfying $r \leq \tau$. Given that the attacker knows how $SE(z)$ is computed and how τ is set, it is not very difficult to determine the optimal α value to be injected.

This work assumes that an attacker attempts to inject a consistent, yet unobtrusive, bias. The bias may be relatively small compared with the measurement variance. The attacker attempts to "hide in the error," so to speak, by keeping the attack residual too small to be distinguishable from the measurement error, but consistently in a direction that benefits the attacker. The benefit could be simple energy theft or overcharging for the amount of supplied energy.

3.2 Graph Approach

State estimation is traditionally considered to be an optimization problem where a power system is modeled as a system of linear equations. The collected data is represented as a vector of measurements whose relations are expressed by a matrix.

This work engages a graph model of the system instead of the standard form involving a system of linear equations. Because an optimization problem is not considered, there are no benefits to using the standard form. Additionally, in a distributed system such as a smart grid, control of the system may be distributed; long delays and response times in such a system render the collection of all the measurements for analysis problematic. Privacy may also be a concern.

Let $G = (V, E)$ be a graph representation of a smart grid where V is the set of nodes representing endpoints in the smart grid and E is the set of edges representing transmission lines between two nodes. Let $N(v)$ denote the set of neighbors of v.

The problem definition becomes simpler under the assumption that every node has an attached battery that stores or releases energy at will. This is not a restriction because a node without a battery is equivalent to a node that chooses never to use its battery. Each node can measure and report its incoming power P_i^+ from each neighbor, outgoing power P_j^- to each neighbor and its battery storage and discharge, P_b^+ and P_b^-, respectively. Each node operates under the conservation of power constraint:

$$\sum_{v_i \in N(v)} P_i^+ + \sum_{v_i \in N(v)} P_i^- + P_b^+ + P_b^- = 0 \tag{5}$$

Each node is required to report incoming and outgoing power readings to each neighbor. To preserve privacy, these readings are not reported to a central operator. Note that, even if a node reports all the measurements to an observer, it is trivial for the node to appear to be perfectly consistent internally even if it reports false measurements. If the node underreports its incoming power by a, it simply has to subtract a from P_b^+ to satisfy the equality.

In order to model economic attacks where an attacker seeks to gain some advantage from false data injection, it is useful to simplify the model further. Consider the case where two nodes, v_1 and v_2, share a transmission line, and v_1 intends to launch a false data attack against

v_2. There are two cases to consider. The first case is that the attack is strictly directed at v_2, which corresponds to a two-node problem. In second case, the attack is directed at multiple nodes, but it would still produce some attack residual between v_1 and v_2. In a situation involving faulty hardware, it may be reasonable to assume that a bad node provides bad data to all its neighbor nodes. However, an intelligent attacker may decide to provide bad data to only one neighbor or a select set of neighbors. Hence, it makes sense to reduce attacks to two-node problems. This may not be the optimal way to detect all attacks because some attacks may be detected faster by considering multiple residuals. But setting optimality aside, it makes for a much simpler problem definition:

- Given a set of edges E in a system graph $G = (V, E)$, determine the edges that are likely to be under attack.

Note the emphasis is on edges not nodes, which differs from the standard problem formulation that emphasizes nodes or state variables. This makes the problem explicitly about relations between nodes and not the nodes themselves. Residual sums represent relations between nodes; attacks, when they are detected, reside in the relations between nodes.

3.3   Distinguishing Victim from Attacker

The problem formulation only mentions determining an attacked edge, not the node that may be the attacker. Although it may be possible in some circumstances to determine which node is the attacker and which node is the victim, it is impossible to do so for all cases. Consider the case where an attacker at v_1 launches an attack strictly at v_2. That is, v_2 is the only node that can attest to the false data reported by v_1. In this case, a third-party observer would only be able to conclude that a disagreement exists between v_1 and v_2. In many practical situations, it would be required to know which node is acting falsely. However, for the purpose of this work, it is sufficient to determine the edge disagreement.

3.4   False Positives and False Negatives

A common approach to attack detection is to set a threshold that distinguishes normal data from corrupted data. The threshold could be derived statistically to have a desired property. Against a sophisticated attacker, the threshold would also define attacks that would be considered to be tolerable. If a threshold for divergence between two measurements is set to 10%, then an attacker who controls one of the measurements may design the attack vector to approach the 10% divergence without exceeding it. If the threshold were to be reduced to 1%, it would impose a tighter limit on the attacks that are tolerated, but it would also increase the false positive rate.

The false positive rate can be adjusted by setting the threshold for attack detection. If the goal is to have fewer false positives, the threshold should be increased; if the goal is have fewer false negatives, the threshold should be reduced. The trade-off between the inversely correlated false positives and false negatives is adjustable, but a practical solution ought to include an effective way to balance them.

3.5 Smart Attacker

If an attacker knows the detection schemes that are employed, a solution must assume that the attacker would actively avoid detection. It is not sufficient to determine the most optimal attack strategy and then defend against it. This is because sub-optimal attacks would go completely unnoticed.

3.6 Smart Grid Example

The smart grid is used to demonstrate a distributed bias attack. Roth and McMillin [7] describe how power mitigation works in a distributed grid infrastructure. The individual nodes report how much power they consume and produce, and an observer then verifies that the reported values are consistent. The model does not take noise into account. However, noise can be handled by checking the difference between two related measurements. If the difference exceeds a certain threshold, then the observer detects the anomaly and takes the appropriate action. If the difference is within the threshold, then the arithmetic mean of the two measurements is agreed to be the true state.

Figure 1 shows how a bias attack is conducted on a smart grid power distribution line between two nodes. The attacker simply underreports the incoming power when consuming electricity and overreports the outgoing power when producing electricity. The amount of bias depends on the threshold for tolerance, which the attacker is assumed to know. In effect, the attack would look like noise to any observer.

The scenario is illustrated in Figure 1, where the attacker underreports the received power, which amounts to theft. The physical connection (1) shared between the nodes has an actual flow of power that both nodes measure (2). The nodes report the measurements to each other, but the attacker injects bias (3). Both the nodes compute the mean state value (4) and residuals (5). If the residuals are small enough, no malicious activity is detected.

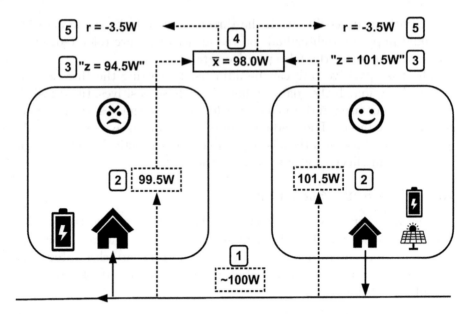

Figure 1. Bias attack on a smart grid power distribution line between two nodes.

In the example, the attacker has gained free power by abusing the noise tolerance. The attack works because the nodes use consensus to determine the real state of the system. In the absence of an attack, this would be the most reliable approach for many noisy distributed cyber-physical systems. The goal is therefore to demonstrate how bias attacks can be detected efficiently.

4. Proposed Solution

This section discusses the proposed solution for distributed bias detection.

4.1 Residual Sum

The residual sum is a central measurement of the integrity of a system. It is defined as:

$$r = z - \hat{x} \tag{6}$$

where $\hat{x}$ is an estimate of the system state x and z is a measurement of x. A large $|r|$ is obviously an indication of erroneous or false data. However, if $r \sim \mathcal{N}(0, \sigma^2)$ is assumed to hold when there is no attack, at any time step, r is expected to be non-zero and $|r| > \tau$ means that an attack is detected at a steady rate where τ is a threshold for the residual. A certain rate of false positives is expected. If an attacker injects $a = \frac{1}{2}\sigma^2$, the false positives will increase, but it is difficult for an observer to determine that an attack is occurring because σ^2 is not known.

In a single time instant, it may be impossible to discriminate between an attack and a random event. If the residual is tracked over multiple time instants, a clearer picture can be obtained. Taking the sum of absolute residuals until time n would yield a monotonically increasing function. However, the following residual sum function $RSUM$ is obtained upon summing the signed values of r:

$$RSUM(n) = \sum_{i=0}^{n} r \qquad (7)$$

The residual sum can be used in much the same way as the residual to determine if the reported measurements are within the expected bounds. A large $|RSUM|$ indicates erroneous or false data, but $RSUM$ has some properties that make it ideal for the problem at hand.

4.2 Statistical Behavior

The residual under no attack is assumed to be $r \sim \mathcal{N}(0, \sigma^2)$ and is $r \sim \mathcal{N}(c, \sigma^2)$ under a bias attack where c is a constant.

The residual sum $RSUM$, which is just the addition of residuals, has the distribution:

$$RSUM(n) \sim \mathcal{N}(0, n \cdot \sigma^2) \qquad (8)$$

This follows from the fact that the sum of two normally distributed variables is a normally distributed variable with mean equal to the sum of the means and variance equal to the sum of the variances. Summing up n residuals yields the following distribution of $RSUM_a$ under a biased attack:

$$RSUM_a(n) \sim \mathcal{N}(n \cdot c, n \cdot \sigma^2) \qquad (9)$$

Over time, the mean of the biased $RSUM_a$ grows at a rate of c whereas the mean of the unbiased $RSUM$ is expected to stay at zero.

This leads to the important observation that too much of a good thing can be a bad thing.

Theorem 1. Let $RSUM_a(n)$ and $RSUM(n)$ be the biased and unbiased residual sums after n measurements, respectively. Let γ be a chosen significance level for confidence intervals. For any γ, there exists some n for which the confidence interval of $RSUM_a(n)$ does not intersect the confidence interval of $RSUM(n)$.

Proof: Let $\pm z_\gamma$ be the confidence interval for $X \sim \mathcal{N}(0, 1)$ with confidence level γ. Let $\pm z_\gamma(n)$ be the confidence interval for $RSUM(n)$ with confidence level γ for some $n > 1$.

By definition:

$$P(X > z_\gamma) = \gamma \tag{10}$$

$$P(RSUM(n) > z_\gamma(n)) = \gamma \tag{11}$$

The distribution of $RSUM(n)$ is standardized as follows:

$$P(\frac{RSUM(n) - \mu}{\sigma\sqrt{n}} > \frac{z_\gamma(n) - \mu}{\sigma\sqrt{n}}) = \alpha \tag{12}$$

Since μ is zero and $RSUM(n)$ is normalized:

$$P(X > \frac{z_\gamma(n)}{\sigma\sqrt{n}}) = \gamma \tag{13}$$

Comparing Equations (10) and (13) yields:

$$z_\gamma = \frac{z_\gamma(n)}{\sigma\sqrt{n}} \tag{14}$$

And ultimately:

$$z_\gamma(n) = z_\gamma \cdot \sigma\sqrt{n} \tag{15}$$

Since z_γ is a constant, $z_\gamma(n)$ is $O(\sqrt{n})$. Let $\pm z_\gamma(n)'$ denote the confidence interval for $RSUM_a(n)$. Since the mean of $RSUM(n)$ is zero and the mean of $RSUM_a(n)$ is $n\mu$, $\pm z_\gamma(n)'$ will grow at a rate of $O(n\mu \pm z_\gamma \cdot \sqrt{(n)}) = O(n)$. Since $z_\gamma(n)'$ is of greater order than $z_\gamma(n)$, there exists some n_i, such that for every n_j where $j > i$, $|z_\gamma(n)'| > |z_\gamma(n)|$. Hence the two confidence intervals do not intersect after n_i measurements. $\qquad\square$

The interpretation of this result is that, no matter what confidence level γ is chosen and how small the bias residual value, eventually the biased $RSUM_a$ will distinguish itself from an unbiased $RSUM$. Figure 2 shows the diverging confidence intervals for biased and unbiased $RSUM$ values. The important point is that a small attack may go undetected for a long time, but eventually it will be detectable with an arbitrary level of confidence.

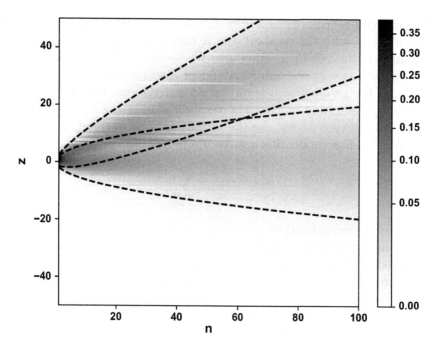

Figure 2. Diverging confidence intervals for biased and unbiased *RSUM* values.

4.3   Resource Requirements

RSUM is not only a useful tool for detecting bias attacks, but it also requires very limited computational resources for a distributed system. In terms of space, since *RSUM* can be computed dynamically, each *RSUM* value requires only a single (numeric) storage location. The solution requires each node to store $2 \cdot deg(v)$ values, where $deg(v)$ is the degree of node v.

In terms of computations, each *RSUM* requires only one addition at each time step. However, the estimate $\hat{x}$ may require additional computations depending on the method.

In terms of bandwidth, at minimum, each RSUM requires a single value to be transmitted between two nodes. However, this value only has to be transmitted between adjacent nodes, so it will not affect the communications network significantly.

4.4   Published Residuals

A valuable property of the residual sum is its potential to protect the privacy of individual nodes. In a traditional cyber-physical system, where data is sent to a central controller, privacy depends on how well the controller is trusted. In a fully distributed system, trust may not be assumed, but with the residual sum it may not be an issue.

Consider the case of a smart grid where the nodes may not wish to publish their energy consumption and production to a third-party controller. If the residual sum is published instead, an observer would not be able to determine much. The residual sum only expresses the disagreement between nodes, not the actual amounts of energy transferred.

The only observation that can be made from the residual sum is:

$$RSUM(n) < \sum_{i=0}^{n}(z) \tag{16}$$

This may be considered to be a privacy loss since a non-zero $RSUM$ would indicate activity, and vice versa. However, the concern can be alleviated by incorporating the following noise addition scheme.

Suppose two nodes share a physical connection and publish their shared residual. To obfuscate activity between them, they add a noise value e to every published value. The noise value e is drawn from a list of values L via the following steps:

1. A random seed value is exchanged between the nodes.

2. At coordinated intervals, n values are randomly generated by a linear congruential generator and added to a list L.

3. Every original element e in L is replaced with $\sigma \cdot (e\%100)/100$ and $-e$ is added to the end of L.

4. For every $2n$ time steps, an element e' is drawn randomly and removed from L. The element e' is then added to the current published $RSUM$.

This scheme makes it impossible for an observer to determine if published values between time 0 and $2n$ reflect activity or inactivity. Since the values in L sum to zero, it also guarantees that the published $RSUM$ is accurate at the end of each interval. Although σ may not be known, a suitable scalar may be used in its place.

4.5   Action and Queue-Based Inspection

This subsection demonstrates how the residual sum is used to discover bias attacks. The solution assumes that inspectors are tasked with finding and handling attacks and abnormalities. Such inspectors already exist in electric grids – they conduct routine inspections of meters for possible tampering. It is assumed that inspectors can identify and handle tampering of any meter, have full access to the entire system and carry specialized equipment. While these assumptions are convenient, they are not far from reality. The main issues are resources and distribution – hiring inspectors and scheduling them effectively.

The solution is to use residual sums to prioritize the work of the inspectors. Simply put, the focus is on the edges in the system that have high residual sums. Since the residual sums are published, the inspectors do not have to travel to the sites and can operate from a central control facility to handle a large region.

The idea is to set a threshold τ for the residual sums and alert the inspectors to edges that exceed τ. Choosing a τ value effectively sets the rates of true and false positives. If τ is too low, more false positives would be generated than the inspectors could handle. If τ is too high, the wait times would be much longer before inspectors can act on any malfeasance. A good threshold should yield manageable true and false positive rates.

However, a simpler approach that does not rely on thresholds exists. This approach sorts the residual sums by magnitude and schedules inspections at the corresponding locations in descending order. Thus, the most likely attacked nodes are inspected first and at the exact rate that the inspection crews can handle.

5. Experimental Results

Simulation experiments were conducted to demonstrate the effectiveness of using residual sums to detect bias attacks. The simulations were conducted using the well-known IEEE 14-bus system [1] and the MATPOWER package in MatLab.

The variance of the measurements was artificially set. It was accomplished by producing a set of base measurements by iteratively running state estimation on an initial set of measurements and replacing them with the estimated values. This yielded a measurement set with a square sum residual close to zero. The measurement set served as the basis for the simulation experiments.

Simulations were executed over 10,000 time steps. At each step, some $\mathcal{N}(0, \sigma^2)$ distributed noise was added to the base measurement of a node with $\sigma = 0.1$. All the simulations used ten unbiased nodes and a varying number k of biased nodes. For the biased nodes, an additional 0.01 was added to each measurement, corresponding to exactly one-tenth of the standard deviation of the noise.

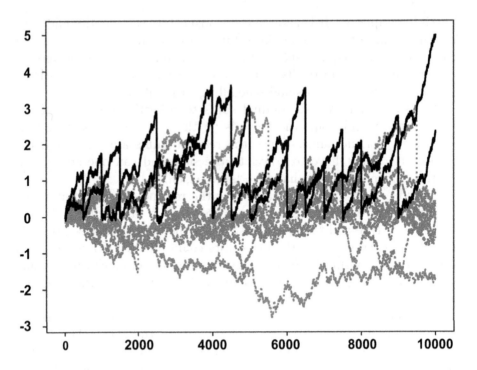

Figure 3. Simulations with ten unbiased (gray) and two biased (black) *RSUMs*.

State estimation of the power system was conducted using MAT-
POWER at each time step using the adjusted measurements. The residual of each variable was then calculated as the difference between the
measurement and estimate, and each residual was added to its corresponding residual sum. At regular intervals h, the highest magnitude
residual sum was identified and reset to zero.

Figure 3 shows the simulation results with ten unbiased *RSUMs*
(gray) and $k = 2$ biased *RSUMs* (black) conducted at regular intervals of $h = 500$ time steps with the highest residual sums reset to zero.
In this particular simulation instance, 13 out of 19 inspections found a
biased node to have the highest *RSUM*, corresponding to a true positive
rate of 68%. The figure highlights the chaotic nature of the noisy measurements, where some of the unbiased *RSUMs* become outliers while
the biased nodes consistently grow in the positive direction.

Table 1 presents the true positive rates obtained for varying numbers
of biased nodes k and inspection intervals with varying lengths (time
steps) h. Note that when there are many biased nodes and the inspection intervals are long, the true positive rate effectively becomes 100%.

Table 1. True positives for varying numbers of biased nodes and inspection intervals.

Biased Nodes (k)	Inspection Intervals (h)				
	100	300	500	700	900
1	0.27	0.45	0.47	0.57	0.73
2	0.42	0.64	0.68	0.64	0.91
3	0.55	0.67	0.74	0.86	0.91
4	0.7	0.82	0.95	1.0	1.0
5	0.74	0.88	0.95	1.0	1.0
6	0.78	0.91	1.0	1.0	1.0
7	0.86	0.94	1.0	1.0	1.0
8	0.86	1.0	1.0	1.0	1.0
9	0.83	0.94	1.0	1.0	1.0
10	0.93	1.0	1.0	1.0	1.0

The table illustrates a practical benefit of the queue approach. Inspectors know the positive rate and can adjust the inspection interval, but they do not have any information about the number of biased nodes. Nevertheless, they can achieve the desired positive rate by adjusting the inspection interval.

The simulation results demonstrate the applicability of Theorem 1. Because the biased and unbiased nodes diverge, it becomes easy to prioritize the edges on which inspections should focus.

6. Conclusions

A sophisticated attacker can easily conduct bias attacks on a noisy cyber-physical system while evading conventional detection methods. The proposed scheme for detecting bias attacks leverages the residual sum, a fundamental measurement of bias in cyber-physical systems. The properties that render the residual sum optimal for detection are discussed and theoretical bounds are derived in the absence and presence of bias attacks. The theoretical treatment and the simulation results demonstrate that the detection scheme is highly efficient, privacy preserving and effectively identifies bias attacks.

Future research will attempt to conduct experiments on a physical testbed. While this work has focused on electricity theft, future research will investigate other economic attacks. Additionally, multiple colluding attackers will be considered, which may lead to new challenges and opportunities.

Acknowledgement

This research was supported by the National Science Foundation under Grant No. CNS-1837472 and by the Missouri S&T Intelligent Systems Center.

References

[1] Illinois Center for a Smarter Electric Grid, IEEE 14-Bus System, Information Trust Institute, University of Illinois at Urbana-Champaign, Urbana, Illinois (`icseg.iti.illinois.edu/ieee-14-bus-system`), 2020.

[2] L. Jia, R. Thomas and L. Tong, Malicious data attack on the real-time electricity market, *Proceedings of the IEEE International Conference on Acoustics, Speech and Signal Processing*, pp. 5952–5955, 2011.

[3] G. Liang, J. Zhao, F. Luo, S. Weller and Z. Dong, A review of false data injection attacks against modern power systems, *IEEE Transactions on Smart Grid*, vol. 8(4), pp. 1630–1638, 2016.

[4] Y. Liu, P. Ning and M. Reiter, False data injection attacks against state estimation in electric power grids, *ACM Transactions on Information and System Security*, vol. 14(1), article no. 13, 2011.

[5] E. Mengelkamp, B. Notheisen, C. Beer, D. Dauer and C. Weinhardt, A blockchain-based smart grid: Towards sustainable local energy markets, *Computer Science – Research and Development*, vol. 33(1-2), pp. 207–214, 2018.

[6] A. Molina-Markham, P. Shenoy, K. Fu, E. Cecchet and D. Irwin, Private memoirs of a smart meter, *Proceedings of the Second ACM Workshop on Embedded Sensing Systems for Energy-Efficiency in Buildings*, pp. 61–66, 2010.

[7] T. Roth and B. McMillin, Physical attestation of cyber processes in the smart grid, in *Critical Information Infrastructures Security*, E. Luiijf and P. Hartel (Eds.), Springer, Cham, Switzerland, pp. 96–107, 2013.

[8] L. Xie, Y. Mo and B. Sinopoli, False data injection attacks in electricity markets, *Proceedings of the First IEEE International Conference on Smart Grid Communications*, pp. 226–231, 2010.

Chapter 13

COMPARISON OF DESIGN-CENTRIC AND DATA-CENTRIC METHODS FOR DISTRIBUTED ATTACK DETECTION IN CYBER-PHYSICAL SYSTEMS

Jennifer Leopold, Bruce McMillin, Rachel Stiffler and Nathan Lutes

Abstract   Cyber-physical systems are vulnerable to a variety of cyber, physical and cyber-physical attacks. The security of cyber-physical systems can be enhanced beyond what can be achieved through firewalls and trusted components by building trust from observed and/or expected behaviors. These behaviors can be encoded as invariants. Information flows that do not satisfy the invariants are used to identify and isolate malfunctioning devices and cyber intrusions. However, the distributed architectures of cyber-physical systems often contain multiple access points that are physically and/or digitally linked. Thus, invariants may be difficult to determine and/or computationally prohibitive to check in real time. Researchers have employed various methods for determining the invariants by analyzing the designs of and/or data generated by cyber-physical systems such as water treatment plants and electric power grids. This chapter compares the effectiveness of detecting attacks on a water treatment plant using design-centric invariants versus data-centric rules, the latter generated using a variety of data mining methods. The methods are compared based on the maximization of true positives and minimization of false positives.

Keywords: Cyber-physical attacks, invariants, data mining, water treatment plant

1.   Introduction

Cyber-physical systems typically contain multiple entry points, especially via edge devices (e.g., smart meters, home monitors and cameras) that provide access via service provider core networks. It is often the case that the distributed architectures of cyber-physical systems have access points that are physically and/or digitally linked. As a result, a

© IFIP International Federation for Information Processing 2020
Published by Springer Nature Switzerland AG 2020
J. Staggs and S. Shenoi (Eds.): Critical Infrastructure Protection XIV, IFIP AICT 596, pp. 261–279, 2020.
https://doi.org/10.1007/978-3-030-62840-6_13

computationally-prohibitive number of (combinatorial) conditions need to be checked in real-time to enforce the security of the overall systems.

Efforts to secure cyber-physical systems must contend with a number of challenges:

- Cyber and physical information flows should be combined in a single representational model. However, the semantics of the combined cyber-physical information flows in security domains are often not well understood. A good understanding of the semantics is needed to automate the task of securing information flows.

- Information flows are fundamentally bidirectional between two security domains [9]. An information flow either simultaneously preserves integrity but not confidentiality, or simultaneously preserves confidentiality but not integrity. This needs to be made clear to system designers.

- Mining system behavior by observing system operations may not uncover all the operational modes or may result in an overly complex model with a surplus of generated rules.

- Observations of physical systems may not be timely, accurate or complete due to malicious information, bad data, noisy data and communications delays.

- The proliferation of individual security domains causes high model complexity. Merging the security domains can result in a trivial, all-encompassing security domain.

A promising solution for addressing cyber-physical system vulnerabilities is to enhance the security of cyber-physical systems beyond what can be achieved through firewalls and trusted components by building trust from the observed and/or expected behaviors. These behaviors are encoded as invariants. Redundant, yet inconsistent, information flows that do not satisfy the invariants can help identify and isolate malfunctioning devices and cyber intrusions. Researchers have employed a variety of methods that analyze the designs of and/or data generated by cyber-physical systems such as water treatment plants and electric power grids. This work empirically compares the effectiveness of detecting attacks on a water treatment plant using design-centric invariants versus data-centric rules generated by several data mining methods.

2. Related Work

An invariant is a condition that should hold during the flow of information through a device or process at it moves from one state to the next. Invariants for a cyber-physical system can be derived using a variety of methods. A design-centric method determines invariants by examining the cyber-physical system design and control algorithms. This method has been employed by Adepu and Mathur [1, 2], with their Distributed Attack Detection (DAD) system [2] being notable for its use of only continuous (i.e., non-discretized) data. In contrast, a data-centric method determines invariants by analyzing the data generated by a cyber-physical system under (labeled) normal and attack conditions. Various data mining and machine learning methods have been employed to generate invariants, including association rule mining, support vector machines, decision trees and neural networks [7, 10].

Umer et al. [10] have compared design-centric and data-centric methods for deriving invariants for a water treatment plant. In the design-centric approach, system component specifications and state condition graphs of the plant were examined and 39 invariants were manually defined (see [3] for a discussion of state condition graphs). In the data-centric approach, association rule mining was employed, which produced hundreds of invariants.

The analysis of Umer et al. yielded two key conclusions. First, the data-centric approach did not find all the invariants defined by the design-centric approach. This was likely due to the loss of information from the data discretization needed to perform association rule mining and the lack of data that tested certain possible/expected conditions. The second conclusion was that the design-centric approach did not include all the invariants defined by the data-centric method, likely due to the comprehensive nature of the data mining method that considered all possible combinations of conditions. Nine invariants were found to be common to the data-centric and design-centric rules. Umer and colleagues mention that an integrated approach for invariant generation might be advantageous, but they did not provide a comparative analysis.

3.   Background

This section describes the cyber-physical system testbed used to analyze design-centric and data-centric rules for detecting attacks. It also discusses the metrics used for evaluating the rule sets.

3.1   Secure Water Treatment Plant

The dataset used in this study was obtained from the Secure Water Treatment (SWaT) plant, a testbed for cyber security research [4]. Figure 1 shows the architecture of the plant. The plant produces five gallons/minute of treated water and can operate non-stop, 24 hours per

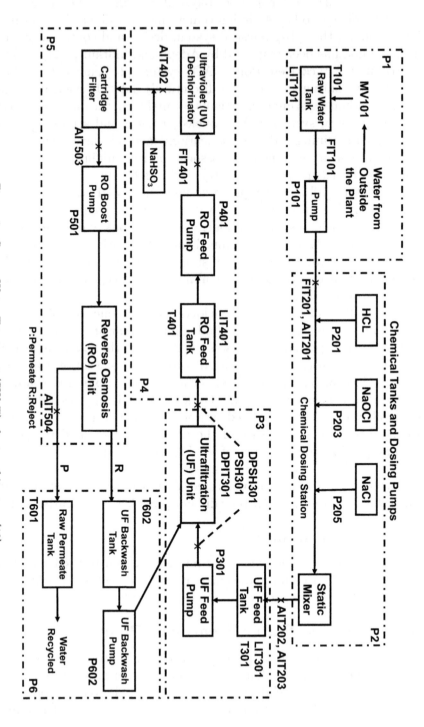

Figure 1.   Secure Water Treatment (SWaT) plant architecture [10].

day, seven days a week in a fully autonomous mode. The plant has six stages (processes), each of which is controlled by a programmable logic controller. The states of the stages are measured by sensors and the control actions are performed by actuators. The plant has 68 sensors and actuators; some of the actuators are standby devices that are used only when the primary actuators fail.

A multi-layer ring network supports plant communications. Programmable logic controllers at one level can communicate with sensors and actuators at another level and in different stages. Plant operations are monitored and controlled by an operator at a supervisory control and data acquisition (SCADA) workstation. Physical attacks include replacing or removing sensors, disconnecting wires between components (i.e., sensors, actuators and programmable logic controllers) and interrupting power flow to electronic components.

Each instance in the dataset corresponds to a discrete or continuous value of a sensor and the timestamp denoting when the reading was taken. The readings were taken every second over 24-hour periods, operating for a certain number of days under normal conditions and a certain number of days under attacks.

The original dataset [5] comprised 890,298 instances labeled as sensors operating normally and 54,621 instances labeled as sensors under attack. However, when the dataset was created, the system was operating under a variety of non-standard (i.e., atypical) conditions with no indications of states. As will be discussed in the next section, some of the design-centric rules were sensitive to the system operating state. Also, the values of some attributes in the dataset were not within normal ranges and/or were fluctuating abnormally during certain states or state changes, although the system was not under attack. Without system state information, the original dataset was inadequate for evaluating design-centric as well as data-centric methods.

The dataset used in this research (currently available at [5]) does not contain data related to atypical states (e.g., initial startup and backwash). Additionally, the dataset maintains state information. It has 13,070 instances labeled as sensors operating normally and 1,926 instances labeled as sensors under attack (a binary attribute is_attack identifies an instance as normal (0) or attack (1)). However, no information is provided about the nature of the attacks.

3.2 Evaluation Metrics

The effectiveness of design-centric versus data-centric rules at detecting attacks was evaluated using the following basic metrics:

- **True Positive (*TP*):** A true positive is an instance labeled as an attack (i.e., is_attack=1) that was correctly detected as an attack.

- **False Positive (*FP*):** A false positive is an instance labeled as normal (i.e., is_attack=0) that was incorrectly detected as an attack.

- **True Negative (*TN*):** A true negative is an instance labeled as normal (i.e., is_attack=0) that was correctly detected as normal.

- **False Negative (*FN*):** A false negative is an instance labeled as an attack (i.e., is_attack=1) that was incorrectly detected as normal.

In the cyber security domain, the highest priority is to maximize the number of true positives and minimize the number of false negatives. A false negative – missing an attack – can have severe consequences. False positives correspond to "crying wolf," so large numbers of false positives are undesirable, but they do carry less severe consequences.

The following metrics are derived from the four basic metrics:

- **Accuracy:** Accuracy is the proportion of the total number of instances that were correctly identified. It is computed as:

$$Accuracy = \frac{TP + TN}{TP + FP + FN + TN} \tag{1}$$

- **Precision:** Precision is the proportion of instances that were correctly identified as positive from among the total number of instances that were correctly or incorrectly identified as positive. It is computed as:

$$Precision = \frac{TP}{TP + FP} \tag{2}$$

- **Sensitivity:** Sensitivity, which is also referred to as recall, is computed as:

$$Sensitivity = \frac{TP}{TP + FN} \tag{3}$$

- **Specificity:** Specificity is the proportion of negative instances that were correctly identified from among the total number of negative instances. It is computed as:

$$Specificity = \frac{TN}{TN + FP} \tag{4}$$

In general, precision and sensitivity are important because they are viewed as metrics of exactness and completeness of testing, respectively. The kappa statistic is also useful for evaluating a decision model:

- **Kappa Statistic:** The kappa statistic indicates how much better a predictive model is compared with random guessing. It is computed as:

$$Kappa = \frac{Non\text{-}Random\ Successes - Random\ Successes}{N - Random\ Successes} \quad (5)$$

  where *Non-Random Successes* is the number of instances correctly predicted by a non-random model and *Random Successes* is the number of instances correctly predicted by a random model and N is the number of instances in the dataset.

4. SWaT Rule Evaluation

This section compares the effectiveness of design-centric and data-centric rules obtained from the SWaT dataset. Rules produced by a variety of methods are evaluated based on their ability to detect attacks in the SWaT dataset.

4.1 Design-Centric Method

Umer et al. [10] manually generated 39 invariants by examining the SWaT specifications and state condition graphs. However, a number of problems were encountered when attempts were made to test the accuracy of these rules on the SWaT dataset.

Rules are specified using the syntax *Antecedent → Consequent*. Each rule was intended to be checked in the following manner where n is the number of seconds to wait for the consequent to become true after the antecedent was satisfied:

> If the *Antecedent* is true
>> Then wait n seconds
>> If the *Antecedent* and *Consequent* are true
>>> Then the system is functioning normally
>>> Else the system is not functioning normally
>> End-if
> End-if

Interestingly, the situation where the antecedent becomes false during the n-second wait period was not considered, a condition that occurred seven times in the SWaT dataset. The only concern was that the antecedent and consequent should be true at the end of the n-second period. This could be a problem if, for example, a water tank reaches a certain level (satisfying the antecedent), leaks some water on the floor due to a malfunction or malfeasance during the wait period (thereby no longer satisfying the antecedent), but refills to a certain level (again satisfying the antecedent) before the end of the wait period.

Umer et al. [10] do not report the time constraints for the design-centric invariants. Therefore, one of the authors (Adepu) was contacted to obtain the time constraint for each rule. Even then, the time constraints for several rules had to be increased by a few seconds to best fit the SWaT dataset (i.e., increase the attack detection accuracy).

Other problems encountered with the original design-centric rules included the specification of attributes that were not in the dataset, unspecified threshold values, reversals of conjunctions and disjunctions, and missing conditions in antecedents and consequents. These problems necessitated the elimination of a few rules (i.e., those involving attributes that were not in the dataset) and resulted in a proliferation of false positives and false negatives. Many of these problems were resolved with the assistance of one of the authors of [10] (Adepu). Other problems were resolved by examining the data and/or specifications in the SWaT operating manual [6].

Tables 1 and 2 show the final set of 31 design-centric rules along with their time constraints in seconds. The order of rules has no significance. Values of 1 and 2 for pumps (e.g., P101) represent off and on, respectively. Values of 1 and 2 for valves (e.g., MV201) represent closed and open, respectively. Attributes with the prefix PLC represent the state of the system (e.g., initial startup and backwash). Interested readers are referred to the SWaT operating manual [6] for more information about the attributes.

The rule set was treated as a set of invariants. Starting from any instance in the dataset, all the rules had to be satisfied or else an attack was considered to have occurred. Because multiple rules with different time constraints had to be satisfied for an attack not to have occurred, it was not possible to compute the true negative rate (i.e., number of labeled normal instances detected as normal). For similar reasons, false negatives (i.e., number of labeled attack instances detected as normal) could not be determined easily. Consequently, the accuracy, specificity and sensitivity values could not be computed.

When the set of design-centric rules was tested on the SWaT dataset, the false positive rate (i.e., instances labeled as normal but detected as attacks) was 55.47% and the true positive rate (i.e., actual attacks

Table 1. Design-centric invariants.

Rule	Rule Specification	Time Constraint (sec)
1	LIT101≤500 → MV101=2	14
2	LIT101≥800 → MV101=1	12
3	LIT101≤250 → P101=1 and P102=1	2
4	LIT301≤800 and PLC1!=1 → P101=2 or P102=2 or PLC1!= 2	12
5	LIT301≥1000 → P101=1 and P102=1 and MV201=1	3
6	LIT301≤800 and PLC2!=1 → MV201=2	10
7	FIT201≤0.5 → P201=1 and P202=1 and P203=1 and P204=1 and P205=1 and P206=1	2
8	AIT201≥260 and FIT201≥0.5 → P201=1 and P202=1	2
9	MV201=2 and FIT201≥0.5 and AIT503≤260 and AIT201≤250 and PLC2!=1 → P201=2 or P202=2	7
10	AIT503≥260 and MV201≥0.5 → P201=1 and P202=1	2
11	MV201=2 and FIT201≥0.5 and AIT503≤260 and PLC2!=1 → P201=2 or P202=2	2
12	AIT202≤6.95 → P203=1 and P204=1	2
13	MV201=2 and AIT202≥7.05 and FIT201≥0.5 and PLC2!=1 → P203=2 or P204=2	8
14	AIT203≥500 → P205=1 and P206=1	2
15	P101=2 or P102=2 and MV201=2 and AIT203≤420 and FIT201≥0.5 and AIT402≤250 and PLC2!=1 → P205=2 or P206=2	6
16	AIT402≥250 → P205=1 and P206=1	2
17	MV201=2 and FIT201≥0.5 and AIT402≤240 and PLC2!=1 → P205=2 or P206=2	6
18	LIT301≤=250 → P301=1 and P302=1	4
19	LIT401≥1000 → P301=1 and P302=1	2
20	LIT301≥250 and LIT401≤800 → P301=2 or PLC3!=7	2

Table 2. Design-centric invariants (continued).

Rule	Rule Specification	Time Constraint (sec)
21	LIT401$\leq$250 $\rightarrow$ P401=1 and P402=1	4
22	LIT401$\leq$250 $\rightarrow$ UV401=1	4
23	P401=1 and P402=1 $\rightarrow$ UV401=1	4
24	FIT401$\leq$0.5 $\rightarrow$ UV401=1	4
25	P401=1 and P402=1 and PLC4=4 $\rightarrow$ UV401=1	4
26	AIT402$\leq$240 $\rightarrow$ P403=1 and P404=1 or PLC4!=4	2
27	AIT402$\geq$250 $\rightarrow$ P403=2 or P404=2 or PLC4!=4	2
28	P401=1 and PLC5=12 $\rightarrow$ P501=1	5
29	UV401=1 $\rightarrow$ P401=1 or P402=1	4
30	FIT401$\leq$0.5 and PLC5=12 $\rightarrow$ P501=1 or P502=1	4
31	LIT101$\geq$1100 $\rightarrow$ P601=1	2

correctly detected as attacks) was 44.53%. In all, there were 446 occurrences of false positives, 14 of which were caused by Rule 1 and 432 by Rule 5. These problems may have been due to faulty components. For example, in the case of Rule 5, a motorized valve (MV201) may have had trouble closing; however, increasing the time constraint for Rule 5 only resolved eight of the 432 false positives attributed to the rule.

Of greater concern than the large number of false positives was the unacceptably low rate of true positives. A possible explanation is that the threshold values in the design-centric rules may not have been realistic with regard to the actual performance of the individual components. For example, the LIT301 attribute was required to be less than or equal to 800 in Rule 4; however, in one of the data-centric rule sets, LIT301 had to be less than or equal to 793.7869. This was the case for several attributes common to the design-centric and data-centric rule sets. Another possible explanation for the low true positive rate may have been the time constraints. Manual examination of the dataset revealed several instances where it took longer than the specified amount of time for the consequent of a rule to be satisfied. When the time constraint was increased for some of the rules, the increase in the true positive rate was often accompanied by an increase in the false positive rate.

4.2 Data-Centric Methods

Several data mining methods were employed to generate rules for detecting attacks in the SWaT dataset. Unlike the set of invariants, each rule has as its consequent a single binary condition that indicates whether or not an attack has occurred. Also, unlike the set of invariants, it is not necessary for an instance to satisfy all the rules in the rule set. Additionally, none of the data mining methods took into account the temporal nature of the physical system; specifically, unlike the design-centric rules, they did not consider that a certain amount of time had to transpire between the satisfaction of the rule conditions. For this reason, 10-fold cross validation was used to test the methods. Breaks in time sequences between instances were not as critical as they were in the design-centric testing.

All the data mining methods were implemented using the R programming language. None of the methods required discretization of the SWaT data. However, attributes with values that did not change from row to row were removed before creating the data-centric models (i.e., AIT401 and all the pump attributes, except for P101, P203, P205, P301, P401 and P601). These attributes were not informative and would not have been included in any decision model.

The data mining methods – some of them ensemble methods – that produced the best accuracy were: J48 and C5.0 (both decision tree methods with pruning), rfRules (random forest specifying a maximum of 300 trees), AdaBoost.M1 (boosting with decision trees), naïve Bayesian network (NB), support vector machine (SVM) (linear with a polynomial kernel), JRip (association rules with reduced error pruning) and multilayer perceptron neural network (NNet). Other methods such as linear regression models and association rule methods were attempted. However, the results of these methods are not discussed here because their accuracy was not competitive or their results were not as informative as the other methods. Interested readers are referred to [11] for details about the data mining methods used in this work.

Table 3 compares the results obtained using the eight data mining methods based only on accuracy and the kappa statistic. Figures 2 and 3 show more extensive comparisons in terms of accuracy, kappa statistic, precision, sensitivity and specificity.

The results indicate that the two ensemble methods (rfRules and AdaBoost.M1) did not improve on the individual decision tree methods (J48 and C5.0), and did not justify the additional complexity and memory requirements of an ensemble method. The naïve Bayesian network and neural network were also eliminated from the top candidates due to

Table 3.   Accuracy and kappa statistic for eight data mining methods.

Method	Accuracy	Kappa
J48	0.998044	0.991256
Naïve Bayesia Network	0.871880	0.212844
Support Vector Machine	0.998311	0.992461
rfRules	0.984352	0.926389
AdaBoost.M1	0.999289	0.996819
C5.0	0.997866	0.990452
JRip	0.998399	0.992863
Neural Network	0.871533	0.000000

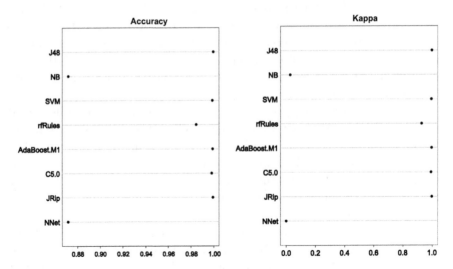

Figure 2.   Evaluation metrics for the eight data mining methods.

their lower accuracy, kappa statistic, sensitivity (in the case of the naïve Bayesian network), precision and specificity. Although the support vector machine performed well, it was decided to investigate only the J48, C5.0 and JRip models because they performed well and were the most comparable models in terms of their expression as rule sets.

Stacking was employed using the three selected methods (J48, C5.0 and JRip) as the base classifiers and the best performing of the three, JRip, as the ensemble method. This was done to see if an ensemble of the best three methods could improve on the performance of the individual

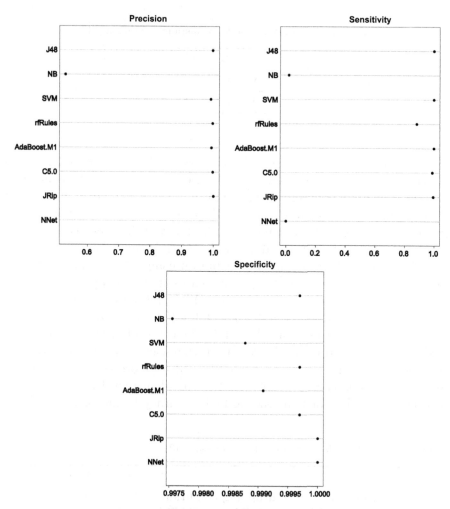

Figure 3. Evaluation metrics for the eight data mining methods (continued).

methods. The accuracy of the ensemble method was 0.998399 and its kappa statistic was 0.992813. Since these results did not improve on those obtained using the individual JRip method, the ensemble method was not considered any further in the interest of memory efficiency.

The J48, C5.0 and JRip predictive models are expressed as rule sets. Even rules derived from pruned decision trees (e.g., J48 and C5.0) can result in unnecessary conditions. Therefore, in order to construct the most efficient rule sets, a program was written in R to check for and drop unnecessary conditions. The strategy that was utilized (originally presented in [8]) is summarized in the following paragraphs.

Table 4.   Contingency table for instances satisfying A'.

	C	$!C$
X	$Y1$	$E1$
$!X$	$Y2$	$E2$

Let R be a rule of the form $A \rightarrow C$ where A is the antecedent, C is the consequent and the antecedent A contains more than one condition. Let R' be a more general rule of the form $A' \rightarrow C$ where A' is obtained by deleting one condition X from A'. Consider the contingency table in Table 4, where the counts $Y1$, $Y2$, $E1$ and $E2$ were collected by considering instances in the dataset that satisfy condition A'.

Let $U_{25}(E, S)$ be a binomial distribution using a 25% confidence level for a sample size S with E negative cases in the sample. The error rate of rule R is estimated as $U_{25}(E1, Y1 + E1)$ and the error rate of rule R' is estimated as $U_{25}(E1 + E2, Y1 + Y2 + E2 + E2)$. If the error rate of R' is no greater than that of R, then the condition X is deleted. Using a greedy approach, the condition that yields the lowest error rate for the rule is successively eliminated until no more conditions can be eliminated. The choice of 25% for the confidence level is considered a conservative value for maintaining high accuracy in rule sets [8].

Table 5.   Profiles of data-centric rules before and after conditions were dropped.

	J48	JRip	C5.0
Number of rules before dropping conditions	25	11	19
Number of rules with conditions dropped	19	2	1
Average number of conditions in antecedents	5.68	2.64	2.42

Table 5 shows the number of rules before dropping conditions, number of rules that had conditions dropped and average number of conditions in the antecedent per rule (after dropping conditions) for the J48, JRip and C5.0 methods.

Table 6 and Tables 7 and 8, show the JRip and C5.0 rule sets, respectively. Due to space constraints, the J48 rule set is not shown.

Only a few identical rules were produced by the methods, specifically J48 and C5.0, both of which are decision tree methods. Nevertheless, there are some commonalties between the rule sets.

Table 6. JRip rule set.

Rule	Rule Specification
1	AIT202≤8.931236 and LIT301≥923.2809 → is_attack=1
2	AIT402≤6.613689 and PIT503≥113.800949 and PIT501≤159.590485 and LIT101≥596.9952 and DPIT301≤1.245278 and DPIT301≥1.229272 → is_attack=1
3	AIT402≤6.613689 and AIT402≥5.075622 and LIT301≤829.274536 and LIT101≤769.3148 → is_attack=1
4	AIT402≤6.664958 and LIT301≥938.781738 and AIT203≥262.4968 → is_attack=1
5	LIT301≥1024 and AIT502≥69.21302 and FIT503≥0.610313 and LIT401≤864.932068 → is_attack=1
6	LIT301≥1027.94153 and AIT203≤240.810043 → is_attack=1
7	LIT301≥1112.57532 and AIT202≥9.202961 and AIT201≥126.24968 → is_attack=1
8	LIT401≤787.2597 → is_attack=1
9	FIT601≥0.000384 and LIT301≥1024 and LIT401≥848.936157 → is_attack=1
10	DPIT301≤1.104424 → is_attack=1
11	Else → is_attack=0

Table 7. C5.0 rule set.

Rule	Rule Specification
1	AIT202≤9.383043 and LIT301≤923.2008 → is_attack=0
2	LIT301≥923.2008 and LIT401≥878.4286 and AIT201≥126.0895 → is_attack=0
3	AIT402≥6.664958 → is_attack=0
4	LIT301≤923.2008 and LIT401≥954.0246 → is_attack=0
5	AIT202≥8.931236 and LIT401≤805.5627 → is_attack=0
6	AIT202≥8.931236 and PIT503≤113.6728 → is_attack=0
7	P301≥0 and AIT202≥8.931236 and LIT401≤849.5514 → is_attack=0
8	AIT202≥8.931236 and AIT202≤8.996923 → is_attack=0

Table 8.   C5.0 rule set (continued).

Rule	Rule Specification
9	AIT203≤262.3686 and FIT501≥0.80223 and AIT201≤126.0895 → is_attack=0
10	AIT203≤262.3686 and FIT504≥0.209781 and AIT201≤126.0895 → is_attack=0
11	AIT202≤9.020315 and LIT401≥865.4319 → is_attack=0
12	AIT202≥8.931236 and LIT301≥923.2008 and LIT301≤938.3812 → is_attack=0
13	LIT301≤793.7869 → is_attack=0
14	AIT202≥9.070623 and FIT503≤0.606984 → is_attack=0
15	AIT402≤3.409382 and FIT401≥0.802484 → is_attack=0
16	AIT202≥8.996923 and AIT402≤6.664958 and LIT401≥805.5627 and LIT401≤849.5514 → is_attack=1
17	AIT202≥9.383043 and AIT203≥243.2453 and AIT402≤6.664958 and LIT401≤954.0246 → is_attack=1
18	AIT202≥9.39554 and LIT301≥793.7869 and AIT402≤6.664958 → is_attack=1
19	LIT301≥923.2008 and AIT402≤ 6.664958 → is_attack=1

Figure 4 shows the attributes that are common and different in the J48, JRip and C5.0 rule sets based on their references in the rule antecedents and consequents. Of particular interest are the six attributes included in all three rule sets: AIT202, AIT203, LIT301, LIT401, AIT402 and AIT201. These attributes could be the primary "canaries in the coal mine" with respect to detecting attacks. In fact, they may have been the direct targets of the attacks.

Not surprisingly, the six common attributes also featured prominently in the design-centric rule set. However, the design-centric rule set was distinctive in that it frequently specified conditions on various pumps (attributes with the prefix P followed by three digits such as P201) and the ultraviolet dechlorinator (UV401), whereas only one pump attribute (P301) was used in the J48 and C5.0 rules and the dechlorinator attribute was never used in the J48, C5.0 and JRip rules. In fact, the P203 and P205 attributes have identical values in the SWaT dataset, eliminating the need to test more than one of them.

Another point of interest is that, of the six SWaT stages (labeled P1–P6 in Figure 1), the least often referenced attributes in the design-

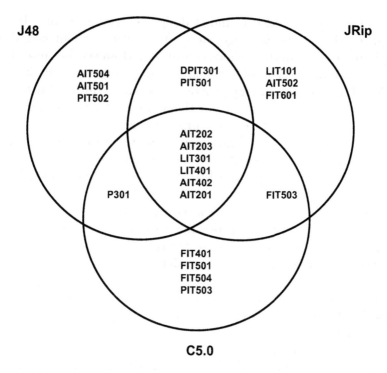

Figure 4. Common and different attributes in the data-centric rule sets.

centric and data-centric rules are from stages P1, P5 and P6. Perhaps the attacks targeted the P2, P3 and P4 stages and/or there is a "ripple effect" between the sensors in these three stages.

5. Conclusions

Detecting attacks on cyber-physical systems is an important but challenging task. A promising approach is to enforce invariants, conditions that must hold during the operation of a physical process and, when violated, are indicative of a component fault or cyber attack. Invariants can be generated by manually examining the design of a system (design-centric method) and/or by deducing patterns observed in data collected under normal and abnormal system operating conditions (i.e., data-centric method).

The comparison of the effectiveness of detecting attacks on a water treatment plant using one design-centric rule set and multiple data-centric rule sets generated by data mining methods reveals that the data-centric methods are far better at predicting attacks and minimizing false negatives. The results of this study cannot be generalized and are not intended to indict design-centric invariants. In fact, a design-centric method leverages domain knowledge about how the system should behave under various conditions. However, because the task is time-consuming (typically manual), it may not cover all the contingencies. Furthermore, design-centric rules may require adjustments to the threshold values to account for the wear-and-tear on system components. In contrast, a data-centric approach can more easily generate an optimal combination of the numerous conditions that identify anomalous behavior. As demonstrated by the results, a data-centric approach learns (and re-learns) from a real-time system that may no longer correspond to the original design specifications. However, a data-centric rule set is only as complete as the data on which it is based; if the underlying dataset does not cover all possible situations, the resulting rule set will not check for all contingencies. Overall, the best strategy is to consider the information provided by design-centric as well as data-centric methods.

The data-centric rules produced in this study are based on a single dataset and may be subject to overfitting, despite undergoing 10-fold cross validation. In future research, it would be interesting to test these rules on the live SWaT testbed, much like the work reported in [2].

Other structured cyber-physical datasets are available from the iTrust Center for Research in Cyber Security [5], including the Water Distribution (WADI) and Electric Power and Intelligence Control (EPIC) datasets. Future work could compare design-centric and data-centric methods for detecting attacks in these datasets. However, this will require design-centric invariants, which could be generated in a semi-automated manner from system schematics and design documents.

Finally, future research will investigate other data-centric methods for detecting attacks. A promising problem is to model a cyber-physical system as a graph and use dynamic graph anomaly detection algorithms to deduce invariants. Modeling a cyber-physical system as a graph is a natural extension of its interconnected physical design and may provide a bridge to developing automated methods for generating design-centric invariants.

Acknowledgements

This research was performed with the assistance of three Missouri University of Science and Technology students – Nathan Lincoln, Michael Macke and Alex Warhover. The research project was supported by the National Science Foundation under Grant No. CNS-1837472.

References

[1] S. Adepu and A. Mathur, Generalized attacker and attack models for cyber-physical systems, *Proceedings of the Fortieth Annual IEEE Computer Software and Applications Conference*, pp. 283–292, 2016.

[2] S. Adepu and A. Mathur, Distributed attack detection in a water treatment plant: Method and case study, to appear in *IEEE Transactions on Dependable and Secure Computing*.

[3] S. Adepu, A. Mathur, J. Gunda and S. Djokic, An agent-based framework for simulating and analyzing attacks on cyber-physical systems, *Proceedings of the Fifteenth International Conference on Algorithms and Architectures for Parallel Processing*, pp. 785–798, 2015.

[4] J. Goh, S. Adepu, K. Junejo and A. Mathur, A dataset to support research in the design of secure water treatment systems, *Proceedings of the Eleventh International Conference on Critical Information Infrastructures Security*, pp. 88–99, 2016.

[5] iTrust Centre for Research in Cyber Security, Dataset Characteristics, Singapore University of Technology and Design, Singapore (`itrust.sutd.edu.sg/itrust-labs_datasets/dataset_info`), 2020.

[6] iTrust Centre for Research in Cyber Security, Secure Water Treatment, Singapore University of Technology and Design, Singapore (`itrust.sutd.edu.sg/testbeds/secure-water-treatment-swat`), 2020.

[7] K. Junejo and D. Yau, Data driven physical modeling for intrusion detection in cyber-physical systems, *Proceedings of the Singapore Cyber Security Conference*, pp. 43–57, 2016.

[8] J. Quinlan, *C4.5: Programs for Machine Learning*, Morgan Kaufmann Publishers, San Mateo, California, 1993.

[9] D. Sutherland, A model of information, *Proceedings of the Ninth National Computer Security Conference*, pp. 175–183, 1986.

[10] M. Umer, A. Mathur, K. Junejo and S. Adepu, Integrating design and data centric approaches to generate invariants for distributed attack detection, *Proceedings of the Workshop on Cyber-Physical Systems Security and Privacy*, pp. 131–136, 2017.

[11] I. Witten, E. Frank and M. Hell, *Data Mining: Practical Machine Learning Tools and Techniques*, Morgan Kaufmann Publishers, San Francisco, California, 2011.

INFRASTRUCTURE MODELING AND SIMULATION

Chapter 14

A MODEL-BASED SAFETY-SECURITY RISK ANALYSIS FRAMEWORK FOR INTERCONNECTED CRITICAL INFRASTRUCTURES

Rajesh Kumar

Abstract   Interconnected infrastructures are complex due to their temporal evolution, component dependencies and dynamic interdependencies, coupled with the presence of adversaries. Much research has focused on safety and security risk assessments of isolated infrastructures. However, extending these techniques to interconnected infrastructures is infeasible due to their complex interdependencies and the lack of generic modeling tools.

This chapter presents a framework for modeling and analyzing interconnected infrastructures. The framework has a two layers. One is the higher modeling layer that expresses the functional dependencies of infrastructures, where each infrastructure is refined to capture component-level disruptions and is represented using a novel combination of dynamic reliability block diagrams and attack-fault trees. The other is the lower analysis layer based on stochastic timed automata that serves as a semantic framework for the higher layer. While the higher layer graphically represents complex dependencies and interdependencies, and temporal and cascading disruption scenarios, the lower analysis layer provides a rigorous foundation for investigating the relationships using formal verification, in particular, statistical model checking. The lower layer also provides a flexible means for incorporating quantitative system attributes such as probability, time and cost. The efficacy of the framework is demonstrated using a real disruption scenario involving interconnected electric power and industrial communications networks, where an analyst can identify weak links, evaluate alternative protection measures and make transparent decisions about risk management investments.

Keywords: Interconnected infrastructures, risk, safety, security, attack-fault trees

© IFIP International Federation for Information Processing 2020
Published by Springer Nature Switzerland AG 2020
J. Staggs and S. Shenoi (Eds.): Critical Infrastructure Protection XIV, IFIP AICT 596, pp. 283–306, 2020.
https://doi.org/10.1007/978-3-030-62840-6_14

1.   Introduction

Modern society relies on several critical infrastructures that are strategically interconnected with each other, exchanging logical and physical flows such as information, power and goods, resulting in a system-of-systems [14, 26]. As these infrastructures have expanded and become increasingly networked and interconnected, they have become extremely vulnerable to numerous threats ranging from natural hazards and mechanically-induced operational failures to human error and terrorist acts. Due to the strong intertwining of critical infrastructure goods and services, a small malfunction in one infrastructure can quickly cascade to other infrastructures, resulting in devastating impacts, perhaps bringing industrial operations to a complete standstill. An example is the Indian blackouts of July 30-31, 2012, where disruptions of the northern sections of the power grid immediately impacted railway and metro services, and proceeded to cause disruptions in many other sectors, including telecommunications, financial services and manufacturing [25].

Given the complex, multi-actor and decentralized nature of interconnected infrastructures, critical infrastructure owners and operators need active risk management frameworks to understand disruption scenarios from the organizational perspective as well as from the system-of-systems perspective. Important questions are – What is the probability of a disruption? Will the countermeasures implemented in a upstream infrastructure impact downstream infrastructures? Where should countermeasures be positioned so that the overall reliability is improved? Answering these and other questions would enable critical infrastructure owners and operators to make transparent decisions about mitigating risk and increasing infrastructure resilience.

This chapter presents a generic model-based quantitative analysis framework that is designed for infrastructure owners and operators. The framework enables an analyst to decompose complex interconnected infrastructures into smaller manageable parts. The individual parts can be analyzed separately or all the parts can be combined and analyzed holistically. The framework combines two popular dependability models – dynamic reliability block diagrams [13, 35] and attack-fault trees [24]. Quantitative functionally-related system characteristics such as cost structures and time-dynamic attributes are incorporated in a stochastic timed automaton model [10] that is derived from the combined dynamic reliability block diagram and attack-fault tree models. The popular UPPAAL SMC tool [10] is used to perform statistical model-checking, allowing the simulation of a complex system when a simple closed-form solution does not exist or a rigorous state-space search is infeasible.

In recent years, several attempts have been made to model inter-dependent infrastructures [29, 32]. Ouyang [27] has classified model-ing techniques into several broad categories – empirical, agent-based, system-dynamics-based, economic-theory-based and network-based ap-proaches, among others. Stergiopoulos et al. [34] identify agent-based and network-based analysis techniques as the most popular approaches for modeling interdependencies in critical infrastructures. Bobbio et al. [5] have conducted an interesting sector-specific analysis of inter-dependencies between the electric power and telecommunications sec-tors. In another paper, Stergiopoulos and colleagues [33] employ graph-based techniques to represent dependencies and concurrent cascading and common-cause failures. However, their work is restricted to a high-level analysis while the framework proposed in this chapter permits high-level and component-level analyses.

Reliability and safety analyses often leverage graphical models such as reliability block diagrams, fault trees and event trees [19, 28]. Quan-titative analyses with these models employ logic and probability theory. Motivated by model-based reliability and safety analyses, model-based security analysis is attracting interest. Ruijters and Stoelinga [30] have conducted a detailed survey of the state of the art in fault tree modeling and analysis.

Other frameworks employ attack trees [20, 21], state-based analy-sis [15] and Boolean-driven Markov processes [7]. Although attack trees and fault trees have been employed in several practical case studies (see, e.g., [16]), they have not been used to model and analyze interconnected infrastructures. As in the case of fault trees and reliability block di-agrams, several tools and techniques have been developed for attack tree analysis [23]. Some techniques translate attack trees to transition diagrams such as Petri nets, stochastic activity networks [31], priced timed automata [22] and Markov chains [2]. Petri net formalisms such as stochastic Petri nets have great modeling power. However, Bouis-sou and Bon [7] note that they are too general in the sense that their processing becomes intractable.

2. Proposed Framework

Figure 1 presents an overview of the proposed framework. The first step is to decompose a network of infrastructures into sub-infrastruc-tures (e.g., power network and telecommunications network). The sub-infrastructures are further decomposed into different systems (e.g., the

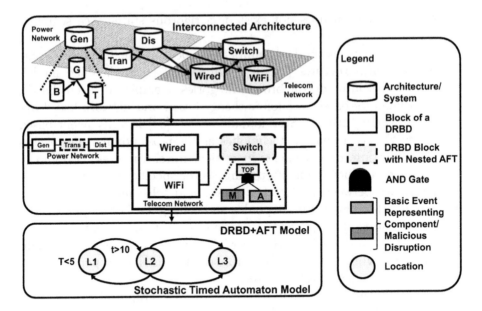

Figure 1.   Proposed framework.

power network comprises the generation, transmission and distribution systems).

The second step is to construct a dynamic reliability block diagram (DRBD) based on a single service output by the synchronized operation of the infrastructures. If the analysis needs to consider additional services, a separate reliability block diagram is constructed for each service. A dynamic reliability block diagram comprises blocks shown as boldface rectangular boxes in Figure 1. These blocks can be connected in different configurations such as series or parallel, depending on the functional descriptions of the system components. For example, in Figure 1, the power network block is connected in series with the telecommunications network block. The traditional dynamic reliability block diagram formalism is extended with additional dashed blocks such as the switch block shown in Figure 1. A dashed block is similar to a conventional dynamic reliability block diagram block, but it additionally embeds an attack-fault tree (AFT) [24]. An attack-fault tree is a succinct representation of all the scenarios that disrupt a dynamic reliability block diagram block.

The third step is to derive a stochastic timed automaton model of the combined dynamic reliability block diagram and attack-fault tree model. Stochastic timed automata are transition diagrams with stochastic semantics. Stochastic timed automata corresponding to the combined dy-

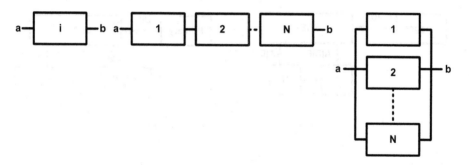

Figure 2. Standard reliability block diagram configurations.

namic reliability block diagram and attack-fault tree model are created in a compositional manner inspired by the compositional aggregation approach of Boudali et al. [6]. The automata are then fed into the model-checker along with metrics of interest that are encoded in temporal logic. Results are obtained using UPPAAL SMC (statistical model checker) [10].

3. Framework Building Blocks

This section describes dynamic reliability block diagrams and attack-fault trees, the two main components of the proposed framework. The combined dynamic reliability block diagram and attack-fault tree model is translated to a stochastic timed automaton model, which is one input to the UPPAAL SMC tool. The other input is the metrics of interest that are encoded using temporal logic.

3.1 DRBD Configurations

Reliability block diagrams (RBDs) [19] consist of blocks that are connected in different configurations by edges. Figure 2 shows three standard configurations (from left to right): (i) block representing the functional system component C_i with end points a as input and b as output; (ii) series configuration with N blocks; and (iii) parallel configuration with N blocks. Reliability block diagram analysis is typically time-invariant [28]. Moreover, reliability block diagrams assume independence of events; this simplifies the analysis, but it is not very practical.

Figure 2 shows the standard series and parallel configurations. In the series configuration, the system is said to be disrupted if any of the blocks is disrupted. In the parallel configuration, the system is said to be disrupted if all the blocks are disrupted.

Dynamic reliability block diagrams [35] extend reliability block diagrams with dynamic features. Specifically, additional syntactic con-

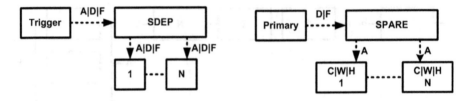

Figure 3. Dynamic reliability block diagram configurations.

structs are introduced to model dynamic dependencies and additional behaviors, such as load sharing, that cannot be modeled by standard reliability block diagrams.

Figure 3 shows the two dynamic reliability block diagram blocks. An SDEP block comprises a trigger block and N blocks, each of which can be a cold, warm or hot spare. When an event (A, D or F) signaled by the trigger occurs, it forces any of the dependent events (A, D or F) to occur. Note that A stands for an activation event that leads to an active state for the component, D stands for a deactivation event that leads to a standby state for the component and F stands for a disruption event that leads to a fail state for the component. Thus, SDEP can model nine types of dependency relationships between system components (A, A), (D, D), (A, F), (D, A), (A, D), (D, F), (F, A), (F, D), (F, F).

A SPARE block models spare management. It comprises a primary and several spare components that can be cold, warm or hot. Upon deactivation or failure of the primary component, the next (second) component is activated, and so on.

3.2   Attack-Fault Trees

An attack-fault tree [24] combines two popular formalisms, attack trees [20] and dynamic fault trees [6].

An attack-fault tree has a top node that represents the unwanted disruption event. The top event is refined using logical AND, OR, SAND and SPARE gates until the child nodes are reached. Figure 4 shows the standard and dynamic fault tree gates (from left to right): AND, OR, PAND, FDEP and SPARE gates. In the case of an AND gate, all its child nodes must be disrupted for the node to be disrupted. In the case of an OR gate, the disruption of any one child node results in the disruption of the parent node. A PAND gate has similar behavior as an AND gate; it models the constraint that the parent node is disrupted only when the disruptions of its child nodes occur in order from left to right. An FDEP gate models a disruption that can be attributed to a common cause. It consists of a trigger event and several dependent child nodes; when the

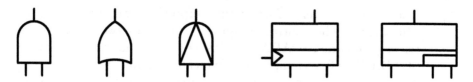

Figure 4. Standard and dynamic fault tree gates.

trigger event occurs, all the dependent nodes are disrupted. A SPARE gate consists of a primary child node (leftmost child) while all the other child nodes are spares. When the primary child fails, the SPARE gate attempts to obtain a working spare child node.

3.3   Rome Scenario

This section presents a power outage incident from the literature called the "Rome Scenario" [4]. This real scenario is used as a running example in the chapter to illustrate model building using the proposed framework and to perform quantitative analysis.

The Rome Scenario refers to the outage of critical supervisory control and data acquisition (SCADA) system communications links in Rome, Italy on January 2, 2004, which rendered other infrastructures such as telecommunications and transportation unavailable. The attention is restricted to the interplay of two interconnected networks, electric power infrastructure and industrial communications networks (communications links that connect the SCADA systems to remote terminal units (RTUs) that cooperate with each other to provide uninterrupted electric power). On one hand, the electric power infrastructure relies on its SCADA systems to perform important tasks such as obtaining telemetry data and performing control actions and remote diagnostics. On the other hand, the telemetry resources such as radio communications and fiber-optic cables rely on an uninterrupted supply of electricity.

Note that the different infrastructures in the scenario are operated by different entities. Hence, the goal of the quantitative analysis of the scenario is to identify which of the shared assets are most vulnerable to disruptions.

The Rome Scenario involves the following assets:

- **Electric Power Infrastructure:** The electric power infrastructure comprises of two major subsystems: (i) power components that comprises bus bars, switches, circuit breakers, medium voltage (MV) transmission lines, high voltage (HV) transmission lines; and (ii) control equipment that comprises the SCADA system, remote terminal units and relays.

The electric power infrastructure supplies power to the control equipment. The control equipment comprises two SCADA systems: (i) manned SCADA (MSC) system and the disaster recovery SCADA (DSC) system, both of which communicate over a redundant single-pair high-speed digital subscriber line (SHDSL) based fiber optic link.

The SCADA systems monitor different portions of the power infrastructure; however, the DSC sends the observed parameters to the MSC for control actions. Apart from the SHDSL that links the two SCADA systems, the SCADA systems are also connected to high voltage (HV) remote terminal units using a default proprietary network (DPN) with the public switched telephonic network (PSTN) serving as backup communications. Each SCADA system is connected to medium voltage (MV) remote terminal units using Global System Mobile (GSM) communications.

- **Spare Power System:** The spare power system is used as a backup to power the industrial communications nodes in case of a power outage in the electric infrastructure. The spare power system comprises a diesel generator and battery.

- **Industrial Communications Network:** The industrial communications network comprises several communications links between the SCADA systems and remote terminal units, as described above.

- **External Infrastructures:** The external infrastructures rely on electricity provided by the electric power infrastructure.

Figure 5 shows the high-level representation of the Rome Scenario using dynamic reliability block diagrams. The blocks `Electric_power_infrastructure` and `Other_infrastructures` are positioned in series, which means that a disruption of the electric power infrastructure would disrupt the other infrastructures that depend on the power it provides.

The electric power infrastructure comprises two subsystems expressed as blocks `Power_components` and `Control_equipment` in series to model the fact that a disruption of any block would disrupt the electric power infrastructure. Block `Power_components` is placed in parallel with block `Power_system_spare`, which means that both blocks would have to be disrupted to disrupt the electric power infrastructure.

Figure 6 shows the nested dynamic reliability block diagrams in the `Control_equipment` block. They are: (i) `MSC`, which represents the MSC SCADA system; (ii) `DSC`, which represents the DSC SCADA system; and

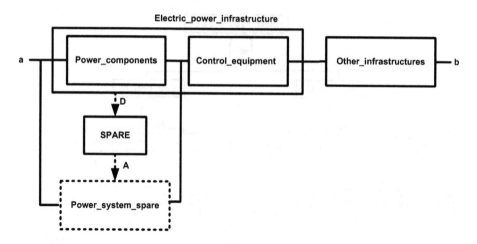

Figure 5. Rome Scenario dynamic reliability block diagram.

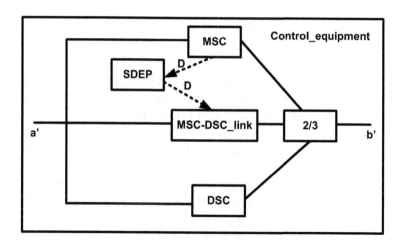

Figure 6. Nested DRBDs in the Control_equipment block.

(iii) MSC-DSC_link, which represents the communications link connecting the two SCADA systems. The MSC, DSC and MSC-DSC_link blocks are placed in parallel and are connected in series with the 2/3 block, which means that if any two of the three blocks are disrupted, the Control_-equipment block would be disrupted. Furthermore, the disruption of MSC immediately leads to the disruption of MSC-DSC_link. Thus, if MSC is disrupted, the control_equipment block would be disrupted. However, if either DSC or MSC-DSC_link is disrupted (but not both), the Control_equipment block would not be disrupted. Of course, MSC, DSC and MSC-DSC_link would be disrupted if their components are disrupted.

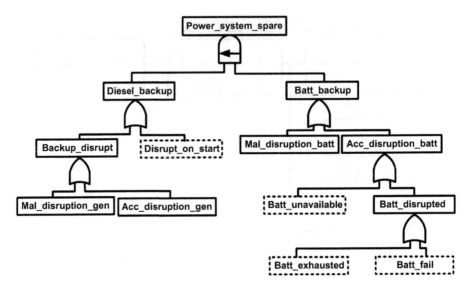

Figure 7. Attack-fault tree for the Power_system_spare block.

As discussed below, the disruption of Power_system_spare is modeled using an attack-fault tree. Attack-fault trees could also be constructed for MSC, DSC and MSC-DSC_link disruptions if a more granular analysis is required.

Figure 7 shows the attack-fault tree for the Power_system_spare block. The leaves with bold-lined rectangles represent malicious failures while those with dashed-lined rectangles represent accidental disruptions.

The attack-fault tree starts with the top event of Power_system_spare signifying the disruption of spare power system. The top event can occur due to the disruptions of Diesel_backup and Batt_backup, both serving as backup power supply options in the event of a main power supply outage. The assumption is that, as soon as a main power outage occurs, the battery backup is activated first and the diesel backup is activated only if the battery backup is disrupted. Hence, Power_system_-spare is refined using a SAND gate. Batt_backup would be disrupted if any of the accidental disruption Acc_disruption_batt or malicious disruption Mal_disruption_batt events occur. The accidental disruption of the battery backup would occur if any of the Batt_unavailable or Batt_disrupted events occur. The accidental disruption of the battery would occur if any of the battery failure Batt_fail or battery exhaustion Batt_exhausted events occur. The Diesel_backup event would occur if any of the Backup_disrupt or Disrupt_on_start events occur; hence, it is refined by an OR gate. Finally, the Backup_disrupt event would

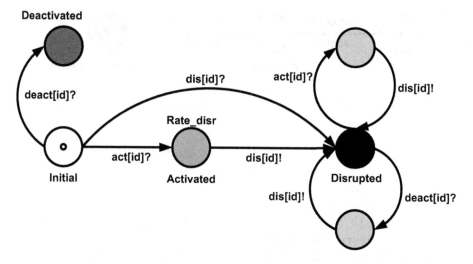

Figure 8. Stochastic timed automaton $\mathcal{S}_v$ for a DRBD basic block v.

occur due to a malicious disruption or an accidental disruption of the diesel generator, `Mal_disruption_gen` or `Acc_disruption_gen`.

4. Stochastic Timed Automata

This section specifies the stochastic timed automata for the elements in the framework. Stochastic timed automata are timed automata models [1] with stochastic semantics.

Figure 8 shows a stochastic timed automaton $\mathcal{S}_v$, for a basic dynamic reliability block v. Note that `id` denotes the block identifier. The disruption of a block occurs with an exponential distribution rate $\lambda \in \mathbb{R}^+$.

The stochastic timed automaton comprises system control states and transitions between the system control states. Additionally, real-valued variable clocks are used to keep track of the global time, which increases linearly but may be reset when a transition is taken. Constraints in terms of clocks are specified as invariants that enforce deadlines or as guards that enforce enabling conditions on transitions. Unlike timed automata that only allow non-determinism, stochastic timed automata incorporate stochastic processes where transition times are governed by probability distributions. Like timed automata, multiple stochastic timed automata can be composed using synchronization signals on transitions. The signal `a?` indicates that some transitions are waiting for signal `a` that can only be taken simultaneously with a transition in another stochastic timed automaton emitting the corresponding signal `a!`.

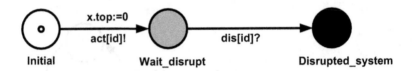

Figure 9. Stochastic timed automaton $\mathcal{S}_{\text{Sys}}$ that starts the system Sys.

Figure 9 shows the stochastic timed automaton that starts the system Sys. Note that x.top is the global clock that keeps track of time. The two automata $\mathcal{S}_v$ and $\mathcal{S}_{\text{Sys}}$ communicate using the broadcast signals act[id], dis[id] and deact[id].

The stochastic timed automaton $\mathcal{S}_v$ has the control states {Initial, Activated, Disrupted, Deactivated} and one delay transition governed by the probability distribution (invariant Rate_dist) over the control state Activated. The stochastic timed automaton $\mathcal{S}_{\text{Sys}}$ has the control ststes {Initial, Wait_disrupt, Disrupted_system}. This automaton initializes the system by emitting a broadcast signal act[id]! and then waits for a broadcast signal dis[id]?. After receiving the signal, it makes a transition to Disrupted_system, which indicates system disruption.

Similarly, stochastic timed automata are provided for all the dynamic reliability block diagram/attack-fault tree elements. The templates are instantiated appropriately depending on the actual dynamic reliability block diagram/attack-fault tree model connections. The compositional theory of timed input/output automata extended to stochastic timed automata [11] is used to compose the stochastic timed automata.

The parallel composition operator || is used to construct a lerger stochastic timed automaton from several smaller ones. Let $\mathcal{S}_{v_i}$ be the stochastic timed automaton corresponding to a node v_i of a dynamic reliability block diagram and let $\mathcal{S}_{w_i}$ be the stochastic timed automaton corresponding to each attack-fault tree element w_i, then the network of stochastic timed automata $\mathcal{N}_T$ for the combined dynamic reliability block diagram and attack-fault tree model T is given by:

$$\mathcal{N}_T = \mathcal{S}_{v_1} \| \mathcal{S}_{v_2} \| \cdots \| \mathcal{S}_{v_n} \| \mathcal{S}_{w_1} \| \mathcal{S}_{w_2} \| \cdots \| \mathcal{S}_{w_n} \| \mathcal{S}_{\text{Sys}}$$

This network of stochastic timed automata is one of the inputs to the UPPAAL SMC tool. The other input is the encoded query of interest expressed using the UPPAAL SMC specification language.

The following are the stochastic timed automaton templates governing the composition of series, parallel, SDEP and SPARE dynamic reliability block diagrams:

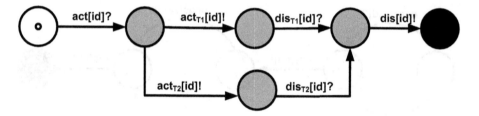

Figure 10. Stochastic timed automaton for a series block configuration.

- **Series Blocks:** Figure 10 shows the stochastic timed automaton template for a series block configuration. The series block configuration has two basic blocks T1 and T2 connected in series. After the stochastic timed automaton receives the activation signal act[id]?, it activates both the blocks by sending $act_{T1}[id]!$ and $act_{T2}[id]!$. The series block configuration is disrupted if it receives dis from any of the basic blocks. Then, it sends dis[id]!, signaling that the series block is disrupted.

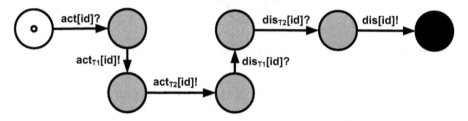

Figure 11. Stochastic timed automaton for a parallel block configuration.

- **Parallel Blocks:** Figure 11 shows the stochastic timed automaton template for a parallel block configuration. The parallel block configuration has two basic blocks T1 and T2 connected in parallel. After the stochastic timed automaton receives the activation signal act[id], it activates both the blocks. The parallel block configuration is disrupted if it receives dis from both the blocks.

- **SPARE Blocks:** Figure 12 shows the stochastic timed automaton template for a SPARE block configuration. The SPARE block has a primary basic block P whose deactivation or disruption results in the activation of a spare block T1. The SPARE block is disrupted if blocks P and T1 are disrupted.

- **SDEP Blocks:** Figure 13 shows the stochastic timed automaton template for an SDEP block configuration. The SDEP block has a

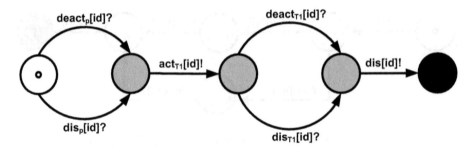

Figure 12.   Stochastic timed automaton for the SPARE block configuration.

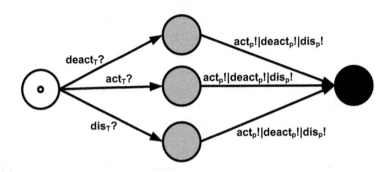

Figure 13.   Stochastic timed automaton for the SDEP block configuration.

trigger and several dependent child blocks. Upon activation (resp. deactivation or disruption) of the trigger, all the dependent child blocks are activated (resp. deactivated or disrupted), depending on the high-level model, permitting several output signals. The SDEP block in Figure 13 has a trigger T and a child P. The SDEP block remains always activated and is ready to accept any of the signals (deactivation, activation or disruption) from the trigger. Depending on the system configuration, it can then signal the activation, deactivation or disruption of its child block.

The semantics of dynamic reliability block diagrams using stochastic timed automata does not alter the semantics of the attack-fault tree elements [24]. Therefore, it is not necessary to repeat the discussion for attack-fault trees.

5.   Property Verification Using UPPAAL SMC

UPPAAL [3] is a platform for modeling, simulating and verifying (via model checking) systems that are modeled as networks of timed automata. In addition to the UPPAAL model checker for timed automata, the UPPAAL tool suite includes a statistical model checker, UPPAAL SMC, which extends the expressiveness of the UPPAAL modeling language by supporting statistical model checking of hybrid models.

The UPPAAL SMC tool was used to conduct the following analyses:

- **Subsystem View:** This view is interested in the probability of disruption of one subsystem. In this case, the focus is on obtaining the reliability over time of the spare power system.

- **System-Wide View:** This view is interested in the probability of disruption of the control system block. The probability of disruption of the electric power infrastructure without a spare power system is also of interest.

- **System-of-System View:** This view is interested in the probability of disruption of the electric power infrastructure taking the disruptions of the spare power system and control system into account. Also of interest is how the probability of disruption changes if all the nodes of the spare power system are disrupted maliciously.

The verification of the properties of interest for the network of stochastic timed automata required their encoding in the UPPAAL SMC specification language, which is a variant of the Metric Interval Timed Logic (MITL) query language [8]. Formally, the reliability $R(t)$ is the probability that a system is undisrupted in the interval from 0 to time t, i.e., $R(t) = P(T > t)$. The unreliability of the network of stochastic timed automata $\mathcal{N}_T$ is expressed in MITL as:

$$P_{\mathcal{N}_T}(\lozenge_{\leq t}\, \mathcal{S}_{\mathsf{Sys}}.\mathtt{Disrupted\_system})$$

The aforementioned formula is a cost-bounded reachability query that asks for the probability that a random run [9] of the network of stochastic timed automata $\mathcal{N}_T$ satisfies the state predicate $\mathcal{S}_{\mathsf{Sys}}.\mathtt{Disrupted\_system}$ within a cost given by t, where time t is the bound. This query is encoded as follows for input to the UPPAAL SMC tool:

$$P[\leq t](<> \mathcal{S}_{\mathsf{Sys}}.\mathtt{Disrupted\_System})$$

The mean time to successful disruption within time t is given by:

$$E_{\mathcal{N}_T}(T : \lozenge_{\leq t}\, \mathcal{S}_{\mathsf{Sys}}.\mathtt{Disrupted\_system})$$

where T is the accumulated time in the mission time t before disruption.

The UPPAAL SMC tool computes the metric in two steps: (i) compute the expected time of disruption under a time bound t given by the

Table 1. Parameters used for the DRBD blocks and AFT leaves.

DRBD Block/ AFT Leaf	Disruption Rate (1/MTTF)	Instantaneous Disruption Probability
Batt_fail	–	0.00023
Batt_unavailable	–	0.000114
Disrupt_on_start	–	0.00046
Mal_disruption_gen	0.0000114 (3,600 days)	–
Acc_disruption_gen	0.000023 (1,800 days)	–
Batt_exhausted	0.00046 (90 days)	–
Mal_disruption_batt	0.00065 (64 days)	–
MSC	0.0000114 (3,600 days)	–
DSC	0.000023 (1,800 days)	–
MSC-DSC_link	0.00046 (90 days)	–
Power_components	0.0000114 (3,600 days)	–

query specified in Equation (1) below; and (ii) divide the value obtained in the previous step by the probability of successful disruption within the time bound t.

The UPPAAL SMC tool query for obtaining the expected time under a time bound t was encoded as follows:

$$E[\text{x\_top} \leq t, N](max : \text{x\_top} \times S_{\text{Sys}}.\text{Disrupted\_system}) \qquad (1)$$

where N is the number of simulation runs.

6.   Evaluation of the Rome Scenario

This section discusses the experimental setup and the experimental results obtained for the Rome Scenario.

6.1   Experimental Setup

All the experiments were performed on a 2.00 GHz Intel Xeon CPU E5335 with 22 GB RAM under Linux. The UPPAAL SMC tool was used to verify the properties.

The statistical parameters chosen were the confidence interval $\alpha = 0.05$ and probability uncertainty $\epsilon = 0.001$. Details about the confidence interval and probability uncertainty are provided in [10]. Furthermore, a second model checker, STORM [12], was used to compare the results.

Table 1 shows the parameters used in the case study. A disruption rate was assigned to each dynamic reliability block diagram that was not further refined using an attack-fault tree. Similarly, each leaf of the attack-fault tree was assigned a disruption rate. The disruption rate corresponded to the inverse of the mean time to failure (MTTF). A few leaves in the attack-fault tree that modeled instantaneous disruptions – `Disrupt_on_start`, `Batt_unavailable` and `Batt_fail` – were not assigned failure rates, but were assigned disruption probabilities instead. These discrete probabilities modeled instantaneous accidental disruptions, for example, when a component failed to start.

The mean time to failure was assigned based on domain knowledge in order to demonstrate the proposed framework. In practical scenarios, it should be based on historical data. Note that, although only one mean time to failure parameter was employed for dynamic reliability block diagrams and attack-fault trees, this is not a limitation of the framework. Instead, the dynamic reliability block diagrams and leaves of attack-fault trees can be associated with different cost structures that express repair costs, disruption costs, etc. Also, although exponential distributions are used in the framework (as in many reliability and security analyses in the literature), the proposed framework supports acyclic phase type distributions that can be used to approximate any probability distribution with arbitrary precision.

Another important aspect is model correctness, given that building a model is a complex task that can introduce subtle errors. Model correctness is verified at the design stage using the UPPAAL SMC tool. UPPAAL SMC incorporates an automatic syntax checker as well as a simulator that can analyze a model and verify its correctness.

6.2 Experimental Results

First, the disruption of a small subsystem – spare power system – modeled by an attack-fault tree was analyzed. Two cases were considered: (i) Case A: only accidental disruptions of the battery and diesel generator; and (ii) Case B: malicious and accidental disruptions of the battery and diesel generator. These were analyzed by enabling or disabling the leaves of the attack-fault tree.

Figure 14(a) shows the cumulative distribution functions of the unreliability of the `Power_system_spare` block for Cases A and B. For Case A, the UPPAAL SMC tool yielded a probability of disruption over a one-year mission time of 0.14. The STORM model checker using the DFTCalc web interface [18] yielded a probability of disruption over the same mission time of 0.138. The small difference in the values can be attributed to differences in their underlying techniques – the UPPAAL SMC tool is based on simulation whereas STORM is based on model checking (which provides more precise results). The results demonstrate that malicious disruptions of components can result in higher probabili-

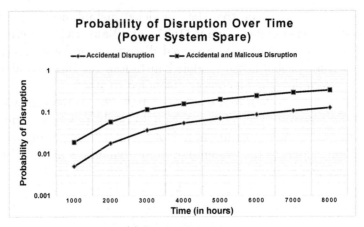

(a) Spare power system.

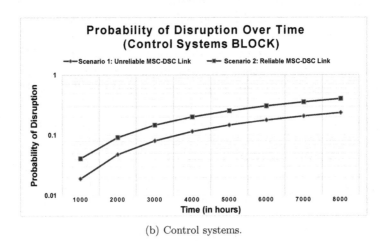

(b) Control systems.

Figure 14.   Disruption probabilities for the spare power system and control systems.

ties of system disruption. The mean times to successful disruption were determined to be 236 days for Case A and 299 days for Case B.

Next, a reliability analysis of the Control_systems block shown in Figure 6 was conducted. Figure 14(b) shows the results. Using the disruption parameters for MSC, DSC and MSC-DSC_link in Table 1 yielded a probability of disruption over a one-year mission time of 0.236.

Various what-if scenarios could be evaluated by configuring subsystems as initially being in the disrupted state. For example, the original model parameters assumed that the MSC-DSC_link was unreliable. However, if it is assumed that the MSC-DSC_link is 100% reliable, then MSC and DSC would both be functional, with MSC taking control of the DSC

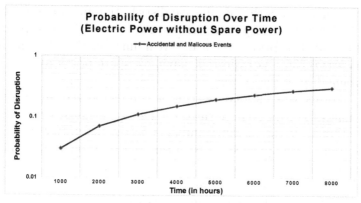

(a) Without spare power.

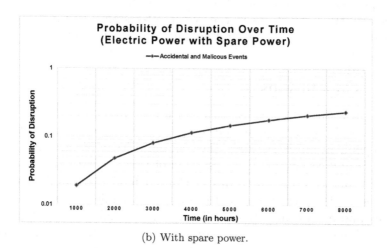

(b) With spare power.

Figure 15. Disruption probabilities for two electrical power infrastructure scenarios.

functions in case of a DSC disruption. This modification corresponds to a `Control_systems` block with the MSC and DSC blocks in a parallel configuration. Executing the query on the modified model yielded the probability of disruption over a one-year mission of 0.168, which is significantly lower than the previous disruption probability of 0.236. This result demonstrates that the `MSC-DSC_link` is a considerable source of system disruption.

Figure 15(a) shows the cumulative distribution function of the unreliability of the `Electric_power_infrastructure` without spare power. The probability of disruption over a one-year mission time for this what-if scenario was 0.303.

Figure 15(b) shows the cumulative distribution function of the unreliability of the `Electric_power_infrastructure` with spare power. The probability of disruption over a one-year mission time for this what-if scenario was 0.236. As expected, having a spare power system reduces the unreliability of the system.

Several other what-if analyses can be conducted. For example, a sensitivity analysis could be performed to identify the most vulnerable components that have the maximal impacts on the disruption probabilities. This would be accomplished by executing several runs of the model, with a different component being disabled in each run.

Furthermore, if cost structures and repair rates are associated with the dynamic reliability blocks and attack-fault tree leaves, then more complex queries could be asked and answered, for example: What are the expected costs of a disruption? The results would enable an analyst to identify the bottlenecks in the system-of-systems, helping implement mitigation measures that would enhance the safety and security of the entire system.

7.   Conclusions

Critical infrastructures by their nature are highly interdependent on each other. However, due to the complexity of modeling and simulating interdependent infrastructures, the vast majority of research has focused on safety and security risk assessments of isolated infrastructures. The generic framework presented in this chapter models dynamic dependencies existing between infrastructures using dynamic reliability block diagrams and attack-fault trees. The dynamic reliability block diagrams express dynamic and complex aspects of infrastructures such as redundancy policy management and load sharing whereas attack-fault trees model combinations of component disruptions that can lead to subsystem disruptions. The application of the framework to a real disruption scenario involving interconnected electric power and industrial communications networks demonstrates its efficacy. Specifically, it enables an analyst to identify weak links, evaluate alternative protection measures and make transparent decisions about risk management investments.

Future research will attempt to automatically generate models from system specifications, important because manual modeling involves the time-consuming, iterative task of capturing all the disruption scenarios. Research will also focus on validating the framework in complex real-world scenarios with reliable data. Also, it will attempt to create a repository of reliability models for interconnected infrastructures that can serve as benchmarks for comparing infrastructure analysis tools.

References

[1] R. Alur and D. Dill, A theory of timed automata, *Theoretical Computer Science*, vol. 126(2), pp. 183–235, 1994.

[2] F. Arnold, D. Guck, R. Kumar and M. Stoelinga, Sequential and parallel attack tree modeling, in *Computer Safety, Reliability and Security*, F. Koornneef and C. van Gulijk (Eds.), Springer, Cham, Switzerland, pp. 291–299, 2015.

[3] G. Behrmann, A. David and K. Larsen, A tutorial on UPPAAL, in *Formal Methods for the Design of Real-Time Systems*, M. Bernardo and F. Corradini (Eds.), Springer, Berlin Heidelberg, Germany, pp. 200–236, 2004.

[4] R. Bloomfield, P. Popov, K. Salako, V. Stankovic and D. Wright, Preliminary interdependency analysis: An approach to support critical infrastructure risk assessment, *Reliability Engineering and System Safety*, vol. 167, pp. 198–217, 2017.

[5] A. Bobbio, G. Bonanni, E. Ciancamerla, R. Clemente, A. Iacomini, M. Minichino, A. Scarlatti, R. Terruggia and E. Zendri, Unavailability of critical SCADA communications links interconnecting a power grid and a telco network, *Reliability Engineering and System Safety*, vol. 95(12), pp. 1345–1357, 2010.

[6] H. Boudali, P. Crouzen and M. Stoelinga, A compositional semantics for dynamic fault trees in terms of interactive Markov chains, in *Automated Technology for Verification and Analysis*, K. Namjoshi, T. Yoneda, T. Higashino and Y. Okamura (Eds.), Springer, Berlin Heidelberg, Germany, pp. 441–456, 2007.

[7] M. Bouissou and J. Bon, A new formalism that combines advantages of fault trees and Markov models: Boolean logic driven Markov processes, *Reliability Engineering and System Safety*, vol. 82(2), pp. 149–163, 2003.

[8] P. Bouyer, Model-checking timed temporal logics, *Electronic Notes in Theoretical Computer Science*, vol. 231, pp. 323–341, 2009.

[9] P. Bulychev, A. David, K. Larsen, A. Legay, G. Li and D. Poulsen, Rewrite-based statistical model checking of WMTL, in *Runtime Verification*, S. Qadeer and S. Tasiran (Eds.), Springer, Berlin Heidelberg, Germany, pp. 260–275, 2012.

[10] A. David, K. Larsen, A. Legay, M. Mikucionis and D. Poulsen, UPPAAL SMC tutorial, *International Journal on Software Tools for Technology Transfer*, vol. 17, pp. 397–415, 2015.

[11] A. David, K. Larsen, A. Legay, M. Mikucionis, D. Poulsen, J. van Vliet and Z. Wang, Stochastic Semantics and Statistical Model Checking for Networks of Priced Timed Automata, *arXiv:* 1106.3961v2, 2014.

[12] C. Dehnert, S. Junges, J. Katoen and M. Volk, A STORM is coming: A modern probabilistic model checker, in *Computer Aided Verification*, R. Majumdar and V. Kuncak (Eds.), Springer, Cham, Switzerland, pp. 592–600, 2017.

[13] S. Distefano and A. Puliafito, Dependability evaluation with dynamic reliability block diagrams and dynamic fault trees, *IEEE Transactions on Dependable and Secure Computing*, vol. 6(1), pp. 4–17, 2009.

[14] I. Eusgeld, C. Nan and S. Dietz, "System-of-systems" approach for interdependent critical infrastructures, *Reliability Engineering and System Safety*, vol. 96(6), pp. 679–686, 2011.

[15] M. Ford, P. Buchholz and W. Sanders, State-based analysis in AD-VISE, *Proceedings of the Ninth International Conference on Quantitative Evaluation of Systems*, pp. 148–157, 2012.

[16] M. Fraile, M. Ford, O. Gadyatskaya, R. Kumar, M. Stoelinga and R. Trujillo-Rasua, Using attack-defense trees to analyze threats and countermeasures in an ATM: A case study, in *The Practice of Enterprise Modeling*, J. Horkoff, M. Jeusfeld and A. Persson (Eds.), Springer, Cham, Switzerland, pp. 326–334, 2016.

[17] T. Gonschorek, M. Zeller, K. Hofig and F. Ortmeier, Fault trees vs. component fault trees: An empirical study, in *Computer Safety, Reliability and Security*, B. Gallina, A. Skavhaug, E. Schoitsch and F. Bitsch (Eds.), Springer, Cham, Switzerland, pp. 239–251, 2018.

[18] D. Guck, J. Spel and M. Stoelinga, DFTCalc: Reliability centered maintenance via fault tree analysis (tool paper), in *Formal Methods and Software Engineering*, M. Butler, S. Conchon and F. Zaidi (Eds.), Springer, Cham, Switzerland, pp. 304–311, 2015.

[19] O. Hasan, W. Ahmed, S. Tahar and M. Hamdi, Reliability block diagram based analysis: A survey, *AIP Conference Proceedings*, vol. 1648(1), pp. 850129-1–850129-4, 2015.

[20] B. Kordy, L. Cambacedes and P. Schweitzer, DAG-based attack and defense modeling: Don't miss the forest for the attack trees, *Computer Science Review*, vol. 13-14, pp. 1–38, 2014.

[21] R. Kumar, Truth or Dare: Quantitative Security Risk Analysis via Attack Trees, Ph.D. Dissertation, Faculty of Electrical Engineering, Mathematics and Computer Science, University of Twente, Twente, The Netherlands, 2018.

[22] R. Kumar, E. Ruijters and M. Stoelinga, Quantitative attack tree analysis via priced timed automata, in *Formal Modeling and Analysis of Timed Systems*, S. Sankaranarayanan and E. Vicario (Eds.), Springer, Cham, Switzerland, pp. 156–171, 2015.

[23] R. Kumar, S. Schivo, E. Ruijters, B. Yildiz, D. Huistra, J. Brandt, A. Rensink and M. Stoelinga, Effective analysis of attack trees: A model-driven approach, in *Fundamental Approaches to Software Engineering*, A. Russo and A. Schurr (Eds.), Springer, Cham, Switzerland, pp. 56–73, 2018.

[24] R. Kumar and M. Stoelinga, Quantitative security and safety analysis with attack-fault trees, *Proceedings of the Eighteenth IEEE International Symposium on High Assurance Systems Engineering*, pp. 25–32, 2017.

[25] L. Lai, H. Zhang, C. Lai, F. Xu and S. Mishra, Investigation of the July 2012 Indian blackout, *Proceedings of the International Conference on Machine Learning and Cybernetics*, pp. 92–97, 2013.

[26] C. Nielsen, P. Larsen, J. Fitzgerald, J. Woodcock and J. Peleska, Systems of systems engineering: Basic concepts, model-based techniques and research directions, *ACM Computation Surveys*, vol. 48(2), article no. 18, 2015.

[27] M. Ouyang, Review of modeling and simulation of interdependent critical infrastructure systems, *Reliability Engineering and System Safety*, vol. 121, pp. 43–60, 2014.

[28] M. Rausand and A. Hoyland, *System Reliability Theory: Models, Statistical Methods and Applications*, John Wiley and Sons, Hoboken, New Jersey, 2004.

[29] S. Rinaldi, J. Peerenboom and T. Kelly, Identifying, understanding and analyzing critical infrastructure interdependencies, *IEEE Control Systems*, vol. 21(6), pp. 11–25, 2001.

[30] E. Ruijters and M. Stoelinga, Fault tree analysis: A survey of the state of the art in modeling, analysis and tools, *Computer Science Review*, vol. 15-16, pp. 29–62, 2015.

[31] W. Sanders and J. Meyer, Stochastic activity networks: Formal definitions and concepts, in *Lectures on Formal Methods and Performance Analysis*, E. Brinksma, H. Hermanns and J. Katoen (Eds.), Springer, Berlin Heidelberg, Germany, pp. 315–343, 2000.

[32] R. Setola and M. Theocharidou, Modeling dependencies between critical infrastructures, in *Managing the Complexity of Critical Infrastructures: A Modeling and Simulation Approach*, R. Setola, V. Rosato, E. Kyriakides and E. Rome (Eds.), Springer, Cham, Switzerland, pp. 19–41, 2016.

[33] G. Stergiopoulos, P. Kotzanikolaou, M. Theocharidou, G. Lykou and D. Gritzalis, Time-based critical infrastructure dependency analysis for large-scale and cross-sectoral failures, *International Journal of Critical Infrastructure Protection*, vol. 12, pp. 46–60, 2016.

[34] G. Stergiopoulos, E. Vasilellis, G. Lykou, P. Kotzanikolaou and D. Gritzalis, Classification and comparison of critical infrastructure protection tools, in *Critical Infrastructure Protection X*, M. Rice and S. Shenoi (Eds.), Springer, Cham, Switzerland, pp. 239–255, 2016.

[35] H. Xu, L. Xing and R. Robidoux, DRBDs: Dynamic reliability block diagrams for system reliability modeling, *International Journal of Computers and Applications*, vol. 31(2), pp. 132–141, 2009.

Chapter 15

CREATING A CROSS-DOMAIN SIMULATION FRAMEWORK FOR RISK ANALYSES OF CITIES

Stefan Schauer and Stefan Rass

Abstract   Cities and their agglomerations are home to a large number of critical infrastructures that provide essential services in a geographically-narrow space. Because the critical infrastructures in a city are physically and logically dependent on each another, an incident in one infrastructure can have impacts on the entire city and its population. Thus, detailed risk analyses that strongly focus on the interactions within and between infrastructures, and on the potential cascading effects on the population are vital to protecting the critical supply infrastructures.

This chapter proposes a general cross-domain simulation framework that describes the major critical infrastructure networks in a large city at appropriate levels of abstraction. Unlike current approaches, the proposed framework focuses on the dynamic relationships between the networks and integrates stochastic models to achieve a realistic representation. The framework supports detailed assessments of the effects of threats on individual critical infrastructures and the potential cascading effects in the network of critical infrastructures.

Keywords: Risk analysis, interdependencies, cross-domain simulation

1.   Introduction

Critical infrastructures are defined as organizations or systems (or parts thereof) that are responsible for maintaining essential economic and societal functions, and whose disruption or failure could have significant impacts on the economic and social well-being of populations [4]. Large cities and their agglomerations are home to large numbers of critical infrastructures that support societal processes such as the supply of essential goods and services. This creates a number of geographical, physical and logical (information-related) dependencies, resulting in a

© IFIP International Federation for Information Processing 2020
Published by Springer Nature Switzerland AG 2020
J. Staggs and S. Shenoi (Eds.): Critical Infrastructure Protection XIV, IFIP AICT 596, pp. 307–323, 2020.
https://doi.org/10.1007/978-3-030-62840-6_15

highly interrelated and sensitive network of organizations and connections [29].

Critical infrastructures in the areas of general utilities (electricity, gas and water), information and communications technologies, distribution of goods (food and fuel) and transportation (road and rail) are extensive networks that have special security requirements. Due to their strong interrelations and dependencies, a failure, or even a disruption, of a single supply network affects the network itself and has direct or indirect (cascading) effects on a number of other critical networks, significantly impacting the economic and social well-being of the population. In 2016, the European Commission issued a directive calling for detailed risk analyses focusing on the interactions of critical infrastructure networks and their potential cascading effects on populations, with the goal of protecting the critical infrastructure networks [5].

Current systems and tools that simulate the functions of supply networks in risk analyses are unable to fully assess the effects on a city as a whole. The simulation approaches focus on isolated solutions, typically just one supply network at a time. This is because they are designed to accommodate the physical characteristics and technical conditions of a single network instead of a collection of interconnected networks. They provide local views where the dependencies on other networks are generally ignored; as a result, a detailed understanding of the dynamics of all the networks in a city cannot be obtained. Additionally, the proprietary systems used by asset owners and operators often do not exchange data or connect to systems of other asset owners and operators to support cross-domain analyses. Because the cascading effects on multiple networks in a city are not considered, the impacts of potential threats cannot be assessed precisely. Understanding and implementing protections against cascading effects on a large scale calls for a holistic view of the network of interdependent critical infrastructures, which requires cross-domain simulation.

This chapter demonstrates how a cross-domain simulation framework that describes central utility infrastructure networks – electricity, gas, water, food and telecommunications (including information and communications technology), and transportation networks (road and rail) in a large city – can be created. The approach, which has been developed under Project ODYSSEUS, seeks to simulate potential threats (natural disasters and human-initiated incidents) with a strong focus on the dynamic relationships between infrastructure networks. Probabilistic techniques such as Markov chains and probabilistic automata are leveraged to achieve flexible, yet realistic, representations of the networks. The resulting framework supports detailed assessments of the

Table 1. Model-based simulation approaches applied in various domains.

Domain	Physical Models
Traffic	Granular flows (macroscopic model, e.g., [11]), agent-based simulation (microscopic model, e.g., [38]) and variants (e.g., [12]).
Water	Incompressible fluids or similar (e.g., [2, 22, 24, 33]).
Gas	Compressible liquids/gases or similar (e.g., [7, 25]).
Communications	Stochastic models (waiting lines, e.g., [27]) or similar (e.g., [14, 36]).
Power	Ohm's law and alternating current technology, Maxwell's equations, induction law, etc. (e.g., [14, 32]).

impacts of threats to individual critical infrastructures as well as potential cascading effects in the network of critical supply infrastructures. The simulation points to the potential compensatory and displacement mechanisms in the multi-domain network of supply infrastructures in the event of incidents. This knowledge assists in deriving and evaluating preventive measures that can minimize the negative effects of incidents.

2. Simulation Approaches

This section discusses various critical infrastructure simulation approaches, including supply network simulation approaches, interdependency graphs and cascading effects.

2.1 Supply Network Simulation

A detailed overview of critical supply networks and their behavior during an incident can be achieved by continuously monitoring the networks (collecting data about network components) and simulating the behaviors of the networks using mathematical models. The combination of these two approaches provides an up-to-date picture of each network and good estimates of its behavior in future situations.

Table 1 summarizes the model-based simulation approaches. The underlying mathematical models are often specific to the domains and are, therefore, based on the appropriate physical approaches. The list of models, which is by no means exhaustive, demonstrates the diversity of simulation approaches. A categorization of the approaches according to their underlying methodologies is possible (e.g., empirical, agent-based, system-dynamics-based, economic-aspect-based and network-based).

A shortcoming of the approaches listed in Table 1 is that they typically only represent a single network (domain) – they do not capture the dependencies existing between multiple networks. As a result, they support simulations and risk analyses of single networks and do not provide perspectives beyond their own network boundaries. What is needed is a holistic view of all the supply networks in a city.

Cross-domain simulation methods can address this deficiency [14, 32, 36]. However, these methods typically interweave only two domains into a common model; an example is energy and information and communications technology in the context of a smart grid [23].

2.2 Interdependency Graphs

Dependencies between critical infrastructures or portions of critical infrastructures have been extensively investigated in recent years. Several approaches have been developed to categorize dependencies [28, 29]. Dependencies are divided into five categories [28, 29]: (i) physical; (ii) informational; (iii) spatial; (iv) procedural; and (v) social. The categorization contributes to a better understanding of the interactions between infrastructures, for example, visualizing them in the form of an interdependency graph can support an assessment of the impacts that an incident would have on the connected infrastructures. However, in real scenarios, the interdependencies are much more complex and the categories are often too general to be applied directly.

Approaches for categorizing and describing the interrelationships between critical infrastructures include the hierarchical holographic model (HHM), input-output inoperability model (IIM) and the hierarchical coordinated Bayesian model (HCBM) [10].

The hierarchical holographic model [8] provides a taxonomy that conveys the interdependencies between critical infrastructures in more detail than in [29], which makes it possible to obtain a more precise idea of the interdependencies.

The input-output inoperability model [9] also provides a detailed overview of the interdependencies between critical infrastructures (or more generally between economic sectors) and describes the impacts of incidents based on linear equations. However, it focuses heavily on economic aspects, which may not always be the appropriate context for considering critical infrastructures.

Extreme events with low probabilities of occurrence and serious consequences pose challenges. This is because little data is available about these rare events. The hierarchical coordinated Bayesian model [37] addresses the problem by enabling data about extreme events from multiple sources to be combined in order to improve the accuracy and variance of impact assessments.

Preliminary interdependency analysis (PIA) [1] is an interesting approach for identifying and assessing interdependencies between critical infrastructures. The methodology involves examining the various types of dependencies (e.g., functional dependencies, similar components or common environments) and refining the findings in an iterative manner. This results in a high-level service model and a detailed service behavior model that convey the abstract services provided by the critical infrastructures and the operations of the services. Preliminary interdependency analysis is similar to the ODYSSEUS approach presented below because it connects services from multiple domains and describes the operational states of the services in the event of incidents.

Stochastic process models are effective at modeling partially-known dynamics and relations between events. These models leverage probability distributions to handle the randomness and uncertainty inherent in the interactions between critical infrastructures. A prominent example is percolation theory [15, 30], but it has rarely been used in the security and risk management domains. Percolation theory was recently used by König et al. [16] to model the spread of malware in a heterogeneous network. Bayesian networks are also used to describe interdependencies between critical infrastructures [31].

2.3 Cascading Effects

Interdependency graphs are also used to simulate cascading effects in critical infrastructures. One of the early approaches is cross-impact analysis, which describes how the relationships between individual events affect future events [34].

A more general approach, interdependent Markov chains, has been used to describe the propagation of cascading effects in a utility infrastructure [26]. Initially, interdependent Markov chains were used in the energy sector to describe system dynamics in order to analyze overload scenarios and estimate the probabilities of blackouts. The approach was subsequently extended to apply to other critical infrastructures [26]. However, Bayesian models and Markov chains are more difficult to apply compared with percolation theory due to the large amount of data required to analyze the overall system and understand the interplays. Other stochastic models can also be used to describe cascading effects because they can capture dependencies between multiple networks [10, 13, 21] and help conduct simulations using percolation theory [20].

However, the models may be difficult to instantiate (parameterize), especially obtaining the probabilities of network node behaviors that are essential to model building. Software support (e.g., [35]) and process-oriented procedure models (e.g., [3]) are available for data collection, but they may be difficult to implement due to the diversity of domains.

König and Rass [17, 18] have proposed a stochastic model that identifies potential cascading effects in networks of interconnected critical infrastructures and supports assessments of the cascading effects. As mentioned above, percolation theory and Markov chains have been combined and extended to determine the possible consequences of scenarios using simulations, such as when an infrastructure has to reduce its capacity or fails completely [6]. Another similar approach augments Markov chains with probabilistic Mealy automata [19] that can simulate cascading effects in critical infrastructures.

3.   ODYSSEUS Simulation Approach

The proposed cross-domain analysis framework developed under Project ODYSSEUS is designed to simulate the effects of various threats to supply networks in a city; these are determined by analyzing the interdependencies existing between the networks. This involves "parallel" simulations of the networks that consider the states of other networks (e.g., electricity $\leftrightarrow$ information and communications technology).

The proposed framework, which is applicable to all domains, relies on a directed graph comprising nodes and edges. A node is not fixed in its physical characteristics – depending on the type of simulation, it can represent a node in a power grid, a distribution point in a water network, etc. Edges represent connections between various types of nodes (physical, logical, etc.). Accordingly, an edge can represent a connection between two nodes in the same domain or in different domains. The general concept of hyperedges that connect three or more nodes and the resulting hypergraphs are not considered in this work. Therefore, the model is divided into an intra-domain level and an inter-domain (or cross-domain) level.

3.1   Intra-Domain Level Simulation

The intra-domain level focuses on the simulation of a single network (e.g., electric power network). It pursues two approaches. The first approach is to describe the dynamics of each network using a proven physical model (see Table 1). The model corresponding to each network is instantiated using information pertaining to the network prior to simulation. This enables the theories and tools developed for the

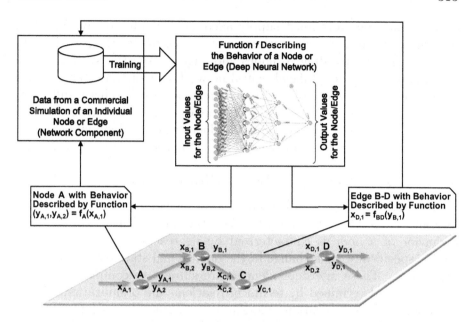

Figure 1. Intra-domain view of the model.

domain-specific models to be leveraged. However, a drawback with the approach is that utility networks are only considered up to a certain level of abstraction (e.g., due to overall network complexity or available information). As a result, the physical models may not always be applicable.

In cases where an "exact" model-based simulation is unavailable or infeasible, the second approach focuses on approximating the dynamics using generic models. More precisely, the behavior of a node A is simulated by an artificial neural network. The artificial neural network is represented as a function f_A with n input parameters and m output values that can be flexibly designed using training data (Figure 1). The same procedure is used for an edge such as $A \to B$ whose behavior is represented by a similar function $f_{A \to B}$. This type of modeling enables physical processes to be abstracted in a purely qualitative manner for any physical quantities (e.g., electric power, water pressure and traffic density) used in the network.

This machine learning approach can approximate single physical systems (e.g., incompressible fluids in water networks, compressible gases in gas networks and granular flows in traffic networks) if there is not enough information available for a complete simulation (e.g., due to the chosen level of abstraction). To achieve this, the stakeholders and network asset owners and operators must supply adequate amounts of training data for the artificial neural network or, more precisely, for the functions f_A and $f_{A \to B}$ corresponding to nodes and edges, respectively. If the data is available, then an artificial neural network can simulate the physical behavior of a node or edge with sufficient accuracy. This results in a network of nodes and edges that can be viewed (mathematically and in the simulation) as a series of function blocks whose individual behaviors can be adapted to the conditions of the simulation (Figure 1).

3.2   Inter-Domain Level Simulation

The inter-domain or cross-domain level focuses on simulations of the overall system (i.e., dynamics between the individual networks). The behavior of a node is characterized by its reaction to external influences, specifically, by a change in the operational states of its neighboring nodes. These interdependencies are subject to complex dynamics that can be determined by technical relations and organizational (non-technical or non-physical) mechanisms such as emergency supply systems and insurance covering the failure of individual suppliers. The dependencies are expressed stochastically as in [6, 17–19].

To obtain a more abstract representation of the general condition of a node separately from its respective domain, each node is characterized by various operational states that range, for example, from "undisturbed operation" to "total failure." In this way, the effects of an incident on a node E in one domain (e.g., electric power network) can be represented by the change in its operational state. Furthermore, due to the dependencies between different domains, a change in the operational state of node E can affect a node A in another domain (e.g., water network) as shown in Figure 2.

Hence, an external event in the electric power network triggers a transition of node A from one operational state to another. From a theoretical perspective, each node is a probabilistic Mealy automaton, which has various defined states and emits symbols denoting the effects that influence other nodes [19]. A key advantage of this representation is that state transitions are probabilistic, which enables the inherent uncertainties about the influences between domains to be expressed. In other words, the node A may or may not react to a state change of the connected node E in the other domain based on some probability value.

The ODYSSEUS framework provides a basis for describing the connections between infrastructure networks. However, the framework has been extended and further developed for cross-domain and generic use to better represent the dynamic aspects of individual networks. There-

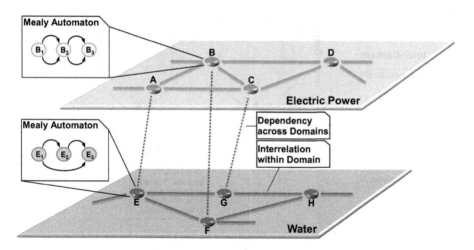

Figure 2. Inter-domain view of the model.

fore, information flows between individual technical and organizational components of the various domains are analyzed and their interplays and interactions are considered to leverage knowledge about the dependencies between nodes. The information flows between the networks help define the transitions of the operational states of each node.

The state transitions also depend on node behavior according to the intra-domain model. Hence, the outputs of the artificial neural networks in the intra-domain model described above are mapped to the operational states of the automaton representations of the nodes. Machine learning is thus applied to model the physical portion of a node and mimic its behavior according to concrete physical processes whereas the Mealy automaton integrates more abstract and informal knowledge about the interdependencies and interplays across domains. Figure 3 shows the combination of the intra-domain and inter-domain models with information from the OpenStreetMap geographical information system.

By jointly simulating the intra-domain and inter-domain levels, the ODYSSEUS framework provides a holistic understanding of the impacts of potential threats across multiple interrelated networks. The framework assists in characterizing the interrelations between domains in a structured, systematic and empirically-underpinned manner.

4.   Application Areas and Limitations

This section discusses application areas for the ODYSSEUS simulation framework along with its limitations.

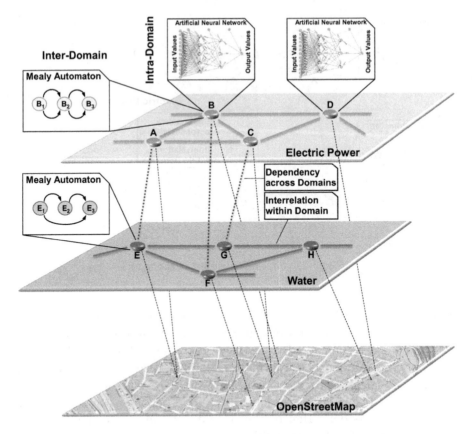

Figure 3. Combination of intra-domain and inter-domain models.

4.1   Application Areas

Due to the growing dependencies and interconnections in critical infrastructures in a large city, the complexity of the overall network is difficult to grasp. Therefore, it is imperative to understand the potential cascading effects that an incident might have on specific infrastructures as well as on social well-being. The main application of the proposed simulation framework is to support regional risk analyses. This can be achieved using cross-domain simulation as part of an impact assessment during the classical risk management process. In addition to the risks to an individual critical infrastructure network, the simulation framework provides a general and holistic view. This would enable risk managers at infrastructure asset owners and operators as well as administrative and political entities to better estimate the potential consequences of incidents. The estimates would facilitate more comprehensive risk analyses and support decision makers at multiple levels. Indeed, in light of the recently established Network and Information System Security Act of Austria, the cross-domain risk analyses would be central enablers to protecting critical supply infrastructures.

The following three user groups would benefit from the proposed cross-domain simulation framework:

- Operators of supply infrastructure networks in a city would benefit from the proposed simulation framework because it would provide accurate risk assessments of the consequences of incidents in their own networks. Furthermore, the consideration of cascading effects from other networks would complement and refine the risk analyses.

- Administrative entities responsible for risk and disaster control in a city would benefit greatly from the holistic view of supply networks. A comprehensive simulation of the overall network would enable these entities to better assess the complex effects of incidents on individual infrastructures as well as on the population, enabling them to proactively work on preventive measures and mitigations.

- National authorities responsible for protecting critical infrastructures would gain improved perspectives from the holistic simulation, especially insights into the impacts of rare and difficult-to-assess events and natural hazards, as well as attacks on soft targets. They would also gain understanding about potential cascading effects at multiple levels that would support the planning of preventive measures and emergency responses.

4.2   Limitations

The principal limitation of the proposed framework is data availability. This limitation manifests itself in three ways. The first pertains to individual infrastructures. Whereas data for some infrastructures may be rather easy to acquire (e.g., road and rail networks), it is more difficult to obtain data for other infrastructures (e.g., electric power and telecommunications networks), especially data about the "last mile" (final connections to consumers). In any case, this is highly sensitive data that infrastructure asset owners and operators would not and should not be disseminating.

The second manifestation involves intra-domain simulations, where machine learning requires large amounts of training data to create adequate models. It would also be difficult to obtain this data from infrastructure asset owners and operators. Under such circumstances, domain-specific simulation models could provide the data needed for machine learning.

The third manifestation involves inter-domain simulations, where substantial knowledge about the interrelations between networks is necessary to instantiate models. Whereas this knowledge may not be overly sensitive, it is still difficult to obtain because much of it is implicit as opposed to explicit.

Future research will attempt to address all three manifestations of the data availability limitation. The effort will rely on openly-available data pertaining to infrastructure networks (e.g., OpenStreetMap and OpenInfrastructureMap). These maps provide good overviews of infrastructure networks at levels of detail that are adequate for creating simulation models. Experts from infrastructure asset owners and operators will also be solicited for data about their networks. Indeed, the dependencies within and between infrastructure networks will be articulated in interdisciplinary workshops with experts from infrastructure asset owners and operators. In addition to obtaining information about dependencies, these venues will help gather implicit knowledge from the experts. With regard to machine learning, efforts will be made to have infrastructure asset owner and operator personnel conduct the artificial neural network training themselves using their sensitive data within their security domains, and provide the trained models. This is a promising approach because it would not be necessary to gain access to the sensitive systems and data belonging to infrastructure asset owners and operators.

Another limitation of the proposed methodology arises from the complexity of critical infrastructure networks in a city. Each network comprises numerous physical and cyber assets as well as multiple kinds of connections (e.g., cables and pipes) between them. It would be inefficient, possibly infeasible, to model every detail of the networks. At a certain point, incorporating additional detail in a model does not yield increased insights. Therefore, efforts will be made to determine and engage the appropriate levels of abstraction in model creation. These levels of abstraction will be identified in partnership with experts from infrastructure asset owners and operators.

5.   Conclusions

This chapter has presented a novel conceptual framework for holistic simulations of multiple critical infrastructure networks in a large city. The framework leverages a two-level structure comprising an intra-domain level and an inter-domain level. In the intra-domain level, each individual infrastructure network is simulated using the underlying physical model of the domain or using machine learning, where the individual components of the individual network are collectively represented by a neural network that is trained based on the available data. The inter-domain level models the interdependencies between the individual infrastructure networks and simulates cross-domain effects using a stochastic approach, where each network component is modeled as a Mealy automaton with probabilistic state transitions. The simulation framework provides infrastructure asset owners and operators, administrative entities and national authorities with holistic views that support detailed assessments of the impacts of threats on individual critical infrastructures as well as the potential cascading effects in the entire network of critical infrastructures. These risk assessment results will steer proactive efforts at implementing preventive measures and mitigations, and planning effective emergency responses to natural and human-initiated incidents.

Acknowledgements

The authors wish to thank Sandra König for invaluable feedback provided during her reviews. This research was supported by Project ODYSSEUS funded by the Austrian Research Promotion Agency under Grant No. 873539.

References

[1] R. Bloomfield, P. Popov, K. Salako, V. Stankovic and D. Wright, Preliminary interdependency analysis: An approach to support critical infrastructure risk assessment, *Reliability Engineering and System Safety*, vol. 167, pp. 198–217, 2017.

[2] M. Chaudhary, S. Mishra and A. Kumar, Estimation of water pollution and probability of health risk due to imbalanced nutrients in River Ganga, India, *International Journal of River Basin Management*, vol. 15(1), pp. 53–60, 2017.

[3] F. Dietrich and C. List, Probabilistic opinion pooling generalized, Part one: General agendas, *Social Choice and Welfare*, vol. 48, pp. 747–786, 2017.

[4] European Commission, Council Directive 2008/114/EC of 8 December 2008 on the Identification and Designation of European Critical Infrastructures and the Assessment of the Need to Improve Their Protection, Brussels, Belgium, 2008.

[5] European Commission, Directive (EU) 2016/1148 of the European Parliament and of the Council of 6 July 2016 Concerning Measures for a High Common Level of Security of Network and Information Systems Across the Union, Brussels, Belgium, 2016.

[6] T. Grafenauer, S. König, S. Rass and S. Schauer, A simulation tool for cascading effects in interdependent critical infrastructures, *Proceedings of the Thirteenth International Conference on Availability, Reliability and Security*, article no. 30, 2018.

[7] S. Grundel, N. Hornung, B. Klaassen, P. Benner and T. Clees, Computing surrogates for gas network simulation using model order reduction, in *Surrogate-Based Modeling and Optimization*, S. Koziel and L. Leifsson (Eds.), Springer, New York, pp. 189–212, 2013.

[8] Y. Haimes, Hierarchical holographic modeling, *IEEE Transactions on Systems, Man and Cybernetics*, vol. 11(9), pp. 606–617, 1981.

[9] Y. Haimes and P. Jiang, Leontief-based model of risk in complex interconnected infrastructures, *Journal of Infrastructure Systems*, vol. 7(1), pp. 1–12, 2001.

[10] Y. Haimes, J. Santos, K. Crowther, M. Henry, C. Lian and Z. Yan, Risk analysis in interdependent infrastructures, in *Critical Infrastructure Protection*, E. Goetz and S. Shenoi (Eds.), Springer, Boston, Massachusetts, pp. 297–310, 2007.

[11] B. Haut, G. Bastin and Y. Chitour, A macroscopic traffic model for road networks with a representation of the capacity drop phenomenon at the junctions, *IFAC Proceedings Volumes*, vol. 38(1), pp. 114–119, 2005.

[12] M. Herty, *Mathematics of Traffic Flow Networks: Modeling, Simulation and Optimization*, Logos Verlag, Berlin, Germany, 2004.

[13] A. Kelic, D. Warren and L. Phillips, Cyber and Physical Infrastructure Interdependencies, Sandia Report SAND2008-6192, Sandia National Laboratories, Albuquerque, New Mexico and Livermore, California, 2008.

[14] B. Kelley, P. Top, S. Smith, C. Woodward and L. Min, A federated simulation toolkit for electric power grid and communications network co-simulation, *Proceedings of the Workshop on Modeling and Simulation of Cyber-Physical Energy Systems*, 2015.

[15] E. Kenah and J. Robins, Second look at spread of epidemics in networks, *Physical Review E*, vol. 76(3), pp. 036113-1–036113-12, 2007.

[16] S. König, A. Gouglidis, B. Green and A. Solar, Assessing the impact of malware attacks in utility networks, in *Game Theory for Security and Risk Management: From Theory to Practice*, S. Rass and S. Schauer (Eds.), Birkhauser, Cham, Switzerland, pp. 335–351, 2018.

[17] S. König and S. Rass, Stochastic dependencies between critical infrastructures, *Proceedings of the Eleventh International Conference on Emerging Security Information, Systems and Technologies*, pp. 106–110, 2017.

[18] S. König and S. Rass, Investigating stochastic dependencies between critical infrastructures, *International Journal on Advances in Systems and Measurements*, vol. 11(3-4), pp. 250–258, 2018.

[19] S. König, S. Rass, B. Rainer and S. Schauer, Hybrid dependencies between cyber and physical systems, in *Intelligent Computing*, K. Arai, R. Bhatia and S. Kapoor (Eds.), Springer, Cham, Switzerland, pp. 550–565, 2019.

[20] S. König, S. Schauer and S. Rass, A stochastic framework for prediction of malware spreading in heterogeneous networks, in *Secure IT Systems*, B. Brumley and J. Roning (Eds.), Springer, Cham, Switzerland, pp. 67–81, 2016.

[21] P. Kotzanikolaou, M. Theoharidou and D. Gritzalis, Interdependencies between critical infrastructures: Analyzing the risk of cascading effects, in *Critical Information Infrastructure Security*, S. Bologna, B. Hammerli, D. Gritzalis and S. Wolthusen (Eds.), Springer, Berlin Heidelberg, Germany, pp. 104–115, 2013.

[22] H. Krieg, D. Nowak and M. Bortz, Surrogate models for the simulation of complex water supply networks, *Proceedings of the First International WDSA/CCWI Joint Conference*, vol. 1, article no. 18, 2018.

[23] H. Lin, S. Sambamoorthy, S. Shukla, J. Thorp and L. Mili, Power system and communications network co-simulation for smart grid applications, *Proceedings of the IEEE Power and Energy Society Conference on Innovative Smart Grid Technologies*, 2011.

[24] D. Paluszczyszyn, Advanced Modeling and Simulation of Water Distribution Systems with Discontinuous Control Elements, Ph.D. Thesis, School of Engineering and Sustainable Development, De Montfort University, Leicester, United Kingdom, 2015.

[25] Y. Qiu, S. Grundel, M. Stoll and P. Benner, Efficient Numerical Methods for Gas Network Modeling and Simulation, *arXiv: 1807.07142v2*, 2018.

[26] M. Rahnamay-Naeini and M. Hayat, Cascading failures in interdependent infrastructures: An interdependent Markov chain approach, *IEEE Transactions on Smart Grid*, vol. 7(4), pp. 1997–2006, 2016.

[27] M. Reiser, A queueing network analysis of computer communications networks with window flow control, *IEEE Transactions on Communications*, vol. 27(8), pp. 1199–1209, 1979.

[28] S. Rinaldi, Modeling and simulating critical infrastructures and their interdependencies, *Proceedings of the Thirty-Seventh Annual Hawaii International Conference on System Sciences*, 2004.

[29] S. Rinaldi, J. Peerenboom and T. Kelly, Identifying, understanding and analyzing critical infrastructure interdependencies, *IEEE Control Systems*, vol. 21(6), pp. 11–25, 2001.

[30] M. Salathe and J. Jones, Dynamics and control of diseases in networks with community structure, *PLoS Computational Biology*, vol. 6(4), article no. e1000736, 2010.

[31] T. Schaberreiter, K. Kittila, K. Halunen, J. Roning and D. Khadraoui, Risk assessment in critical infrastructure security modeling based on dependency analysis, in *Critical Information Infrastructure Security*, S. Bologna, B. Hammerli, D. Gritzalis and S. Wolthusen (Eds.), Springer, Berlin Heidelberg, Germany, pp. 213–217, 2013.

[32] F. Schloegl, S. Rohjans, S. Lehnhoff, J. Velasquez, C. Steinbrink and P. Palensky, Towards a classification scheme for co-simulation approaches in energy systems, *Proceedings of the IEEE International Symposium on Smart Electric Distribution System and Technologies*, pp. 516–521, 2015.

[33] M. Sunela and R. Puust, Real time water supply system hydraulic and quality modeling – A case study, *Procedia Engineering*, vol. 119, pp. 744–752, 2015.

[34] M. Turoff, V. Banuls, L. Plotnick, S. Hiltz and M. Ramirez de la Huerga, A collaborative dynamic scenario model for the interaction of critical infrastructures, *Futures*, vol. 84(A), pp. 23–42, 2016.

[35] J. Wachter, T. Grafenauer and S. Rass, Visual risk specification and aggregation, *Proceedings of the Eleventh International Conference on Emerging Security Information, Systems and Technologies*, pp. 93–98, 2017.

[36] T. Wen, X. Lyu, D. Kirkwood, L. Chen, C. Constantinou and C. Roberts, Co-simulation testing of data communications system supporting CBTC, *Proceedings of the Eighteenth IEEE International Conference on Intelligent Transportation Systems*, pp. 2665–2670, 2015.

[37] Z. Yan, Y. Haimes and M. Waller, Hierarchical coordinated Bayesian model for risk analysis with sparse data, presented at the *Society of Risk Analysis Annual Meeting*, 2006.

[38] N. Yuhara and J. Tajima, Multi-driver agent-based traffic simulation systems for evaluating the effects of advanced driver assistance systems on road traffic accidents, *Cognition, Technology and Work*, vol. 8(4), pp. 283–300, 2006.

Chapter 16

MODELING TELECOMMUNICATIONS INFRASTRUCTURES USING THE CISIApro 2.0 SIMULATOR

Elena Bernardini, Chiara Foglietta and Stefano Panzieri

Abstract   Telecommunications is a vital component of industrial automation and control systems that are used widely in the critical infrastructure. However, the integration of telecommunications infrastructures in critical infrastructure assets increases the risk of cyber threats. Telecommunications infrastructures can amplify and expand the impacts of an adverse event such as a cyber attack (or fault or natural disaster) on a single infrastructure, leading to cascading disruptions and major crises.

Modeling critical infrastructures is a complex and multi-disciplinary problem that is vital to understanding the domino effects encountered in complex interdependent networks. This chapter models interconnected infrastructures using a mixed holistic reductionist approach that divides each infrastructure into components (reductionist layer), services (service layer) and nodes (holistic layer). The CISIApro 2.0 agent-based simulator, which has been adapted to model and simulate telecommunications infrastructures in terms of network routing and the allocation of differentiated services, is employed. The modeling and simulation approaches enable telecommunications infrastructure operators to assess the consequences of adverse events such as failures, cyber attacks and natural disasters, and to identify restoration actions.

Keywords: Telecommunications infrastructure modeling, agent-based simulation

1.   Introduction

The use of telecommunications infrastructures has risen exponentially in recent decades. These infrastructures are vital to modern society during normal operations as well as during crisis situations [27].

Telecommunications infrastructures are constantly evolving to adapt to new challenges. The massive volumes of mobile data traffic have led to

© IFIP International Federation for Information Processing 2020
Published by Springer Nature Switzerland AG 2020
J. Staggs and S. Shenoi (Eds.): Critical Infrastructure Protection XIV, IFIP AICT 596, pp. 325–348, 2020.
https://doi.org/10.1007/978-3-030-62840-6_16

the development of fifth-generation (5G) networks [3]. A new challenge is to provide the massive connectivity that will be needed when the Internet of Things becomes all-pervasive.

The Internet of Things paradigm is seeping into the critical infrastructure because it supports automated connection and collaboration between humans and computing systems and devices [29]. Internet of Things technologies are attractive for use in industrial control systems, especially advanced supervisory control and data acquisition (SCADA) systems that are widely used in all the critical infrastructure sectors [5]. Unfortunately, the integration of Internet of Things in the critical infrastructure significantly increases the cyber attack surfaces of critical infrastructure assets as well as the negative impacts brought about by cascading disruptions in the interconnected infrastructures.

Assessing and mitigating the risks to critical infrastructure assets are important problems. The U.S. Department of Homeland Security defines risk as "the potential for an unwanted outcome resulting from an incident, event or occurrence, as determined by its likelihood and the associated consequences" [26]. Risk is traditionally defined as a function of three elements: (i) threats to which assets are susceptible; (ii) vulnerabilities of assets to the threats; and (iii) consequences of attacks that occur when threats exploit vulnerabilities. Risk management involves understanding the threats and hazards that could affect assets, assessing the vulnerabilities of the assets and evaluating the impacts on the assets.

Resilience is also a key concept with regard to the critical infrastructure [7]. The resilience of an entity is its degree of preparedness and ability to respond to and recover from negative events. Critical infrastructure assets are lifeline systems because they are intimately linked to the economic wellbeing, safety and security of society; robustness to disruptions and rapid recovery are vital to resilience [6].

The concepts of risk and resilience are similar and they are tightly connected – improving the resilience of a system means decreasing the risk. This chapter draws on the two concepts to understand the consequences of adverse events such as faults, cyber attacks and natural disasters, and the consequences of mitigations and restoration actions. The focus is on telecommunications infrastructures – their integration in the critical infrastructure sectors amplifies and expands the negative impacts of an adverse event on a single infrastructure, leading to cascading disruptions and major crises. Interconnected infrastructures are modeled using a mixed holistic reductionist (MHR) method, where each infrastructure is divided into components (reductionist layer), services (service layer) and nodes (holistic layer). The CISIApro 2.0 agent-based simulator, which has been adapted to model and simulate telecommunications infrastructures in terms of network routing and the allocation of differentiated services, is employed to assess the consequences of adverse events such as failures, cyber attacks and natural disasters, and to identify restoration actions. The efficacy of the modeling and simulation approaches are demonstrated using a scenario involving the disruption of 5G service in interconnected telecommunications, manufacturing and health care infrastructures.

2. Literature Review

Three principal methodologies have been proposed for modeling critical infrastructures, agent-based simulation, input-output analysis and network modeling; other methodologies include heterogeneous and unclassified approaches [15].

An agent-based simulation considers each infrastructure as a complex adaptive system comprising agents that represent single facets of the infrastructure. Each agent may be represented at various degrees of abstraction depending on the desired modeling resolution. The principal advantage of agent-based simulation is its potential to establish synergistic strategies when agents communicate with each other [23].

Input-output analysis methodologies are based on the economic theory pioneered by Leontief in the early 1930s. Haimes and Jiang [16] developed the (linear) input-output inoperability model to analyze the impacts of interdependencies on the inoperability of interconnected networked systems. To illustrate the concept, consider a model of two subsystems. If a failure in Subsystem 1 results in Subsystem 2 being 80% inoperable and a failure of Subsystem 2 renders Subsystem 1 being 20% inoperable, then the impact of functional loss due to an external interference can be determined by solving the Leontief equations. The input-output inoperability model is efficient and versatile, but its application has largely been restricted to modeling economic cost interdependencies.

Researchers have been developing new ways of modeling infrastructure interdependencies. The most promising solutions are based on graph/network theory, where infrastructures are defined using abstract graphs/networks comprising nodes representing infrastructure components and arcs representing relations between components. These approaches leverage closed-form expressions and numerical simulations to characterize topology, performance and uncertainty. Readers are referred to [12, 21, 24] for details about methodologies for modeling interdependencies between critical infrastructures.

The telecommunications infrastructure is important and complex because it is integrated in every critical infrastructure sector. In the critical infrastructure protection field, researchers have primarily focused on SCADA networks [9, 13, 14, 18]. SCADA systems are used to monitor and control industrial processes across the critical infrastructure. SCADA networks are essentially telecommunications networks that employ industrial control protocols such as DNP3 [28] and Modbus TCP/IP [11].

Telecommunications networks have typically been analyzed using domain simulators such as ns-3 [22] or queue models [2]. For instance, ns-3 has been used to analyze the consequences of perturbations on network operations [8].

This chapter considers the problem of modeling telecommunications networks in complex scenarios involving multiple interdependent infrastructures. The integration of telecommunications in other critical infrastructure assets increases the risk of cyber threats that can seriously impact the other infrastructures. Additionally, telecommunications infrastructures can amplify and expand the impact of an adverse event on a single infrastructure, leading to cascading disruptions and major crises.

3.   Modeling Interdependencies

This section describes the mixed holistic reductionist method [10] for modeling interdependent infrastructures. The method, which exploits the advantages of holistic and reductionist approaches, provides guidelines for carefully modeling critical infrastructures and their interdependencies.

In holistic modeling, infrastructures are considered to be individual entities with well-defined borders and functional properties. The volume of data needed for holistic modeling activities is relatively small and much of it can be found in public datasets.

The reductionist paradigm considers the functions and actions of individual components to properly understand the overall system. The reductionist approach drills down to the inputs and outputs of the individual components. The level of abstraction enables the relationships between individual components to be readily established.

Different systems require varying degrees of analysis and their limits can be lost when conducting complex case studies. The mixed holistic reductionist method enables network relationships to be articulated at various levels using a top-down or bottom-up strategy. The other main benefit is the ability to model infrastructures at different levels of abstraction based on the amount of available data.

The connection point between the two layers of complexity corresponding to the holistic and reductionist approaches is the assessment of service efficiency (abbreviated as "service"), which is a critical aspect for infrastructure owners and operators. It expresses the functional relationships at various rates or granularities between components and infrastructures. Indeed, the mixed holistic reductionist method specifically identifies services to customers and other linked infrastructures that reside in the middle layer between the holistic and reductionist levels.

Despite the presence of limited data about critical infrastructures, the mixed holistic reductionist method helps achieve the appropriate level of detail. The following are some essential considerations with regard to the method:

- Each network is modeled by identifying its components and their interactions.

- An effective level of abstraction is established for the layer based on inputs from end-users, stakeholders and open documentation.

- Every component (called an agent) is defined so that it is decoupled from other components. The behavior of each component depends on its internal state and on inputs from components that are directly connected to it.

- The simulator that applies the mixed holistic reductionist method must represent the behavior of agents in the reference scenario.

The mixed holistic reductionist method supports the definition of three types of agents: (i) holistic agents; (ii) service agents; and (iii) reductionist agents.

Figure 1 shows a holistic agent that represents an infrastructure as a whole (or its general functional divisions). It provides a means to understand the global interactions in the infrastructure that reflect actions relevant to policies, strategies, etc.

Figure 2 shows a service agent that represents a functional or operational function, which offers an integrated resource as a remote control (i.e., a supervisory mechanism typically implemented by software or data collection). In the case of a geographically-dispersed system, data can be obtained via a telecommunications network from field equipment. A service agent may: (i) provide a service to customers; (ii) produce resources: (iii) adjust its topology; and (iv) assess the aggregated state of a set of components, usually reductionistic components.

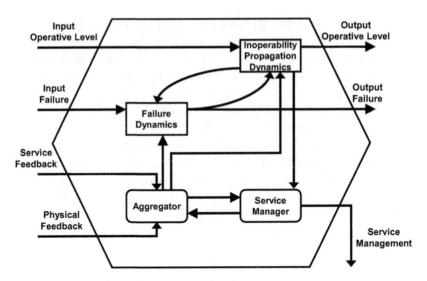

Figure 1.   MHR representation of a holistic agent.

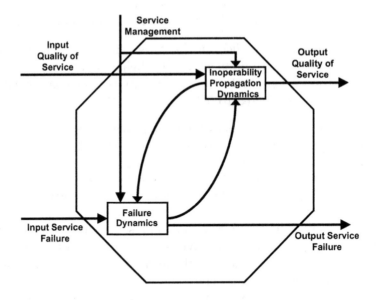

Figure 2.   MHR representation of a service agent.

Figure 3 shows a reductionist agent that describes the actual or aggregated aspects of a system at an appropriate level of abstraction. Note that input failure in the figure includes the effects of failures, cyber attacks and/or natural disasters.

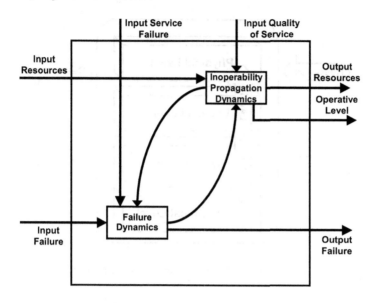

Figure 3. MHR representation of a reductionist agent.

The mixed holistic reductionist method enables a developer to represent a scenario using various functional components. The layers can model a complex scenario with multiple interconnected infrastructures at various degrees of abstraction. One infrastructure can be modeled using all the layers (reductionist, service and holistic) whereas another infrastructure can be modeled using just the holistic layer without posing any problems aside from the granularity and precision of the results.

4.   Dynamic Risk Propagation via CISIApro 2.0

The CISIApro 2.0 (Critical Infrastructure Simulation by Interdependent Agents) [14, 19] software engine is capable of measuring cascading effects induced by dependencies and interdependencies, and fault propagations in a complex system. CISIApro 2.0 also suggests prevention and restoration methods by determining their positive effects. CISIApro was built from scratch in 2011 under the EU H2020 ATENA Project [1] to enhance the modeling of infrastructure interdependencies. It was upgraded to CISIApro 2.0 during the EU H2020 RESISTO Project [4], incorporating several significant functionalities for simulating telecommunications infrastructures.

Each agent's operational level is a risk metric. CISIApro 2.0 is an agent-based simulator in which each agent has the same structure. As shown in Figure 4, an agent receives resources and faults from upstream

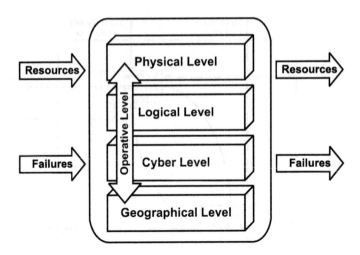

Figure 4. CISIApro 2.0 agent representation.

agents and distributes them to downstream agents. The various levels are derived based on resource and fault propagation. A resource is a commodity or data generated and/or consumed by an agent (called an entity) in CISIApro 2.0. The agent may produce or receive failures (generally malfunctions) that reflect physical failures or possible cyber attacks. The malfunctions are distributed among agents according to propagation models that take into account the interdependency class (i.e., level) and information reliability. The interdependency levels are physical, logical, cyber and geographical. The capacity to generate resources is expressed by the operational level, which is based on the availability of resources, proliferation of faults and agent functionality.

The risk is typically a numerical measure based on the magnitude of the effect, probability of the incident or threat, and measurement of the vulnerability. In CISIApro 2.0 implementations, the probability of an event is generally considered to be more related to the trustworthiness of the information. A user may also add a vulnerability variable for each agent, but the vulnerability depends only on the distance from the source and the duration of the attack.

The operational level of an agent is correlated with a risk rating. The risk, which denotes the amount of harm due to a specific incident (e.g., cyber attack), is measured as:

$$\text{Risk} = 1 - \text{Operational Level} \tag{1}$$

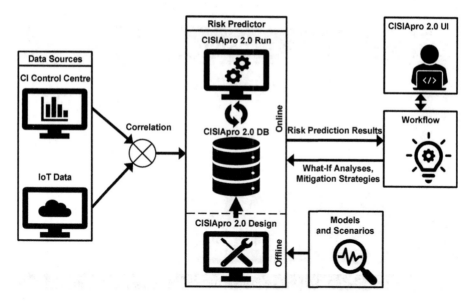

Figure 5. CISIApro 2.0 architecture.

where the maximum value of the operational level is one and a higher operational level value means a lower risk. The operational level reflects a complex risk evaluation that considers the cascading consequences of adverse events (failures, cyber attacks and natural disasters). The operational level of each infrastructure is standardized by considering the quality of service to customers and other infrastructures.

4.1 CISIApro 2.0 Implementation Details

Figure 5 shows the CISIApro 2.0 architecture. CISIApro 2.0 has two main units. The first is the CISIApro 2.0 Design offline tool that enables dynamic and highly interdependent scenarios to be planned and implemented. The second is the CISIApro 2.0 Run online tool that uses Simulink MathWorks as its real-time engine (the tool is currently linked to near real-time data sources).

CISIApro 2.0 is a software platform built on a database-centered architecture (CISIApro 2.0 DB in Figure 5). The distributed design allows for horizontal scalability, where every element in the risk propagation architecture independently interacts with the centralized database to collect the latest field data and CISIApro 2.0 output data.

Figure 6 shows the CISIApro 2.0 graphical user interface. The CISIApro 2.0 Run engine generates impact estimates of the observed ab-

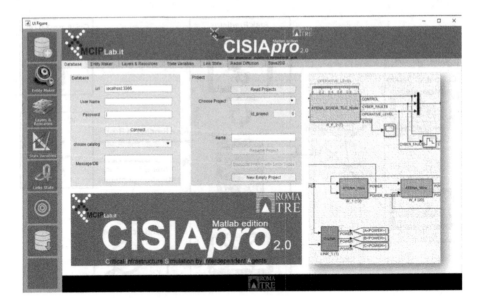

Figure 6. CISIApro 2.0 graphical user interface.

normalities. A decision maker, often assisted by a workflow manager, selects potential reaction techniques that minimize the negative results, often taking into account the CISIApro 2.0 outputs. When presented with a real scenario and the quality of service levels of the systems under consideration, CISIApro 2.0 simulates what-if scenarios to provide decision makers with practical knowledge about potential incidents and their impacts.

4.2 CISIApro 2.0 Mathematical Structure

This section describes the mathematical structure underlying CISIApro 2.0, which takes the form of a multilayer network.

A graph (i.e., single-layer network) is a tuple $\mathcal{G} = (\mathcal{V}, \mathcal{E})$, where $\mathcal{V}$ is a set of nodes and $\mathcal{E} = \mathcal{V} \times \mathcal{V}$ is a a set of edges that connect pairs of nodes. Two nodes are adjacent if there is an edge between them.

In order to model critical infrastructures, the graph definition must be expanded to incorporate layers. Using the multilayer network formalism [17], a complex system has d layers denoted by $\mathcal{L} = \{\mathcal{L}_a\}_{a=1}^d$, where other variables may be used to indicate whether or not a node is present in a given layer.

First, a set $\mathcal{V} \times \mathcal{L}_1 \times \cdots \times \mathcal{L}_d$ is constructed, following which a subset $\mathcal{V}_M \subseteq \mathcal{V} \times \mathcal{L}_1 \times \cdots \times \mathcal{L}_d$ is specified that only contains the corresponding node-layer combinations. Let u and α_i be a node and layer, respectively, then $(u, \alpha) \equiv (u, \alpha_1, \ldots, \alpha_d)$ represents the set containing each topological connection (u, α_i) between node u in layer α_i.

Next, the edge set $\mathcal{E}_M \subseteq \mathcal{V}_M \times \mathcal{V}_M$ is defined as the set of all possible combinations of node-layers. Note that different connections can be modeled using this set, including self-node connections in different layers as well as links between layers.

Finally, a multilayer network M is defined as the quadruple:

$$M = (\mathcal{V}_M, \mathcal{E}_M, \mathcal{V}, \mathcal{L}) \tag{2}$$

Note that a single-layer network is a special case of a multilayer network in which $d = 0$ and $\mathcal{V}_M = \mathcal{V}$ are redundant. Furthermore, given a subset $D \subseteq \mathcal{L}$ of the layers of a multilayer network M, a special set of nodes that can be reached by any edge starting from a generic node v from any of the layers in D is called the "neighborhood" and is formally defined as $\Gamma(v, D)$.

In the following, the multilayer network structure of CISIApro 2.0 is specified and interdependency modeling for risk assessment is discussed.

In general, the first two elements in a multilayer network M generate a graph $\mathcal{G}_M(\mathcal{V}_M, \mathcal{E}_M)$. Therefore, a multilayer network can be viewed as a graph with labeled nodes and edges.

A multilayer network M is directed if all the underlying graphs $\mathcal{G}_M$ are directed. Mathematically, $\mathcal{E}_M$ is an ordered set of edges and, therefore, $((u, \alpha), (v, \beta)) \neq ((v, \beta), (u, \alpha))$.

The CISIApro 2.0 structure is a directed multilayer network where each agent is a node that exists in at least one layer, but it may be included in all the layers. CISIApro 2.0 disallows multilayer network self-edges by avoiding self-edges in the underlying graph, i.e., $((u, \alpha), (u, \alpha)) \notin \mathcal{E}_M$.

The CISIApro 2.0 structure connects each agent with the set of nodes identified by the same agent in different layers. Therefore, the coupling edges $\mathcal{E}_C$ are always present in the CISIApro 2.0 structure:

$$\mathcal{E}_C = \{((u, \alpha), (v, \beta)) \in E_M | u = v, \ \forall u, v \in \mathcal{E}_M, \ \forall \alpha, \beta \in \mathcal{L}\} \tag{3}$$

Each node (u, α) that is in at least one layer of M has a status vector $x_u(t)$ associated with it that defines the evolution of component u at time t. The CISIApro 2.0 structure describes a layer using a propagation, diffusion or consensus model among the nodes in a layer.

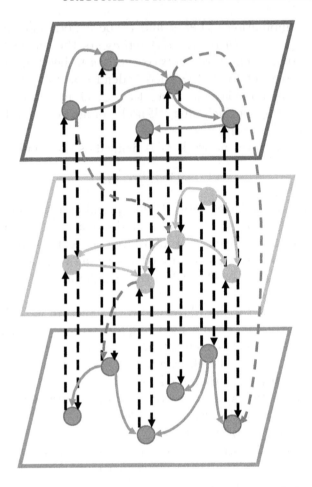

Figure 7.   Multilayer network in a CISIApro 2.0 simulation.

Figure 7 shows an example multilayer graph in CISIApro 2.0. The multilayer network has three layers, where the dark dotted lines denote the coupling edges and the light dotted lines denote the inter-layer edges. In general, the set of inter-layer edges $\mathcal{E}_{inter}$ is given by:

$$\mathcal{E}_{inter} = \{((u,\alpha),(v,\beta)) \in E_M | u \neq v, \alpha \neq \beta\} \tag{4}$$

and the remaining edges are the intra-layer edges $\mathcal{E}_{intra}$:

$$\mathcal{E}_{intra} = \{((u,\alpha),(v,\beta)) \in E_M | u \neq v, \alpha = \beta\} \tag{5}$$

The status vector of each component is governed by a non-linear discrete dynamical equation, where the status changes for each u are modulated using its internal state $x_i(t)$ and the neighboring data.

Formally, the discrete-time nonlinear dynamics of the status vectors at time k is specified as:

$$
\begin{aligned}
x_u(t+1) &= g_u\left(x_u(t), y_{\Gamma+(u,\mathbf{L})}(t), z_u(t)\right) \qquad (6)\\
y_u(t) &= h_u(x_u(t), z_u(t))
\end{aligned}
$$

where g_u and h_u are nonlinear functions, $z_u(t)$ is the external input to node u and $y_{\Gamma+(u,\mathcal{L})}(t)$ is the data received from the incoming neighborhood.

The incoming neighborhood of node u is defined as:

$$
\Gamma^+(u, \mathcal{L}) = \{v \in \mathcal{V}_M | ((v, \beta), (u, \alpha)) \in \mathcal{E}_M, \alpha, \beta \in \mathcal{L}\} \qquad (7)
$$

Without loss of generality, the status vectors of the different layers x_u can be stacked in a state vector $\hat{x}(t) = [x_1(t) \ldots x_u(t)]^T$, $\forall u \in \mathcal{V}_M$ and the inputs in an input vector $\hat{z}(t) = [z_1(t) \ldots z_u(t)]^T$, $\forall u \in \mathcal{V}$. Thus, the resulting dynamical system can be rewritten as:

$$
\begin{aligned}
\hat{x}(t+1) &= \hat{g}\left(\hat{x}(t), \hat{y}_{\Gamma+(\cdot,\mathcal{L})}(t), \hat{z}(t)\right) \qquad (8)\\
\hat{y}(t) &= \hat{h}(\hat{x}(t), \hat{z}(t))
\end{aligned}
$$

where $\hat{g}$ and $\hat{h}$ are the column vectors of g_u, $\forall u \in \mathcal{V}$ and h_u, $\forall u \in \mathcal{V}$, respectively, and set $\Gamma^+(\cdot, \mathcal{L})$ expresses the incoming neighborhood of a generic node in the multilayer graph.

Kivela et al. [17] have demonstrated that the dynamical model specified in Equation (8) is general enough to cover classical approaches in the multilayer network literature, including percolation cascades and susceptible-infected-recovered models.

4.3   CISIApro 2.0 Dynamics

This section describes the CISIApro 2.0 dynamics, which uses the maximum consensus approach. For simplicity, a single layer in a multilayer graph generated by the propagation of a single resource is considered. The extension of the maximum consensus approach to a multi-layer graph is straightforward.

Consider a directed graph $\mathcal{G} = (\mathcal{V}, \mathcal{E})$. To replicate the propagation algorithm in CISIApro 2.0, the set of nodes is partitioned into three subsets: (i) source nodes $\mathcal{V}_f \subset \mathcal{V}$; (ii) sink nodes $\mathcal{V}_t \subset \mathcal{V}$; and (iii) transmitting nodes $\mathcal{V}_m \subset \mathcal{V}$. Each node belongs to only one of these subsets and $\mathcal{V}_f \cup \mathcal{V}_m \cup \mathcal{V}_t = \mathcal{V}$. For each resource, some nodes generate information (i.e., $\mathcal{V}_f$), some nodes receive information (i.e., $\mathcal{V}_t$) and the remaining nodes (i.e., $\mathcal{V}_m$) simply resend the information they receive.

The propagation algorithm in the CISIApro 2.0 simulator is based on the following rules:

1. Each source node $i \in \mathcal{V}_f$ generates a resource (or specific information) corresponding to its state (i.e., operating level) x_i and broadcasts it to its successor nodes. The information transmitted by each source node is orthogonal (or better distinguishable) from the messages propagated by the other source nodes.

2. The propagation of information from each source node to a destination node takes place via the transmitting nodes as follows:

$$x_i(k+1) = \max_{j \in \mathcal{J}_i} \{x_j(k)\} \qquad i = 1, \ldots, n \qquad (9)$$

where $\mathcal{J}_i$ is the set of predecessors of node i and k identifies the kth communications event.

3. Each sink node must receive at least one resource from one of the source nodes.

4. The sink nodes do not re-transmit any information they receive.

5. A fault in a transmitting node means that all its successors do not receive information propagated after the fault.

The propagation algorithm is defined when the destination nodes receive the information transmitted by the source nodes. Specifically:

$$x_i(k) = \max_j \{x_j(0)\} \qquad i \in \mathcal{V}_t, j \in \mathcal{V}_f \qquad (10)$$

The main concept is that the sink node needs the information transmitted by at least one source node. If two nodes transmit a resource, then the receiver just needs the resource and usually does not care which node provides it. The propagation algorithm is a specific case of the maximum consensus algorithm where the destination nodes are defined explicitly.

Assuming that the topology of the telecommunications network is fixed and that communications between nodes are synchronous (i.e., each node exchanges information with its neighbors simultaneously), the maximum consensus algorithm [20] is defined as follows:

$$x_i(k+1) = \max_{j \in \mathcal{J}_i} \{x_j(k)\} \qquad i = 1, \ldots, n \qquad (11)$$

where $\mathcal{J}_i$ is the set of predecessor nodes of node i and k identifies the kth communications event. Note that only source nodes can have self-loops (i.e., $i \in \mathcal{J}_i, \forall i \in \mathcal{V}_f$).

Under these conditions, given a graph $\mathcal{G}$ and vector of the initial information states $\hat{x}(0) = (x_1(0), \ldots x_i(0), \ldots, x_n(0))^T$, it is guaranteed that maximum consensus is reached if $\exists l \in \mathbb{N}_0$ such that:

$$x_i(k) = x_k(k) = \max \{x_1(0), \ldots, x_n(0)\} \qquad \forall k \geq l, \ \forall i,j \in \mathcal{V} \quad (12)$$

5. Telecommunications Network Scenario

The scenario considered in this chapter involves a 5G telecommunications network that supports a smart factory and a hospital ward. 5G networks are beginning to be deployed across the critical infrastructure [25].

Figure 8 shows the telecommunications network model. The network comprises a backbone network, metro network and access networks.

The optical packet backbone (OPB) network is a multi-service platform that provides voice, data and video services. This network leverages IP/MPLS (multiprotocol label switching) technology to ensure high quality of service. It is completely redundant in all its components and immune to failure conditions.

The optical packet metro (OPM) network is a metropolitan and regional collection and aggregation network that handles Ethernet, IP or MPLS traffic flows depending on the configuration. Like the optical packet backbone network, the optical packet metro network is a multi-service network in which all fixed and mobile services converge, and it must guarantee scalability, reliability, availability and flexibility.

The access networks provide services to customers. Multiple technologies, each with different coverage and performance, are used in the "last mile" – the portions of the network that connect access nodes to customer sites. The bottom-left of Figure 8 shows a new generation access network (gigabit passive optical network (GPON)) that employs optical line transmission (OLT) and optical network units (ONUs). The distinctive feature of this technology is the creation of an architecture in which a single optical fiber can reach multiple recipients, reducing infrastructure costs by eliminating the deployment of individual fiber connections between the control panel and recipients. The bottom center portion of Figure 8 shows a broadband network, which is popular because the same

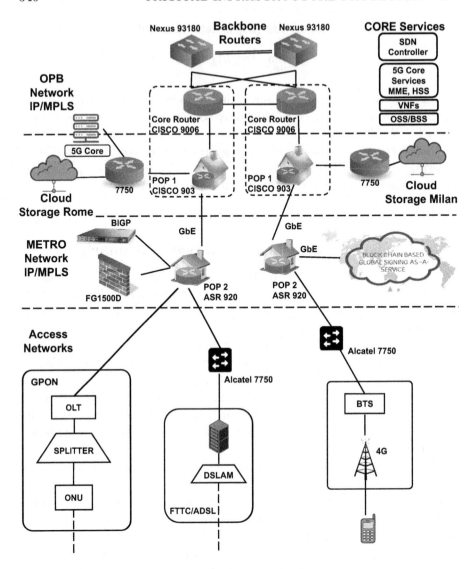

Figure 8. Telecommunications network representation.

copper cables of traditional telephone networks are shared by voice and data services. The data traffic sent by a user is separated from voice traffic by a splitter and is collected by a digital subscriber line access multiplexer (DSLAM), where the broadband lines of users assigned to a central station terminate. The bottom right-hand side of Figure 8 shows a GSM (mobile telephone) network with a base transceiver station (BTS) comprising antennas and transceivers responsible for radio coverage in the service area.

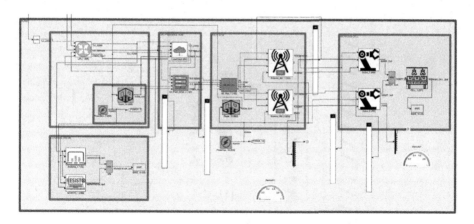

Figure 9. Smart factory representation in the CISIApro 2.0 simulator.

The security fabric of the data center layer incorporates next-generation security devices and application controllers such as Fortinet Forti-Gate (with URL filtering, centralized antivirus, intrusion detection and protection systems, e-mail filtering and layer 4 firewalls, along with F5 BIGIP (web application firewalls).

Figure 9 shows a smart factory that relies on the telecommunications network. The smart factory incorporates a radio access network architecture that is expected to be implemented in factories of the future (Industry 4.0). The local architecture, which is completely autonomous, has a picocell site and an on-premises data center hub for local data processing and storage.

The 5G network presents itself as the best solution for this scenario; it even supports virtual control of the robots. In this paradigm, robot control functionality can be located in the cloud instead of locally on the robots. Clearly, any remote systems that provide control functionality must be protected from cyber attacks to the maximal extent.

Figure 10 shows a hospital ward that relies on the telecommunications network. The hospital ward infrastructure includes electric power, water and heating, ventilation and air conditioning system components. The hospital building has eight rooms, two operating rooms, a post-surgery room, doctors' room, staff room, visiting room, waiting room and storage room. The rooms are modeled differently based on their importance. Specifically, the operating and post-surgery rooms, which are dedicated to patient care, must provide medical services during a telecommunications network failure whereas the other rooms can still provide reasonable quality of service during a failure.

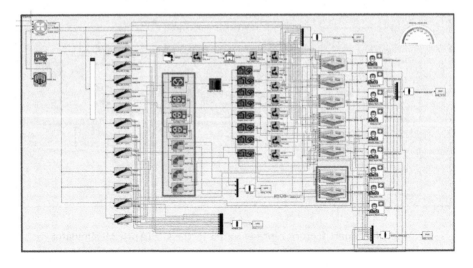

Figure 10.   Hospital ward representation in the CISIApro 2.0 simulator.

The telecommunications network enables medical records and hospital ward data to be stored in the cloud. Also, it supports networked medical devices and systems.

6.   Scenario Simulation Results

The telecommunications network scenario provides several services, each of which is modeled as a service agent in CISIApro 2.0. First, the 5G service presented in Figure 8 is discussed. 5G technology supports the remote monitoring and control of robots, human-machine interactions and real-time collection and management of information processed by the intelligent systems. In the hospital ward, the goal is to pervasively interconnect doctors, patients and healthcare personnel with healthcare systems to enhance medical care. In this context, 5G supports remote surgery, patient monitoring and communications between doctors, patients and healthcare personnel in real time.

CISIApro 2.0 was used to evaluate the consequences of a cyber attack, specifically a denial-of-service attack on the 5G core component. The focus was not on how the attack was conducted, but the possible impacts on the interconnected infrastructures.

As shown in Figure 11, the cyber attack on the 5G core reduced its operative level to zero, a complete outage. The other agents in the telecommunications infrastructure were not affected by the outage because they did not rely on 5G services.

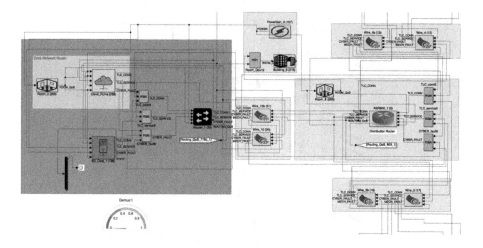

Figure 11. Consequences in the 5G core.

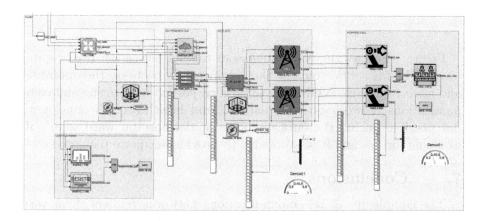

Figure 12. Consequences in the smart factory.

However, the 5G outage did have consequences on the smart factory and hospital ward. Figure 12 shows the domino effects of the 5G outage on the smart factory. Four agents, 5G-PGW-SGW, 5G-Pico and the two antennas RU, needed 5G services to operate. Since the 5G outage was total, the operative levels of the four agents dropped to zero because they could not properly produce their outputs. On the other hand, the two robots had operative levels of 0.4. This is because, although information from the robots could not be collected and processed and they could not be controlled remotely, the autonomous capabilities implemented in the robots enabled them to continue to operate during the outage.

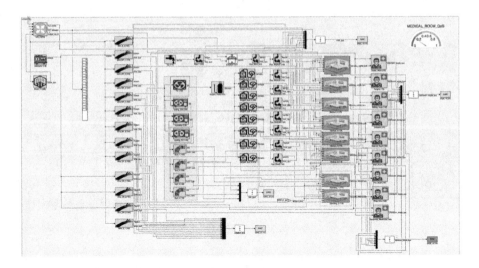

Figure 13. Consequences in the hospital ward.

Figure 13 shows the consequences of the 5G outage on the hospital ward. The 5G service outage had significant impacts on the operating and medical rooms. While remote surgery, patient monitoring and communications between doctors, patients and healthcare personnel were not possible during the outage, rooms in the hospital ward were still available for use and it was possible to provide adequate patient care.

7.   Conclusions

The complexity of telecommunications networks renders them very difficult to model, let alone simulate them in order to evaluate the impacts of network disruptions. The CISIApro 2.0 suite has been upgraded over the past two years to model and simulate telecommunications networks in terms of network routing and the allocation of differentiated services with high fidelity.

The case study involving interconnected telecommunications, manufacturing and health care infrastructures demonstrates the efficacy of using CISIApro 2.0 for infrastructure modeling and simulation. Two distinct phases were involved. The first phase was to model the interconnected infrastructures – telecommunications networks, smart factory and hospital ward – using a mixed holistic reductionist approach that divides each infrastructure into components (reductionist layer), services (service layer) and nodes (holistic layer). The second phase was to use the CISIApro 2.0 real-time simulator to evaluate a scenario involving the disruption of 5G services and its impacts on the interconnected infrastructures. The results reveal that the modeling and simulation approaches enhance the situational awareness of telecommunications infrastructure operators and enable them to assess the consequences of adverse events in the telecommunications infrastructure on connected infrastructures.

Future research will apply the CISIApro 2.0 modeling and simulation techniques to evaluate the behavior of more complex interconnected infrastructures under various faults, cyber attacks and natural disasters.

Acknowledgement

This research was partially supported by the European Union Horizon 2020 Research and Innovation Programme under Grant Agreement No. 786409 (RESISTO – Resilience Enhancement and Risk Control Platform for Communications Infrastructure Operators).

References

[1] F. Adamsky, M. Aubigny, F. Battisti, M. Carli, F. Cimorelli, T. Cruz, A. Di Giorgio, C. Foglietta, A. Galli, A. Giuseppi, F. Liberati, A. Neri, S. Panzieri, F. Pasucci, J. Proenca, P. Pucci, L. Rosa and R. Soua, Integrated protection of industrial control systems from cyber attacks: The ATENA approach, *International Journal of Critical Infrastructure Protection*, vol. 21, pp. 72–82, 2018.

[2] A. Alfa, *Queueing Theory for Telecommunications: Discrete Time Modeling of a Single Node System*, Springer, New York, 2010.

[3] N. Al-Falahy and O. Alani, Technologies for 5G networks: Challenges and opportunities, *IT Professional*, vol. 19(1), pp. 12–20, 2017.

[4] E. Aonzo and A. Neri, RESISTO: Resilience Enhancement and Risk Control Platform for Communications Infrastructure Operators, *POLARIS Innovation Journal*, no. 41, pp. 13–15, 2020.

[5] H. Boyes, B. Hallaq, J. Cunningham and T. Watson, The Industrial Internet of Things (IIoT): An analysis framework, *Computers in Industry*, vol. 101, pp. 1–12, 2018.

[6] M. Bruneau, S. Chang, R. Eguchi, G. Lee, T. O'Rourke, A. Reinhorn, M. Shinozuka, K. Tierney, W. Wallace and D. von Winterfeldt, A framework to quantitatively assess and enhance the seismic resilience of communities, *Earthquake Spectra*, vol. 19(4), pp. 733–752, 2003.

[7] M. Bruneau and A. Reinhorn, Exploring the concept of seismic resilience for acute care facilities, *Earthquake Spectra*, vol. 23(1), pp. 41–62, 2007.

[8] E. Cetinkaya, D. Broyles, A. Dandekar, S. Srinivasan and J. Sterbenz, Modeling communications network challenges for future Internet resilience, survivability and disruption tolerance: A simulation-based approach, *Telecommunication Systems*, vol. 52(2), pp. 751–766, 2013.

[9] P. Chopade and M. Bikdash, Critical infrastructure interdependency modeling: Using graph models to assess the vulnerability of the smart power grid and SCADA networks, *Proceedings of the Eighth IEEE International Conference and Expo on Emerging Technologies for a Smarter World*, 2011.

[10] G. Digioia, C. Foglietta, S. Panzieri and A. Falleni, Mixed holistic reductionistic approach for impact assessment of cyber attacks, *Proceedings of the European Intelligence and Security Informatics Conference*, pp. 123–130, 2012.

[11] N. Erez and A. Wool, Control variable classification, modeling and anomaly detection in Modbus/TCP SCADA systems, *International Journal of Critical Infrastructure Protection*, vol. 10, pp. 59–70, 2015.

[12] I. Eusgeld, D. Henzi and W. Kroger, Comparative Evaluation of Modeling and Simulation Techniques for Interdependent Critical Infrastructures, Scientific Report, Laboratory of Safety Analysis, Swiss Federal Institute of Technology Zurich, Zurich, Switzerland, 2008.

[13] C. Foglietta, D. Masucci, C. Palazzo, R. Santini, S. Panzieri, L. Rosa, T. Cruz and L. Lev, From detecting cyber attacks to mitigating risk within a hybrid environment, *IEEE Systems Journal*, vol. 13(1), pp. 424–435, 2019.

[14] C. Foglietta, C. Palazzo, R. Santini and S. Panzieri, Assessing cyber risk using the CISIApro simulator, in *Critical Infrastructure Protection IX*, M. Rice and S. Shenoi (Eds.), Springer, Cham, Switzerland, pp. 315–331, 2015.

[15] K. Gopalakrishnan and S. Peeta (Eds.), *Sustainable and Resilient Critical Infrastructure Systems: Simulation, Modeling and Intelligent Engineering*, Springer, Berlin Heidelberg, Germany, 2010.

[16] Y. Haimes and P. Jiang, Leontief-based model of risk in complex interconnected infrastructures, *Journal of Infrastructure Systems*, vol. 7(1), pp. 1–12, 2001.

[17] M. Kivela, A. Arenas, M. Barthelemy, J. Gleeson, Y. Moreno and M. Porter, Multilayer networks, *Journal of Complex Networks*, vol. 2(3), pp. 203–271, 2014.

[18] A. Kwasinski and V. Krishnamurthy, Generalized integrated framework for modeling communications and electric power infrastructure resilience, *Proceedings of the IEEE International Telecommunications Energy Conference*, pp. 99–106, 2017.

[19] D. Masucci, C. Palazzo, C. Foglietta and S. Panzieri, Enhancing decision support with interdependency modeling, in *Critical Infrastructure Protection X*, M. Rice and S. Shenoi (Eds.), Springer, Cham, Switzerland, pp. 169–183, 2016.

[20] B. Nejad, S. Attia and J. Raisch, Max-consensus in a max-plus algebraic setting: The case of fixed communications topologies, *Proceedings of the Twenty-Second International Symposium on Information, Communication and Automation Technologies*, 2009.

[21] M. Ouyang, Review of modeling and simulation of interdependent critical infrastructure systems, *Reliability Engineering and System Safety*, vol. 121, pp. 43–60, 2014.

[22] G. Riley and T. Henderson, The `ns-3` network simulator, in *Modeling and Tools for Network Simulation*, K. Wehrle, M. Gunes and J. Gross (Eds.), Springer, Berlin Heidelberg, Germany, pp. 15–34, 2010.

[23] S. Rinaldi, J. Peerenboom and T. Kelly, Identifying, understanding and analyzing critical infrastructure interdependencies, *IEEE Control Systems*, vol. 21(6), pp. 11–25, 2001.

[24] G. Satumitra and L. Duenas-Osorio, Synthesis of modeling and simulation methods in critical infrastructure interdependencies research, in *Sustainable and Resilient Critical Infrastructure Systems*, K. Gopalakrishnan and S. Peeta (Eds.), Springer, Berlin Heidelberg, Germany, pp. 1–51, 2010.

[25] M. Shafi, A. Molisch, P. Smith, T. Haustein, P. Zhu, P. De Silva, F. Tufvesson, A. Benjebbour and G. Wunder, 5G: A tutorial overview of standards, trials, challenges, deployment and practice, *IEEE Journal on Selected Areas in Communications*, vol. 35(6), pp. 1201–1221, 2017.

[26] U.S. Department of Homeland Security Risk Steering Committee, DHS Risk Lexicon: 2010 Edition, Washington, DC (`www.dhs.gov/xlibrary/assets/dhs-risk-lexicon-2010.pdf`), 2010.

[27] H. Wang, B. Alidaee and W. Wang, Critical infrastructure management for telecommunications networks, *Proceedings of the Eighth International Conference on Active Media Technology*, pp. 493–501, 2012.

[28] H. Yang, L. Cheng and M. Chuah, Modeling DNP3 traffic characteristics of field devices in SCADA systems in the smart grid, *Proceedings of the Workshop on Modeling and Simulation of Cyber-Physical Energy Systems*, 2017.

[29] Q. Zhao, Presentation of the technology, protocols and new innovations in the Industrial Internet of Things (IIoT), in *Internet of Things for Industry 4.0*, G. Kanagachidambaresan, R. Anand, E. Balasubramanian and V. Mahima (Eds.), Springer, Cham, Switzerland, pp. 39–56, 2020.

Correction to: Cyber-Resilient SCADA Systems via Secure State Restoration

Zachary Birnbaum, Matthew Davis, Salman Salman, James Cervini,
Lanier Watkins, Saikiran Yamajala, and Shruti Paul

Correction to:
Chapter "Cyber-Resilient SCADA Systems via Secure State Restoration" in: J. Staggs and S. Shenoi (Eds.): *Critical Infrastructure Protection XIV*, IFIP AICT 596, https://doi.org/10.1007/978-3-030-62840-6_9

In an older version of this paper, the surname of the fourth author was different. This has been updated in order to accommodate a name change.

The updated version of this chapter can be found at
https://doi.org/10.1007/978-3-030-62840-6_9

Printed in the United States
by Baker & Taylor Publisher Services

Printed in the United States
by Baker & Taylor Publisher Services